The Collectors
A History of Canadian Customs and Excise

The Collectors
A History of Canadian Customs and Excise

Dave McIntosh

Published by NC Press Limited
in association with Revenue Canada, Customs and Excise
and the Canadian Government Publishing Centre, Supply and Services Canada

THE COLLECTORS
Jacket Illustration: The Toll Gate, *Cornelius Krieghoff,*
National Gallery of Canada, Ottawa
Painting of Dave McIntosh by Shirley Van Dusen
Jacket Design by Doe Pon
Typesetting by Jay Tee Graphics
Colour Separations by Herzig-Sommerville Ltd.
Printed and Bound in Canada by Aprinco Ltd.

© Minister of Supply and Services Canada—1984
Catalogue Number: RV31-18-1984E
All rights reserved. No part of this publication may be reproduced, stored in a retrieval system, or transmitted by any means, electronic, mechanical, photocopying, recording or otherwise, without the prior written permission of NC Press Limited.

Canadian Cataloguing in Publication Data
McIntosh, Dave.
   The collectors: a history of Canadian customs and excise
Published also in French under title: Les receveurs.
Bibliography: p.
Includes index.
ISBN 0-920053-29-7

1. Customs administration – Canada – History.
2. Taxation of articles of consumption – Canada – History. 3. Tariff – Canada – History. I. Title.
HJ6751.A6M25 1985   354.710672'46   C85-098175-1

New Canada Publications, a division of NC Press Limited
Box 4010, Station A, Toronto, Ontario, Canada M5W 1H8

CONTENTS

Introduction 7

SECTION I
Customs and Excise in History

Chapter I Beginnings in Europe and North America 11
Chapter II New France 22
Chapter III British North America 34
Chapter IV Customs and the Fight for Responsible Government 44
  in Nova Scotia
Chapter V Customs in the Canadas 56
Chapter VI Customs Duties versus Free Trade 66
Chapter VII Macdonald's National Policy 70
Chapter VIII The Tariff as an Issue between Ottawa and the Provinces 89
Chapter IX Creation of a Department 102
  Historical Illustrations 113
Chapter X Customs and Excise in the West 157

SECTION II
Development of the Canada-United States Border

Chapter I Sea to Sea, Acrimoniously 185
Chapter II Customs Holds the Pass 200

SECTION III
Smuggling

Chapter I The Golden Age 215
Chapter II The Fur Smugglers of New France 220
Chapter III Smuggling in British North America 229
Chapter IV Early Canadian Anti-Smuggling Directives 242
Chapter V The Customs Scandal of 1926 253
  Colour Illustrations: Customs Ports of Entry 257

SECTION IV
The Lives and Times of Customs and Excise Officers

Chapter I "Conduct Yourself with Urbanity" 291
Chapter II Kerby of Fort Erie 301
Chapter III John Carmichael Haynes, Agent of the Governor 322
Chapter IV Busby of the Yukon 331

APPENDICES

Maps: Border Customs Ports   *353*
Appendix I   Border Customs Ports   351
Appendix II   The Customs Act of 1886   381
Appendix III   Customs Instructions in 1870   385
Appendix IV   A Customs Affair of 1876   391
Bibliography   *399*
Index   *407*

INTRODUCTION

For a great deal of its history, Canadian Customs and Excise has operated on the far frontier. Some of its posts are still remote from any settlement. The customs officer often accompanied, and sometimes preceded, the pioneers. Before the Mounties appeared, John Godson collected duties on the Klondike Trail in the southern Yukon by camping on the shore of a lake and wading out in his hip boots to meet the gold seekers in their boats.

Customs and Excise has been a most vital arm of our government from its very beginnings, if for no other reason than that administrations cannot prevail without revenue. Until 1917, when income tax was first introduced here, three-quarters of the revenue of the Canadian government, and of the several preceding colonial governments, came from customs and excise duties.

The long history of Customs and Excise is here arranged in four main sections, each complete in itself: a general history; the development of the land frontier; smuggling, including the 1926 customs scandal; and the lives and times of customs and excise officers. This account does not dwell on the details of headquarters administration, but concentrates, instead, on the experiences of customs and excise officers in the field — that is, out where the real work is done. It is the author's great fortune to have been able to talk with David Sim, a towering figure in the department for thirty-five years, and to meet a still zestful band of former and present-day collectors, who, without exception, regard the department with humor and goodwill despite the stern slogan drummed at them decade after decade: "The Revenue must be protected." It was Sim who said, "There are bound to be whispers about any organization which collects money." The department has been very hard on its members who stole even a nickel of the money that passed through their hands, but has been readier sometimes to excuse drinking on the job as an occupational hazard, especially among excisemen working in distilleries and breweries. Some of the stories here recorded, like the highlights of the career of La Couvée, the master of a patrol boat, have come directly from customs officers with near total recall of a long life of service. Others, like the accounts of Jeffery of early Halifax, Kerby of Fort Erie, Haynes of Osoyoos, and Godson and Busby of the Yukon, have been kept alive in customs archives, in letters and telegrams and the painstaking and earnest reports of officers keeping in touch "from the field."

A project to gather historical material and artifacts of Customs and Excise was initiated in 1980 by J.P. Connell, then deputy minister of National Revenue. The writing and publication of the history have been keenly supported by the present deputy minister, R.J. Giroux, the late Alex Morin, assistant deputy minister for field operations, and Jacques Laurin, former director of public relations. Many people outside the department have assisted the writer, in particular: Shirley B. Elliott, Librarian, Legislative Library, Halifax; Ray Sheehan, Library of Parliament; Gilles Desormeaux, Public Archives of Canada; Patricia M. Somerton, Saskatchewan Provincial Library; Lindsay Moir, Glenbow Museum, Calgary; T. de. Goede, Legislative Library, Victoria; Eric L. Swanick, Legislative Library, Fredericton; Graham Smith, librarian and archivist, Customs and Excise, London, England; and Lorraine Fairley, Toronto, editor. The cartography is by Richard P. Shaw, Ottawa. Within the department, great assistance has been given by Diane Parsonage and Gilles Gélinas, Customs and Excise library; and Dianne Parisien and Claire Pelletier, wizards of the word processor.

SECTION I

Customs and Excise in History

CHAPTER I

Beginnings in Europe and North America

The revenuer, it is generally conceded, is not universally loved. Indeed, his chief opponent, the smuggler, has received a far better press throughout history.

But the customs officer has long been and is today Canada's first line of protection, not in military terms of course, but in economic, social, and other senses. Contrary to the political rhetoric of more than a century, our border, commercial as well as geographic, *is* defended.

Customs and Excise, the oldest department of government in nearly all countries, has played a long and mostly honorable role in the development of Canada. Until the First World War, when income and sales taxes were introduced as "temporary" financial measures, Customs and Excise provided the biggest part, by far, of national revenue. Even today, customs and excise duties rank only behind income taxes in the federal government's sources of revenue.

The battle over whether crown or legislature had the right to impose and dispose of customs duties was vital in the achievement of responsible government in the several provinces before Confederation and in the attainment of national independence after it. The issue of tariffs has been vital — and debate bitter — in the economic development of this country.

The customs and excise man or woman is a protector of the revenue in the sense that the country can function only through the proper collection of taxes. When customs collector William Wanton of Saint John informed Governor Thomas Carleton of New Brunswick August 22, 1792, of a robbery at the customs house, he didn't write of a crime but of "this violent outrage committed on the Revenue." Revenue was always spelled with a capital R then, and often still is. Since Wanton's day, countless collectors and their seniors have echoed him in the phrase "the Revenue must be protected" and, apart from some aberrations such as the customs scandal of 1926, have done so. The customs or excise officer is a defender of the principle that taxes be shared equitably. Slipshoddiness or undetected fraud means that somebody has to pay more than his or her fair share.

Customs go back to Biblical times, at least. The prophet Ezra wrote in the Old Testament: "There have been mighty kings also over Jerusalem, which have ruled over all countries beyond the river; and toll, tribute, and custom was paid unto them." (Ezra 4:20) In the New Testament, we read the much more familiar: "And it came to pass in those days, that there went out a decree from Caesar Augustus, that all the world should be taxed." (Luke 2:1) Luke also refers to Zacchaeus, a customs collector, with the comment "and he was rich." Saint Matthew sat "at the receipt of customs" (Matthew 9:9) as a collector for the occupying Romans.

Income tax is a johnny-come-lately compared with the oldest fiscal expedient: taxes on goods, under whatever name. Customs duties apply on goods imported into a country or exported from it (the latter now very rare) and are designed as revenue producers, their original purpose in Canada at least, or as protection for domestic production and manufacture, the main purpose since 1879. Customs duties, or the tariff, are lower now, generally, than at any time since the early Confederation period. Excise duties and taxes usually apply to domestic manufacture and production, though this was not always the case, and are considered simply revenue producers. The word tariff, incidentally, comes from Tarifa, a fortress in Spain from which the Moors sailed to exact tribute from ships carrying goods through the Strait of Gibraltar. (Some importers still consider the tariff an act of piracy.)

The English word excise appears to come from the Dutch *accijus*, derived from the French *assise*, derived in turn from the Latin *assidere*, a tax. On the other hand, excise may come directly from the Latin *excidere*, to cut out. In any event, placing a duty on articles of home production and consumption has a long history. In ancient India there was a tax of a one-fiftieth part on cattle, gems, gold and silver. Byzantium taxed imports as much as 12 per cent and Athens had a 20-per-cent duty on corn and other goods as well as a tax on several exports. The tax collectors were *telonae*, from the Greek *telos*, a tax. The Roman historian Tacitus notes that Emperor Augustus (63 BC to 14 AD) introduced an excise tax of one per cent on all articles sold in public markets in Rome (it was two per cent on slaves). The tax caused clamor and discontent, Tacitus informs us. The Romans called customs *portoria*. When the Romans conquered Egypt, they established a general sales tax which amounted to as much as ten per cent and they carried a similar tax into France and Spain. When the Romans departed, the tax of course did not depart with them.

Salt duty also dates from the earliest Roman times. In Latin it was *gabalum*, which became the French *gabelle*, Arabic *kabala* and Spanish *alcavala*. The word in all these languages originally stood for all taxes levied on commodities, but later was limited to the hated salt duty. In France, *gabelle* is first found in an ordinance of 1246. Increases in the tax between 1542 and 1548 produced three revolts. As many as eighteen hundred peasants were sent to prison and three hundred to the galleys each year for avoidance of the *gabelle*. Although salt could be produced in New France, the colony was required to import it from France.

The Spanish *alcavala* in the mid-14th century started at one per cent and went to ten per cent. It was a cumulative tax which was levied at every stage of production and distribution. The Spanish introduced this tax into their colonies in the 16th century. Canada tried the cumulative (or turnover or cascade) tax in 1920 but it was so unpopular and unworkable it was abandoned in 1923.

The Roman excise tax was similar to the *octroi*, the King's eighth or town duty of a later period. These duties were charged on commodities entering the great cities of France and Italy and endured until fairly recent times. In Scotland, taxes on goods entering cities and towns from the country were called "small custom" to distinguish them from the "great custom" paid on goods from foreign countries.

The first written record of Customs in Britain is dated 742, when King Aethelbad refers to dues "which shall be there demanded by the collectors . . . of London Town." Richard I in the late 12th century imposed a tax called prise or prisage on imported wine. It had probably come into use under another name soon after the Norman conquest in 1066. Prisage was not a monetary tax. It was a share of the imported wine appropriated for the royal household. It was taken by the King's butler (from the French *bouteilleur*) and was eventually commuted into money payments called butlerage. Other old English tributes, some of them self-explanatory, included anchorage, ballastage, busselage (duty paid by the bushel or other measure), keelage, lastage (payable by traders at fairs), towage, moorage, tennage (payment for use of ground), cranage, wharfage, keyage, housellage (fee for storing goods), tronage (a charge on goods weighed at the tron, or beam for weighing), pesage (another tax for weighing), measurage, poundage and tunnage (a tax on wine at so much a tun, or hogshead). Later (1845) Canadian versions were slidage and boomage, taxes on government timber slides and booms on the Ottawa River and its tributaries.

The French word for customs, *douanes*, dates from about 1372 and has the same derivation as divan, whose original meaning was a meeting place for financial administrators. *Douanes* comes from the Arab *diouan* and Italian *doana* and *dogana*. People all over the then known world became so accustomed to paying "customary dues" that they simply shortened the word to customs.

King John, who signed Magna Carta, imposed a tariff of one-fifteenth on all imports in 1205. In 1206, the entire customs revenue of England, including tolls and licences for fairs, was £5,000. By 1590, it was only £50,000. The Magna Carta of 1215 dealt with "ancient and rightful customs," or taxes on imported wine and exported wool and hides. The customs tariff was first imposed by statute during the reign of Edward I (1272-1307). The first customs house in England was established in 1304 at London. By 1326, all goods of a specific kind had to pass through a certain port; each type of goods used a different port. The port became known as a staple and the goods passing through as "staples." The original staples were wool, woolfels (sheepskins) and leather. This system aided tax collection but not transportation or distribution. The poet Geoffrey Chaucer was appointed Comptroller of the Customs and Subsidy of Wool, Skins and Leather in the port of London June 8, 1374. Not until 1385 was he permitted to hire a deputy so that he could devote more time to poetry. Chaucer had begun his *Canterbury Tales* a year before entering customs service and continued writing them all the time he served as comptroller.

Collection of customs was farmed out for centuries in both Britain and France: the highest bidder, whether a single company or consortium, won the right to collect the revenue in exchange for an annual payment into the royal treasury. Farming, as it was called, was applied by both the English and French to their colonies in North America. It was brought to an end in Britain in 1671 (in the Excise in 1683) but lasted in France until 1791, that is, until after France had lost all her North American possessions, except St. Pierre and Miquelon, by the Treaty of Paris in 1763.

Because Canadian customs laws were adopted from Britain, and from France until — and even for some years after — Wolfe's victory at Quebec in 1759, we will deal briefly with the British and French systems.

Although farming the revenue started as early as 1275 in England, it gradually became apparent that some revenue was being lost to the crown under this system, and direct collection by some permanent government officials was begun. Later, the king frequently ordered collectors to make payments to certain persons for services rendered the crown. One of the earliest payments of this type was recorded in the port of Bristol when money was paid to explorer Jean Cabot. The most famous collector at Bristol was Richard ap Amerycke or A'Meryke, who served there from 1486 to 1499. Early in 1496, Cabot received a patent from Henry VII authorizing him to sail from Bristol and annex any "new found land" in the name of the king, the patentees to be exempt from customs duties on any goods brought back. Cabot himself didn't have the funds to finance this enterprise but it is possible that A'Meryke helped finance the venture or persuaded merchants to do so. In any event, Cabot received a pension of £20 from the king for his successful voyage. The pension was paid to him by A'Meryke out of Bristol customs duties. Modern British historians conjecture that Cabot repaid his benefactor by naming America after him.

The first "rate book," forerunner of the present-day tariff, was published in England in 1507. It did not give the actual rates of duty but the official values of all goods to which the rates were applied.

Early smuggling concentrated on the export of sheep, wool and hides. It was not until much later that the big smuggling items were liquor, wine and tobacco. In 1565, Parliament laid down this penalty (it was often exacted) for smuggling sheep out of the country: "Every such offender shall suffer imprisonment by the space of one whole year without bail or mainprize [a form of bail], and at the year's end shall in some open market town, in the fulness of the market, on the market day, have his left hand cut off, and that to be nailed up in the openest place of such market." A second offence called for hanging.

An elaborate system of privileges came into being and excused some personages from payment of import duties. For instance, in 1571, the entire Queen's household received its wine duty-free. Ten bishops were each allowed as much as twelve tuns free per year (a tun was 252 gallons), seven deacons three tuns each, the ambassadors of France and Spain twelve tuns each and more if required, the nobility four to twelve tuns and privy councillors one to ten tuns. In 1611, the drawback, a term still in use today, was authorized. It is a refund of duty on the exportation of previously imported goods.

The English civil war was brought about partly by the quarrel between Charles I and Parliament over which had the right to collect and spend customs duties. In 1643, Parliament imposed the first excise tax, copying Holland's excise tax system, and the term "customs and excise" came into tandem use. Excise taxes fell — and still fall — mainly on liquor and tobacco. Customs duties are imposed on these items as well when they are imported, of course.

Cromwell's Excise Act of 1657 authorized searches for goods without a specific warrant, a system which endured in Canada until comparatively recent times. We will have occasion later to quote directly from Canadian law on the subject of searches made under a legal procedure known as the "writ of assistance."

In France, there were states within states for customs purposes. What is today northern and central France contained the *Provinces des cinq grosses fermes*. In most of the rest of the country were the *Provinces réputées étrangères* which were treated as foreign countries when it came to imposition of customs tariffs. Jean-Baptiste Colbert, finance minister from 1661 to 1683, attempted in 1664 to impose one national tariff for all of France at roughly seven per cent on value of goods. But the *provinces étrangères* objected on the grounds that they would lose certain exemptions and privileges, such as taxing a foreigner more than a Frenchman. Like the clergy of England, some monastic orders in France received exemptions on wine — for example, thirty duty-free hogsheads of wine a year as long as it came from their own vineyards. Students at the University of Bordeaux were allowed fifteen jars of tax-free wine a month from their parents.

In 1667, a new tariff was imposed to protect French industry, particularly textiles, from Dutch and English imports. It became known as the *"tarif de guerre"* because it was one of the causes of war between France and Holland in 1672. The paradoxical situation was reached in which imported goods, once past the frontier, circulated freely throughout the kingdom while domestic products still continued to be taxed at various rates by the various provinces. Some imported goods became cheaper than the same domestic products. Elaborate frontier zones were established, four miles in depth. On entry into the zone, goods were stamped and taxes paid. The goods then had to be conveyed by prescribed routes and stops made at subsidiary customs houses where the original receipt was again stamped — and stamped again. At the last check point, the goods were examined all over again. The entire zone was patrolled by guards on horseback and on foot.

In 1726, French law graduated customs penalties in accordance with the amount of the fine levied. For instance, if a fine of 200 *livres* was not paid, the delinquent was flogged and branded with a C on the shoulder. If the unpaid fine was 300 *livres*, the penalty was three years in the galleys. For women and girls, the penalty was the lash. Judges were not allowed to reduce any fines on pain of payment themselves.

L'administration des douanes en France sous l'ancien régime, published in Paris in 1976 by *l'Association pour l'histoire de l'administration des douanes*, records this comment on customs officers in 1687: "Il a été bientôt reconnu que pour les exciter à remplir leurs fonctions avec attention il convenait de leur donner des récompenses sur le produit des saisies dues à leur vigilance." (It was soon discovered that to bestir them to fulfil their duties competently they should be recompensed for their seizures.)

The *ferme générale* was constituted in 1726, with one revenue collection contract between the king and a company of financiers known as *La Ferme*. The contract was renewed every six years. The number of *fermiers-généraux* varied from forty in 1726 to eighty-seven in 1774. In 1726, the king received 80 million *livres* from *La Ferme* and the *fermiers* took in 91 million *livres* for a tidy profit. *La Ferme* had 24,000 employees. In 1738, it is recorded, hours of business at customs were 6 a.m. to midnight from October 1 to April 1 and 4 a.m. to midnight from April 1 to October 1.

Customs officers carried arms and were exempt from *la gabelle* and some military duties.

Baron de Corméré gives this rather mordant picture of going through customs in 18th century France:

> Le Citoyen qui voyage est tenu de faire sa déclaration, d'acquitter des droits dont il ne connaît ni la cause, ni la quotité; il faut qu'il s'en rapporte à la bonne foi des commis; inutilement il murmure contre les retards, les formalités des visites, le ravage qu'elles occasionnent dans les malles, et contre l'établissement des droits qui l'expose à ces désagréments; il paye, en maudissant les auteurs de pareilles acquisitions. (The traveller is obliged to make a declaration and pay without knowing the reason or rate of tax; he must rely on the honesty of the clerk; uselessly, he may complain of delays, the formalities, the unpleasant search of luggage, the laws which result in these annoyances; but he will pay while cursing the authors of such regulations.)

Has anything really changed, in France or anywhere else?

Despite all the duties, and the rigmarole associated with them, France profited greatly from re-exporting to the rest of Europe the products of her colonies in the West Indies: sugar, tobacco, coffee, cocoa, ginger and dyes such as indigo and roucou. (Canadian furs did not rank high in this re-export trade.)

New France knew no other customs system than *La Ferme* because the French colonial empire in North America was swept away before the revolution of 1789 when the mobs attacked not only the Bastille but the headquarters of *La Ferme* itself. The French customs system was reformed in 1791 though perhaps not to the extent claimed at that time in a government directive: "Chez un peuple éclairé l'organization des Douanes n'est qu'une institution bienfaisante." (An enlightened nation looks on customs as a beneficial institution.)

The Europeans brought rum and religion to North America but they did not introduce customs duties to this continent. They were already here; the Indians exacted tribute from each other as goods passed from one tribe's territory to the next. A tribe particularly adept at imposing this toll was the Kichesipiirini, a family of the Algonquins who occupied a strategic island in the Ottawa River and were known to the French as *nation de l'Isle*. The island is called Morrison today. They took a percentage of furs, corn meal, sunflower oil, herbs and other goods in exchange for unharassed passage of the portage around the rapids in the Ottawa.

The Indians were great traders (Ottawa, from the Indian *adawa*, means a place for buying and selling) and party-givers. Those who paid toll were often feasted by the toll-takers. In the Jesuit Relations of 1636 Paul le Jeune refers to the Indian trade and customs system as "*les lois du Pays*" (the laws of the country) and says they were strictly observed by all Indian tribes. The whites, though accustomed to paying taxes, objected to paying tribute to the Indians on the Ottawa, one of the many factors which led to the bloody wars between the Indians and the French. In Indian terms, the whites were smugglers.

Le Jeune wrote:

> The Hurons, and the French who are now staying in their country, wishing to come down here, pass first through the lands of the Nipisiriniens, and then come alongside this Island, the inhabitants of which every year cause them some trouble. These Islanders would prefer that the Hurons should not come to the French nor the French go to the Hurons, so that they themselves may carry away all the trade; for this reason, they have done all they could to block the way; but, as they fear the French, those who accompany the Hurons make the journey easier for them. It is strange that although the Hurons may be ten against one Islander, yet they will not pass by if a single inhabitant of the Island objects to it, so strictly do they guard the laws of the Country. This portal is usually opened by means of presents, sometimes greater and sometimes smaller, according to the emergency. They ought to be very rich this year; for, a Captain of the Island having died this Spring, and their tears being not yet dried, no strange Nation can pass by there without making them some gift, to make them more easily swallow, as they say, the grief occasioned by the death of their Chief. When he who has been given to another, and presents have been offered to his relatives, — then it is said that the body is "cached," or rather, that the dead is resuscitated; and then only the usual tribute is paid when one passes over the highways and boundaries of these Islanders.

Joseph François Lafitau, in *Moeurs des sauvages amériquains, comparées aux moeurs des premiers temps* (Paris, 1734) wrote that Indians had certain duties to pay when they were on a trading mission and passing through the territory of another tribe among whom they did not wish to stop. Jesuit Gabriel Sagard, in his *L'Histoire du Canada* of 1636, maintained that the Indians who exacted toll on the Ottawa were the most discourteous and ill-tempered Indians in Canada. This prompted Clyde C. Kennedy, a more recent historian of the Ottawa Valley, to reflect in 1970 that Sagard's remark was merely the general and accepted characterization of anybody, anywhere in the world, who collects tolls and taxes. In 1775, trader Alexander Henry had to pay tribute to a village of Chippewas near Rainy Lake as the price of taking his goods farther into the interior; and trader Ross Cox tells us that several tribes on the Columbia exacted toll as late as the 1820s.

Before the Europeans arrived, the population of the beaver (*castor canadensis*) was about ten million and increasing by 20 per cent a year. The beaver migrates little and travels slowly on land. They were easy prey in their lodges to the new iron instruments and guns (to the Indians, the French were *gens du fer*) which the Europeans brought with them and traded to the Indians. The wave of beaver killing swept west as the demand for skins continued in Europe. In New France, companies holding fur-trading monopolies by royal charter rose and fell in dizzying succession. Some got rich quickly, but more went bankrupt. For the Indians, the loss was more than financial. Forsaking the bow-and-arrow and their bone and stone axes in favor of the new-age tools, they gave up their own culture, including agriculture, and turned to hunting for fur, the only tradeable good they had. As the beaver population was decimated and the hunting fanned out farther and farther west, the Indians competed among themselves. Their land fell into disuse, and the Hurons, the great middlemen-traders on whom the French depended to bring out the furs, were scattered. Not least, the Indians became heavy users of one of the Europeans' chief trading items: rum.

In the end, historian Donald Creighton wrote, "white settlement had conquered the empire of the St. Lawrence; and the Indians had been driven before it, driven irresistibly through defeat and shame toward their final degradation — towards the reserve, the shapeless alien clothes, the crafts debased and meaningless in a new age, and the dull, uncomprehending, haunted search for something which had irrevocably vanished."

But the fur trade was not Canada's first industry. Newfoundland codfishing was — the manna of Europe, in Champlain's phrase.

Jean Cabot found what now is Atlantic Canada in 1497 and named Newfoundland *Baccalaos*, from the Portuguese for codfish. He and Gaspar and Miguel Corte-Real reported that the sea was so full of fish that sailors caught them by lowering a basket with a stone in it and hauling it up again. Sebastian Cabot, the son, said "fyshes somtymes stayed his shyppes" and Marc Lescarbot (*L'Histoire de la Nouvelle France*, 1609) tells us that the fish got crowded by their numbers into shore where the dogs caught them. It did not take long for the European revenuers to see the tax possibilities in this bountiful state of nature. In 1501, Henry VII of England granted letters patent to some merchants of Bristol and Portugal which gave them a trade monopoly for ten years, with permission to enter one vessel duty-free. By 1506, Portugal had a duty on cod landed from the Newfoundland banks. Two decades before Jacques Cartier's discovery of the St. Lawrence, as many as sixty French ships from Normandy and Britanny alone were fishing on the banks. Cartier had trouble crewing his ships for exploration because the fish trade was so brisk and sailors scarce.

The first traders in Canada appear to have been dry fishermen — that is, fishermen who salted and dried their cod on land in scores of tiny harbors where they returned year after year. They began bartering for furs with the Indians in Newfoundland, then in Acadia, Gaspé, the Saguenay. "Green" fishermen filleted and salted their catch aboard ship.

In the early 1500s, fishermen sailed from small harbors in Portugal, Spain, France and the West of England in their fragile vessels, daring storm, fog, ice and, worst of all, rovers, pirates and sea-robbers. These early western Atlantic fishermen at first escaped the notices of kings, chroniclers — and customs men — and traded happily among themselves. Oil, wine and fruit from France, Spain and Portugal were exchanged for English cutlery, cordage, caps and hosiery thousands of miles out of sight of a customs house of any nationality. The dry fishermen gave names to their ports which attest to this day to their origins — Portugal Cove, Spaniard's Bay, Frenchman's Cove, English Harbour — and every year they congregated at St. John's before the long sail home. Lescarbot says one old master, Captain Savalit of St. Jean-de-Luz, made forty-two annual voyages to Newfoundland. Only after governments became involved did territorial squabbling begin, leading, as usual, to raid, plunder and war.

The first English Act of Parliament relating to North America was designed to give protection to English fishermen on the Grand Banks. In 1541, Henry VIII imposed a fine of ten pounds on any subject buying fish in Flanders or at sea to be sold in England.

By the end of the 16th century, St. John's was a free port for international trade and shipowners sailed to Newfoundland in their own vessels to superintend trade. Newfoundland historian D.W. Prowse says that "the character of this business . . . was an absolutely free trade; no Custom House officer [was present] to trouble the merchant's pocket or his conscience." The master and his crew fished; the owner had his store and traded. There were hundreds of ships, about fifteen thousand fishermen, and trade was extensive, lucrative — and untaxed. In 1578, Anthony Parkhurst of Bristol reported 150 French sail, 130 Spanish, 50 Portuguese and 50 English on the Newfoundland banks. He also reported the presence of "rovers and other violent intruders" among the fishing fleets and shore settlements. In 1586 André Thevet put the total at three hundred ships, including the Dutch.

The fish merchants and their seagoing representatives, known as the fishing admirals, opposed settlement because it would interfere with their dry fishing. As late as 1663 there was an English Act of Parliament which prohibited the levying of any tax on codfish in Newfoundland — the only product Newfoundland had to tax — to make certain there would be no revenue to sustain any government on the island.

But the bounteous free trade days were bound to come to an end. As the British and French empires expanded, especially in North America, they both adopted similar mercantile policies: the colonies could trade only with the mother country. The rationale was that the colonies supplied natural products and had to take manufactured goods in return. It was a profitable arrangement for a long time, but in the end it cost Britain and France their empires.

CHAPTER II

New France

France was the first to penetrate the North American continent. Cartier traded for furs on his 1534 voyage and as early as 1542 Jean François de la Rogue, Seigneur de Roberval, authorized the masters of two of his company's fishing vessels in the St. Lawrence to retain one-third of all furs obtained from the Indians.

In 1581, merchants of St. Malo outfitted a ship especially to trade in furs in the St. Lawrence. This proved so successful they hired a larger, eighty-ton vessel the next year. To try to keep the trade to themselves and thus secret, they hired the ship in the Channel Islands and the crew elsewhere. Three ships followed in 1583, five in 1584 and ten in 1585. But it soon developed that too many ships laden with trade goods were seeking too few pelts and the competition among the French traders led to ruin for some of them. As a result, royal grants of monopolies for trading in New France were established in 1588. Etienne de la Jannaye and Jacques Nouel, both captains in the navy, successfully petitioned Henry III for a twelve-year monopoly. There was an immediate outcry from the merchants — and the fishermen who traded in furs on the side — and the charter was revoked four months later. But the principle had been established. However, when Henry IV granted a monopoly, on the grounds that only a royal charter with a clause requiring colonization would induce merchants to settle colonists in a remote and forbidding land, his subjects showed little or no inclination to emigrate to the colony. Besides, the monopolists were interested only in furs and largely evaded their undertakings to settle New France. By 1628, after five different charter companies had been launched in twenty-eight years, there were still only two families of settlers on the St. Lawrence.

An example of how things went wrong is the experience of Pierre Chauvin who was granted a trade monopoly in 1599 on condition that he take out fifty colonists a year for ten years. In 1600 he landed sixteen colonists at Tadoussac and left them in a small log hut. They had to take winter refuge with some friendly Indians and scrambled home to France at the first opportunity the following year. No other settlers were landed and Chauvin lost his charter in 1602. In 1603, Dupont-Gravé and Champlain sailed up the St. Lawrence looking for a suitable site for colonists and then received some glowing reports from Indians about the Bay of Fundy. In 1604 the colony went, not to the St. Lawrence, but to Ste.

Croix in Passamaquoddy Bay where scurvy carried off thirty-five of the seventy-nine persons. The colony moved to Port Royal. An even more disastrous attempt had been made to set up a colony on Sable Island in 1598. There, sixty convicts were landed, but no relief was sent until 1603, when only eleven persons were found alive.

In 1604, Pierre de Gua (or Guast), Sieur de Monts, was given a ten-year monopoly covering an area between the Ste. Croix River (now the border between New Brunswick and Maine) and Tadoussac on the St. Lawrence River. A clause in his commission empowered him to impress "idlers and vagabonds" as colonial laborers. Trade was forbidden to all except shareholders in de Monts' company and any other ship, French or foreign, caught bartering for furs within its limits was subject to seizure and a fine of 30,000 *livres* (the *livre* was equivalent to 18 cents). In the first summer, eight vessels were seized as smugglers.

When the company vessels arrived back in France, twenty-two bales of pelts were seized for insufficient payment of import duties. Customs officers deemed New France a foreign country and imposed the same level of duty as on goods from Spain. The company's agent would pay only the duty which applied among the provinces of France. De Monts won on appeal but the decision took so long that the money from sales of the seized bales was not available in time to buy fresh stores for the Port Royal colony in 1605. Poutrincourt took charge of the colony in 1606 but Basque traders reached the area ahead of him and picked up all six thousand furs the Indians had to trade. Again, many of the colonists returned to France.

In 1608, Champlain went up the St. Lawrence again and established a settlement at Quebec. He stayed that winter with twenty-eight men (factors for the fur trade, interpreters, workmen to build a fort) of whom ten died of scurvy, five of dysentry and five from other causes. Wherever Champlain went in his explorations up the St. Lawrence and Ottawa, the fur traders were never far behind; they relied on him to intercede on their behalf with the Indians. Champlain complained that he was doing all the work finding fur-trading grounds and others were reaping the profits.

Seven ships engaged by the Prince de Condé, who held the fur monopoly at the time, had a good trading year with Champlain's help in 1613, but some of their furs were stolen between Quebec and Tadoussac by "strangers and pirates," that is, traders barred from the fur business by the monopolist of the day. In 1616, Condé was locked up in the Bastille for rumored designs on the crown and the man who arrested him, Thémines, took over the fur trade. Huguenot William de Caen was granted the fur monopoly in 1620 on the condition that there be no Protestant psalm-singing on his ships once the Newfoundland banks had been passed en route to Canada.

H.P. Biggar in his book *The Early Trading Companies of New France* makes the point:

> The history of all the companies formed during these years for trade in New France is the same; first a monopoly is granted under circumstances ostensibly most favourable to the government and to the privileged merchants; then follow the growls of the excluded traders, the lack of good voluntary colonists, the transportation to the colony of a few beggars, criminals or unpromising laborers; a drain on the company's funds in maintaining these during the long winter; a steady decrease in the number taken out; at length no attempt to fulfill this condition of the monopoly; the anger of the government when made aware of the facts; and finally the sudden repeal of the monopoly several years before its legal termination.

In 1627, Armand, Cardinal de Richelieu, ruler of French commerce, formed *La Compagnie des cents Associés*, also known as *La Compagnie de la Nouvelle France*, with a fifteen-year trading monopoly on condition that four thousand colonists be settled by 1643 and that three priests be supported in each village. One of the attractions of the contract was that no duty was to be paid on goods from New France for fifteen years: for instance, goods made in Canada and sold in Paris and elsewhere in France by returning artisans would be tax-exempt. There was another attraction: royal conferment of twelve titles of nobility on shareholders in the company. This made it easy to raise the initial capital of 300,000 *livres*. The formal instrument establishing the company was a blend of proselytism and commerce:

> Le seul moyen de disposer ces peuples à la connoissance du vrai Dieu étoit de peupler les dits pays de naturels François catholiques, pour, par leur exemple, disposer ces nations à la religion chrétienne, à la vie civile, et même y établissant l'autorité Royale, tirer des dites terres nouvellement découvertes quelques avantageux de commerce pour l'utilité des sujets du Roi. (The only way to attract these people to knowledge of the true God is to settle in the country French Catholics who, by their example, will instill in these people a feeling for the Christian religion and civilization and, by establishing royal authority, will draw from the new-found country commercial advantages for the benefit of the King's subjects.)

The colonists could trade with the Indians for furs, but they had to sell to the company.

In 1628-29, a Scottish and English company was formed for trade in the St. Lawrence and a fleet under David Kirke starved Quebec into surrender July 20, 1629. New France was English until 1632, when it was returned to France by the Treaty of St. Germain-en-Laye. *La Compagnie de la Nouvelle France* picked up where it had left off as if nothing had happened.

In 1629, another English fleet had landed Lord Ochiltrie and some sixty settlers on Cape Breton where the Scottish nobleman built a fort and promptly began demanding one-tenth of the catch of the French fishing fleet in the area. Captain Charles Daniel, in charge of a fleet of *La Compagnie de la Nouvelle France*, suddenly appeared, razed the fort and tossed Ochiltrie into a Dieppe prison for a month. Ochiltrie, when he gave his account, claimed that the French under Daniel had been received as friends but once inside his fort had turned on the inhabitants and seized them.

As far as colonizing New France went, *La Compagnie de la Nouvelle France* did not make much more of a dent in the problem than all its predecessors. By 1641, the colony comprised only three hundred souls living in two trading posts: Quebec and Trois-Rivières. A quarter-century later, the number had crept up to 3,418 of whom half were non-farmers living in Quebec, Trois-Rivières and Montreal. Agricultural settlement could not hold a candle to the lure of profit in the fur trade. The true first Canadien was not the settler-farmer but the voyageur, who paddled ever westward, singing in rhythm with his blade, living on corn maize and rum, and dying on the wilderness trail of drowning, of accidental falls under enormous back-packs, and of heart attacks and terrible hernias on the ninety rough portages between Montreal and Lake of the Woods.

The large Indian canoe (*canot de maître*) carried four tons of supplies and eight to ten men. It was made of thick birch bark sewn together with wattap (spruce roots) and was thirty-five feet long, four and a half feet wide and thirty inches deep. The trade goods, returning furs and provisions were bound in packages of ninety to a hundred pounds of which a voyageur usually carried two, one on his back anchored by a head band and the second on top of that at the back of his neck. Each of the big canoes carried sixty packages. At Grand Portage on Lake Superior, the voyageur switched to the smaller *canot du nord* which carried four or five men and one and a half tons of goods. The ratio was usually two-thirds goods and one-third provisions. The trip from Montreal to Michilimackinac near the junction of Lake Huron and Lake Superior took twenty-six days. From Grand Portage, the voyageurs ventured another one to two thousand miles into the continent. Each voyageur was allowed forty pounds of personal provisions, corn and pemmican obtained from Indians. In return, the Indians got ironwork such as kettles, firearms, axes and ammunition, and rum and tobacco. Out of a load of beaver pelts worth 8,000 crowns, each voyageur got only 600 crowns for a trip which might take up to three years. Put another way, his pay was 150 to 300 *livres* (or $25 to $50) for a supply run from Montreal to Michilimackinac and return.

Alexander Henry in his *Travels and Adventures in Canada and the Indian*

Territories tells us that at Fort des Prairies a gun brought twenty beaver skins, a blanket eight to ten pelts, an axe three skins, and half a pint of gunpower or one foot of Spencer's twist tobacco, one skin.

The fur trade began on the Atlantic coast, then moved to the Saguenay, the St. Lawrence, the Ottawa, the Great Lakes, the headwaters of the Hudson Bay drainage basin, Lake Winnipeg, the Saskatchewan, the Churchill, the headwaters of the Mackenzie River basin, the Mackenzie itself, the Peace, the headwaters of the Pacific Coast rivers and the Columbia.

The fur traders did not want or welcome settlers. They saw them as potential competitors for furs, not as farmers. By the same token, the governing authorities depended on the fur trade for revenue (25-per-cent export tax on beaver pelts). The greater and more widespread the trade, the heavier the competition from the English and the Iroquois, who traded with them, the sharper the threat of Indian warfare on the far frontier, the more compelling the need for forts and troops, the larger the sacrifice of settlement and agriculture to military expenditures, and the wider the vicious circle until the ultimate breach and collapse. The farmers of the St. Lawrence Valley produced not for export but for very subsistence. All the energy and initiative of the government, of traders and of at least half the population was poured into the western wilderness and its product, the beaver fur. As Donald Creighton notes, the expansion of the French westward was penetration, not occupation; travel, not home-building; commerce, not agriculture.

La Compagnie de la Nouvelle France fell upon hard times and in 1645 for 1,000 beaver pelts a year ($100,000) it leased its fur monopoly to the colonists themselves, or *La Communauté des Habitants* (or *Habitans*). Jesuit Paul Le Jeune gives some indication how restrictive the monopoly was: the colonists could use the pelts for barter but could not themselves send them to France; the monopolists did not care where the skins came from as long as they went through their storehouse and crossed the sea to France in their ships. Le Jeune notes in passing that codfish had to be shipped from France to Quebec because there were not enough people to go to the Gaspé to catch cod. They were pursuing furs.

La Communauté des Habitants, like many of its predecessors — and successors — went bankrupt. Between 1632 and 1718 at least a dozen different traders, companies or consortiums — or combinations of these — held the fur trade monopoly. A few prospered but most withered and vanished into new mergers which in turn languished and died. Oddly, the nobles and businessmen of France did not appear much interested in the fur trade, apart, perhaps, from those who were wearing rich Canadian fur hats and coats. They were more interested in the possibilities for viticulture in Canada. Pierre Boucher, governor of Trois-Rivières, recounted that on a visit to France in 1661, the question put to him most often was: do vines grow well in New France? The next question was: is wine dear? The answer was ten sous a quart; wine was served in the best houses, beer in some others and bouillon in all. Boucher added that the poorer people drank water which was very good and very plentiful.

The first government in Canada was ordained by Louis XIV of France, March 27, 1647, when he appointed a Conseil de Québec to administer the colony's affairs. It comprised the governor, the superior of the Jesuits, the governor of Montreal and a secretary. One of its first orders forbade merchants from landing goods "furtively" from vessels anchored at Quebec. Two residents of the colony were added to the Conseil the next year and, in 1657, five more persons were appointed.

In 1663, New France became a royal province: la Province du Canada. The Conseil souverain replaced the old council. It comprised the governor, the intendant, the bishop, five councillors, the attorney-general and a recording clerk and met every Monday at 8 a.m. in the Chateau St. Louis, later in the Palais de Justice, a renovated brewery.

One of the Conseil's administrative difficulties was that some recording clerks refused to give the records to their successors and, often, governors and intendants not only kept the originals of edicts and regulations but took them to France when they were replaced in their jobs. This problem was to recur, as we shall see, in the customs department of the United Province of Canada more than a century later. Indeed, it is interesting to note that the same Canadian problems crop up time and again regardless of period or circumstance and whether the regime is French or English. Another example is the order of the Conseil, in 1664, which barred local judges and attorneys from asking fees for public duties and threatened to replace them with the persons who informed on them for doing so. The exaction of fees, particularly customs fees, became an acute problem in all the colonies of British North America in the early 1800s and a key factor in the drive for responsible government in some of them. We will have occasion to deal with this at some length in a later chapter.

It was the civil law of the *Coutume de Paris* that was introduced into New France rather than the *Coutume de Normandie*, although four-fifths of the population was Norman. The first intendant, Robert, never arrived in Quebec and was succeeded in 1665 by Jean Talon. Talon made no bones about his intention to make Canada a revenue-producer for the king. In 1667 he wrote to Colbert, minister of marine and colonies as well as of finance, that the colony would not become a charge on France but rather would produce enough for its own needs:

et par la douane et ses sorties du Royaume elle contributera à l'augmentation des fermes et revenus du Roy, et accommodera ses sujets de l'ancien état en les deschargeant de leur surabondant. Et pour ce qu'elle ne paye pas en argent monnoyé ce qu'elle emprunte, elle donne des denrées par retour, consistantes en pelleteries tournent au bénéfice des sujets de Sa Majesté, lesquelles, si la Colonie de la Nouvelle-France n'étoit soustenue, tomberoient entre les mains des Anglois, des Hollandois ou des Suédois; et cet avantage n'est pas si peu considérable que la compagnie (de l'Occident) ne doive convenir que cette année il passe de la Nouvelle en l'Ancienne-France pour près de cinq cent cinquante mille francs de pelleteries. (and through customs and exports contribute to the king's revenue and relieve France of surpluses of goods. And the colony will pay for its goods in furs instead of cash, a profitable system for France. If New France had no support, it would fall into the hands of the English, Dutch or Swedes. That advantage (the fur trade) is not so insignificant that the (charter) company must admit that for that year nearly 550,000 francs worth of pelts had been exported from New to Old France.)

Talon took extraordinary measures to advance the projects he had in mind; for example, to encourage the growing of hemp he seized all the available thread in the shops and gave notice that no one could buy it except in exchange for hemp. But his optimism about economic prospects was never borne out and the fourteen intendants who succeeded him until the death of New France saw the colony become increasingly a financial drain on France, especially in the final years when it became mainly a military base.

On December 16, 1663, the Conseil souverain ordered that merchants selling goods imported from France be permitted to charge 65 per cent more than the selling price in France — 100 per cent more on wine — and that out of this markup they were to pay a revenue tax of ten per cent on imports. There had long been markups on goods as well as an export tax on furs, but apparently this was the first form of import duty used in Canada. It did not last long. In 1664, Colbert gave *la Compagnie de l'Occident* the trade monopoly for Canada, the West Indies and South America for forty years. But it failed like so many others and closed in 1674. The taxes of 1663 were immediately re-imposed at Quebec. The Conseil even fixed retail prices, its agents going to stores and shops and tagging each item of merchandise with a price slip bearing the royal arms. Merchants had to keep records of sales and inventory. Evasion of the ten-per-cent duty was difficult in the extreme. The best the merchants could do was to complain about the tax collector, First Councillor Villeray, and his collection methods. Frontenac fired Villeray but Colbert countermanded him. In 1682, Frontenac himself was recalled to France for arresting some members of the Conseil for purportedly insulting him, but was re-appointed in 1689.

During the summer, the season of open navigation, the population increasingly turned to the quick profits of the fur trade, to the neglect of agriculture. The coureurs de bois roamed farther and farther west. They insisted on the right to trade, with or without official permission, and undid the Conseil's best efforts to keep the settlers on the farm and away from furs. But they ran into American settlers moving into the Ohio country, a rich ground for beaver, and Hudson's Bay Company traders moving down from the north. The French countered by building forts, forging Indian alliances and mounting expensive military campaigns which ultimately devastated the economic life of the colony.

The construction and garrisoning of Fort Niagara in 1720-26 intensified the conflict between the French and English traders. The English maintained it was an infraction of the 1713 Treaty of Utrecht whereby France had ceded Acadia, today's Nova Scotia and New Brunswick, to England (and retained Canada, Isle Royale (Cape Breton), l'Ile de St-Jean (Prince Edward Island), Labrador and Anticosti). The French, for their part, ordered their voyageurs to hug the north shore of Lake Ontario en route to Niagara from Fort Frontenac (Kingston) so their goods would not be seized by the English operating out of Oswego.

Year after year, the governors of New France begged the home government to send out more and better goods for trade with the Indians. The loss of trade was often charged to the drying up of the brandy supply through the temperance efforts of the missionary-priests, while the English traders generally operated under no such restriction. Governor Beauharnois wrote that nothing so kept the Indians from trading with the French as the refusal to let them have liquor. To regain trade from the English, the French had to keep lowering the prices of their goods.

Still, import duties were not high. They were applied on a very limited number of products in the first half of the 18th century: the usual wine, eau-de-vie and tobacco. The fur companies did not police customs strictly, on the grounds that the cost would be higher than the revenue. It was not until 1748 (and only then as a war measure) that the king imposed duties on a wide range of goods (305 imported items and 39 exports). They were not immediately enforced and, even when they were, the duty was a modest three per cent. But the heavy export duty on furs continued throughout this period.

There were other types of customs tariffs, used for specific purposes. In 1714, at the French settlement of Plaisance in Newfoundland, liquor was taxed to pay for a hospital and in an attempt to reduce drunkenness among the fishermen and soldiery. At Louisburg, between 1722 and 1727, taxes were imposed first on the fish catch, then on fishing boats, to pay for the hospital, church and presbytery in the fortress.

After France lost Acadia, a brisk smuggling trade grew up between Cape Breton, still French, and the Acadians, particularly those around Minas Basin, and between Cape Breton and New England. The French took wine and brandy to the Acadians and New Englanders and took back wheat and cattle. When the English traders arrived to exchange their manufactured goods for agricultural products, the Acadians and New Englanders had little left to trade. The English colonies went so far as to build and sell ships to the French in Cape Breton, taking mainly liquor in return. This naturally caused some hostility in England: trader John Bradstreet complained to the authorities in 1719 that the French "reap as much benefit from Nova Scotia as if they were still proprietors thereof." (Historian Thomas C. Haliburton maintained that it was partly as a measure to check the export of contraband farm products to Cape Breton that the English expelled the Acadians from Nova Scotia.) On November 3, 1751, Governor Edward Cornwallis of Nova Scotia, who had founded Halifax two years earlier, reported to London that at least one hundred and fifty ships from New England had carried 12,000 barrels of flour and other goods to Louisburg in exchange for rum and molasses. "I doubt if Louisburg could subsist if it was not supported from our colonies," he said. "What could induce [New Englanders] to carry on a trade so pernicious to their Mother Country?"

There was a peculiar reverse side to this. The French merchants of St. Malo complained to the king that when they tried to sell goods to Cape Breton they found the English from New England had been there first and they were stuck with untradeable cargoes of flour, beef, lard, salt, sailcloth and so on.

Farming out the revenue from furs for a fixed sum was temporarily halted in New France in 1700. The leading merchants agreed to buy furs on their own account and turn over the 25 per cent tax to the government. But this did not work satisfactorily and was soon abandoned and the fur monopoly restored — to yet another company.

It irritated the monopolists that the officers, soldiers, clerks and workmen at Niagara, Frontenac, Fort Rouillé (Toronto) and other posts all engaged privately in the fur trade. Certain posts became favorites for officers because of the opportunities for profit. If the fur traders protested, the officers made it as difficult as possible for them to trade with the Indians. Some traders were driven to bankruptcy by military entrepreneurs.

And the drive west for new fur-trading territory continued feverishly. Between 1731 and 1748, La Vérendrye and his sons established trading posts from Grand Portage to the fork of the Saskatchewan: Fort St. Pierre on Rainy Lake, Fort St. Charles on Lake of the Woods, Fort Maurepas at the mouth of the Winnipeg, Fort Dauphin northwest of Lake Manitoba, Fort La Reine south of Lake Manitoba, Fort Rouge at the junction of the Assiniboine and the Red, Fort Bourbon on Cedar Lake, Fort Poskoyac on the Saskatchewan, and Fort La Corne at the junction of the north and south branches of the Saskatchewan.

Furs accounted for more than two-thirds of Canadian exports and in an average year the trade was worth 1,250,000 *livres* or about $2,500,000. The trade in pelts was not confined to beaver by any means. The furs received at Niagara and Frontenac in 1727 totalled 2,850 beaver, 3,014 deer, 4 bison, 7 moose, 448 racoon, 167 otter, 8 wolverine, 4 wolf, 247 marten, 438 bear, 84 fisher, 104 polecat, 6 red fox, 5 mink and 8 muskrat. And this was not counting the large illegal trade through Albany and Louisburg. By the census of 1754, of the fifty-five thousand people in New France, four thousand were regularly employed in the fur trade.

Still, New France was a drain on old France. As early as 1696, Baron Lahontan, who had seen much military service in Canada, wrote in his Instructive Summary of the Affairs of Canada (*Abrégé instructif des affaires du Canada*):

> Canada returns nothing directly to the King of France, since the sums accruing from the beaver lease and the import of goods and the export of all kinds of furs are used to maintain forty companies of marines, a governor general, four local ones, an intendant, a sovereign council, and a hundred other offices of justice, a bishop and all his clergy, two or three seminaries, as many hospitals, seven or eight convents of either sex, thirty missions among the Indians, besides the cost of a large amount of munitions; yet that country is of indirect advantage to him, inasmuch as France has only to send ships to Muscovy to trade there with the skins, while at the same time the Indians consume a quantity of goods made in the kingdom, in exchange for the beavers, martens, foxes, otter and moose which would have to be procured from foreign countries.

Three centuries later, Canada's position is little changed: we still export raw materials and import manufactured goods.

Lahontan said that eight hundred crowns' worth of goods taken in one canoe to the Indians — the goods comprised guns, powder, lead, axes, kettles, knives, needles, thread, cloth, blankets, overcoats and shirts — brought back 4,000 crowns worth of beaver skins. He added:

> The merchants of Canada sell their goods at an excessive price to the inhabitants of the coasts or villages, as well as to the Indians of the colony, and so become rich and opulent in a few years, because the money sent thither by the King of France for the maintenance of troops, by passing through the hands of the peasants who board them during the winter, falls into the coffers of the said traders, who keep it from circulating further. The Governor General gives twenty or thir-

ty permits a year to anyone he pleases to go and trade goods for skins in the country of all the friendly Indians, to wit, in all the lakes. Besides this number certain others go to the Illinois and other places, as if for the maintenance of the Jesuit missionaries, who care much less for the salvation of all these poor barbarians than for increasing the revenues of their houses by the prodigious number of canoes of beaver which they send to Quebec.

We can get some idea of why New France experienced economic difficulties throughout its life if we trace the price of a barrique (hogshead) of wine about the year 1755. The cost of putting it on board ship in France was 50 *livres* and the insurance 52 *livres*. (Of twenty ships leaving France, roughly six survived war, piracy and storm.) The freight charges were 150 *livres*, ordinary wastage ten *livres*, import duties 12 *livres* and unloading 3 *livres*, for a total of 277 *livres*. Interest on money to handle such a transaction came to at least 30 *livres* so that the merchant in Quebec would have to charge at least 330 *livres* to make even a modest profit of eight or nine per cent. The markup from the harbor price in France was nearly 700 per cent. Little wonder that Canada's imports totalled 8,000,000 *livres* in 1758 against exports of furs, fish and lumber worth 2,500,000 *livres*. Talon's dream of a colony whose surplus goods would enrich the coffers of France remained only that.

In the last eleven years of the French regime, *La Grande Société Gradis* of Bordeaux held a virtual monopoly on Canadian trade. Bigot, the intendant of New France, owned 30 per cent of the company and Bréard, controller of marine at Quebec, 20 per cent. With the connivance of Bigot, it was comparatively easy to evade customs duties, ignore the ceiling prices and cheat both the king and the colonists. Within twenty-four hours of a ship's arrival at Quebec, a complete and detailed declaration of the goods on board had to be handed to the *Bureau du Domaine* in the intendant's palace. Import duties were then assessed, although, as noted previously, only wine, brandy and tobacco and some dry goods were subject to tax. After 1748, there was a general customs duty of three per cent, except on salt and rope, but enforcement was lax. All duties were supposed to be payable before a landing licence was granted, but this proved impossible to enforce. Though the merchants often claimed they didn't have the money to pay the duty before they sold their goods, a score of them reached millionaire status during the last decade of France's rule in Canada.

Although the Treaty of Paris of 1763 lost France her North American empire (except for St. Pierre and Miquelon), the fur trade went on, just as if nothing had happened. In the articles of surrender, dated at Montreal, September 8, 1760, it was stipulated that the Canadiens could keep their furs, sell them, take them to France or elsewhere, and send canoes to fetch furs still at posts in the interior. No duties would be imposed beyond those established under the French regime.

But the treaty also forbade settlement of Indian territories in the Ohio and Mississippi Valleys, and the Quebec Act of 1774 extended the now English province to south of the Ohio River and west to the Mississippi. Thus a great fur-trading empire was formally established that stretched from the Labrador coast to the valley of the Mississippi. Because the Quebec Act blocked — or was seen to block — the American colonies' westward expansion, it was a contributing cause of the American Revolutionary War, which, in its turn, changed the shape of Canada while it created the United States.

CHAPTER III

British North America

Raising money through imposition and collection of taxes has been a central problem for all forms of government from the earliest and most primitive administrations.

The right of taxation itself was long a conflict between Crown and Parliament in the British provinces of North America as well as in England. The colonies all equally resented imperial taxes which raised money simply for Britain. They also disliked the rigid British control of trade and commerce. To Britain, the colonists were merely consumers of British manufactured goods sent to them in British ships. As Samuel Johnson said of them: "Sir, they are a race of convicts, and ought to be thankful for anything we allow them short of hanging." The difference between New England on the one hand and Canada and Nova Scotia on the other was one of degree: the New Englanders felt strongly enough to revolt, which they did in 1776, after a modest beginning made by hurling 340 chests of taxed tea into Boston Harbor, December 16, 1773. (Some demonstrations in sympathy with the New Englanders were held in Nova Scotia despite the attempt of John Newton, collector of Impost and Excise, to ban them. But there was no consignment of tea to the ocean.)

It has been suggested that the only reason Canada and the Maritime colonies did not join the revolution was that they were expert smugglers and consequently were not as enraged by customs duties as were the Americans. For instance, the law said tea could not be imported into Canada except from England and that it had to be supplied by the East India Company. In 1839, it sold in Upper Canada for three shillings, sixpence a pound while Chinese tea sold in the United States for one shilling, ninepence. Instead of dumping India tea into the harbor, the Canadians smuggled Chinese tea from the States. Three-quarters or more of the tea consumed in Upper Canada was smuggled.

Canadians showed no remorse for disregarding trade regulations imposed by a faraway imperial authority without their consent. Moreover, economic protection through import duties did not have then — as it had later — the status of a respectable political philosophy in British America. Generally, taxes were not heavy anyway. John Howison in *Sketches of Upper Canada* (1821) wrote that "taxes are so trifling that they scarcely deserve notice." And Robert Gourlay wrote in 1822: "No country in the world is less burdened with taxes. In no other country is the produce of labor [so] left to the laborer's own use and benefit, more undiminished by public exactions or deductions.''

The character of the change-over from French to British rule is no more apparent than in this order, taken from the *Quebec Gazette* of February 9, 1769:

> Public notice is hereby given, that, in pursuance of Orders lately received in this Behalf, by the Receiver-General of this Province, from the Lords Commissioners of His Majesty's Treasury, the said Receiver-General proposes to demand and collect from all Vessels that shall arrive in this Port, this ensuing Season, a Duty of,
>
> Ten Shillings Sterling per Hogshead upon Wine.
>
> Twenty Shillings per Hogshead upon Rum.
>
> One Shilling per Velte, or Measure of Two Gallons, upon Brandy.
>
> One half-penny Sterling per bottle of ordinary Wine.
>
> Three half-pence Sterling per bottle of sweet Wine.
>
> Five Pence Sterling per Gallon upon Eau de Vie de Liqueur.
>
> And Three Farthings Sterling per Pound on all Tobacco and snuff.
>
> But upon all British Brandies and other Spirits imported in Vessels from Great-Britain and being the Manufacture thereof, only one Half of the aforesaid Duty, which was levied by the French Government, in the year 1757, on Brandies and Spirits of the like Quality imported into Canada, is to be demanded and Collected; His Majesty being Graciously Pleased to remit one Moiety of the Duties on British Brandies and Spirits, and the whole of the Duties on Dry Goods imported and exported, except the Duty on Tobacco and Snuff imported, as well in Tenderness to His Subjects in the Province of Quebec, as in favour of the Manufactures of Great-Britain.

So, "graciously" and "in tenderness," was British trade preference established. It was not discarded until the 1980s.

In 1775, the British Parliament passed an act "to establish a fund towards further defraying the charges of the administration of justice and support of the civil government within the province of Quebec in America." This act wiped out any remaining duties of the French regime and established customs duties on goods brought into the province by "land carriage" or inland navigation. Duty had to be paid "at the port of Saint John's near the River Sorrel." The penalty for smuggling was forfeiture of all the goods as well as of all horses, cattle, boats, vessels or any other carriage used in the conveyance of the goods, and a fine three times the value of the goods. St. Jean was off to a brisk start as a customs port of entry. It remained the sole inland customs port in Canada until 1801.

Britain seemed to lean toward protection of Canadian agriculture and industry, such as they were. By order-in-council, in 1785, Britain forbade all trade by sea between Canada and the United States and the next year prohibited "the importation of all goods and commodities of the growth and manufacture of the U.S. into any of the ports of the Province of Quebec."

This upset the Canadians and, in 1787, the British Board of Trade recommended that the Canadian legislature be allowed to regulate inland trade with the United States. The following year the legislative council of Quebec opened Canada to free importation, by way of Lake Champlain and the Richelieu River, of American timber, cereals, dairy products, cattle, poultry and fresh fish.

Lower Canada accepted customs duties, at least on manufactured goods and on the usual wine, liquor and tobacco, as the inevitable means of raising revenue. But the merchants of Upper Canada resisted this form of taxation, preferring a land tax.

The division of Canada in 1791 into Upper and Lower provinces provided a partial solution to certain political problems, but it resulted in further economic difficulties, among them the collection and disposition of customs duties.

Although Britain had finally and formally discarded the customs tariff of the old French regime in Canada as inadequate and had imposed a new schedule of import duties to meet Quebec's revenue needs, when Upper and Lower Canada were carved out of Quebec in 1791, no provision was made for apportioning the customs revenue between the two provinces.

The catch was that Upper Canada had no seaport. Quebec was the main port of entry for Canada for all goods imported from Europe, from the other British provinces of North America and from the United States. All customs duties on these imports were collected at Quebec. And the only inland port of entry for the first decade of the Constitutional Act was also in Lower Canada, at St. Jean. British law forbade Upper Canada to import European goods through the United States and only a meagre flow of American products on which duties could be levied crossed the Great Lakes. Lower Canada conceded that, because customs duties were paid on goods consumed in both provinces, Upper Canada was entitled to a share of those duties. The question was: how big (or small) a share?

The first provincial Parliament of Upper Canada, at its second session at Niagara, in 1793 approved:

> an act to authorize the Lieutenant-Governor to nominate and appoint certain commissioners to treat and agree in behalf of this province with a like number of persons in behalf of Lower Canada of and concerning the establishing such regulations as may regard the collection of duties or payment of drawbacks to be imposed or allowed on goods passing from one province into the other, by the legislature of each

province respectively, and of and concerning any proportion to be received and paid of any equal duties already imposed, or hereafter to be imposed, by the said legislatures respectively, on any article or commodity passing from one province into the other, and of and concerning any regulations, provisions, matters, and things which may regard the commerce, manufactures or produce of the said province.

The quarrelling began almost at once, and it took four years to work out a financial arrangement whereby Upper Canada, whose population then was scarcely more than a few thousand, received one-eighth of all duties collected at Quebec under the Provincial Revenue Act of Lower Canada. (At its very first session, the Assembly of Lower Canada imposed a new tax on imported wine, exempting wine consigned to Upper Canada; the difficulty came in distinguishing which wine was to be consumed in Lower Canada and which in Upper Canada.)

The division of revenue was worked out by the Board of Commissioners with representatives from both provinces. But there were difficulties in the very composition of the board. The Upper Canadian representatives were appointed more or less permanently but those from Lower Canada were named only when an old agreement expired and it came time to work out a new arrangement. In any event, the 1795 agreement lasted until 1817, mainly because a war intervened and the very survival of Canada took precedence even over customs duties.

Upper Canada depended on this agreement for four-fifths of its income and, by its terms, turned over to Lower Canada its own authority to determine which articles entering Upper Canada were to bear customs duty and the amount of that duty. A "joint inspector" was stationed at Coteau-du-Lac to check all boats and carriages for the actual amounts of dutiable goods entering Upper Canada. This was the only record Upper Canada had of its imports and thus the only means of measuring the revenue due it.

In 1810, goods entered at Coteau-du-Lac included 87,692 gallons of Jamaica rum, 11,748 gallons of brandy and 24,949 gallons of wine, bringing in customs revenue of £3,143. This amount was paid over by Lower Canada under the agreement. At the same time, Upper Canada collected £1,300 in tavern and shop licences and £1,500 on goods, mainly liquor and wine, imported directly from the United States. Robert Gourlay observed, in 1822 in his *Statistical Account of Upper Canada*, that "in such an extended line of water communication there are places of landing where, it is supposed, dutied goods are sometimes smuggled into the province." For a civil servant, George Heriot, deputy postmaster general of British North America, treated the matter of revenue very casually. He said, merely, (in his 1807 *Travels through the Canadas*) that at Coteau-du-Lac "a certain duty is payable on spiritous liquors, wines and some other articles imported into Upper Canada." We learn from Gourlay and others that the other articles were molasses, sugar, coffee, tea, tobacco, playing cards and salt.

In 1817, Upper Canada managed to negotiate a new agreement under which it received one-fifth of the customs revenue. This agreement was for two years only and contained no provision for any payment to Upper Canada if the Board of Commissioners could not reach a new arrangement in 1819. At the same time, Upper Canada put in a bill of £5,178 for "arrearages" accumulated during the 1812-14 war, claiming that a great deal of port wine had entered Upper Canada without being marked down by the inspector at Coteau-du-Lac. Before long, Upper Canada upped its claimed "arrearages" to £10,845. Lower Canada agreed to pay £1,585 on account for 1816, but balked at the rest.

In 1819, the very thing that Upper Canada feared might happen, happened. The two houses of the Lower Canada legislature — assembly and council — quarrelled over the appointment of the commissioners who would negotiate with Upper Canada on a new agreement, and no one was appointed for two years. Not a penny of customs revenue moved from Lower Canada to Upper Canada, which complained of the "detention" of its revenue. Lower Canada had kept piling on new customs duties and increasing the old ones so that nearly every article which had been duty-free was now taxable. It had neglected to inform Upper Canada of these additions and increases and, moreover, had failed to inform the inspector at Coteau-du-Lac who was supposed to keep track of dutiable goods. This meant a smaller total of dutiable goods accounted for and thus a smaller portion of revenue for Upper Canada. Even though Upper Canada consumed one-third to one-half of all the goods imported at Quebec, it was getting only one-fifth of the customs duties levied on them.

Lower Canada was not impressed with this argument. The legislature of Upper Canada had long consented to the arrangement and therefore had nobody to blame but itself. Upper Canada conceded this, at least to some degree, when it replied that it had "unwisely assented" to the exclusive control of the port of Quebec by Lower Canada.

In 1821, the negotiations between the two colonies reopened after Lower Canada managed to agree on its members for the Board of Commissioners, chief among whom was the redoubtable Louis-Joseph Papineau. Upper Canada presented an even bigger bill for "arrearages" and asked for one-quarter of the customs revenue. Lower Canada responded by saying that if that was the way Upper Canada felt about it, it could levy its own customs duties at the colonial border. As frustrated as it was, Upper Canada declined to fall into that trap. Not only would it have had to bear the heavy expense of establishing customs houses on a new frontier — it had been reluctant to install them in the first place on its U.S. border — but, far worse, it would have meant double taxation. A second round of tariffs would have paralyzed trade in Upper Canada. Who would want to do business in Upper Canada when everything would cost less in Lower Canada?

Lower Canada also maintained that Upper Canada could get goods more cheaply from the United States because it was lax in collecting duty, and because the "extent and openness of the frontier" permitted a great deal of smuggling. (A select committee in Upper Canada two decades later corroborated this charge.) Besides, Papineau said, Upper Canada was importing so much liquor and salt from the United States that the European trade had practically dried up, thus cutting the customs revenue at Quebec. Upper Canada said that Lower Canada had placed it on the footing of foreigners by adding a 2 1/2 per cent tax on goods consigned to Upper Canada alone. It was, in effect, "a foreign country interposing between us and the Parent State." Lower Canada said it had a perfect right to tax goods arriving at Quebec however it wished.

The legislature of Upper Canada formed a joint committee of the legislative council and the assembly to gather up all its complaints in one petition to the king that swam in piteous cries: "The Executive government is embarrassed, the public creditors are delayed, all means of advancing works of general utility withheld; and it has at last become necessary to borrow . . . to pay pensions to veterans wounded in maintaining the cause of your Majesty's empire in a national war"; "every branch of the public service is threatened with ruin"; "it is impossible to foresee how the government of this province can be long carried on"; "the public faith must be broken."

The immediate aid of the "Parent State" was required. The imperial Parliament should assume "exclusive and entire control of all imports and exports in and from the Port of Quebec" and make provision for the payment of "arrearages." The petition concluded with a request for the appointment of three arbitrators to settle the apportionment of customs duties: one from Upper Canada, one from Lower Canada and one from Nova Scotia or New Brunswick.

In response to this and to other signs of restlessness in the Canadas — the fight for responsible government was well under way by this time — the British government decided on a general reorganization of the affairs of the two provinces. As originally drafted by John Beverley Robinson, attorney-general of Upper Canada, at the request of the colonial office, the Union Bill was designed to accomplish three things: regulation of trade between Canada and the United States; an arbitration system for the division of duties collected at Quebec; and a united legislature. The first two objectives were achieved in 1822 in the Canada Trade Act but political union was abandoned (temporarily, it turned out) after opposition led by James Mackintosh in Britain and acrimonious argument waged by petition, pamphlet and public gathering in the Canadas.

Under the Trade Act, the customs tariff was to be decided by the Lower Canada legislature as it had been since 1791. Three arbitrators were chosen but Upper Canada often found itself in the minority on the Board of Commissioners. It continued to fight for a larger portion of the customs revenue though Lower Canada was better about making payments. The *Montreal Gazette* of November 2, 1822, asked plaintively: "Will perpetual arbitration not increase rather than remove the causes of provincial discord about revenue?" And, "Is it possible with one common port of ingress to continue a system for imposition of import duties which will not give to the one or the other legislature an unfair influence?"

In the same cause, the commercial class proposed annexation of Montreal to give Upper Canada a seaport. The legislative council of Upper Canada passed a resolution in 1826 advocating such a move, prompting Papineau to remark that Upper Canada's only principle was that of a highway robber.

In 1830, shippers and merchants and "others interested in the trade between Upper and Lower Canada" sent a petition to Sir John Colborne, lieutenant-governor of Upper Canada:

> That in the prosecution of their trade they have for several years been subjected to vexacious delays and (as they are advised) illegal exactions in the nature of fees, demanded by the officer of Customs at Coteau-du-Lac, a tax of twenty shillings on each Durham boat and five shillings on each bateau being demanded on their arrival at Coteau-du-Lac from Upper Canada.
>
> That the fees alluded to are demanded in direct violation of the provisions of an act to regulate the trade of the Provinces of Upper and Lower Canada. . . .
>
> Aware of the injustice and illegality of the exactions complained of, your petitioners through the committee of the Board of Trade of Montreal caused a remonstrance to be made to His Excellency Sir James Kempt during the last summer, who referred the matter to the attorney-general of Lower Canada whose opinion is hereunto annexed and a copy of which was transmitted to Mr. Simpson, the officer of Customs at Coteau-du-Lac.
>
> That notwithstanding this opinion the officer at Coteau-du-Lac has continued to demand the above illegal fees and in some instances has even fired upon boats to compel them to come in. Your petitioners beg leave to suggest that the authority upon which the officer of Customs at Coteau-du-Lac relies in receiving the exorbitant fees alluded to is a provincial act of the Lower Province passed in the ninth month of the reign of his present Majesty, that by this act the

fees therein enumerated are only demandable on vessels coming from a foreign country or from Upper Canada laden with the produce of a foreign country, and nothing therein contained can be construed to authorize any charge on vessels going from Upper into Lower Canada laden exclusively with the produce of the former and that no report is necessary until their arrival at Montreal, the general port of destination.

This petition was fully backed by the Upper Canada House of Assembly February 10, 1830, which added that Upper Canada was being deprived of "the free and uninterrupted navigation of the River Saint Lawrence" and that means should be taken "for the recovery and return of all monies thus illegally extorted from the people of this Province."

Another attempt around the problem was a suggestion that goods warehoused in Quebec and Montreal be shipped and rewarehoused in Kingston, enabling Upper Canada to collect duty when they came out of the warehouse. The Board of Customs, London, rejected the idea on the grounds that Upper and Lower Canada were two separate possessions of Her Majesty and sending goods from Quebec to Kingston would class them as exports liable to a second import duty.

The two provinces continued their independent and quarrelsome existence; arbitration in 1833 that awarded Upper Canada one-third of the customs collections failed to settle the problem. Meeting in 1835, a select committee of the Upper Canada House of Assembly complained that Lower Canada owed a portion of at least £178,000 in collections at Quebec, but added resignedly, "It appears that an act of the Imperial Parliament is deemed necessary before the claim of Upper Canada can be satisfied."

In 1837, Upper Canada returned to its proposal that the island of Montreal be annexed to it to provide a seaport. By a vote of 29 to 14, the assembly approved a resolution which maintained that, when the border was fixed between Lower and Upper Canada in 1791, the authorities had overlooked "a natural and obvious boundary line" at the island of Montreal. All that was required was to shift the border only thirty miles or so to the east. The resolution again dwelt on some of Upper Canada's favorite complaints: the division of customs duties was unfair because it was based on population instead of actual consumption of goods; every "boat, raft and craft" going down the St. Lawrence from Upper Canada had to clear customs as if it were going to a foreign country; Lower Canada was financing public works out of revenue which properly belonged to Upper Canada but was neglecting improvement of canals on the St. Lawrence; the St. Lawrence was a "common highway" for both provinces but Upper Canada had been deprived of its "natural right" of free access to the sea.

The assembly then offered with a flourish the assumed benefits from Montreal's annexation: an increase in demand for British commerce and consequently in the employment of British seamen; the export of as much grain and flour through Quebec as from all U.S. seaports combined; a doubling in the value of property in the annexed section, and enhancement of the value of all property in Lower Canada; a new spirit of enterprise in both provinces; completion of the ship canal from the Great Lakes to the ocean; and an increase in revenue. Moreover, this union of Montreal and Upper Canada would do no injustice to the residents of Lower Canada: Montrealers would retain every privilege except that they would be under the jurisdiction of the Upper Canada legislature in all matters connected with trade and commerce. The "evil result of dividing the country above Montreal" would at last be eliminated. The assembly concluded: "Your Majesty's faithful Commons despair of ever having a free access to the ocean until the Boundary Line is altered so as to give the Legislature of this Province the entire control of a Sea Port, which of right they should long since have possessed."

Lower Canada saw the proposed annexation as the forerunner of union of the Canadas, consequent subjugation of the French by the "British Party" of Montreal and eventual swamping of the French-language population by the English. All through the piece, Lower Canada did not seem to blame Upper Canada so much as it blamed some misguided Upper Canadians who had been led on by the "enemies of Lower Canada" in Montreal. (The population of Lower Canada in 1834 was 600,000 of whom 525,000 were French-speaking. But 157 civil servants were English-speaking and only 47 French-speaking.)

The Assembly of Lower Canada naturally protested against any excision of 60,000 of its inhabitants and declared that annexation of Montreal to Upper Canada would be a violation not only of the terms of surrender of Montreal in 1760, but of solemn acts of Westminster. Fighting off annexation became one of the rallying points for the revolutionists in the uprising which came later that year.

The lieutenant-governor of Upper Canada, Sir Francis Head, mailed off the annexation resolution to London as Despatch No. 25, and received the usual polite acknowledgement from Downing Street that the assembly's petition would be placed before the throne. Nothing, of course, came of the proposal, and Montreal remained, as some Upper Canadians lamented, in "bondage."

The customs problem was never settled until the two colonies became the United Province of Canada in 1840. The peripatetic capital of the single colony jumped around from Kingston to Toronto, Montreal to Quebec, until it finally came to rest, by royal decree, in a remote lumber village called Ottawa in 1858. Ottawa had changed its name from Bytown in 1855 but the customs department did not get around to making the official change on its books until 1870, three years after Confederation.

CHAPTER IV

Customs and the Fight for Responsible Government in Nova Scotia

A far more profound and important argument was raging between Britain and her colonies in North America over the imposition and disposition of customs revenue. The principle at stake was the winning of responsible government, in this context a government entrusted to a ministry (or cabinet, if you prefer) possessing the confidence and support of the majority of the members of the elected Parliament or legislature.

This issue was fought in all the legislatures in the British colonies of North America but Nova Scotia was the first colony to achieve responsible government — without the civil wars of the Canadas — and its case clearly demonstrates the prominent role played by Customs.

It would be well, first, to clear up a couple of constitutional points. The reorganization of the Baldwin-Lafontaine ministry in 1848 inaugurated responsible government in Canada. But it had existed from 1846 in Nova Scotia by virtue of a dispatch from Lord Grey to Sir John Harvey, lieutenant-governor, in which the Colonial Secretary declared that the executive council could be retained as long as it had the confidence of the legislature. Responsible government was not the only major change in Canadian autonomy in this period, however; in 1846 a British statute authorized the colonies to enact their own customs laws. From that date we were able to regulate our own commerce to suit ourselves, without outside intervention. At about the same time, the colonies also obtained command of the civil list — that is, the power to make civil service appointments.

England had ended the farming of taxes in 1671, and began appointing customs collectors in the colonies (plantations, they were called) in 1696. They collected imperial taxes for England, to be spent as London judged and not as the colonies wished. Yet control of North American Customs from London became almost impossible, and an American Board of Customs was established at Boston in 1767. It departed at the first shot in the American Revolutionary War in 1776, never to return to this side of the Atlantic. But for nine years, Customs in Canada was run from Massachusetts.

The colonial collectors had to administer all kinds of acts besides the tariff. There were 3,000 acts governing navigation, trade and customs. They included the Navigation Act of 1651 which dictated that colonial goods must be shipped to England in English ships, the Woollens Act of 1698 which said wool and wool products could not be shipped from one colony to another without first being shipped to England, and the Molasses Act of 1733 which imposed heavy duties on rum, sugar and molasses from the French and Dutch West Indies to protect the British West Indies product. These were all part of British mercantile policy, which might be described as England First.

When Cornwallis founded Halifax in 1749, he was charged, among other things, with "protection of the revenue." Customs duties and excise taxes date from 1751, all on liquor. The Nova Scotia assembly was bound and determined to collect its own revenue. At the first assembly in 1758 the first act passed was duty of three pence a gallon on rum and other liquor. It was specified that this was a provincial tariff "to provide bounty and premiums for clearing and fencing lands, catching and curing codfish and other necessary encouragements to labor and industry." Thus Nova Scotia had double duty: the imperial tariff and the provincial tariff, and a collector for each. Naturally, the offices of the two collectors were in different locations. More than a dozen documents were required to enter and remove goods from a Halifax warehouse. In 1759, merchant ships were taxed at Halifax to support the Sambro lighthouse and in 1802 Nova Scotia taxed all imports from the United States "for the better support of the poor."

But as long as Nova Scotia was a colony, it was obvious that the provincial tariff would be only a subsidiary measure because London could disallow it at any time. Before the colony could take charge of all customs revenue, it had first to get control of the appointment of customs collectors.

It is not clear when and where the first crown-appointed customs collector did business in Canada but we do know there was a collector at Annapolis Royal in 1719, and that ten years later he was serving Canso as well. Hilbert Newton was collector for Nova Scotia in 1744 at a salary of £60 a year and his son, Henry, born in 1732, was the first collector in Halifax, a post he held for fifty years. Hilbert Newton's superior was Thomas Lechmere, surveyor-general for "the northern district of America," which included Jersey, New York, Connecticut, Rhode Island, New England, New Hampshire, Nova Scotia and Newfoundland.

The officers of Customs were appointed by the Commissioners of the

Customs in England who came under the authority and direction of the Lords Commissioners of His Majesty's Treasury. These appointments were sought, not because of their salaries, which were low or nonexistent, but for the fees which could be charged legally. The table of fees was drawn up in England for each customs position — collector, comptroller, surveyor, searcher (or jerquer), waiter (or watchman) — and specific charges were made against importers and merchants for each document used: harbor clearances, warehouse clearances, bonds, certificates and registers. Samuel Pepys, secretary of the Royal Navy, observed: "It is not the salary of any place that did make a man rich, but the opportunity of getting money when he is in place."

As early as 1775, the assembly of Nova Scotia asked that the fee system ("these horrid charges") be abolished and that customs officers be paid salaries. The assembly petitioned London "that you will appoint good and sufficient Salarys, to the Officers of the Customs, and absolutely forbid them to take any fee, in any case whatsoever, as we have found, that the detail of Revenue duty, in all its Departments, have been clogged with unnecessary forms and trifling Regulations, to increase fees and perquisites of the Officers . . ." Governor Francis Legge was recalled to England for impropriety when he tried to sue for default the collectors at Halifax, Louisburg, Canso, Annapolis, Lunenburg and Cobequid.

The assembly's petition did not bear immediate fruit. The system lasted another fifty years in British North America, though it ended in Britain in 1807. By 1814, there were fourteen different charges at Halifax ranging from 13 shillings for registering a vessel to ninepence for cancelling a bond. At Liverpool, the fees in one year amounted to £2,330.

In 1820, the assembly found, for instance, that customs fees had amounted to more than £3,000 at Windsor in 1816-19 while the actual duty collected was only 18 shillings, ten pence.

Just how brazenly the customs officers looked on customs as their own tightly knit preserve is indicated in the testimony before the assembly. For instance, the responsibilities of comptroller were to examine and verify the collector's quarterly accounts and to check all proceedings in the port which might have been irregular or improper. John Slayter, comptroller at Halifax for thirty years, stated in 1820: "I keep no clerk, book, or paper separately from the collector, whose books and papers are open to my inspection, nor have I ever since the collector came into office regulated, comptrolled or altered any of that officer's proceedings."

In 1786, the assembly had complained about exaction of customs fees from fishing vessels and other small boats taking produce to market. In 1790, a compromise was worked out: coasting vessels could obtain three-month "passports" for five shillings, 7½ pence. But the fact remained that Customs was still charging fees on trade moving within the colony.

In 1820, the assembly turned its economic grievance — the protest against customs fees — into a much larger question of constitutional rights. Two petitions came before the assembly. The first complained that high fees injured the coastal trade. Thirty-four shipowners compared fees charged at Barrington, Nova Scotia, and Saint John, New Brunswick, for the same ship. The 44-ton *Rainbow* paid fees of 16 shillings, nine pence at Saint John compared with four pounds, 17 shillings, seven pence at Barrington — more than five times as much. The 38-ton *Robin* paid 16 shillings, nine pence at Saint John and four pounds, 19 shillings, and half pence at Barrington. The 83-ton *Armistice* paid one pound, six shillings, six pence at Saint John and six pounds, 19 shillings, half pence at Barrington. The second petition came from twenty-nine coastal traders at Windsor, and asked whether it was equitable that a vessel of fifty tons, valued at £500, should pay £60 in customs fees in one summer.

Thomas Nicholson Jeffery, collector at Halifax, was called before the assembly for an explanation. He refused to give any. The ports of New Brunswick, Prince Edward Island, and Cape Breton (though annexed to Nova Scotia that year) were "foreign." Furthermore, said Jeffery, the amount of fees received by customs officers was "of a private nature" and "I am not bound to give any information to this Honourable House thereon." The assembly instructed Jeffery to specify the items which comprised the fees schedule, or bill of charges. Jeffery replied: "If you furnish me with that bill of charges, I will take time and consider whether I will answer it or not."

The assembly found that "evils and violations of law do exist in the Halifax Department of the Custom-House in this Province" and that officers were charging 60 per cent more than the authorized fee schedule at Halifax and as much as 200 per cent more in the outbays. And it maintained that the assembly itself was the only authority which could tax Nova Scotians.

Jeffery was a son-in-law of Attorney-General John Richard Uniacke who himself, during the war of 1812-14, made £50,000 in fees as advocate-general in the admiralty court of Halifax. Both men were members of the legislative council, which did not act on, or take particular notice of, the assembly's strictures.

In 1778, two years after the start of the American Revolution, Britain had slightly relaxed the mercantile policy that had done so much to bring on the revolt. It determined that at least some of the proceeds of taxes collected in the colonies would be for expenditure in the colonies in which they were raised. But Britain continued to appoint the collectors. The colonial legislatures had first to wrest this control from London before they could hand the collectors laws to implement.

In 1821, that goal seemed as far away as ever in Nova Scotia. Jeffery relented to the extent of telling the assembly that he had stuck to the legal fee schedule but had had other expenses, such as hiring extra staff at £800 a year. Three governors — Wentworth, Dalhousie and Kempt — expressed confidence in Jeffery, and Jeffery himself said the assembly's attack on customs fees was aimed at the establishment itself and not at the customs officers.

The Commissioners of Customs in London, finally taking note of the complaints from Nova Scotia and the other colonies, asked the treasury to revise the fee schedule and even found that Jeffery had been "in error" in a few instances in collecting unauthorized fees. But, concluded the commissioners, flying in the face of what Jeffery had himself said, the assembly's charges stemmed from "personal hostility" toward Jeffery and there was no ground for further investigation.

The assembly kept up the pressure. It produced a case, for instance, where a ship wrecked off Cape Negro near Barrington Passage had been charged a £6 entrance fee by Barrington Customs though she had never reached port. Jeffery launched a counter-attack. He said shipowners had made accusations of exorbitant fees as a smokescreen to divert attention from their smuggling, or attempted smuggling.

Not all customs collectors were as unpopular as Jeffery. Collector William Johnstone was appointed at Liverpool, Nova Scotia, in 1771. He was lax about collecting duties. When he was seventy-six, he was replaced by an enforcer, John McAlpine, whose efficiency raised such a hue and cry that Johnstone was re-appointed and served until 1795, when he was eighty-three, apparently to the satisfaction of all importers there.

At last, in 1825, Britain abolished the fees and substituted regular salaries for customs officers. *The Acadian Recorder* of April 30, 1825, recorded "jubilation" and *The Novascotian* of March 23 gushed: "What bounds are there not to the vast liberality of our Parent State!" *The Recorder* joined in: "The generous flame of enthusiastic joy burst forth into the most ardent and heartfelt expressions of congratulations among our delighted citizens . . . Such a day of cheerfulness has not been witnessed in this place for ten years." But the celebration was a little premature. True, customs officers were to be paid salaries. But the salaries were to be taken out of the revenue, and in some cases were as large as the discarded fee. And Britain still appointed the collectors, and determined how much duties were to be, and how the revenue was to be spent.

Some customs officers were very upset by the turn of events. At Saint John, Collector Henry Wright and Comptroller Henry Bowyer-Smith complained by letter to London on February 12, 1826, that there was "great disparity between the amount of salaries now allotted to the officers and their former incomes." This had caused the "most serious alarm." Business had increased and was still increasing at the port, greatly adding to their labors and responsibilities. Wright had taken in £3,204 in fees in 1825; in 1826 his annual salary was set at £1,000. Bowyer-Smith had taken in £1,410 in fees; now his salary was £600 a year. The Saint John customs house had revenue of £18,278 in 1826, keeping £8,696 to cover the salaries of the staff, including the senior officers, and operating expenses.

In 1825, fees charged at St. John's, Newfoundland, amounted to £4,251; the new salary schedule was £2,971. In Nova Scotia, fees charged came to £5,801; salaries now were £6,430, higher because salaries had already been in use in the outbays where fees were scanty. Fees collected in New Brunswick ports in 1825 amounted to £9,133; salaries in 1826 were £6,397. At Charlottetown, fees had been £673; salaries were £525. The biggest drop was in Canada; £10,398 collected in fees fell to £5,762 in salaries.

Not all fees ended. We have a good example of this from the records of the Fort Erie, Ontario, customs house. On July 25, 1829, there was an auction of seized goods: whisky, pork, beans and a scow. A sum of £121, ten shillings and 10 1/2 pence was realized. The expenses were: £1 for the auctioneer, £1 for the clerk, ten shillings for the appraisers, £2, 13 shillings and threepence for loading, storage and guarding, and £9, four shillings, ten pence as a fee to Attorney-General Robinson for a one-page document authorizing the sale.

The Board of Customs in London issued orders at least three times that salaries were to come out of customs revenue: "Apply the produce of such duties in the first instance towards defraying the charge of the salaries of their respective departments." And again: "Salaries of officers employed in the collection of customs are to be the first charge upon the net produce of any duties of that branch of the revenue collected in each colony or possession of the Crown abroad."

In cases where duties were insufficient to meet the salaries, provision should be made "out of any colonial funds," even if this meant getting the money from another colony. Only as a last resort was the Board of Customs to be billed for customs officers' salaries. The Lords Commissioners of His Majesty's Treasury enthusiastically endorsed this policy as "most just and proper" and under the date December 12, 1825, wrote that "neither government nor parliament could have contemplated imposition of a new and considerable burden upon the public funds of this country." The reference, of course, was to the public funds of Britain.

In 1828, the Board of Customs cautioned the governors of the colonies against assenting to any act of colonial legislatures which might give the legislatures power to withhold customs salaries or to regulate them. At the same time, it repeated its order that salaries were to be paid out of customs duties collected in the colonies. Under no circumstances, it warned, was the relief of the colonies from customs fees to be made the means of additional and unreasonable burden at home.

Charles Fairbanks, chairman of a special committee of the Nova Scotia Assembly, reported in 1829 that the abolition of fees, including "vexacious and illegal exactions," had provided general relief for the shipping interests. But, he went on, "the most essential of the Prerogatives of this House" was control of the customs revenue raised in the province "and the right of the province to the whole produce of these duties."

Without consulting the assembly, the Board of Customs in London instructed its officers in Nova Scotia to appropriate nearly half the duty collected and use it for salaries. These customs officers, of course, were neither accountable to, nor under the control of, the assembly.

The assembly declared: "The House conveyed, in firm and respectful terms, to His Majesty's Government, their complaint against the intended infringement of the constitutional rights of the Assembly — and asserted, in distinct terms, that no other authority than this legislature can legally direct the collector of His Majesty's Customs to pay over the duties levied under the new [1826] statutes to any person but the treasurer of the Province." The Board of Customs, in effect, rejected this position. The assembly came right back again: ". . . the duties imposed by the Imperial Parliament do of right belong to, and are by the statutes placed at the sole disposal of, the colonial legislature and . . . their appropriation can originate only in this House."

Meanwhile, Joseph Howe published Judge Thomas C. Haliburton's *An Historical and Statistical Account of Nova Scotia*. Haliburton wrote that British colonial policy meant British monopoly of supply, monopoly of provincial (colonial) produce, monopoly of manufacture, and monopoly of shipping. In short, colonial policy, said Haliburton, created poverty in the colonies, mistrust and rebellion. He quoted the Earl of Chatham declaring in Parliament: "The British colonists in America had no right to manufacture even a nail for a horseshoe."

At about the same time, John McGregor was preparing his two-volume history, *British America*. The British prohibition on trade in manufactured goods among the colonies, he said, "was in itself considered a kind of insult to the understanding, more intolerable than pecuniary oppression."

Another travelling historian, R. Montgomery Martin, tried to show how important customs revenue was to the colonies. In 1832, Nova Scotia revenue from ad valorem duties on wine, liquor, sugar, tobacco, beef, pork and flour brought in £105,386. The next most productive sources of revenue were rent from coal mines, £4,000, lighthouse dues, £2,000, and rent of crown lands, £1,063. In 1831, total revenue in New Brunswick was £68,769. Customs duties at Saint John and twelve outports accounted for all of it except £1,113 in duties for support of lighthouses and £620 in duties to provide for sick and disabled seamen. By the same token, customs provided nearly all Prince Edward Island's revenue of £5,068 in 1833 and about £15,000 of Newfoundland's £17,956 revenue in 1831. The cost of customs service in that year in Newfoundland was £4,498.

At long last, the nervous Lords of the Treasury offered to split customs revenue and expenses with the colony. But the assembly refused, adhered to the principle of its right to all the duties. Then, in 1830, the British government approved a bill passed unanimously by the Nova Scotia Assembly. This legislation was an "Act to provide for the Custom-House." It granted funds out of revenue from customs duties to defray the expenses of the entire customs establishment and declared that the assembly had the inherent and undoubted right to appropriate and dispose of all the produce of all duties collected.

The customs officers had vigorously opposed the bill, fearing, correctly, that it would make them dependent on the colonial legislature. From their lofty bureaucratic positions in the civil service and through their impeccable political connections, customs officers at that time wielded considerable influence in government circles and often, as in the case of Jeffery, were members of those very circles themselves. (In his book *A Subaltern's Furlough*, published in 1833, Lieut. E.T. Coke wrote that he was on the Windsor-to-Halifax stagecoach when he noted a farm which was "quite a treat": it had lagoons for trout fishing. It was the property of the collector of customs at Halifax, T.N. Jeffery. His near neighbor was Attorney-General Uniacke, whose imposing home now is a provincial museum. Mount Uniacke, like the farm with the trout ponds, attested to the lucrative fees which public offices then produced.)

The Nova Scotia Assembly had scored one victory over the customs officers. And yet — Britain still appointed these officers and set their salaries, which were substantial. A collector was paid £1,500 and allowed £500 in expenses, a sum not surpassed for more than a century. At least the principal officers and clerks of the Customs at Halifax had to take a prescribed oath to receive "no fee or perquisites while in the discharge of their official duties." This regulation soon became a standing instruction throughout Customs.

On February 11, 1837, in his first session of the assembly, Howe introduced his famous twelve resolutions, the third of which dealt with the "long struggle" over customs. He accused "a little knot of persons selected from a single town" (the legislative council in Halifax) of denying the "representations of a majority of this House, representing the whole Province."

In 1838, the assembly protested again that London appointed Nova Scotia's customs collectors and fixed their salaries. "Your Majesty's subjects in this Province are studiously overlooked in the selection to fill places, however inferior and subordinate, in the Department of Your Majesty's Customs."

When Britain began swinging heavily to free trade, it gave the colonies permission to pass acts reducing or repealing any or all imperial customs duties. The Nova Scotia Assembly immediately repealed certain duties and, in 1848, passed a consolidated tariff as substitute for duties payable under imperial acts. With British free trade, imperial customs officers became redundant, and those who could not be re-employed in the new provincial department of customs were pensioned off by London. The last formality was declared by customs order on January 5, 1855, when imperial control of colonial customs ceased entirely, and local legislatures replaced the Lords of the Treasury as the official dispensers of patronage of the customs — that is, of customs appointments.

New Brunswick

Customs fees represented a lesser issue with the legislature in Fredericton than with the assembly in Nova Scotia. The key issue in the New Brunswick House during the fight for responsible government was the revenue from the sale of crown lands. The money from these sales was collected by crown officials not responsible to the government or people of the province. Other issues included Governor Sir William Colebrooke's appointment of his son-in-law, Alfred Reade, as provincial secretary in 1844.

This is not to say that the dispute over customs fees was unimportant. Protests about fees began soon after New Brunswick became a separate province in 1784. In 1788, the inhabitants of Sunbury filed a petition with the assembly asking the governor to publish a list of fees collected by the officers of customs, but it was not until 1799 that Governor Thomas Carleton reported that he had received these instructions from London: "that Tables of Fees be publicly hung up in all places where such fees are to be paid; and you are to transmit copies of all such Tables of Fees to Us by one of our principal Secretaries of State and duplicates thereof to the Committee of our Privy Council for Trade and Plantations for their information."

It was a very small victory to have the Commissioners of Customs announce the fees charged by customs officers. The collector at Saint John was a powerful man in the colony who reported only to the Colonial Secretary in London. The first collector at Saint John was Francis Peabody, who arrived in 1762 when New Brunswick was still part of Nova Scotia. William Wanton was collector until 1816, when he died at the age of eighty-two. His successor was Henry Wright, whose fees in the first year on the job were £2,900, or £1,000 more than the maximum charged by Wanton and £900 more than the governor's salary and expenses combined. The legislature conducted an investigation into Wright's fees. Wright ignored it. Fees at Saint John at this time ranged from one shilling, eight pence to £1, one shilling and there were only eleven seizures of goods in one three-year period.

The New Brunswick Assembly sent off a petition to the king on March 16, 1827. It started off by saying that the abolition of customs house fees was additional proof of the care and kind regard which the sovereign had so often evinced for the welfare of his New Brunswick subjects. But then it added:

> It was not without feelings of extreme regret that this House heard just before the close of the last session that the Custom House officers in this province had received instructions from the Commissioners of Customs to retain for their salaries a large proportion of the duties. . . . The House considers the order, which so materially affects their dearest interests and which appeared to them at variance with the Acts of Parliament, to have been intended as a temporary arrangement to continue in operation only until the subject should be submitted to this House, with whom they humbly conceive the appropriation of the Provincial Revenue for payment of those salaries, or for any other purpose, should originate.

The address to the king noted that duties collected in the previous year (1826) amounted to less than £20,000, but that little more than half this sum had been paid to the provincial treasurer, "the salaries of the officers at several places far exceeding the amounts of duties collected, or of the fees under the other system."

The legislature declared that customs duties could be collected at a cost of no more than £2,000 annually, a polite way of saying that customs was skimming off the top four times the amount to which it was legitimately entitled, and that customs officers' salaries should be fair and reasonable in relation to salaries of other officers in the colony. It concluded its handwritten, nine-page entreaty: "The House is waiting with great anxiety in hope of arrival of Your Majesty's most gracious order to direct the whole amount of the duties collected be placed in the provincial treasury and at the disposal of the provincial Assembly to whom, they humbly conceive, it rightfully appertains to fix the amount of the appropriation for collection, as well as for other purposes."

It was another eight years, however, before anxiety was assuaged and New Brunswick was permitted to take over the financing of the customs establishment. The legislature's claim that customs duties could be collected for far less than the salaries approved by London was borne out almost immediately. The Journal of the legislature for 1837 records that £3,050 was appropriated that year for a customs staff of ten. On February 18, 1840, Governor Sir John Harvey submitted a proposal to the assembly for a new customs house at Saint John which would be of "eminent advantage to the commercial prosperity, credit and beauty of the city of Saint John." There was no mention of the real purpose: tax collecting.

Newfoundland

In Newfoundland, the first early pressure for abolition of fees was exerted by the merchants of St. John's, which then came under the administration of Boston. The first collector there, a Mr. Hamilton, appointed in 1762, could not prevail on the merchants to pay his fees and finally threw up the job in disgust. He was followed the next year by a stern Scot, Alexander Dunn, who collected his fees but, on the other hand, usually found mitigating circumstances to turn loose vessels which had been seized for smuggling rum.

The customs laws of Newfoundland were so stringent that, in 1784, sixteen men were charged with stealing flotsam from a wrecked ship. One was convicted and sentenced to be hanged but was pardoned by the governor. All his worldly possessions remained seized by admiralty court, however, and he died of grief.

A source of revenue peculiar to the Atlantic colonies was privateering, not to be confused with piracy. Privateering was an accepted and honorable way of life for many Maritime seamen during the long wars between England and France and between Britain and the United States. An official letter of marque, granted by the governor, was in effect a legal licence to prey on the shipping of an enemy state. Privateers often raided shore communities and carried off hostages for ransom. Customs, of course, levied duty on captured goods imported by privateers — when they could find them. A customs directive at St. Andrews, New Brunswick, dated August, 1793, says property "taken at sea from the King's enemies" is subject to duties or seizure, just like everything else.

As a postscript on fees, the practice of charging them did not die easily.

As late as April 19, 1881, Commissioner A. Brunel of Inland Revenue had to issue this circular (No. 227) to collectors: "It has come to the knowledge of this Department that in one instance a collector of canal tolls has received fees for making out ships' reports. This is entirely inconsistent with Act 31 Victoria Chapter 5 and contrary to the policy of this Department. You will therefore not only refrain from accepting any such fees for yourself but you will prohibit your subordinate officers — if there are any — from doing so."

CHAPTER V

Customs in the Canadas

In Upper and Lower Canada, the collection of customs was a constant source of irritation for the colonial legislatures, just as it was, as we have seen, in the Maritime colonies. The legislative assembly of the Province of Canada met for the first time in 1841 and one of the first things it did was to set up a special committee to look into customs.

Before that time, the assembly of Upper Canada had had to deal at almost every session with some problem surrounding the collection of customs. This was apart from the running feud with Lower Canada on the division of customs revenue collected at Quebec. Customs collectors (seven in 1834 alone) frequently defaulted on their payments to the treasury, and their salaries were stopped until payment was made. The collectors would then petition the legislature to get salaries which they claimed were due them. William Hands, the collector at Sandwich, petitioned three times for £34 in back pay which had been withheld because he was late making a payment in 1816. Three times he was refused, but each petition had to go through all the usual stages of presentation, committee hearings, drafting of a bill and so on. Robert Brown, collector at Cobourg, William Kingsmill, collector at Port Hope, and William Chisholm, collector at Oakville, petitioned for the same reason, but they were luckier. The latter two had the excuse that they were off on militia duty. Customs collectors were patronage appointments, of course.

In 1835, two collectors — Francis Caldwell at Amherstburg and William Merrit at Port Dalhousie — were members of the assembly, and two others, Chisholm at Oakville and Richard Fraser at Brockville, were former members. Customs collectors had to put up financial guarantees when they took appointments. When a Mr. Beeston, collector at Hallowell, was declared a defaulter in 1839, two men who had been his guarantors petitioned the assembly not to be prosecuted as sureties for Beeston. At the 1839-40 session, the assembly approved a bill to regulate the times at which collectors must make returns and payments. It had little effect because public officials did not feel themselves especially accountable to an elected legislature, nor were they. Responsible government was still a decade away. In 1833, Inspector-General George Markland found it necessary to issue instructions that collectors must reside at the ports under their charge or they would be fired. Some collectors lived where they pleased and appointed deputies at their ports, however small.

Patrick Shirreff, in *A Tour through North America*, tells how annoyed he was when he had to pay a fee at the Sandwich customs house for the horse he was riding from Detroit to Chatham. He refers scathingly to Sandwich as "this metropolis of western Canada." He adds: "I am not sure if it is absolutely necessary to enter a horse at the customhouse on crossing the Detroit river, and at the time suspected it was as much with the view of obtaining the fees as complying with the law. The owner of the horse requested me to apply at the customhouse with which he was connected."

In 1837, a committee of the legislature found that the number of ports of entry was greater than necessary. For instance, there were customs ports at Johnstown and Prescott, only three miles apart, making for needless expense. Maitland and Brockville were almost as close to each other. On examination of collections for 1833-35, the committee found that fourteen ports accounted for only £3,755 in revenue but had cost £1,877 to operate. Seven other ports had collected £34,428 at a cost of £2,100. Some collectors were overpaid, others underpaid. Kingston and Toronto required warehouses, but the "present state of the finances" forbade any such recommendation.

It is not surprising that the special committee of 1841 was instructed to find out exactly how duties were collected, how the revenue was accounted for, and whether there were any abuses in either process. Not yet used to the fact that Upper and Lower Canada now were united in a single province, the committee looked only at the customs department's western section — that is, Upper Canada. It found, in short, low revenue, almost non-existent accounting and plenty of abuses. It also found some collectors who refused to give it information on the grounds given by Collector Jeffery in Halifax: the information was private.

There were thirty-seven customs ports of entry in Upper Canada, yet the annual net revenue amounted to only £16,000 or about $80,000. Collectors at that time received as salary 50 per cent of collections up to £200 and lesser percentages between £200 and £4,500, but maximum salary was pegged at £300 a year, three times greater than in 1801 when customs operations were beginning. Collectors also were entitled to charge fees for supplying clearance papers and were awarded one-third of what seized goods brought at auction (half when the seizure was under £40).

John Macaulay, Inspector-General of Customs and a member of the legislative council, testified that the collectors made quarterly returns to him and he admitted that some were in default. He said that collectors did not have to name importers or state the value of goods in making their returns. Some kept no books at all and one, John Bostwick at Port

Stanley, owned the wharf and warehouse used by Customs. (William H. Smith in *Canada Past and Present*, 1852, remarked that early customs collectors had no schedule of tariff rates but simply charged what they saw fit, kept the money in their pockets and from time to time sent some to the government.)

The committee commented that collectors' "books of account are considered private property and are not delivered up to the government on removal or death of the officer." Anthony Manahan told the committee that when he took over as collector at Toronto he had to buy a fresh set of books because the ones used by the former collector were "withheld from me."

Inspector-General Macaulay was asked: "Are you aware of smuggling being carried on to any extent?" "Yes, there is a great deal," he said. "The only way of preventing it is to reduce duties and to admit prohibited articles at a moderate duty." This was a frequent theme in the committee's investigation. Collector Chisholm at Oakville suggested a lower tax on tea to reduce smuggling and thereby increase revenue.

The committee found that collectors were not subject to any local supervision whatever, and that many of their returns were far from satisfactory. Revenue would be materially increased, it said, if the collectors were subjected to the constant supervision of an officer whose duty it should be to inspect their accounts personally and act as a "check upon this class of public accountants."

The witness quoted at the fullest length was the Kingston merchant John Roy:

> I know of several instances of goods consigned to Kingston having been entered at Bath, Gananoque and Brockville. On asking the owner of a parcel which had been entered in this way at Bath, what was his reason for doing so, he informed me that he had had a quarrel with Mr. Kirkpatrick, the collector of Kingston, and would not give him the benefit of any duties arising from his importations . . .
> No person from the Custom House attends to verify that the goods and the entry correspond; for example, a person might enter 300 barrels of salt at half a dollar per barrel duty and without the least risk of detention [*sic*] land 600. A barrel of salt contains 280 pounds but the people in the Canada trade generally take care that their barrels contain as much over that quantity as possible, indeed, I have known them contain 360, while the Custom House, without any reference to this mercantile usage, take it for granted that a barrel contains neither more nor less than the former quantity. The whole system of the Custom House business in this section of the country is conducted on so loose and unsatisfactory a principle that I am perfectly satisfied not more than half the amount of duties is collected that the law authorizes; for instance, I have known tobacco, which cost, in New

York, 10 cents, entered at 3 and 4 cents per pound. Paper for printing newspapers, imported always in bundles of two reams each, and costing from 4 1/2 to 5 dollars per ream, is entered at the Custom House by the bundle, which is supposed to contain but one ream, and pays duty accordingly at a valuation of 3 dollars for what cost 8 or 9 dollars.

Leather is an article upon which the greatest frauds are practised on the revenue; and there is a vast variety of other articles of considerable importance such as buckskin mittens, furs, various descriptions of French dry goods, sewing silks, cut velvets, etc. which are generally imported without paying any duties whatever.

Collector Chisholm at Oakville testified that valuations on goods varied from port to port. Importers therefore entered goods at ports where the collector was known to be less stringent in his appraisals than collectors at nearby customs houses. Because salaries depended on collections, customs officers vied with each other in attracting the most imports at valuations as high as possible as long as they did not drive the importer elsewhere. Inspector-General Macaulay noted that importers often got into rows with collectors and consigned their goods to other ports.

Manahan, the Toronto collector, said that because there was no Queen's warehouse there was no proper security for goods. Forty chests of contraband tea had easily been stolen (re-seized, as it were) by smugglers. There wasn't even a customs office (one was built the next year). Manahan testified that he had had to rent an office at £20 a year, buy £7 1/2 worth of furniture for it, procure new books and supply stationery and stamps — all out of his own pocket. Manahan also suggested that a comptroller should be appointed to ensure "more diligent attention on the part of the collectors" who should all be placed on fixed salaries and made to account for their revenue from fees.

James Cull, a civil engineer, gave evidence of nepotism run wild in the customs district of Hamilton:

— The collector of tolls on the Burlington Bay Canal was John Chisholm Sr.

— The deputy collector of tolls on the Burlington Bay Canal was John Chisholm Jr.

— The collector of customs at the Canal, Wellington Square and Hamilton was John Chisholm Sr.

— The deputy collector at Hamilton was a son of John Chisholm Sr., unnamed.

— The deputy collectors at Wellington Square were another son of John Chisholm Sr. and Mr. Smith, son-in-law of John Chisholm Sr.

Cull testified that canal tolls and customs duties were mixed in together so that neither could be accounted for and that the revenue from tolls alone could be increased to £4,000 from £1,150.

None of the Chisholms appeared before the committee, but questions were submitted in writing to John Chisholm Sr. as collector of customs. Asked for the amount of annual receipts, Chisholm said he could not get the figures without a great deal of trouble and referred the question to the inspector-general. And as for the canal tolls, well, he didn't know the number of vessels passing through, or their tonnage. At the same time, Chisholm had a complaint: "The remuneration is too small to the collector."

An early traveller to Upper Canada was le Duc de la Rochefoucault Liancourt. He visited there in 1795 at the invitation of Governor Simcoe and reported that duties were low and revenue consequently the same. The population of Upper Canada was about 30,000 and the total revenue of the colony was £900, or $3,600, thanks mainly to a tavern licence fee of $11 a year and duty of fourpence a gallon on Madeira and twopence on other wines. Members of the legislative assembly received $2 a day — and had to prove their attendance before they got it. The expenses for the civil and military administration were $400,000 a year, paid by London. Liancourt wrote:

> The high duty laid by England upon all the commodities exported from her islands provides a powerful encouragement to a contraband trade with the United States where, in many articles, the difference of price amounts to two-thirds. The government of Canada is very vigilant to prevent this contraband trade; but a certain prospect of gain excites to exertion, which will frequently succeed in eluding the law as well as the vigilance of the executive power. The shopkeepers know perfectly well how to favor this contraband trade, the only means for destroying which would be to lower the duties, and, of consequence, the price of the commodities. The Governor has it in contemplation to encourage such manufactures as produce these articles, which are run in large quantities into this province from the U.S., such as hats. But all his exertions to this effect will fail in regard to sugar, coffee, tea; in short, with respect to all commodities, which are directly imported from the U.S., without being there subjected to as high a duty as in Canada.

William Dunlop in his *Statistical Sketches of Upper Canada*, published in 1832, wrote that "the taxes on articles required for the consumption of the inhabitants are not one-twelfth so great in Canada as in the United States. All British goods pay at Quebec only 2 1/2 per cent ad valorem whilst at any American port they pay from 33-1/3 to 60 per cent." He reported these sources of revenue for Upper Canada in 1832: customs duties on imports at Quebec, £37,600; sale of land, £25,935; duties on goods from the United States £6,390; and tolls at the Welland and Burlington Bay Canals, £3,000. Dunlop had this advice for immigrants:

"A man of fortune, in my opinion, ought not to come to Canada. It is emphatically the poor man's country but it would be difficult to make it the country of the rich." And this: "It cannot be too strongly impressed upon emigrants (from the United Kingdom) the inexpediency of carrying to the woods of Upper Canada heavy, lumbering articles of wooden furniture."

After the assembly's harsh committee report on revenue collection, the government of Upper Canada appointed a special commissioner, Malcolm Cameron, to investigate Customs. His report, in 1843, was, if anything, even more damning. For instance:

> From the experience the undersigned [Cameron] had long had in commercial business in this Province, he was aware that the collection of the Revenue derived from Customs had been carelessly managed, easily evaded, and subject to many frauds; that the system pursued was loose and corrupt; that the tariff was unequal and unjust; that the appointments to office had been generally made without the least regard to the qualifications of the parties; and that there was very little, if any, supervision over them; but he must confess that he was wholly unprepared to believe the extent of the negligence, frauds and peculations which he found had been practiced.

Cameron visited all forty ports of entry from Goderich on Lake Huron to Lancaster, near Cornwall, and found that the only check on collectors was "their own folly or insatiable avarice." Because of the "vicious method" of relating collectors' salaries to revenue, customs officers held out inducements to importers to enter goods at their ports by offering lower tariff rates and lower valuation of goods. The manner of keeping books was as various as the characters and eduction of the collectors. No system of accounts existed. No instructions had been given to collectors and each was left to put his own construction on Acts of Parliament, many of which he had never seen.

Cameron quoted a letter of May, 1843, from Collector James Kerby of Fort Erie to Joseph Cary, deputy inspector-general: "I beg leave to state, that for want of a uniform table of Duties ready at hand, embracing all articles subject to Duty under the different heads, I am often thrown into confusion."

Cameron's report resulted in action by the inspector-general's office. Detailed instructions and copies of the statutes went to the collectors and in 1845 salaries were detached from collections, though officers continued to share in the proceeds of seizures and some preventive officers were paid only in that way. Another result was the dismissal, for "irregularities," of William Moore Kelly, collector at Toronto.

The practice of applying different valuations on similar goods did not cease immediately. In 1846, John Gray, preventive officer at Farren's Point, an outport of Cornwall, wrote that Customs was being brought into contempt because, "A person going to the collector with an article on which there is an ad valorem duty, and saying how much will you enter this article at; if you will not enter it at so much, I will go to such a collector and he will enter it at that value."

Lower Canada

In Lower Canada, the legislative assembly made brave attempts to cut the salaries of civil servants, including customs collectors, in retaliation for the high fees they charged, but was over-ruled by the executive council. Between 1820 and 1825, eight pounds were spent on customs collection for every pound of revenue realized. In 1812, the assembly passed a bill to tax salaries of civil servants to help finance the war effort; it was thrown out by the council, which substituted for it a tax on imported goods. Citizens of Lower Canada were taxed at a rate of 2½ per cent, foreigners at five per cent.

In 1823, Michael Henry Perceval, customs collector at Quebec, was accused of exacting undue fees from traders. A relative and protégé of Spencer Perceval, chancellor of the exchequer, he lived in splendor at Spencer Wood and enjoyed fees and benefits of £8,000 a year (not to mention his wife's inheritance of £100,000). The assembly demanded his suspension pending an inquiry, but the executive council refused, saying he was thoroughly honest. It helped Perceval that he was a member of the executive council, like Jeffery in Nova Scotia. At the same time, Colonel Henry Caldwell, the receiver-general, was found in default of public funds by £96,000, a sum equal to two years' revenue. Caldwell kept the provincial revenue in his house and dipped into it as his personal needs arose. He was dismissed but never charged. (The special investigator in the case was a Mr. Davidson, Caldwell's brother-in-law.) In light of this "roguery" among officialdom, the assembly refused to vote money for any civil servants' salaries unless the salaries were cut by 25 per cent. Once again, the executive council rejected the assembly's demand. Lord Dalhousie, the governor, noted in his diary that the assembly resolution to cut salaries, including his own, was the first order of business and passed with applause.

The assembly's displeasure and resentment with the executive council and bureaucracy were caused by far more than fraud, of course. When a select committee of the British House of Commons looked into the civil government of Canada in 1827 it found, for instance, that of the seven members of the executive council only one was a native of Lower Canada — and he was English-speaking. A memorandum prepared for Governor

Sir James Kempt in 1829 said the "Canadian gentry" had been excluded from appointments of honor or emolument and disregarded "in matters of politeness and attention." "English colonists" were favored over the French-speaking "native proprietors of the soil." Positions carrying a salary in the civil service were almost universally filled by "place hunters, strangers to the laws of the country, enemies to the religion of the people, ignorant of their language and prejudiced against their manners and customs." In other words, things hadn't changed since General James Murray, the first English governor of Quebec, had made a similar complaint to London about English popinjays with political connections being given handsome jobs in the colonies.

But at least the governor-in-council did have some regard for the Canadien as a consumer. In 1780, in an effort to reduce the price of wheat and flour, Customs was ordered to stop the export of all wheat, pease, oats, biscuit, flour and meal. The penalty was seizure of the ship and goods and a £100 fine. The ban lasted four years. The council also had some regard for the voyageurs: liquor could not be sold to them on the stretch of the Ottawa River between Allumette Island and the lower carrying-place of the Chaudière (Ottawa) where the rapids were most dangerous.

Traveller Isaac Weld reported the following encounter with Customs and Immigration on Lake Champlain in his book *Travels Through the States of North America and the Province of Upper and Lower Canada during the years 1795, 1796 and 1797*: "A short time after sunset we passed the boundary between the British dominions and the United States. Here we were brought to by an armed brig of twenty guns, under English colours, stationed for the purpose of examining all boats passing up and down the lake; the answers which we gave to the several questions asked being satisfactory, we were accordingly suffered to proceed."

Weld does not specify what the questions were. One speculates that one of them might well have been: "On business or pleasure, sir?" Weld continued: "Immediately on our landing [at St. John's] we were conducted to the guard house, where we had to deliver to the sergeant on duty, to be by him forwarded to the commanding officer, an account of our names, occupation, and place of abode, the strictest orders having been issued by the governor [Dorchester] not to suffer any Frenchman or other foreigners, or any people who could not give an exact account of their business in Canada, to enter into the country." (Lord Dorchester had stopped Liancourt from visiting Lower Canada.) Weld tells us that a total of eleven articles were subject to duty — all the usual (brandy, rum, madeira wine, sugar, molasses, coffee, tobacco, regular wine, all other foreign liquor) plus salt and playing cards — and adds in an odd juxtaposition: "There are no game laws, nor any excise laws whatsoever."

One early traveller made an unusual call at the Magdalen Islands, now

Iles-de-la-Madeleine. John Lambert wrote in his *Travels through Canada and the United States of North America in the years 1806, 1807, 1808* that the islands belonged to Admiral Sir Isaac Coffin and were inhabited by 1,000 souls. Each settler paid two quintals of fish per year to the admiral through a collector who was also justice of the peace and was paid £100 a year by Sir Isaac. Lambert added: "The Americans carry on a small lucrative trade with the inhabitants, in articles chiefly contraband." (Lower Canada sent customs inspectors on visits to the islands beginning in 1831 but it was not until 1844 that an officer was appointed there in the person of J.C. Belleau. Neither he nor any of his successors in the last century hit it off with the inhabitants. The islanders contrived to evade duties and the government might have given up trying to collect them but it feared that the islands, in the middle of the Gulf of St. Lawrence, might become a huge smuggling depot. John Fox succeeded Belleau in 1852 and his position was not made more comfortable when he was ordered to collect 12 1/2-per-cent duty on goods salvaged by the islanders from shipwrecks. Somehow, Fox persevered until 1880 when he was replaced.)

From Quebec City, Lambert reported a wide discrepancy between customs revenue and costs. In 1803, customs duties had brought in £22,775 but the expenses to collect them were £43,220. The gap had widened: in 1794, collections had been £15,449 and expenses £22,206.

Thomas Knox was appointed collector at Quebec in 1762. In the same year, Brigadier General Thomas Gage, Governor of Montreal and District, in typically flowery language announced appointments at Montreal, then a lowly outport with a population of 5,500:

> Whereas the Right Honourable the Lord Commissioners of the Royal Treasury have by their ordinances resolved and enjoined the Commissioners of His Majesty's Customs that it would be desirable for the welfare of the State and for good order to establish a Customs in the City of Montreal and to that end the said Commissioners have deemed it proper to appoint and establish Thomas Lamb, Esquire, as Collector and Mr. Richard Oakes to be waiter of the said Customs at Montreal, we therefore order all citizens of the said Montreal and its Dependencies to regard and recognize Messrs. Thomas Lamb and Richard Oakes in the said capacity. We require all officers, civil and military, to lend assistance at all times when they will be called upon by the said officers for the said service and to support them with all their authority conformably to our orders.

The merchants began petitioning in 1790 for a Montreal customs house separate from Quebec's to avoid the necessity of unloading goods at Quebec for customs inspection and reloading them for shipment to Montreal. But Montreal did not become a port of entry until 1831, nor get a customs house, as noted earlier, until 1838. Its first French-speaking collector was not appointed until 1851; Quebec had to wait even longer for such an appointment — until 1883 — in the person of J. G. Blanchet, former speaker of the House of Commons.

Traveller John McGregor reported in 1852 that the customs staff at Quebec City numbered 18, including collector, controller, surveyor, naval officer, three clerks, four searchers and waiters, a tide-surveyor, two tidesmen, an admeasurer of ships, a warehouse keeper, a locker and a messenger. Twenty customs men were scattered throughout the rest of Lower Canada, including five at St. Jean, three each at Montreal and Coteau-du-Lac, and one each in nine other locations, including the Magdalen Islands.

The problem of inconsistent application of customs duties plagued Lower Canada as well as the Upper province.

In 1846, Collector James Thompson at Stanstead complained that collectors at nearby Eastern Townships ports were charging less duty on similar goods than he was. Not only that, but importers were contributing financially to improvement of roads to his rival ports to make them even more enticing.

CHAPTER VI

Customs Duties versus Free Trade

By the John Jay Treaty of 1794, Britain and the United States signed a convenant of "amity, commerce and navigation," though it took two years for the redcoats to leave the American forts which the British had formally surrendered in 1783. The forts had been retained ostensibly against an Indian uprising, to protect the fur trade, or as collateral against the reparations demanded from the States by the United Empire Loyalists. Yet, eighteen years later, the two sides were at war again.

The third article of the Jay Treaty provided that goods of the type admitted duty-free into Canada from Britain could also be admitted free from the Unites States. As Hugh Gray said in his *Letters from Canada*, published in 1809, it carried the appearance of reciprocity, but there was in fact no reciprocity in it. Reciprocity applies on goods passing between two countries; in this case, three countries were involved. It might suit British policy not to charge duty on certain British exports to Canada, but be contrary to British policy to allow the United States to send the same articles into Canada duty-free.

In the event, the United States placed a duty of about 15 per cent on almost everything it imported from Canada, while sending three times as much to Canada duty-free. Gray warned that it might be an advantage for the colonies to get cheap imports from the States but disadvantageous to Britain commercially and politically for her colonies to draw supplies from any source other than Britain. In time, he said, this would render the colonies independent of Britain and attached, instead, to the country from which they received supplies. He was right.

However, there were many articles imported from the United States subject to customs duties so, in 1796, Lower Canada placed the same levies on them as were payable on imports from Europe. Upper Canada did not follow suit immediately, nonplussed as it was by the physical difficulties of collecting duties along a frontier of a thousand miles of lake and forest and especially at the prospect of the States reciprocating by slapping more duties on Upper Canadian products. Pay a pound and collect a penny, as Richard Cartwright, later a finance minister, put it. The

United States began to establish customs ports on the border in 1799. Lower Canada had had a customs house at St. Jean since 1788, but Upper Canada put off such a day until 1801 when eleven ports of entry were set up. The tariff fell chiefly on wines, liquor, sugar, tea, coffee and tobacco.

An effect of Britain's blockade of Europe in 1806, during the Napoleonic wars, was to cut off the supply of Baltic timber for the British fleet and thereby bring the Canadian timber trade into being, to grow by leaps and bounds. The timber trade prospered but the war between England and France had some adverse effects on Maritime trade, an indication, long before Confederation, that regional interests in Canada might conflict. On May 11, 1804, the "merchants and other inhabitants of New Brunswick" addressed a petition to Lord Hobart, Secretary of State, concerning the West Indies trade, traditionally the economic generator for the Maritimes.

The petition began by saying that, in the first decade after 1783, the Loyalists in the province had built ninety-three square-rigged vessels and seventy-one sloops and schooners which in turn had built up increased trade with the British West Indies in fish and lumber. Then war had broken out and the West Indies had admitted free all goods from the non-belligerent United States. American ships were exempt from the ruinous war insurance rates and even from the transient or "stranger's" West Indies duty of 2 1/2 to 5 per cent which New Brunswick vessels had to pay. So flourishing was the U.S.-West Indies trade in fish that the U.S. Congress had provided subsidies for American vessels to encourage them to catch codfish in the Bay of Fundy.

The petitioners said New Brunswick and "neighboring colonies" could easily supply the fish and timber wants of the West Indies and proposed that American ships be barred from the Indies. Otherwise, the "industrious inhabitants" of New Brunswick might "forgo the blessings of the British constitution" and "seek for an establishment in the United States of America." Moreover, an expanded New Brunswick trading fleet would provide "valuable nurseries of seamen for the British navy, that grant security to the commerce and prosperity of His Majesty's Kingdoms and Colonies."

Nova Scotia fired off a similar petition to London. It appealed not only on its own behalf but for Newfoundland, Cape Breton, Prince Edward Island and New Brunswick. Such petitions became a regular feature of Canadian economic life. Sixty-four years later, in 1868, Nova Scotia sent a petition, this time to Ottawa, declaring that the Canadian tariff was ruining its fish trade with the West Indies.

But the admittance of American goods into the West Indies, duty-free, was only a signal of worse things to come. Britain was swinging to free trade. This move began with acts of Parliament in 1824 and 1826 and was more or less completed in 1846. The merchants of the British colonies in North America abhorred free trade. They wanted the old colonial preferences — and prohibitions against others — in the British and West Indies markets and successfully sought free entry of U.S. agricultural products into Canada at the expense of the Canadian farmer.

All the same, Britain continued on its free-trade course and by the Free Trade Acts of 1845 and 1846 revoked hundreds of customs rates and virtually repealed the Corn Laws — the heavy duties on cereal grains. Prime Minister William Gladstone further reduced tariffs in 1860 and Britain prospered in foreign trade. The customs tariff ceased to provide any real protection for British production and manufacture and duties were imposed on only twenty-six classifications of goods, including beer, playing cards, chicory, dice, spruce, hops, malt, paper, vinegar and plate.

But free trading was not extended to the colonies. Far from it. The British act of 1825 to regulate the trade of British possessions abroad listed very few items as duty-free: hay, salt, fresh fruit and vegetables, cotton, firewood (!) and anything used to catch fish. There were far more items banned or dutiable. The East India Company had the tea monopoly; coffee, sugar, molasses and rum of foreign production were kept out; only British fish could be imported into the colonies; import duties were imposed, not only on the customary liquor, wine and tobacco, but on wheat, bread, lumber, horses, coffee, sugar, spices, pickles, turpentine, clocks, musical instruments and ostrich feathers. The tariff was generally 15 per cent ad valorem. Opium could be imported, but was dutiable.

The colonies themselves swooped into the customs field. In 1836, for instance, New Brunswick began taxing a limited range of imports: one shilling and sixpence on wine, a penny on molasses, a penny a pound on coffee and sugar, five per cent on tobacco, ten per cent on soap and 25 per cent on furniture and clocks. The most important item, tea, was duty-free.

In 1829, Nova Scotia raised revenue of £60,000 through import duties, principally on wine and "ardent spirits." Half of this amount was spent for roads, the rest on public buildings, government administration, legislature and courts, schools and the militia. Also in 1829, resentful of a renewed and successful U.S. re-entry into the British West Indies market, the Canadians said Americans would no longer buy good Jamaica rum because they had switched to bad American whisky.

In this period people began to migrate to Canada from the British Isles in large numbers: 50,254 in 1831 alone. In 1827 the population of Upper Canada was 177,174; by 1834 it had grown to 321,145. Most of the immigrants went into agriculture, and the old battle of commerce versus settlement (or merchant versus farmer) which had plagued the country from the earliest days of New France was renewed. This time the argument was over spending money on canals or roads and, in Lower Canada, the conversion of seigniorial rights to free land tenure.

Most immigrants arrived destitute in stinking cargo vessels. In 1832, Canada imposed a poll tax of $1 on immigrants who sailed with government authority, $2 without such authority. The money was supposed to be used for sick and destitute arrivals, but some Upper Canadians claimed that Lower Canada intended the tax to slow English immigration. Another furore arose in Lower Canada when the British American Land Company acquired more than 500,000 acres in the Eastern Townships of Quebec for settlement by English immigrants. In 1832, a cholera epidemic hit the immigrants and spread to the inhabitants, provoking protests in Lower Canada that immigration brought disease and pestilence.

The issue of customs duties versus free trade has caused anger and unpleasantness throughout Canadian history, even rebellion. In 1834, in Upper Canada, William Lyon Mackenzie's reformers sought protection for Canadian agriculture; they argued that Canada-U.S. trade was completely inequitable because the American tariff prevented the Canadian farmer from seeking markets in the United States. They won the election that year and soon proposed heavy duties on imports of U.S. grain, flour and meal. The merchants, on the other hand, complained that this would wreck the carrying trade and prospects for the Welland Canal, and the measure was vetoed by the legislative council.

In Lower Canada, the governor was permitted by the British government to appropriate provincial revenue (most of it from customs) without the sanction of the legislature. The *patriotes* showed their resistance by refraining from buying dutiable articles, maintaining that smuggling was perfectly honorable in the circumstances.

In Upper Canada, rebellion began in Doel's brewery and ended ingloriously in Montgomery's tavern. In Lower Canada, there was bloodshed in Montreal, St. Denis and St. Eustache. Respect for constituted authority won out in both provinces, but 1837 culminated in political and financial chaos: political hatred, stagnant commerce, suspended public works and disorganized finances.

Legislative union between Lower and Upper Canada was accomplished in June, 1841, when the first Parliament met. But responsible government was not. That took another seven years.

CHAPTER VII

Macdonald's National Policy

There had never been any great dispute in Canada about the necessity of raising revenue through modest tariffs to help defray the cost of public works and to run government, courts and schools.

Yet, until the last years of the French regime, there was no systematic tax in Canada. In the reorganization of the colonial government in New France in 1663, there was not even a mention of taxation. Louis XIV (*L'état, c'est moi*) did not delegate royal taxing powers to anyone. He was even annoyed about the name *conseil souverain* (sovereign council) given his governing body in New France and changed it to *conseil supérieur* (supreme council). When Montreal was fortified, around 1716, a special tax was imposed to raise 6,000 *livres*, and this became a precedent for raising sums, large or small, for public purposes. In a letter to Paris, October 31, 1725, Intendant Michel Bégon said the fund for the Montreal fortifications should have been raised through leases on the interior trading posts. He despaired of raising revenue through taxes:

> Les peuples de cette Colonie sont si peu accoutumés à des dispositions et il y a tant de difficulté et d'inconvénient à les forcer de payer que nous vous supplions très instamment de les en décharger, l'avantage qu'on en pourroit retirer n'etant pas à comparer aux mauvais effets que ce recouvrement pourriot produire . . . (The people of this colony are so little used to taxes, and there is so much difficulty and inconvenience in compelling them to pay, that we beg you very urgently to discharge them from it, the profit to be derived not being equal to the ill effects which this collection may produce . . .)

Louis XV stuck firmly to his predecessor's position that the king's taxing authority was non-transferable. He issued a specific order in 1742 declaring that governors and intendants in the colonies of France did not have permission to impose taxes; it was a sovereign right which the king transferred to no one. François Bigot, the last intendant (from 1748 to 1759) raised too much money for himself (about 12,000,000 *livres*), was recalled, thrown into the Bastille, tried for fraud and embezzlement, and banished for life. All his property was seized, including the silver plate on which he had served lavish feasts at Quebec and for which, he claimed, he had paid out of his own pocket. But as corrupt as Bigot and his underlings were (Bigot brought many of his troubles on himself by defending his scapegrace subordinates and appointees), customs duties on imports were not heavy. And, under the English regime, import duties did not grow appreciably; indeed, they did not increase at all for a decade or more. Moreover, neither Britain nor France expected Canada always to pay its own way and, traditionally, spent more in the colony than was collected in taxes. There were, of course, heavy military costs in garrisoning the North American colonies.

With the exception of wine, brandy and tobacco, no article was dutiable in Canada until 1753, when most merchandise was taxed three per cent and duties on liquor, especially rum, were increased. Customs produced nearly 300,000 *livres* ($60,000 a year) but in 1729, for instance, France was already spending $80,000 a year on Canada and, by 1749, this amount had grown to more than $300,000. There was no system of bonding, a detriment to importers who had to pay duty on arrival of commodities. In its time, the English regime also made up the large difference between revenue and the cost of civil administration. In 1794, revenues from customs duties on wine, liquor and molasses, from licences paid by innkeepers, and from fines and confiscations, accounted for only one-third of the cost of government, which was £25,000 ($100,000). In other words, taxation was practically unknown. The following year, duties were also placed on a few other products such as sugar, coffee and salt, in an attempt to make revenue approach costs; it didn't.

John J. Bigsby, secretary of the British section of the Boundary Commission in the 1820s, found that prices of British manufactured goods were moderate in the Canadas, partly because of "the low rate of Customhouse duties," though he still advised the poorer settlers to spin, weave, dye and make soap and candles at home so they could sing: "I grow my own lamb,/My own butter and ham;/I shear my own sheep, and I wear it."

Many settlers had to do this anyway because there was little Canadian industry. William Evans tells us in the first issue of his *Canadian Quarterly Agricultural and Industrial Magazine* published in Montreal in May, 1838, that the principal Canadian manufactures were woollen and linen cloth, "manufactured chiefly by the agricultural class"; the tanning of leather; the distillation of whisky and gin; and the brewing of ale and beer. The few other manufactures, he wrote, were not worth noticing.

If there was no particular argument over the need of tariffs as revenue producers, there was dispute — and it goes on to this day — over the use of tariffs to provide protection for Canadian producers. But just when Canada turned toward a protective tariff, Britain opted for free world trade. Between 1842 and 1846, twelve hundred dutiable articles were freed of duty in Britain, no single duty exceeded ten per cent, all export duties were abolished, and only forty-eight articles remained on the tariff.

The results were nearly disastrous for Canada.

Britain complied with a Canadian request to reduce or eliminate tariffs in Britain on breadstuffs (wheat had been exported since 1752 when New France sent shipments to France; by 1801, exports exceeded a million bushels for the first time) but at the same time it also cut the tariff on timber, removing the protected market for Canada in the United Kingdom. And, while seeking assured markets for wheat in Britain, Canada also sought protection for Canadian agriculture at home against heavy imports of U.S. wheat and flour. A large milling industry grew up in Canada between 1843 and 1846, based on free admission of Canadian flour into the British market. The industry collapsed almost overnight when Britain repealed the Corn Laws in 1846 and all foreign breadstuffs entered the country free of duty. The repeal of the British Corn Laws spelled the end of Canadian preference in the British market.

Meanwhile, in 1845, the U.S. commercial invasion of Canada was extended by a drawback law which remitted duties on American imports from foreign countries when these imports were re-exported to Canada. In 1846, another U.S. statute removed duties on produce imported from Canada and re-exported abroad. This established an all-American trade route from Canada West (Upper Canada) to the Atlantic, bypassing Montreal and Quebec. Montreal saw this as a disaster, but for Toronto it was a boon. Now it had an all-season route to the Atlantic seaboard and a counter to high freight rates on the St. Lawrence. Imports dropped at Montreal while Canadian exports via the Erie Canal increased.

Britain's renunciation of imperial preferences in favor of world trade brought immediate economic depression in Canada. More than half the Canadian merchants went bankrupt. Some towns lost half their population. George S. Workman, president of the Montreal Board of Trade, announced: "We are in the same condition as a man suddenly precipitated from a lofty eminence. We are laboring under concussion of the brain." Many Canadians saw the British action as rejection of the colonies. Reprisals followed. In 1847, Canadian tariffs on U.S. manufactures were reduced and on British goods increased to a uniform level of 7 1/2 per cent ad valorem. The first protective tariff — on farm implements — was imposed. In 1841, tariffs had been raised generally by a modest 2 1/2 per cent to five. But in 1849 they were raised to 12 1/2 per cent. From 1852 on, protection was a popular subject of debate in the assembly of the United Province of Canada.

One traveller to Canada in these troubled times was James Dixon, a Wesleyan preacher and friend of educator Egerton Ryerson. He compared Canada unfavorably with the United States:

On the American side, the people are all life, elasticity, buoyancy, activity; on the Canadian side we have a people who appear subdued, tame, spiritless, as if living much more under the influence of fear than hope . . . On the American side, you are placed in the midst of incessant bustle, agitation; the hotels are filled, coaches are in constant movement, railroad trains passing and repassing with their passengers, while men of business are seen pushing their concerns with impassioned ardour. On the Canada shore we have comparatively still life; delicate, genteel, formal . . . I found [Canada] full of complaints and dissatisfaction from one end to the other. The people everywhere, and all shades of politics, spoke the same language. Their fortunes were wrecked, their commerce destroyed, their agriculture, the sinews of the colony, enfeebled, ruined.

Dixon reached this conclusion:

Canada now only belongs to Great Britain by a figment, a tradition, a loyalty, a recollection of heroic deeds; and not by any material interest or benefit. Nay, in the present state of things, cast off by the Mother country, and left to their own resources, with the United States just by their side, possessing vast political power and influence; a growing credit, and monetary resources; a prodigious mercantile and commercial navy; an active, industrious, and virtuous people; a government capable, in all respects, and equally disposed, to foster, protect, and strengthen all its possessions; — we say, with all these things staring them in the face, the policy of this country [Britain] has made it the plain, palpable interest of the Canadians to seek for annexation.

Dixon accurately forecast the movement, especially pronounced in Montreal where the British element had lost its traditional control of the government, for the annexation of Canada to the United States. The annexation manifesto appeared in 1849.

The movement for "separation from Britain" (this was the actual phrase used at the time) and union with the States was short-lived and, in the end, the least important of the four movements which sprang up when Britain plumped for free trade. The annexation manifesto said in part: "What but ruin or rapid decay meets the eye? Our Provincial Government and civic corporations embarrassed, our banking and other securities greatly depreciated, our mercantile and agricultural interests alike unprosperous, real estate scarcely saleable upon any terms, our unrivalled rivers, lakes and canals almost unused, whilst commerce abandons our shores, the circulating capital amassed under a more favourable system is dissipated, with none from any quarter to replace it." The remedy: "A friendly and peaceful separation from British connection and a union upon equitable terms with the Great North American Confederacy of Sovereign States." The manifesto listed among the presumed advantages of union "the ability to dispense with the costly but ineffectual revenue establishment over a frontier of many hundred miles."

The second movement was for free trade. It was organized by John Young, a cabinet minister in 1848-52, who seized the floor at the start of an early protectionist meeting at Montreal's Bonsecours Market and offered a free trade resolution which was, of course, doomed to failure with that audience. Free trade never had the support of any political party in Canada in those days.

The third movement, reciprocity, was espoused by the Liberal Party until its defeat on that issue in 1911. The fourth, tariff protection for Canadian industry, was part of Sir John A. Macdonald's National Policy, launched in 1879 to endure for a century. The Association for the Promotion of Canadian Industries was organized in Toronto in 1858 by Isaac Buchanan; it persuaded the government to make immediate tariff changes in favor of industry. Buchanan, a member of the legislature, once wore a suit of *étoffe du pays* (gray homespun) in the assembly to illustrate his program. Present at the first meeting of the association was Mackenzie Bowell of Belleville, later minister of Customs and, briefly, prime minister of Canada. The association was the forerunner of the National Policy League of 1876 and of the Canadian Manufacturers' Association of 1886. Though the idea of union with the United States died quickly, it had a long life as a threat wielded by protectionists over supporters of reciprocity and free trade. Reciprocity would lead to annexation, the protectionists swore, and made their rhetoric stick in the minds of Canadian voters.

The five British colonies in North America turned to the United States in the hope of finding a new protector to replace the turncoat British who had just abandoned them to the economic storm. First, Canada demanded abolition of the British navigation laws which required goods traded between Canada and Britain to be carried in British ships; this was done in 1849, opening the St. Lawrence to American shipping. The next step was reciprocal Canada-U.S. reduction of customs duties charged on each other's products. At the same time, there was a movement for free trade among the five colonies: Canada, Prince Edward Island, New Brunswick, Nova Scotia and Newfoundland. Nova Scotia, in fact, proposed a customs union — except for liquor — but the United Province of Canada in particular shied away from the proposal after its customs experience as two colonies between 1791 and 1841. In 1862, Canada proposed such a union itself but, by this time, the Maritimes feared increased competition from Canadian manufacturers.

As a major policy objective, reciprocity lasted sixty-five years, from 1846 to 1911. In May, 1846, William Hamilton Merritt introduced in the Parliament of United Canada a resolution in response to Britain's declaration of free trade that called for Britain to negotiate duty-free admission of Canadian goods into U.S. markets. The negotiations waxed and waned, but finally brought forth a treaty eight years later, due mainly to the tireless efforts of Israel D. Andrews, American consul at Saint John, and in reality a lobbyist for reciprocity on behalf not only of his own government (Congress had to be convinced) but for Canada and the Maritime colonies as well.

In 1846, Canada allowed manufactured goods to come in from the States on the same terms as those from Britain and, in return, asked that Canadian agricultural products enter the United States free. The Americans maintained that such conditions were not equitable and asked Canada to open the Welland and St. Lawrence canals to free passage for U.S. shipping. This demand was met when Britain repealed the navigation laws, but still the United States hung back. The slave-owning South thought reciprocity would lead to Canada's annexation and thus increase the free-state, non-slave, territory. Another factor was plain American indifference.

The turning point was the U.S. desire to fish in Canadian coastal waters. Britain said it would consider giving fishing rights to the United States as part of general negotiations which would include discussion of reciprocity. Lord Elgin concluded a ten-year treaty with William L. Marcy, U.S. Secretary of State, in May, 1854, at Washington. It came into force in 1855 with ratification by the U.S. Congress, the British Parliament, and the legislatures of Canada, New Brunswick, Nova Scotia, Prince Edward Island and Newfoundland.

The treaty established qualified reciprocal fishing rights. Canada (and here is meant the five colonies, though Canada still comprised only Quebec and Ontario) gained free entry to the United States for timber, fish, coal and a number of farm products, including grain, flour and all other breadstuffs, dairy products, meat and vegetables. The United States gained in a number of ways: no export duty was charged by Canada on U.S. lumber floated down the St. John River; U.S. ships paid the same tolls as Canadian vessels on the St. Lawrence system; and the Canadian market was opened up for American fruits and tobacco.

Some people, including merchants and traders, had the mistaken notion that reciprocity meant free trade in everything instead of in a limited range of some fifty items. To the rescue came John Cameron, first clerk at the customs house in Toronto. He said in the preface to his invaluable handbook on tariffs: "Since the passing of the Reciprocity Treaty, several who have not taken the trouble to ascertain its extent have expressed astonishment and indignation on being charged duty on importations from the United States." Cameron's book, published in 1856, was exhaustive, but it was not the first such guide in Canada. In 1834, the *Daily Advertiser* of Montreal printed *A Guide to the Business of the Customs House and Harbour of Montreal* containing the tariff, directions for clearing ships and merchandise, forms of entries, harbor dues, steamer freight charges, canal tolls, storage rates, and so forth. There were similar guides in Halifax, Saint John and St. John's.

Canada's increasing trade with the United States and its first faint moves toward protectionism sent some British manufacturers haring off to the colonial office with cries of unfair competition. The British government more than once disallowed early Canadian attempts to favor home industry, an example being a New Brunswick bounty (subsidy) for hemp-growing. In 1859, the Duke of Newcastle, acting for some aggrieved Sheffield manufacturers, made the mistake of criticizing the Macdonald-Cartier government for the introduction of some incidental protection in the new Canadian tariff. The result, a strong reply by Finance Minister A. T. Galt, became a classic in the lexicon of responsible government:

> Self-government would be utterly annihilated if the views of the Imperial Government were to be preferred to those of the people of Canada. It is therefore the duty of the present government distinctly to affirm the right of the Canadian legislature to adjust the taxation of the people in the way they deem best, even if it should unfortunately happen to meet the disapproval of the Imperial ministry. Her Majesty cannot be advised to disallow such acts, unless her advisers are prepared to assume the administration of the affairs of the colony, irrespective of the views of its inhabitants.

Canada's population was 3,000,000, that of the United States 34,000,000. Trade between the two countries increased: to $46.2 million in 1860 from $14.6 million in 1850. In 1856, wheat and flour comprised two-thirds of U.S. imports from Canada. Exports of Maritime fish doubled between 1853 and 1860. Canadian lumber exports doubled in a decade. But the Atlantic colonies found the treaty generally disappointing: they exported more fish, coal and lumber but did not find the big, expected market in New England for their agricultural products. Opposition to the treaty also developed in the United States. Farmers, lumbermen and the coal industry were hostile from the start. And opposition grew, in 1858-60, when Canada increased duties on U.S. wood, iron, hardware, leather and cotton and woollen clothing to meet demands from Canada's infant manufacturing industry for protection — and from its own governments for more revenue. Galt also provided encouragement for importing via the St. Lawrence instead of through the United States.

For its part, the States tried to keep out some Canadian lumber and wheat, contrary to the treaty, and Canadian resentment grew during the

American civil war. A committee of the U.S. House of Representatives offered Canada an insulting free list which comprised, in its entirety, unwrought burr-millstones, unfinished grindstones, unground gypsum or plaster, firewood and cotton or linen rags. The upshot was that the United States abrogated the treaty, effective March 17, 1866, and a new one was not negotiated until 1935 when Canada and the States extended most-favored-nation treatment to each other in tariff matters. Trade fell sharply with denouncement of the treaty in 1866, but, in the long run, the effects were not disastrous. The United States still needed Canadian products, though now the American consumer had to pay duty on them.

Abrogation gave some impetus to the movement for Confederation. The representatives of the five provinces meeting at Quebec in 1865 talked of a "common commercial policy." Their only common commercial policy up to that point was for each province to tax the manufactured goods of the others as readily as they would those of Russia or Zanzibar. The tariff of the Canadas showed favor toward manufacturers but the general principle underlying customs duties was simply to obtain revenue. The general tariff in Nova Scotia and Newfoundland was ten per cent, in Prince Edward Island eleven per cent, in New Brunswick 12 1/2 per cent (it had a then rare compound duty, specific and ad valorem, on wine), and in Canada 20 per cent, though the levy on liquor was 100 per cent. (The government had proposed a 50 per cent duty on liquor in 1859 but there were objections that such a low rate would encourage intemperance, and it was doubled.)

Obviously, one of the chief difficulties to be overcome if Confederation was to be achieved, was the difference in tariffs. In the Atlantic colonies, the tariff was used strictly for revenue. About the only protectionist voice raised in the Maritimes was that of Abraham Gesner who published *The Industrial Resources of Nova Scotia* in 1849. It advocated tariff protection of industry as a means of stopping emigration to New England. In the Canadas, protection was a strong feature of the tariff. In 1859, Galt increased the general tariff to 20 per cent after an increase to 15 per cent only the year before. Seventeen items, including soap and starch, were taxed at 30 per cent. Galt advanced the argument that some protection of industry — "incidental protection," he called it — was required to provide employment for men (nothing was said of women) who were not suited to farm work. In fact, the year 1859 saw the last great advance for the protectionists until the Conservatives began advocating higher tariffs, when they were in opposition in 1876, on the grounds that Canada must not become a dumping ground (the phrase then was "slaughter market") for foreign manufacturers. The early favorites for Canadian tariff protection were the soap, sugar, coal, coaloil and cotton goods industries, iron and steel coming later.

In the 1860s, other political questions took precedence over protection. One was the attempt, renewed frequently until 1911, to restore the reciprocity treaty with the United States. And then there was the question of Confederation itself. The Confederation negotiations were responsible in 1866 for lowering the United Province's tariff from 20 to 15 per cent to bring the Maritimes in. The Atlantic provinces generally did not favor protection, that is, until the coal industry was established in Nova Scotia. The Maritimers were free-traders because, first of all, free trade aided the shipping and ship-building industries. The big advantage they saw in Confederation was the removal of trade barriers among the five colonies. The easterners were still hesitant (so much so that Prince Edward Island and Newfoundland stayed out) and Nova Scotia and New Brunswick, entering Confederation, found to their dismay that when tariffs rise, whether for revenue or for protection of home production, it is the necessities of life which furnish the bulk of the customs duties. Luxuries always seem to fluctuate in demand and cannot be counted on for that steady income to which governments become accustomed. So the squabbling over the terms of union went on long after Confederation and, in one impasse, Nova Scotia elected a separatist provincial government.

Here, in this issue, the tariff as an internal problem in early Confederation becomes mixed up with the tariff internationally. Indeed, it is difficult to separate the two, but we propose to deal first with the international (that is, Canadian-American) side, and then, in the next chapter, discuss the intricate and deadly fighting between the provinces and Ottawa.

For the first seven years of Confederation, the tariff remained at 15 per cent. At least two major attempts were made during that time to renew reciprocity with the United States: Prime Minister Macdonald tried it, in 1871, and in 1874 so did the editor and parliamentarian, George Brown. Protectionist sentiment was strong enough on both sides of the border to defeat them. The U.S. tariff rose to nearly 50 per cent. There was a world-wide depression in 1874-78. It was the policy of the Liberal government of Alexander Mackenzie to impose duties for revenue only, and the tariff was raised to 17 per cent in 1874. Sir Richard Cartwright, the finance minister, held that "duties should be levied only for the purpose of creating revenue to provide for the necessities of the government." Cartwright was the last Canadian finance minister to impose tariffs for revenue only. But he did not escape budget deficits. Meanwhile, protectionism was growing in Canada. Boards of trade and manufacturing associations were furious when they discovered that Brown's proposals to Washington for reciprocity included thirty-seven Canadian manufactures and all agricultural implements. By the time of the election in 1878, the

Conservatives were responding to the protectionist trend. They formulated what Macdonald called, and what has been known ever since as, the National Policy.

There were three pillars supporting this policy. The first two were western settlement and the Pacific railway — together, the transcontinental consolidation of Canada. The third was tariff protection. During his first ministry, Macdonald had dabbled at protection. A duty placed on American coal in 1870 had to be abandoned the next year because of lack of parliamentary support; a levy on cereals also had to be repealed; but a tax on salt stayed, with Britain excused from it, the first British preferential tariff since Confederation. The Conservatives tried to use the protection issue in the 1874 election but were swamped by the Canadian Pacific scandal of the previous year, and the Liberals came to power for one term.

At one point, Mackenzie tried to put the tariff up to 20 per cent, but Maritime members of his own party prevented it. In opposition, Macdonald was frequently worried that the Liberals, despite Cartwright, would adopt protectionism as a vote-getting policy before he could. But there seemed little real danger of that: "There is no policy more consistent with what we call the Dark Ages of the world than that of protection," said Mackenzie in the Commons. "There is no principle more consonant with the advance of human freedom than absolute freedom of commerce. Our policy at the present time is to avoid, as far as possible, placing a burden of taxation upon the people; and to endeavor to make everything as cheap as the state of the revenue will admit."

In 1875, the U.S. Senate rejected a draft trade agreement between Canada and the United States which was, in effect, Canada's third attempt at restoring reciprocity. In 1876, in an opposition motion, Macdonald called for "readjustment of the tariff" which would "not only tend to alleviate the stagnation of business . . . but also afford fitting encouragement and protection to the struggling manufacturers and industries, as well as to agricultural products of the country."

"We must trust to our customs as the principal source of our future revenue," Macdonald said. "Now, what can be more reasonable than to so adjust the tariff for revenue purposes that it will enable us to meet our engagements and to develop our resources, the duties falling upon the articles we ourselves are capable of producing." By "engagements," he meant the railways, roads and canals required to open up the country, especially the west. And by "articles we ourselves are capable of producing," he meant manufactured goods and agricultural produce. The Liberals defeated the Conservative motion by a vote of 119 to 64. The issue was clear for Canadians: free trade versus protection. Macdonald, sensing the opportunity to put the Canadian Pacific scandal far behind him and scramble back to power on a popular issue, put his motion again in 1877, and again in 1878. "Canada is for the Canadians," he told a meeting at Stanstead, Quebec. In the final session of Parliament before the 1878 election, Cartwright delivered his famous dictum, one all politicians might well read at breakfast every day: "All taxation, however disguised, is a loss per se; it is the duty, and the sacred duty, of the government to take from the people only what is necessary to the proper discharge of the public service; taxation in any other mode is simply in one shape or another legalized robbery." (Importer Daniel Sutherland of Dundee, Canada East, in 1846 referred to customs officers as "licensed robbers.")

A confident and jaunty Macdonald put his 1878 resolution:

> The welfare of Canada requires the adoption of a National Policy which, by a judicious re-adjustment of the tariff, will benefit and foster the agricultural, the mining, the manufacturing, and other interests of the Dominion; such a policy will retain in Canada thousands of our fellow-countrymen who are now obliged to expatriate themselves in search of the employment denied them at home; will restore prosperity to our struggling industries now so sadly depressed; will prevent Canada from being made a sacrifice market; will encourage and develop an active inter-provincial trade; and, moving, as it ought to do, in the direction of a reciprocity of tariffs with our neighbors, so far as the varied interests of Canada may demand, will greatly tend to procure for this country eventually a reciprocity of trade.

For too long, Macdonald said, Canada had been inundated with the sweepings of American factories. Canada had played the policy of conciliation and humiliation with the United States long enough. Now it was time to establish retaliatory tariffs. Only in this way could reciprocity in tariffs be achieved with the Americans: "It is only by closing our doors, and by cutting them out of our markets, that they will open theirs to us." The resolution was defeated 114 to 77. But Macdonald won the general election in a walk and, in 1879, introduced the protective tariff which endured in basic outline until well into the period following the Second World War.

Finance Minister Sir Leonard Tilley introduced the tariff in the Commons on March 14, 1879. In schoolmasterish fashion, he outlined increases in duties ranging from 20 to 40 per cent and special protection for certain industries. He put the policy clearly and succinctly: its purpose was "to select for a higher rate of duty those articles which are manufactured or can be manufactured in the country, and to have those that are neither made nor are likely to be made in the country at a lower rate."

On 245 dutiable articles, the average ad valorem duty was 22.26 per cent. There was also specific duty on some items. The duty on agricultural implements (Canada was a farming country) was 25 per cent. This tax brought big political trouble for both Conservatives and Liberals in the next three decades, especially the Liberals. To protect the farmer to some extent, the 1879 tariff imposed duties on cereals, including wheat, barley, corn, buckwheat, oats, rye, rice, peas and beans. Cartwright condemned the tariff policy as one which allowed "certain sections of the community to tax the rest of the people for their private gain." At the last minute, for fear of U.S reprisals, the government discarded its plan to give Britain trade preferences. Macdonald assured Lord Dufferin, the governor-general, that his government was not going to sink into pure protectionism. Britain frowned darkly on, but did not disallow, the Canadian tariff policy, and saw it correctly as the opening wedge in Canada's assumption of her own foreign policy.

The Commons tariff debate went on and on. "Another day of profitless debate," Macdonald wearily told the governor general two weeks after introduction of the tariff. The debate continued another month before the tariff became law. What emerged over-all was a strongly nationalistic commercial program which, within a year, began bearing the desired economic results.

An odd sidelight on tariff policy in this period was provided by a customs official at Toronto, C.C. Taylor. He wrote a book praising Toronto as a haven for British immigrants and then sent copies of it to many public libraries in England. He followed this up by going to England to be interviewed by the newspapers and to praise the librarians for being astute enough to stock his book, until he became well enough known in the cities of northern England to be invited to make speeches in which he extolled Canada, especially Toronto, upheld trade protection, and damned British free trade.

Meanwhile, the protectionist trend strengthened in the United States and, in 1888, President Cleveland lost office partly because he favored lower tariffs. Protective duties were extended by the McKinley tariff of 1890.

In the 1880s, Canadian economic growth was slow, despite a healthy revenue from customs duties — in 1883 there was a surplus of $6,625,000 against an estimate of $4,460,000, and $1,125,000 in taxation was remitted — and this disappointment led to some second thoughts about protection, including the possibilities of closer relations with the United States. Some consideration was given, not only to reciprocity (again), but to commercial union, that is, abolition of all customs duties between the two countries and a common tariff against others, with division of customs income in agreed proportion (shades of Upper and Lower Canada in 1791-1841). Many Ontario farmers were in favor of commercial union, and essayist Goldwin Smith, who supported it, became president of the Commercial Union League in 1887. The arguments of the league were accepted by some Liberals, including the free-trader, Cartwright, but Sir Wilfrid Laurier refused to endorse the idea, and the party adopted a policy of unrestricted reciprocity, meaning complete removal of customs duties between Canada and the United States, a stand which appalled Canadian manufacturers. In the 1891 election, the Conservatives accused the Liberals of leading Canada down the road to political annexation. On the eve of the election, after Parliament had been dissolved, the government announced that it was sending a delegation to Washington to negotiate a treaty of "limited reciprocity" and appealed for a large majority to show Washington that Canadians generally were behind a treaty-making effort. Macdonald won the election handily, at the age of 76.

A Canadian delegation went to Washington after the election, working at a leisurely pace until it announced failure in 1892 on the grounds that the United States would negotiate only on the basis of free trade in natural and manufactured products and a combined tariff against all other countries. The Liberals accused the Conservatives of deceit and of being controlled by the "monopolies and combines."

Sir John Thompson went to Washington in 1892 soon after he became prime minister — Macdonald had died in June the previous year — and once more proposed a renewal of the 1854 reciprocity treaty. He was refused, like Sir Charles Tupper in 1887. In 1893, the opposition Liberals turned to limited instead of unrestricted reciprocity. At its convention that year in Ottawa, the party passed a resolution which said, in part:

> The customs tariff of the Dominion should be based not as it is now upon the protective principle but on the requirements of the public service; . . . the tariff should be reduced to the needs of honest, economical and efficient government; it should be so adjusted as to make free, or to bear as lightly as possible upon, the necessaries of life, and should be so arranged as to promote freer trade with the whole world, more particularly with Great Britain and the United States; . . . we denounce the principle of protection as radically unsound and unjust to the masses of the people.

Laurier himself described protection as a fraud, a robbery, slavery and "a servile copy of the American system." William Paterson, who was to become his minister of Customs for fifteen years, said that "regard should be had only for the necessities of the revenue." When they got into office in 1896, however, the Liberals enacted a moderately protective tariff. Cartwright was shunted off to trade and commerce and W.S. Fielding became finance minister. Public hearings were held to get the views of the manufacturers who said, of course, that any removal of protection would be inexpedient, unwise and impolitic. Paterson announced, finally, that no government would be justified in risking sweeping tariff changes which would dislocate industry and cause widespread unemployment. In the 1897 tariff, the only significant departure from Conservative policy was a trade preference for Britain. There were duties of 25 per cent on eighty-three items, 30 per cent on seventy items and 35 per cent on fifty others.

In the same year, the Dingley tariff in the United States hit Canadian trade the hardest blow since 1866. In 1898, a Joint High Commission to consider "all controversies" between Canada and the United States, including reciprocity, met for five months without agreement on anything. Laurier did not actively seek reciprocity, despite the urgings of Maritime and Prairie Liberals who wanted lower duties on manufactures, especially farm machinery. But he did not yield to the wing of his party that wanted even higher tariffs. In the 1907 tariff, the farmers actually won a 2 1/2 per cent cut — from 20 to 17 1/2 per cent — in the duty on farm implements, though the benefit was promptly undone by an increase in the appraised value of imported machines and a lower duty on parts used by Canadian manufacturers. Indeed, the farm machinery makers, concentrated in three or four Ontario cities, were allowed drawbacks no matter whether their goods were exported or sold in Canada. A drawback, or remission in tariff, normally applies only to imported parts used in the manufacture of an article which is exported.

Reciprocity suddenly became a public issue again in 1910. President Taft was disturbed by the widespread criticism of the U.S. tariff of the previous year, the Payne-Aldrich Act which had again put up prices on many everyday items. On May 12, 1910, P.C. Knox, the U.S. Secretary of State, let it be known through the usual channels — the British ambassador in Washington — that Taft wanted to initiate tariff negotiations with Canada. The Canadian government, given the futility of many previous pilgrimages to Washington, demurred. But then Laurier took a trip west in July and August. Everywhere he went — Brandon, Manitoba, Yellowgrass, Saskatchewan, Red Deer, Alberta or Golden, British Columbia — the message was the same: start doing what you used to preach and lower the tariff. Prairie farmers quoted back to him speeches he had made for years in opposition to the wicked protective tariff. A farm publication of the time put it this way (quoted in *Corner Stones of Empire: the Settlement of Crystal City and District, 1970*):

> About 41,000 cream separators are worn out in Canada each year and must be replaced. If your separator is worn out, and you buy a new one from the United States, you pay 25 per cent duty, or tariff, or indirect tax, whichever name suits the way you vote. In that case

the tax comes out of your pocket and goes into the government treasury. If you wish to be loyal to the eastern Canadian manufacturer, who lends money to you to buy your machinery at a high rate of interest, you still pay 25 per cent over the value of the separator and in this case the extra money goes into the vaults of our Canadian millionaires. New Zealand is Canada's strong competitor in butter making. The New Zealand farmer imports his cream separator free of duty and is able to undersell the Canadian farmer and still make money. How to do you like our Canadian tariff?

Laurier decided that his government was ready to talk to Washington about a trade agreement. The Americans were certainly ready, because the Republicans were trounced in the Congressional elections of November, 1910, and the Democrats had taken control of the House of Representatives. Fielding and Paterson went to Washington on January 10, 1911, and an agreement was signed eleven days later. The two governments proceeded by concurrent legislation instead of treaty to avoid the constitutional necessity of formal British participation. The agreement was for free trade in farm products and low rates on a range of other goods, including farm machinery, engines and building materials. In all, forty-two items were to be duty-free, including grains, vegetables, fruit, dairy products, fish and wood; and tariffs were to be reduced on sixty-seven others.

The 62nd Congress met in special session in April to pass the reciprocity legislation. It cleared the Senate by 53 to 27 on July 22. But a funny thing happened on the way to Canadian ratification. The Liberals did not foresee much trouble and their belief was strengthened in March when the new tariff won a preliminary vote in the Commons, albeit the Liberal MP for Brantford, home of farm machinery firms, bolted the party. Opposition Leader Sir Robert Borden attacked the agreement as of benefit to the United States only. On July 28, Laurier suddenly dissolved Parliament and took the issue to the electorate.

The Liberals did not seem worried. After all, they had preached freer trade and here they were delivering their promise. And the Conservatives had been driven from office as the party of the protective tariff in 1896. But far from being afraid of the issue, the Conservatives welcomed it; indeed, in 1910, Borden had begun devising an election strategy in which the Conservatives would remain dedicated to Macdonald's National Policy. The Conservatives waved the flag: reciprocity would lead to commercial if not actual military invasion by the Americans, political annexation, and the breakup of the British Empire. The Conservatives had some wealthy allies. The main economic interests opposing reciprocity were the manufacturers, millers, packers, canners, brewers and the railroads.

In the election, September 21, the Commons standing changed abruptly from the 132 Liberals and 89 Conservatives sitting at dissolution to 133 Conservatives and 84 Liberals in the new Parliament. Both Fielding and Paterson, the negotiators of reciprocity, lost their seats, along with five other cabinet ministers. Two elections, 33 years apart, in 1878 and 1911, had been fought on exactly the same issue. In both cases, free trade lost and protection won. Reciprocity died away as a major public issue. Canadians obviously did not feel that special tariff arrangements with the United States were either the main danger to their independence or their main hope for economic growth. The treaties of 1935 and 1938 were not reciprocity but small breaches in a high tariff wall made possible by the U.S. Reciprocal Trade Agreements Act of 1934. Canada gained in two ways: the Americans slackened some tariffs and at long last acknowledged that Canada was being severely ground between the millstones of U.S. and British trade policies. The agreements were a prelude to the General Agreement on Tariffs and Trade, two decades later.

There has been no noticeable champion of unrestricted free trade in Canada for a long time. The farmers' movements of the prairies and Ontario sprang into being partly as protests against the high tariff. (The 1913 *Grain Growers' Guide* of Winnipeg advised its readers: "Always bear in mind that the good old patriotic slogan of the Canadian Manufacturers' Association, 'Canada for Canadians' means 'Canada for 2,500 Canadians.'") But after the collapse of the Progressive Party in the late 1920s, the west gave up attempts to have duties lowered in its own interests. It turned, instead, to seeking a larger share of the national income by other means: guaranteed wheat prices, low freight rates, and exploration for — and discovery of — oil and gas.

Over the years, a myth emerged that the high tariff was simply the price of being Canadian, but, especially since the post-war multinational trade agreements, that legend has been under serious examination. Of course, there were always strenuous objections to high tariffs, but after they had become the accepted government policy of the land, or at least of central Canada, for some seventy years, they had taken on an aura of respectability and natural continuance to which most people were more or less resigned.

But as early as 1893, Cartwright, still the believer in tax-for-revenue-only, had estimated the cost of protection from the start of Macdonald's National Policy in 1879 at one billion dollars. Cartwright often referred to the notorious "Red Parlor," a Toronto meeting place where the Conservatives were said to call together the manufacturers of tariff-protected goods and demand pledges to their campaign funds. He once accused the Conservatives directly of giving tariff protection to two Ontario rice-cleaning mills in return for a cash donation of $15,000 handed over at a

Red Parlor conference. Bowell, the minister of Customs, didn't deny it. He simply said Cartwright's statement was unworthy of a gentleman.

In the 1907 tariff, dutiable items numbered four hundred and eighty compared with three hundred and forty in 1879. Most manufacturers, except stove and coffin makers, were granted additional protection ranging from 2 1/2 to 7 1/2 per cent, but the greatest public outcry was caused when prices went up before the tariff law had been given royal assent. This renewed the old charge that Canadian manufacturers lived up to the limit of tariff protection and advanced their prices as soon as — in this case sooner than — additional protection was granted.

H.C. Eastman and Stefan Stykolt found in their study, *The Tariff and Competition in Canada*, published in 1967, that excessive tariff protection permitted firms to operate plants of sub-optimal scale. In other words, the height of the tariff was greater than needed to preserve those industries. J.H. Dales in *The Protective Tariff in Canada's Development* argued, in 1966, that the tariff increased immigration (to provide a captive consumer group) and the gross national product, but lowered individual income. J.H. Young in *Canadian Commercial Policy* estimated the cost of the Canadian tariff in 1956 at close to $1 billion or four per cent of gross national product, or $180 for each person in the labor force. In 1981, the North-South Institute of Ottawa estimated that protection for the Canadian textile industry alone costs each Canadian family $100 a year.

Arguing the merits or otherwise of the tariff is beyond the scope of this work, but this mere reference to the issue indicates that the use of the tariff for protection of Canadian manufacturers has not always been as acceptable as one might suppose today from recent developments. Besides, there are many other forms of protection. For instance, beginning in 1900, there were clauses in the Railway Subsidies Acts requiring the use of Canadian-made steel, bridging and rolling stock; there were anti-dumping measures adopted in 1904; and offers of largesse to attract industry have been made since 1879.

By 1900, ninety-five Ontario municipalities had granted aid in one form or another to factories, Canadian or American, which established in their areas. This was done through free industrial sites, loans, bonuses, tax exemptions, free water and electricity, and so on. And, as in the case of some industries today, the tariff has also been used to conciliate divergent regional interests: in 1879 imported coal was taxed so as to secure a central Canadian market for Nova Scotia coal; the 1887 tariff increase on iron was intended to help protect the Nova Scotia iron and steel industry and quell that province's secession movement. It is interesting to note that customs officials did not stand apart from the tariff discussion. They were an integral part of it, with much more to do than provide advice to cabinet. Before the amendments to the tariff act in 1894, for instance, to obtain the views of the public and industry, the government sent customs and excise officers to interview representatives of industry. The interviews, drafting of the bill, committee hearings and passage of legislation were all accomplished within a single year.

It has been extremely difficult to change the tariff (especially to lower it) when, on the one hand, the government needs more revenue and when, on the other, protected industries keep up a clamor for continued or additional protection. Any change must be gradual. Prime Minister Sir Charles Tupper once said that he considered fifteen years enough protection before an industry stood on its own feet without a tariff umbrella. That fifteen years has stretched into something like eighty-five but, almost imperceptibly, the tariff, with some obvious exceptions, has been gradually coming down, until soon it will be somewhere around what it was when Confederation began. The federal government declared in the Commons on January 23, 1981: "Canada would have suffered a great loss [in multi-national trade negotiations] today had we witnessed a strengthening of protectionism and restrictive trade practices."

In the 19th century, Britain did not object to Canada and the United States talking trade. But it became considerably provoked when Canada began putting out its first feelers for trade agreements with European countries. Soon after his return to power in 1878, Macdonald appointed Galt high commissioner in London — and concurrently ambassador at large for Europe — with the specific intention of broadening Canadian trade. The Canadian cabinet felt an "absolute need" for direct negotiation with Europeans to ensure "proper protection" for Canadian interests. Macdonald had had some experience in this field as a member of the five-member commission appointed in 1871 to settle outstanding differences between the United States and Britain and Canada. Macdonald later said that the four British commissioners had "only one thing in their minds — that is, to go home to England with a treaty in their pockets, settling everything, no matter at what cost to Canada." Still, Galt's talks with Europeans had to be filtered through the appropriate British ambassadors.

By 1883, however, the new high commissioner, Tupper, managed to get himself appointed joint plenipotentiary in trade negotiations with Spain. At the Colonial Conference in 1887, other Empire members such as New Zealand sought the same negotiating freedom as Canada, if freedom is the right word. By 1892 Canada was seeking its own representation in Washington and elsewhere, and the following year Tupper conducted successful trade negotiations in Paris. The United States, France, Germany and Italy, through their consuls-general in Canada, established quasi-diplomatic channels for direct communication with Ottawa. By the early 1900s, British participation in Canadian trade negotiations with these and other countries, including Belgium and the Netherlands, became a mere formality. Canada had used tariff discussions as one avenue to full independence.

Until early in this century, Canada had a single tariff — apart from the 1854-66 reciprocity agreement with the United States. Then a preferential tariff was added for the British Empire and a little later an intermediate tariff level for most-favored-nation reciprocating countries. Britain, a free trader since the 1840s, did not give trade preferences to Canada and other Empire members until 1919. At the Imperial Economic Conference in 1932, Canada concluded separate tariff agreements with Britain, the Irish Free State, South Africa and Southern Rhodesia. They were partly in response to the higher U.S. Smoot-Hawley tariff of 1930. Almost automatically, the United States raised tariffs in depression times.

Tariffs did not really start to come down until international trade bargaining began in earnest in 1947. Canada was one of the nine original members of the General Agreement on Tariffs and Trade signed at Geneva that year. There now are some ninety member countries carrying on 80 per cent of the world's trade. There have been seven rounds of tariff-cutting negotiations, the longest and most complex of them begun in Tokyo in 1973 and concluded in 1979. The latest round cut tariffs by 30 per cent on average, the reductions to be gradually brought into effect by 1987. At the same time, the British preferential tariff was to be absorbed into the most-favored-nation tariff rates. It was automatically eliminated, in fact, when Britain joined the European Economic Community, disregarding the open objections of the Canadian government. As far as Canada-U.S. trade is concerned, there are few tariff barriers. More than 60 per cent of U.S. imports come into Canada duty-free and about 70 per cent of Canadian exports enter the United States the same way. Defence production-sharing and the automotive agreement of 1965 have had a large impact on two-way, duty-free trade.

CHAPTER VIII

The Tariff as an Issue between Ottawa and the Provinces

The national tariff was an abrasive issue between Ottawa and the provinces in the early years of Confederation. But this was hardly surprising: there was already a tradition of regional antagonism. At any given moment in Canada, there is one province or region which considers that it is being mistreated by one or more other provinces or regions or by the national authority. There is an example from the very first session of the New Brunswick Assembly in 1786.

The assembly had just passed its first revenue act: a tax of two shillings and sixpence was to be placed on every imported barrel (thirty gallons) of rum, brandy, shrub "or any other liquor of which the greater part is distilled spirits"; a 2 1/2-per-cent tax on all merchandise belonging to or consigned to non-residents, and a five-per-cent tax on goods for residents, except on lumber, livestock, Indian meal, grain and salt. The assembly then addressed the Nova Scotia Assembly on the subject of customs duties, claiming that Nova Scotia, out of the western part of which New Brunswick had been formed only two years before, owed it money. The infant legislature said that,

> sundry bonds for duties in spirituous liquors were given by merchants and importers on this side of the Bay of Fundy. The monies secured thereby have been probably paid by the Consumers, Inhabitants now of this province. . . . Those bonds are deposited in your Treasury uncancelled. Your Honourable House will not consider it an unreasonable Requisition that they should be transmitted to our Treasurer and the money applied for the purpose of opening roads. The principles of Justice and Candor which actuate the Members of your House render it needless to be more explicit in pointing out the Equity of our Claim . . . Your advanced progress of Population, your Resources, and Revenue, so much Superior to what that of your younger Sister can be for many years, may warrant an Appeal to your generosity and Disinterestedness; and that we flatter ourselves we may at all Times hope for that reciprocal Aid and friendly Communication which our similar Sentiments and Situation naturally point out as advantageous to both Provinces and which on our part we shall ever be happy to promote to the utmost of our Power.

The Nova Scotia legislature was so mesmerized by this unctuousness that it overlooked a reply — and return of any bonds.

The Maritime opposition to Confederation expressed itself in several ways. In 1865, just two years before Confederation, New Brunswick elected a government opposed to any union with the Canadas. Its premier, the respected Albert Smith, objected to the Quebec Resolutions for union on the grounds that the Canadians (that is, Ontario and Quebec) would assume complete control of the new country and that New Brunswick would be hit by higher tariffs. For years, the New Brunswick Assembly had been clogged with petitions for remission of import duties on agricultural machinery. For example, on February 24, 1854, a petition of the Carleton County Agricultural Society sought remission of duties on an American horsepower machine and a thresher imported the previous fall, mainly for demonstration purposes. There were scores of other such requests that year. And the colony had had two traumatic tariff experiences in the quarter-century preceding Confederation. In 1841, British preferential duties on colonial timber had been drastically reduced, resulting in high unemployment in New Brunswick and heavy emigration to the United States.

In 1848, Britain had repealed all its duties on timber, a staggering blow for the province because its lumber was effectively shut out of the British market by Baltic products close at hand. Governor Sir Edmund Head had written to Lord Grey: "The principal inhabitants of New Brunswick have been and are by descent and by inclination loyal in their feelings and strongly attached to the British Crown. They have felt a pride in forming an integral part of a mighty empire and the sense of self-importance connected with this feeling receives a shock from every expression or every fact which seems to impair this unity. In addition, therefore, to the immediate effect on their material interests produced by the withdrawal of full protection to their timber trade their sympathies received what may be called a moral blow." And now here was Britain encouraging union.

Leonard Tilley and his pro-Confederation government went down to shattering defeat in 1865, and Smith formed a ministry. A Canadian delegation led by Macdonald himself went to London to try to undo the New Brunswick decision. Smith also went to London to plead the anti-Confederation case, but he was rebuffed by the colonial office. It was even rumored at the time that the colonial office tried to bribe Smith with a fat administrative post in one of the colonies. He and his colleagues could agree on being against Confederation but on little else, and their government gradually fell apart. A new election, May 7, 1866, returned Tilley who became minister of Customs in the new federal government. Tilley was greatly assisted, as he conceded later, by the nervousness caused by the Fenian Brotherhood in raids on New Brunswick in the month preceding the election. On April 14, the Fenians seized the customs flag on Indian Island near Campobello and a week later burned down the customs warehouse at the same location.

At Confederation, the individual provinces gave up the tariff to the national government. Article 122 of the British North America Act provided that customs duties of the "different provinces shall remain in force until altered by the Parliament of Canada." The Customs Act of 1866 of the United Province of Canada was adopted in 1867 by the first Parliament of the Dominion and, in 1868, the average tariff was set at 15 per cent. The goods of Quebec, Ontario, New Brunswick and Nova Scotia were duty-free when traded among each other.

It did not take long before complaints began coming in about the ramifications of Confederation, especially as felt in the Maritimes. In a petition to the minister of Customs dated February 28, 1868, Halifax merchants protested higher tariffs on rum and sugar and argued that if Nova Scotians could not buy West Indies rum, the West Indies would not continue to buy Nova Scotia fish. The petition continued:

> The duty on rum has been advanced upon our late [pre-Confederation] too high rates that the poorer classes, who chiefly consume this class of spirits, are seriously burdened by its increased cost. It is true that the duty on whisky has been reduced; but this does not, nor will not have, the effect of forming anew the tastes of those of our people who will use West India rum even if the cost be enhanced by a high duty. Another serious objection to a high duty on rum is the encouragement it affords to the illicit trade. It is well known that when the duty was reduced at one time in Nova Scotia, the revenue was increased. Advance the duty and the reverse must inevitably occur, owing to the numerous facilities afforded along our extended coasts for the operations of the smuggler.

The petition failed.

Canada's first tariff, with its relatively short list of dutiable goods (only three pages) and much longer list of duty-free articles, was approved by Parliament December 21, 1867. But the dutiable list soon began to grow. The tariff was amended May 22, 1868, adding books and snuff, to mention two items, to the dutiable list. To the list of prohibited books, papers, drawings, paintings and prints "of an immoral or indecent character" were added photographs of the same ilk. Export duties were imposed for the first time: on oak, spruce and pine logs.

Joseph Howe wrote Prime Minister Macdonald in the fall of 1868 that Nova Scotia, "if not confederated, could have met all her obligations and, under her old tariff, have had a small surplus in the treasury. By imposing one per cent upon imports we could have raised money enough to keep our roads and bridges, now left almost without any provision, though our tariff has been raised to 15 per cent and sundry direct taxes have been imposed.''

Provincial complaints about the financial terms of union were so common that, in 1885, the federal government bundled them all up in one big document of 604 pages which it tabled in the Commons. It is a litany of woe. One should bear in mind that the sums in dispute, though they appear miniscule by today's governmental standards, were imposing at the time. And it must be remembered also that, in the quarter-century between 1868 and 1893, 74 per cent of all taxation derived from customs duties. The per capita payment of customs duties in 1893 was $4.22 in Canada, $3.05 in the United States and $2.50 in Britain.

Nova Scotia argued that it imported more goods from abroad than Canada did and therefore was hurt more by higher tariffs. Its provincial treasurer, A.W. McLelan, wrote to John Rose, the federal minister of finance: ''(Nova Scotians) ask what concessions are the people of Canada making for Confederation and when you fail to show that it is an act of mutual concessions — when you cannot place your finger upon a single right of privilege, or dollar of money, that you concede — they naturally and determinedly rebel against a surrender of at least one-third their average allowance for local purposes.'' In both Nova Scotia and New Brunswick, the phrase ''better terms'' became the fulcrum of political rhetoric. It meant simply that the two provinces wanted a better deal from Ottawa for giving up, among other things, one of their articles of faith, the low tariff. Nova Scotia was the squeakier wheel and was oiled first. In 1869, Parliament passed an Act Respecting Nova Scotia which provided an additional subsidy of $82,698 a year for ten years, beginning in 1867. (In January, 1877, Nova Scotia came right back with a request for a ten-year extension. Prime Minister Alexander Mackenzie protested that payments to the provinces were already so large that very little money was left to the federal government.)

New Brunswick considered that it had an even more deserving case than Nova Scotia because the federal tariff had hit the very staples of consumption such as flour, meal, corn, sugar, tea and molasses. It rankled that Nova Scotia received better treatment because it had raised more fuss. The demand for better terms was supported by all federal members of Parliament from New Brunswick and the entire provincial legislature. John W. Cudlip of Saint John, who stood for repeal of Confederation and annexation to the United States, was elected to the legislature by acclamation.

On July 14, 1870, the New Brunswick government wrote to Howe, now secretary of state for the provinces, that $92,340 was owing the province. It had been treated unfairly in view of the special subsidy given Nova

Scotia and better terms granted to the Northwest Territories and offered to British Columbia, Prince Edward Island and Newfoundland — and on a new basis instead of on that of the original four-province Confederation. In October, 1871, New Brunswick's "better terms delegation" (it was called that officially), told Ottawa that "when . . . this unjust pressure of taxation shall be fully felt by the people at large, general public irritation and disquietude must succeed the attitude of petition, and swell the voice of popular remonstrance." It reminded Ottawa that George Brown had said in a speech at Saint John, September 14, 1864, that Confederation "would place us all on an equal footing as British Americans, instead of being sectional provincialists, with divided interests."

But now, after Confederation, other provinces saw financial relief for New Brunswick as a "draft upon the purse of the people of the other provinces." If the province had remained out of Confederation and continued its own tariff, it would have had a surplus. Now it was paying $150,000 more into the federal government than it received, and drifting further into debt every year. For the year ended June 30, 1871, Ontario and Quebec had paid $13,504,647 in customs, excise and stamp duties, or $4.80 per capita. New Brunswick had paid $1,452,837, or $5.08 per capita. The delegation poured out its data. New Brunswick had come into Confederation with a surplus of $214,000. Four years later it was going into debt at the rate of $50,000 a year although the revenues for the Dominion government, mainly from customs, had increased by 83 per cent in the same period.

Union would not have been possible without New Brunswick, lying as it did between Canada and Nova Scotia. If the province had stayed out, but had adopted the Canadian tariff, it would have had a surplus of $336,555 by 1871. The actual revenue of the province in 1870, including the federal subsidy, was $1,088,845. But New Brunswickers had paid $1,245,896 to Ottawa, including $1,015,111 in customs duties and $149,322 in excise taxes on liquor and tobacco. In the meantime, Ontario and Quebec were bragging about substantial surpluses, even after heavy spending on public works.

And there was another sour note:

> A list of the officials of the Dominion, their number, salaries and place of birth or residence would reveal a state of things anything but complimentary to the inhabitants of the Maritime Provinces ... (We) do claim as a right that in appointments to office and in the distribution of honors, New Brunswick receive that full consideration due to a Province which contributes so largely to the exchequer and to the effective government of the country.

It was not until 1873 that New Brunswick achieved better terms, mainly on the strength of an annual grant of $150,000 for the loss of export duty on Maine lumber floated down the St. John River. But the new Intercolonial Railway, instead of opening central Canadian markets to New Brunswick and other Maritime merchants and manufacturers, achieved the reverse. In the 1878 federal election, all the provinces except New Brunswick gave Macdonald a majority.

Meanwhile, Ontario complained that the Confederation subsidies paid to the two Maritime provinces were being matched to their increase in population, while those for Ontario were remaining stationary. Ontario was sure that it would have to pay out $1,100,000 of the $2,000,000 that Nova Scotia's subsidy would increase by, in the first ten years of Confederation. It sought disallowance of the subsidy increases to Nova Scotia and New Brunswick on the grounds that the increases were outside the British North America Act. Howe had the (no doubt pleasant) task of forwarding Ontario's complaint to London, where it was rejected. Earl Granville, secretary of state for the colonies, said: "Her Majesty's Government would not feel justified in proposing to the Imperial Parliament to deprive the Parliament of Canada of any power which that Act [BNA Act] has assigned to them."

A combined new customs house and post office in Halifax was the centre of another post-Confederation squabble. For three and a half years, Nova Scotia and Ottawa bickered over who was going to pay how much of its cost, now that it was to become a federal building.

In 1863, four years before Confederation, Nova Scotia authorized construction of the building as a provincial customs house and post office. But the building was not completed until 1868, the year after Confederation. The total cost was $189,080.64. Under the terms of Confederation, all public buildings in the provinces which were to be used for federal purposes (Customs and the mail were, of course, federal) were to become the property of the federal government. Nova Scotia argued that Ottawa owed it $66,385 for construction of the part of the building completed after Confederation, and refused to vacate it until the federal authority paid up. For its part, Ottawa claimed that as long as Nova Scotia continued to occupy the building it would have to pay five per cent a year to Canada on its cost. Ottawa could collect this amount easily, and did, by simply deducting it from the annual subsidy to the province.

Federal Finance Minister Sir Francis Hincks said that the Nova Scotia government was inflicting a large annual loss of $10,000 on Nova Scotians by refusing to comply with the law. In exasperation, Ottawa said that if Nova Scotia did not quit the building it would build another customs house elsewhere. Nova Scotia retorted that the voters could decide on the liberality of a federal government which had just spent $200,000 for a new customs house in Montreal, $75,000 for one at Saint

John and $50,000 for one at London, Ontario, but would not pay $66,385 for Nova Scotia's.

Prime Minister Macdonald declared in 1870 that the federal government had no legal power to submit the question to arbitration. But a year later, on the Commons motion of Sir George E. Cartier, Macdonald's righthand man, the federal authority agreed to do so. Although dispute over the instructions to the arbitrators lengthened the dispute another six months, finally, on November 13, 1871, the arbitrators decided, after meeting four days, that the building should be jointly owned and occupied, that all claims and counter-claims be disallowed, and that the federal government should pay Nova Scotia $80,000. The arbitrators also submitted their own bill — for $4,000.

Manitoba's entry into Confederation in 1870 was eased with the favor of three, later extended to four, years' grace from Canadian customs duties. The old (and lower) tariff of Rupert's Land applied during that time. By 1875, Manitoba was complaining of the "entire inadequacy" of the revenue despite the strict economy of providing no Parliament House (the legislature sat in the provincial courtroom), no residence for the lieutenant-governor, and no jail. All the revenue Manitoba received from Ottawa was $71,172 a year, while Ottawa was collecting more than $300,000 annually in tariffs from the customs port of Winnipeg. Other provinces had received better terms: Nova Scotia was getting an extra $82,698 a year, New Brunswick an extra $63,000. Manitoba's population now was estimated at 36,000 or nearly three times more than when, as it was put, "this country was annexed to Canada." There was no money to build roads. Would-be settlers took one look and promptly moved to the United States. The federal government finally agreed to raise the annual grant to $90,000 a year, and to bear the annual rent of $2,000 for Hudson's Bay Company premises in Winnipeg as a government house — if the province would pay for the repairs and get rid of its seven-member legislative council and thereby save $3,715 a year. The legislature could use the two upper storeys of the new customs house in Winnipeg. In 1879, the annual allowance to Manitoba was increased to $105,653.

A council of the North West Territories was constitued for the prairies (except for Manitoba, already a province) in 1873. It was denied any powers of taxation. The first assembly of the North West Territories, meeting in 1888, demanded more federal funds. It maintained that the people of the Territories contributed "a greater proportion of taxation per head" than other Canadians, and therefore were "entitled to receive a return on the amount paid by them into the federal treasury of a sum similar to that received by the various provinces."

But in the whole history of the early application of the terms of union, no province was harder done by than the smallest member of Confederation, Prince Edward Island, which joined July 1, 1873. On that same date, the Treaty of Washington took effect, giving Canada and the United States free fishing access to each other's coasts and free import of fish and fish oil. The treaty had been signed by Britain and the United States in 1871, when Prince Edward Island was still a separate colony, and had been ratified in 1872 by Canada, Newfoundland and P.E.I. Pending ratification, the three colonies had continued to pay the American customs tariff on their fish landings in the United States on assurances from the American Secretary of State, Hamilton Fish, that these duties would be reimbursed when the treaty became effective. The United States reneged on the promise, and in 1879 the Fishery Commission awarded Britain $5,500,000 in recompense for the customs duties paid the States.

Under the British North America Act, fisheries came under federal authority. Prince Edward Island, Ottawa said, was a part of Canada when the Treaty of Washington had taken effect July 1, 1873, and was therefore not entitled to its claim of $1,250,000 as part of the $5,500,000 award. Newfoundland, being still a separate colony, got $1,000,000, and Canada the rest. Why, asked Prince Edward Island, should wealthy Ontario share in the award when it had been earned by P.E.I. fishermen. In vain, the province appealed to the Queen, but London declined to intervene. In the Canadian Commons, Prime Minister Macdonald finally moved that the claim be rejected and he was upheld by a vote of 126 to 30, April 8, 1880. Prince Edward Island made one last try: through Ottawa, it asked the British treasury for compensation. Ottawa even had the gall to endorse the request, knowing that it would be turned down by Britain, which it was. The island province then started a new campaign in what might be called the Wars of Confederation. It pointed out that the federal government could build a railway for thousands of miles to British Columbia, but could not provide a decent steamship service across nine miles of Northumberland Strait between Prince Edward Island and mainland New Brunswick. But that, for once, was not a tariff issue.

However, the tariff did become a serious bone of contention between Ottawa and British Columbia, even though British Columbia relied less on customs duties for revenue than other provinces did in the colonial period.

Vancouver Island became a crown colony in 1849; British Columbia became one in 1858. Victoria was a free port, so Vancouver Island was therefore free of customs duties and taxes (revenue was raised mainly from land taxes). British Columbia had a general tariff of ten per cent ad valorem on everything. It also had specific duties, and some ad valorem levies as high as 50 per cent; poultry and opium carried identical duties of 25 per cent. Arthur Harvey, in *A Statistical Account of British Columbia*, published in 1867, says that total revenue in British Columbia in 1864 was $508,596, of which customs accounted for $232,839 and road tolls $121,423. In 1866, customs revenue amounted to $320,650 out of a total of $598,400. A rare export duty — on gold — was repealed in 1865. Excise duties and licences included a distiller's licence of $25 a year and $1 a gallon on spirits of every kind; a licence to sell liquor was $100 every six months in town, $30 in the country, plus $5 for each billiard table; a dancehall licence was $100 and a bowling alley licence $5. Miners also required licences, and stagecoach operators, drovers, bankers, livery owners, lawyers, land agents and auctioneers. Unsurprisingly, when British Columbia and Vancouver Island became one colony in 1866, it was the flourishing tariff of British Columbia which was adopted, rather than the zero tariff of Vancouver Island. Duties on imports increased until British Columbia joined Confederation in 1871; some were meant to protect local industry, like the duty on flour.

If British Columbia were to throw in with Canada, there would need to be an early start and fast completion of the transcontinental railway. Under the seventh clause of the terms of union, the customs tariff and excise duties prevailing in the colony would continue in force until it was built, unless, by a decision of the legislature, the tariff and excise laws of Canada should be adopted sooner, in anticipation of an early completion. Unfortunately for British Columbia, in the euphoria of railway building, or, more accurately, of Canadian promises to build, her legislators gave away this leverage and adopted the tariff of Canada.

The tariff needs of British Columbia naturally did not coincide with those of Ontario, Quebec and the Maritimes. There was, as has been noted even in recent times, a continent between them. In January, 1873, there was a 12-12 tie in the British Columbia legislature on the question of whether to petition Ottawa to raise the tariff on barley, oats, potatoes, cheese, butter, hops and hay to the level of the old B.C. tariff, and to excuse brewers and maltsters from excise duties. Speaker James Trimble cast the deciding vote, against, on the grounds that he had made an election promise to support the Canadian tariff.

On March 12, 1875, another petition for temporary protective duties for agriculture came before the legislature. The preamble said that the legislature had been "induced" to accept the Canadian tariff and to enter union on certain ratified stipulations, including the start of the railway. But the railway had not been started, and "the Canadian tariff after a trial of four years, and under circumstances in many respects peculiarly favorable, has resulted in failure and disaster and has operated as a dimunition of productive power, a restriction on growth, and a premium on foreign importations." This petition was approved, 13-6, after the preamble was struck out, and sent to a select committee on the tariff. The committee declared that, "for various considerations still having force," the province was allowed the option of retaining its own tariff until completion of the railway. "We had faith," the committee said, (in a way which read, between the lines, "We must have been idiots") that Canada would fulfil the terms of union, and therefore had elected to adopt the Canadian tariff.

Non-commencement of the railway meant that British Columbia had no easy access to Canadian centres of supply, and imports from the United States prejudiced home production. The committee sought protection for stock and grain and set out the specific extra duties it had in mind on cattle, sheep, hogs, salted and fresh meats, butter, cheese, grain and potatoes. It suggested ingeniously that Canada could even out increases in duties on agricultural products by reducing by the same amount the ad valorem duties on certain manufactured articles. In this way, the total customs revenue from British Columbia would remain the same and, in effect, there would still be one national tariff.

Undismayed by the deaf ear Ottawa turned to the problem, the legislature's select committee on the tariff question took up the battle again at the 1876 session. It presented figures showing how British Columbia had been done out of revenue by the Canadian tariff. The committee declared that the total value of imports to British Columbia in the year ending June 30, 1875, was $2,490,593. Duty paid of $413,991 would have amounted to $541,387 under the old B.C. tariff. The difference was accounted for almost entirely by smaller revenue from two products: $70,674 lost on spirits, and $47,006 lost on flour. In the meantime, the committee said, agriculture had suffered severely in the province. The Canadian tariff admitted some farm products free and put low duty on all others. But the neighboring part of the United States had a surplus of farm commodities which was overflowing into British Columbia to the cost of provincial producers. The committee set out a complete proposed tariff for horses, cattle, sheep, hogs, butter, bacon, eggs and grain (other than wheat or corn) which would bring in $30,313 in a year compared with $13,392 realized from the Canadian tariff. This proposal, like the others, was not even considered by the federal government. It could hardly establish individual tariffs for the provinces, even temporary ones.

In the middle of British Columbia's protests about the tariff and railway, Governor-General Dufferin paid an official visit (by sea, necessarily). He was scheduled to drive under a triumphal arch erected in Victoria but had a look at it in advance and found the word "Separation" inscribed on one of its most prominent banners. Lord Dufferin later reported, through his private secretary: "I sent for the mayor of Victoria and told him that I must have a small — a very small — alteration made in the inscription before I could consent to drive under it; an alteration of one letter only. The initial S must be replaced with an R and then I would pledge my word that I would do my best to see that reparation was made to the province." The alteration was made, and Dufferin drove through the arch.

The protests finally died away as a start was made at last on the railway. It was not completed until 1885. In the meantime, the legislature had turned its attention to another customs and immigration problem which lasted for decades: the heavy influx of Chinese immigrants. In 1878, the legislature resolved that no Chinese be employed on provincial public works and, by 1882, it was protesting that the employment of Chinese, especially on construction of the Canadian Pacific Railway, was "practically establishing a system of slave labor in the province." In 1883, it was estimated that there were 15,000 Chinese in British Columbia, at least half of them working on the CPR. There were 6,000 white immigrants that year and 3,000 Chinese. (Customs put a value of $35,424 on all settlers' effects, which works out to an average of $4 apiece.) Incidentally, fifteen residents of Victoria offered to put up $100 each to bring in "good servant girls from the country villages and districts of Ontario."

Back on the east coast, Nova Scotia's attempts to extract more money out of Ottawa raged on unabated. The federal government refused to pay any more, pointing out that Ontario, with a population of 1,620,851, received a subsidy of $1,196,872 from Ottawa under the terms of Confederation; Quebec, with a population of 1,191,516, received $959,252; and Nova Scotia, with a population of 387,000, received $450,000, excluding some extras it had wangled. The federal authorities did not mention it in their statement — though Nova Scotia did in its reply — that New Brunswick, with a population of 285,599, received $428,752.

Nova Scotia presented per capita figures on federal subsidies to the provinces: British Columbia, $20; Manitoba, $7.50; Prince Edward Island, $1.65; New Brunswick, $1.50; Nova Scotia, 98 cents. In 1880, the Nova Scotia Assembly sent a petition straight to the governor-general, the Marquis of Lorne: "We are desirous of again asking Your Excellency's attention to the position of financial embarrassment in which this Province is involved, and what is, in our opinion, the urgent necessity of some means of relieving that embarrassment." Revenue was $455,000 annually; expenditures were $600,000. The assembly wanted to express "the deep sense of uneasiness which possessed us in view of the fact that our revenue had become inadequate to maintain the various public services in the manner in which we had become accustomed." One concession was wrung from the federal government. It cancelled the ten-cents-a-ton duty on coal which it had collected from Nova Scotia mine owners and, in compensation, gave the province $200,000 a year for five years. The precedent for this was the subsidy given New Brunswick to make up for its former export duty on lumber.

One is not to gather from this recitation of complaints by Nova Scotia, New Brunswick, Prince Edward Island, Ontario, Manitoba and British Columbia — Saskatchewan and Alberta were not yet provinces — that Quebec held itself aloof from such matters. It's just that it chimed in later than the others. Quebec asked for a larger subsidy because, when the right to levy customs and excise duties was transferred from the provinces to the federal authority, a payment of 80 cents per capita was substituted for it, based on the 1861 census. This was in sharp contrast to federal revenues from customs and excise in 1868 of $3.75 per capita or $11,580,968. In 1871 revenues were $16,137,049, or $4.63 per capita; in 1881 revenues were $23,749,114, or $5.49 per capita. The subsidy for Quebec and Ontario remained at 80 cents, although the grants for the other provinces were based on later ten-year censuses. In 1868, Quebec reminded Ottawa, 80 cents per capita had represented 21 1/2 per cent of the receipts of customs; but in 1881 this 80 cents represented only 14 1/2 per cent of these receipts. Furthermore, the population increase in Quebec had not brought a larger subsidy, although it had resulted in increased expenditures. The example Quebec gave was that the cost of maintaining its lunatic asylums had increased from $420,182 in 1868 to $651,318 in 1881.

All these subsidies, grants, tax concessions and the like — today they are called "transfer payments" — have continued to occupy a good part of the foreground of Canadian political and economic life. The arguments are as partisan and as full of resentment now as they were when Joseph Howe told Ottawa that his beloved Nova Scotia would have been far better off if it had stayed out of Confederation. For a long time after union in 1867, it was difficult for Canadians in general, and many officials in particular, to recognize that four colonies were now one confederated colony and that there was, indeed, a single national tariff.

Two months after Confederation, R.S.M. Bouchette, Commissioner of Customs, had to issue this directive:

> The returns from several of the ports of entry continue to treat as imports all goods brought therein from ports or places in other provinces of the Dominion; I have to direct your attention to the following sections of The British North America Act, 1867, governing the trade

between the several provinces united since 1st July last, the day upon which that Act was proclaimed as coming into force, viz: All articles of the growth, produce, or manufacture of any one of the provinces shall from and after the Union be admitted free into each of the other provinces . . . You are, therefore, in your returns of external or foreign trade, to take no notice of goods coming into your port, from any port or place in any other of the provinces, whether such goods are in transit or for consumption there, provided such goods be of the growth, produce or manufacture of those provinces.

Even this directive was ignored in some instances, and regular passenger and freight packets plying between Saint John in New Brunswick and Digby, Annapolis and Windsor in Nova Scotia had to report in detail the cargoes carried on each trip. Finally, it took a special order-in-council of May 31, 1870, to authorize a yearly coasting licence "subject to the same conditions as provided in the case of vessels trading between ports in the same province." On May 7, 1874, Commissioner A. Brunel of the inland revenue department had to remind his officers that there were no restrictions on sending goods to Manitoba and British Columbia from the other provinces. Manitoba had joined Confederation four years earlier, British Columbia three.

CHAPTER IX

Creation of a Department

No one was sorry to see the end of British administration in the North American colonies, and particularly the end of British-appointed administrators. Even the British themselves did not think very highly of their officials, especially in Customs. The Earl of Shaftesbury had declared (about 1662): "When anyone fails in business or a gentleman wants to part with an old servant, interest is made to get them into the Customs as if into a hospital."

General James Murray, the first British governor of Quebec, railed about the colonial staff sent out from Britain. He was speaking of customs officers, too, when he reported to the Lords of Trade and Plantations in 1765:

> The improper choice and numbers of the civil officers sent out from England increased the inquietude of the colony. Instead of men of genius and untainted morals, the very reverse were appointed to the most important offices; and it was impossible to communicate, through them, those impressions of the dignity of government by which alone mankind can be held together in society. The judge fixed upon to conciliate the minds of 75,600 foreigners to the laws and government of Great Britain was taken from a jail, entirely ignorant of civil law, and of the language of the people. The attorney-general, with regard to the language of the people, was not better qualified. The offices of secretary of the province, registrar, clerk of the council, commissary of stores and provisions, provost-martial, etc., were given by patent to men of interest in England, who let them out to the best bidders, and so little did they consider the capacity of their representatives, that not one of them understood the language of the natives.
>
> As no salary was annexed to these patent places, the value of them depended upon the fees which, by my instructions, I was ordered to establish, equal to those of the richest ancient colony. This heavy tax, and the rapacity of the English lawyers, were severely felt by the poor Canadians; but they patiently submitted and, though stimulated to dispute it by some of the licentious traders from New York, they cheerfully obeyed the Stamp Act, in hopes that their good behaviour would recommend them to the favour and protection of their sovereign.

John William Dunscomb, the first Canadian-appointed Commissioner of Customs (1844-1851) and collector at Quebec (1851-1883), was even harsher in his judgment: "The English appointments were made from representatives of decayed families from England, Ireland and Scotland, the Army and Navy, canvassers for Parliamentary elections and men from the race course."

John J. Bigsby, secretary of the boundary commission which established the Canada-U.S. frontier along the St. Lawrence and the Great Lakes, remembered de Rouville Pothier of the Quebec legislature telling him: "The greatest number, and the most lucrative, of our public offices are given to strangers. Every vacant place almost is filled up by the second cousin of a member of the Imperial Parliament, or by someone who has been useful to the ministry in some obscure county election." He specifically included appointments in the customs branch.

The Nova Scotia and New Brunswick legislatures often complained to London about Britons repeatedly being given all the choice government positions in the colonies.

Thomas C. Haliburton in *The Old Judge, or Life in a Colony*, reported that the normal course was for the customs department in Halifax to nominate suitable persons and for the governor to appoint. But nominations of Nova Scotians were set aside by the governor who deferred to the Board of Customs in London. This "improper interference is severely felt and loudly complained of by colonists," he said, and added that they "are so situated as to be unable to obtain any employment or promotion out of their own country; and, therefore, very naturally feel that they are at least entitled to those offices, the salaries of which they furnish themselves." Haliburton spoke of the case of a Mr. Bayley, collector at Rainy Cove, who had been summarily superseded in his job by an Englishman who had appeared on his doorstep on a Sunday night while he was at prayers, announced that he had been appointed by the Board of Customs in England, and demanded immediate turning over of all books and papers. Then Haliburton quoted a friend on how he would deal with such an Englishman:

> First, I'd take him by the nape of the neck with one hand; and then I'd take him by the slack of the seat of his trousers, which gives another good hold, with the other hand, for that makes a good balance of the body, and then I'd swing him forward this way (and he put himself into attitude, and illustrated the process); and I'd say, 'Warny oncest,' then I'd swing him a-head again with a 'Warny twicest,' and then oncest more, with a 'Warny three times!' By this see-saw — do you mark? — I'd get the full sling of my arms with all the weight of my body and his too and then I'd give him the last shove, with 'Here yow go!' and I'd chuck him clean across the street, into neighbour Green's porch, and neighbour Green would up, and kick him into the road, without saying a word, for smashing his stoop-door in and stranger, English-like, would turn to and give him lip, and the constable would nab him, and lug him off to gaol, for making an indecent noise of a Sabbath night.

As Britain turned to free trade and the colonies, one by one, won their battles for responsible government in the 1840s and 1850s, the imperial customs officer quietly vanished from the scene, unsung and unlamented. Canadians could at last be chosen to fill all the positions for which they supplied the salaries, mainly through customs duties.

In 1796, a new office had been established in Lower Canada: inspector-general of provincial accounts, with responsibility for customs administration. Upper Canada followed suit in 1801. The Customs Consolidation Act of 1841 created a single system for the new province of United Canada. But it was a long time before all the differences between the customs procedures of Lower and Upper Canada were smoothed out into one coherent administration. In 1844, Dunscomb made a painstaking and successful attempt to compress customs law into a single volume in his *The Provincial Laws of the Customs*. He said in the preface that the laws were dispersed through so many cumbrous and expensive volumes that they were "very difficult of access to most officers who have to enforce them." There was not even anything in them, he added, to show which laws were still in force and which repealed or expired.

Dunscomb listed customs acts and regulations which applied in Canada generally, those which applied in Lower Canada only, and those which had effect in Upper Canada only. Each of the provinces on its own had as many regulations as the country, generally. A couple of examples show the wide variance of the law in a single colony. Upper Canada had an act to protect the public against accidental injury from machinery used in steamboats, mills and so on. It was one of the duties of customs officers to inspect such machinery and order installation of proper guards where they were lacking. The penalty for non-compliance was up to thirty days in jail. In Lower Canada only, customs officers could not vote in elections for the House of Assembly or for the first year after leaving Customs. The fine for contravention was £100. Even the hours of business were different in the two parts of the United Province: in Lower Canada they were 7 a.m. to 5 p.m. from April 1 to November 30 and 8 a.m. to 4 p.m. December 1 to March 31. In Upper Canada they were 9 a.m. to noon and 3 p.m. to 6 p.m. May 1 to September 30 and 10 a.m. to 3 p.m. October 1 to April 30. They kept the same holidays: Sundays, Christmas Day and Good Friday. In New Brunswick, in 1855, merchants took up a petition asking that the customs house at Saint John be kept open until 4 p.m. instead of 3 p.m. to permit receipt of duties and clearance of vessels.

In 1845, there were 63 customs ports in Canada, the three largest being Quebec, Montreal and St. Jean. At that time, Toronto was described merely as an outport in the district of Home 17 miles from Port Credit.

The total number of customs officers was 132. Most of the collectors, on taking office, were required to put up security of as much as £4,000, a guarantee against embezzlement, fraud, theft or other depradation on the public revenue.

During this early period, there was considerable experimentation with the use of free ports, which were simply locations where dutiable imported goods could be entered and stored without payment of customs duty. When the goods were removed for sale outside the free port, they were, of course, subject to duty.

Halifax and Saint John were created free ports as early as 1818 in an attempt to encourage trade and settlement. Other ports naturally complained of discrimination, so by 1833 there were free ports at St. Andrews, Pictou, Sydney, Quebec, St. John's and Charlottetown. Gaspé and Sault Ste. Marie were made free ports in 1860. But merchants weren't very enthusiastic about them and the only real beneficiaries seemed to be shipping companies which could conveniently use the free ports as transshipment points. The Americans were put out, particularly in the case of Gaspé and Sault Ste. Marie, which they regarded as little more than smugglers' havens. The customs regulations of 1861, governing the free port of Sault Ste. Marie, specified that there was to be no trading or giving of liquor to Indians. Masters of ships carrying liquor had to post a $200 bond to this effect. The free port legislation was repealed in 1866.

The use of the free port at St. Andrews caused a nasty argument between New Brunswick and Nova Scotia in 1824. At that time, the duty on flour was five shillings a barrel. The New Brunswick legislature decreed that this duty would be returned to the importer provided the flour was entered and cleared through St. Andrews and shipped to another British port. The idea was to attract business to St. Andrews, but it did not take long for a smart ship's owner to see the possibilities of gain. The British schooner *Herald*, with a load of American flour, cleared through St. Andrews, giving a promissory note to cover duty. She then sailed immediately to Halifax and sought to discharge the cargo there as duty-paid goods. The collector at Halifax was not fooled. He warned the provincial secretary that the master of the *Herald* would take a certificate to the collector at St. Andrews, declaring that he had landed the flour at Halifax, and get back an amount equal to the promissory note.

Nova Scotia Attorney-General Uniacke said that the Halifax collector was perfectly correct in levying duty on the flour despite the *Herald's* document claiming duty had already been paid at St. Andrews. He gave his opinion for the governor:

The duty in point of fact was not in my opinion paid there, and the whole proceeding is a fiction contrived to pervert the operation of a British Act of Parliament. It is painful to me to observe that in my opinion the officers of the Customs at New Brunswick whose peculiar duty it was to carry the Act of Parliament into effect, have lent their act to the Legislature of that country in execution of a plan to defeat the operation of an Act of Parliament, and to make it subservient to their interests at the expense of all the fair traders in this province and the other British colonies. This ship did not load this cargo in a British port, and therefore could not have it lawfully cleared out of there. If clearances and cockets from the British Customs Houses are granted for cargoes of goods which were never shipped within the jurisdiction of such Customs Houses, and which had no lawful sufferance for the loading or inspection of the same before shipment, there must be an end to all fair trade. Under colour of such clearances, all kinds of unlawful goods can be introduced into the other colonies. Indeed that is now the case; throughout the Bay of Fundy smuggling there is so organized by the measures adopted in New Brunswick that all the fair traders in the Bay of Fundy are nearly ruined, and the same system is fast extending over the rest of the province. Fair trade is, by the contrivance of the Legislature of that country, turned from its natural and legitimate channels, and by drawbacks and bounties artfully contrived, the fisheries of this province are deranged, and the consumption of its inhabitants supplied with articles free from duty to the ruin of the fair trader.

The Nova Scotia solicitor-general, S.B. Robie, suggested that there was an easy remedy: the king had merely to strike down the act of the New Brunswick legislature which was causing all the trouble. But in those days, a collector of customs could ignore acts of colonial legislatures. So the rebuke went from the Board of Customs in London to the St. Andrews collector: "We have received their Lordships' [Lords Commissioners of His Majesty's Treasury] commands to apprize you that they are of opinion that the whole of your conduct with respect to this schooner and the cargo has been highly culpable and deserving of their Lordships' severest animadversion which we communicate to you accordingly."

Victoria and Esquimalt were free ports in the mid-19th century when Vancouver Island was a separate colony. Dr. Charles Forbes informs us, in his treatise *Vancouver Island*, published by the colonial secretary's office in Victoria in 1862, that revenue presented no problems, however. In 1861, £25,252 had been raised through a one-per-cent tax on all real estate, harbor dues, a Victoria street tax, liquor licences, land sales, postage and fines.

Official documents dispatched home from England's North American colonies, were intended to be carried free of charge in the care of the master of the vessel carrying them. Failure to observe this arrangement brought this circular from the customs house, London, July 1, 1801, to all collectors:

> Several packets containing accounts of the collectors in the plantations [have] been put into the post office by the commanders of vessels to whom the same were entrusted on their arrival in the outports, whereby the Revenue has been put to very considerable expense for postage; in order to avoid the same in future — we direct you in all cases to address your accounts to us, and to insert the following words on the cover in which the same are contained, viz : 'Recommended to the particular care of the captain of the ship - - - - who is requested to deliver this packet himself to the collector and comptroller of the Customs (if a merchant vessel) when he reports at the Custom House; or, if a ship of war, to the collector and comptroller at the first port in England at which the ship shall arrive, and on no account to put it into the post office.'

In the United Province of Canada, Customs also had responsibility for collection of canal and road tolls, administration of ferries, immigration, ship registration and enforcement of navigation regulations. In 1859, the inspector-general of accounts became the minister of finance, and Customs became a branch of the finance department. At Confederation, a separate ministry of Customs was established with S. Leonard Tilley as its first minister. A department of Inland Revenue responsible for collection of excise duties was also established, with William P. Howland as first minister. R.S.M. Bouchette, the Commissioner of Customs since 1851, continued in that capacity, that is, as deputy minister, until 1874. Thomas Worthington became first Commissioner of Inland Revenue in 1868.

The first letter sent out by Customs after Confederation shows how smoothly the department eased into its new status. Dated July 2, 1867, it is addressed to Lanman and Kemp, a company in New York City:

> Sirs: In acknowledging the receipt of your communication of the 26th ultimo, requesting a reconsideration of the classification of 'Florida water' for duty, I have the honor to inform you that as the law now stands, all spirits perfumed or 'perfumed spirits to be used as perfumery only' is properly liable to the duty of $1.20 per gallon, with the addition of 15 per cent ad valorem for the bottles — without reference to the question of its being made potable or otherwise as an alcoholic drink. I have the honor to be, sirs, your obedient servant, Tho. Worthington, assistant commissioner, Customs and Excise.

For whatever reasons, of caution or exploitation, Canada is the only country in the world ever to establish a separate department to collect its revenue. In Britain, the United States, and elsewhere, finance or treasury departments, however named, both impose and collect taxes. But in Canada there were and are two departments: finance, which imposes taxes, and national revenue, which collects them. Canadians may have felt, theoretically at least, that the collector exerts some kind of check on the imposer. David Sim, a deputy minister in national revenue for thirty-five years until his retirement in 1965, told the writer in 1981 that the Canadian system of divided responsibility for imposition and collection of taxes has worked well: "Because we (national revenue) are responsible for the administration, we could usually talk finance out of introducing measures which we knew would outrage the public. It's a good thing finance doesn't have to implement its own decisions. By the same token, finance has been able to talk us out of some pretty ludicrous things." As an afterthought: "And Parliament has always been glad to unload responsibility for taxes."

The chain of command in Customs and Excise was carefully engineered so that each person passed up the line ALL the revenue for which he or she had to account to the person one rung higher on the administrative ladder. Historically, the customs collector was always carefully watched. The watcher occupied a position known at first as customer, later as comptroller or surveyor, and the watching consisted of checking the collector's books and making sure that the money collected for the crown got to the treasury.

Because nearly all revenue derived from Customs and Excise, the ministers of these two departments were key members of the cabinet. Three of them became prime minister: Sir Mackenzie Bowell and Sir Charles Tupper (customs) and Sir Wilfrid Laurier (inland revenue). One attempt was made to reduce the political standing of Customs and Excise. Between 1892 and 1897, customs and inland revenue (excise) were divisions of trade and commerce, each headed by a controller. During these five years, the controllers were sometimes — and sometimes not — full members of the cabinet, that is, members of the Privy Council. Under the prime ministership of Sir John Thompson, for instance, between 1892 and 1894, the controllers of customs and inland revenue were members of the ministry but not of the cabinet. They were responsible to the minister of trade and commerce, who was Bowell, formerly minister of Customs. In the even briefer succeeding regime of Bowell as prime minister, the two controllers were given full cabinet rank, but in 1896 Laurier demoted them again and in the following year abolished the two offices and once more established the separate departments of customs and inland revenue.

In 1918, Prime Minister Borden's Unionist government amalgamated the two departments into a single department of customs and inland revenue under a single cabinet minister, initially Arthur Lewis Sifton. The name of the department was changed to Customs and Excise in 1921. In 1925, income tax collection, started in 1917, was taken from the finance department and placed under Customs and Excise. Two years later, the department's name was changed again, to National Revenue, which it bears to this day, and in 1926 three commissioners were appointed to serve under the single minister: a commissioner of Customs, a commissioner of Excise, and a commissioner of Income Tax. In 1943 the commissioners were replaced by two deputy ministers of national revenue, one for Customs and Excise and the other for Taxation, and that administrative system still applies.

Because the revenue depended so heavily on customs duties, customs officers had wide and stringent, almost draconian powers, which were spelled out in the customs acts of the individual colonies and in the notorious writs of assistance. The customs act of the United Province of Canada, for instance, laid down, in 1847, that evasion of customs meant forfeiture of goods and their means of conveyance — if a ship, not only the ship itself but all its rigging, tackle and apparel, if a horse and carriage, the whole outfit plus all the harness. (The current Canadian law says the same thing, substituting car and equipment for horse, harness and carriage.)

In pre-Confederation times, every customs officer had full power "to detain, open and examine any package suspected to contain prohibited property or smuggled goods, and to go on board of and enter into any vessel, boat, canoe, carriage, waggon, cart, sleigh, or other vehicle or means of conveyance of any description whatsoever, and to stop and detain the same, whether arriving from places beyond or within the limits of the Province, and to rummage and search all parts thereof for prohibited, forfeited or smuggled goods." No officer was liable "to any prosecution or action at law for any such search, detention or stoppage."

The writ of assistance said "it shall be lawful for any officer of the customs" to enter any building and "to search for and seize and secure any goods liable to forfeiture" and, in the case of necessity, "to break open any doors and any chests or other packages."

Writs were not for a single seizure only but remained in force for the entire reign of a sovereign — and for twelve months afterwards. A writ taken out in the first year of Queen Victoria's reign therefore remained in force for more than sixty years, if the officers named in it survived that long. It might be pertinent to quote in full a writ of assistance issued in New Brunswick in 1823. The quotation is taken from the actual writ, in longhand, preserved in the British Public Record Office in London:

> George the fourth by the Grace of God of the United Kingdom of Great Britain and Ireland, King, defender of the faith, To Henry Wright, Esq., Collector of our Customs for the Port of Saint John in our province of New Brunswick, Robert Parker, Esq., Comptroller of our Customs for the same port, Henry George Clapper, Preventive

Officer of our Customs for the Port of Fredericton and the vicinity thereof, and all other officers of our own Customs for the same ports, Greeting: We do hereby authorize and empower you, and each and every of you by virtue of this writ to take a constable or other public officer inhabiting near unto the place; and in the daytime to enter and go into any house shop cellar warehouse or room or any other place within our said port of Fredericton or the vicinity thereof and in the case of resistance to break open the door thereof and all chests, trunks and other packages therein and there to seize and from thence to bring any kind of goods and merchandize whatsoever prohibited and uncustomed and to put and secure the same in our Storehouse in our said port of Fredericton and we do hereby authorize and strictly enjoin and require all justices of the peace mayors sheriffs and bailiffs and all our officers ministers and subjects whatsoever to be aiding and assisting to you and each and every one of you in the due execution hereof Witness John Saunders Esquire, Chief Justice, at Fredericton the twenty second day of February in the fourth year of our Reign A.D. 1823.

It is a blanket writ. Three men are specifically named, but it also covers all the rest of the customs officers in both Saint John and Fredericton; there is no time limit; the officers are empowered to break in anywhere in Fredericton or in an undefined "vicinity thereof"; any policeman can be required to assist — or any other public officer, including ministers, justices of the peace, mayors, sheriffs, bailiffs, and any "subjects whatsoever." There was one condition: the writ must be used in daylight hours only. The powers allowed by the writs and the numbers of officers exercising them to break in and search did not contract as time went by. They expanded. A writ of assistance issued in 1861 to Richard Graham, Esquire, Collector of Customs at the Port of Fort Erie, "and any other officer of Customs in Upper Canada," covered all of Upper Canada and applied not only to the current customs act but to any customs act Parliament might pass in future. It was not sent to Ottawa for formal cancellation until 1933, or 32 years after Queen Victoria's death. There is no record to show how often the writ was used or whether it was used at all after Upper Canada became Ontario in 1867. In this century, writs have remained in force, not until the death of the sovereign, but until the death of the holder, or his retirement from Customs. A writ issued in 1962 says:

Elizabeth II, by the Grace of God of the United Kingdom, Canada and her Other Realms and Territories Queen, Head of the Commonwealth, Defender of the Faith. To David Russell Staines, Officer of our Customs, and to all others whom these presents may concern, Greeting: We do, by this our Writ, give to you said David Russell Staines, Officer of our Customs aforesaid, full power and authority, and we do strictly command you in accordance with the provisions of the Revised Statutes of Canada, 1952, Chapter Fifty-eight, Sec. 137, to enter at any time in the day or night into any building or other

place within Canada, and to search for and seize and secure any
goods which you have reasonable grounds to believe are liable to
forfeiture under the said Revised Statutes of Canada, or under any of
the Acts of Parliament of Canada already passed, or to be hereafter
passed amending the said Revised Statutes or imposing duties of
Customs in Canada, and in case of necessity to break open any door
or doors and any chest or chests or other packages for that purpose.
And we do further command all Justices of the Peace and other Peace
Officers that they be aiding and assisting you in the premises.
Witness the Honourable J. T. Thorson, President of Our Exchequer
Court of Canada, at Ottawa this 19th day of October, in the year of
Our Lord one thousand nine hundred and sixty-two and in the
eleventh year of our reign.

The writ was a printed form, with only the typewritten names of the customs officer and judge, date and signature of the court registrar to be filled in. Similar writs still exist and have been used, mainly by police forces, (very infrequently by Customs), to combat the narcotics traffic. A moratorium on their issuance was declared by the federal government in 1976 and all customs writs have since been withdrawn.

The Customs Act of 1886 consolidated the very considerable powers given to customs officers and the heavy obligations on the citizen to observe the law. In the case of the latter there was Section 33, for instance:

> The person in charge of any vehicle, arriving by land in any place in Canada, and containing goods, whether any duty is payable on such goods or not, and the person in charge of any vehicle so arriving, if the vehicle or its fittings, furnishings or appurtenances, or the animals drawing the same, or their harness or tackle, is or are liable to duty, and every person whosoever so arriving in Canada from any port or place out of Canada, on foot or otherwise, and having with him or in his charge or custody, any goods, whether such goods are dutiable or not, shall come to the nearest Customs House or to the station of the nearest officer of Customs, before unlading or in any manner disposing of the same, and make a report in writing to the collector or proper officer of Customs, stating the contents of each and every package and parcel of goods, and the quantities and values of the same; and shall also then answer all questions respecting such goods or packages, and the vehicle, fittings, furnishings and appurtenances, and animals, and the harness or tackle appertaining thereto, as the said collector or proper officer of Customs requires of him, and shall then and there make due entry of the same, in accordance with the law in that behalf.

That was for arrival by land. For arrival by sea:

> No goods shall be unladen from any vessel arriving at any port or place in Canada, from any place out of Canada, or from any vessel having dutiable goods on board brought coastwise, nor shall bulk be broken within three leagues of the coast, until due entry has been

made of such goods, and warrant granted for the unlading of the same; and no goods shall be so unladen (unless for the purpose of lightening the vessel in crossing over or getting free from a shoal, rock, bar or sand-bank) except between sunrise and sunset, and on some day not being a Sunday or statutory holiday, and at some hour and place at which an officer of the Customs is appointed to attend the unlading of goods, or at some place for which a sufferance has been granted by the collector or other proper officer, for the unlading of such goods; and if, after the arrival of the vessel within three leagues of the coast, any alteration is made in the stowage of the cargo so as to facilitate the unlawful unlading of any part thereof, or if any part thereof is fraudulently staved, destroyed or thrown overboard, or any package is opened, it shall be deemed a breaking of bulk; and all goods unladen contrary to this Act shall be seized and forfeited; and if bulk is broken contrary to this Act, the master shall forfeit two hundred dollars, and the vessel may be detained until the said sum is paid, or satisfactory security is given for the payment thereof; and unless payment is made or security is given, within thirty days, such vessel may, at the expiration thereof, be sold to pay the said sum.

There was a similar, appropriate, clause for trains, and aircraft were added in due course.

A carryover from old laws about goods salvaged from wrecks appeared in the act of 1886 as clause 18: "Goods derelict, flotsam, jetsam or wreck, or landed or saved from any vessel wrecked, stranded or lost, brought or coming into Canada, shall be subject to the same duties and regulations as goods of the like kind imported are subject to."

The powers and duties of customs officers were set out in clauses 133 to 144 (the writ-of-assurance clauses are 141 to 143) and may be found in the appendices.

There were thirty clauses outlining forfeitures and penalties for contravening the Customs Act, including imprisonment of up to two years. There was also provision for a $500 fine and dismissal from the civil service for customs officers caught conniving at any evasion of the revenue laws. Any person offering a bribe to a customs officer was to receive the same fine and be sentenced to prison. The penalty for smuggling was forfeiture of the goods (to be sold at public auction), a fine of up to $200, and imprisonment for up to one year. Anyone knowingly harboring smuggled goods had to forfeit them and pay a fine three times the value of the goods.

The first customs tariff passed after Confederation in 1867 imposed duties on only two-dozen classifications of goods, including "spirits and strong waters," playing cards, petroleum products, sugar, tobacco, patent medicines, shoe leather, coffee and tea. Items admitted free included busts, dyes, gems, medicines for hospitals, candle wick, church bells, wire for hoop skirts, sailcloth, locomotive connecting rods, coal, eggs, rice,

Colonel the Honourable James Kerby.

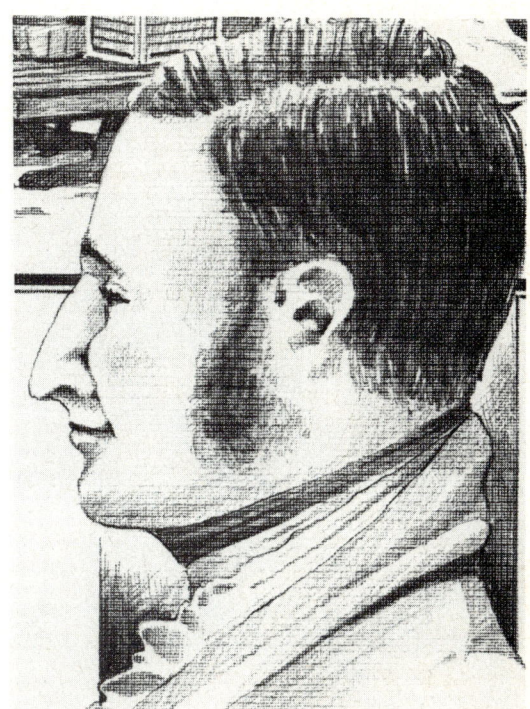

Fort Macleod, Alta., 1879, five years after NWMP established a Customs outpost (Public Archives of Canada).

Wells, found to be in Alaska instead of British Columbia in 1903 boundary settlement (Sheldon Museum, Haines, Alaska).

Summit, Chilkoot Pass, Klondike Trail, 1898 (Yukon Archives).

Customs House, Tagish Lake, on Klondike Trail, 1898. Customs officer John Godson waded out to passing boats. (Yukon Archives).

Quebec City Customs House, c. 1900

Customs House, Halifax, 1906 (Public Archives of Canada).

E.S. Busby, central figure in Skagway flag incident, chief inspector, Customs and Excise, 1912-1929.

Customs patrol plane escorts liner into Vancouver, 1928. The pilot was A.J. Ashton, the observer Preventive Officer N.J. DeGraves, looking for cans of opium tossed overboard to be retrieved later by small boats.

Capt. Alfred La Couvée, standing beside port gun, Margaret, *1927.*

Customs patrol boat Margaret, *1927.*

Seized rum cargo, Pictou, N.S., 1928.

Customs air harbor, St. Hubert, Que., 1930, New York to Montreal flight.

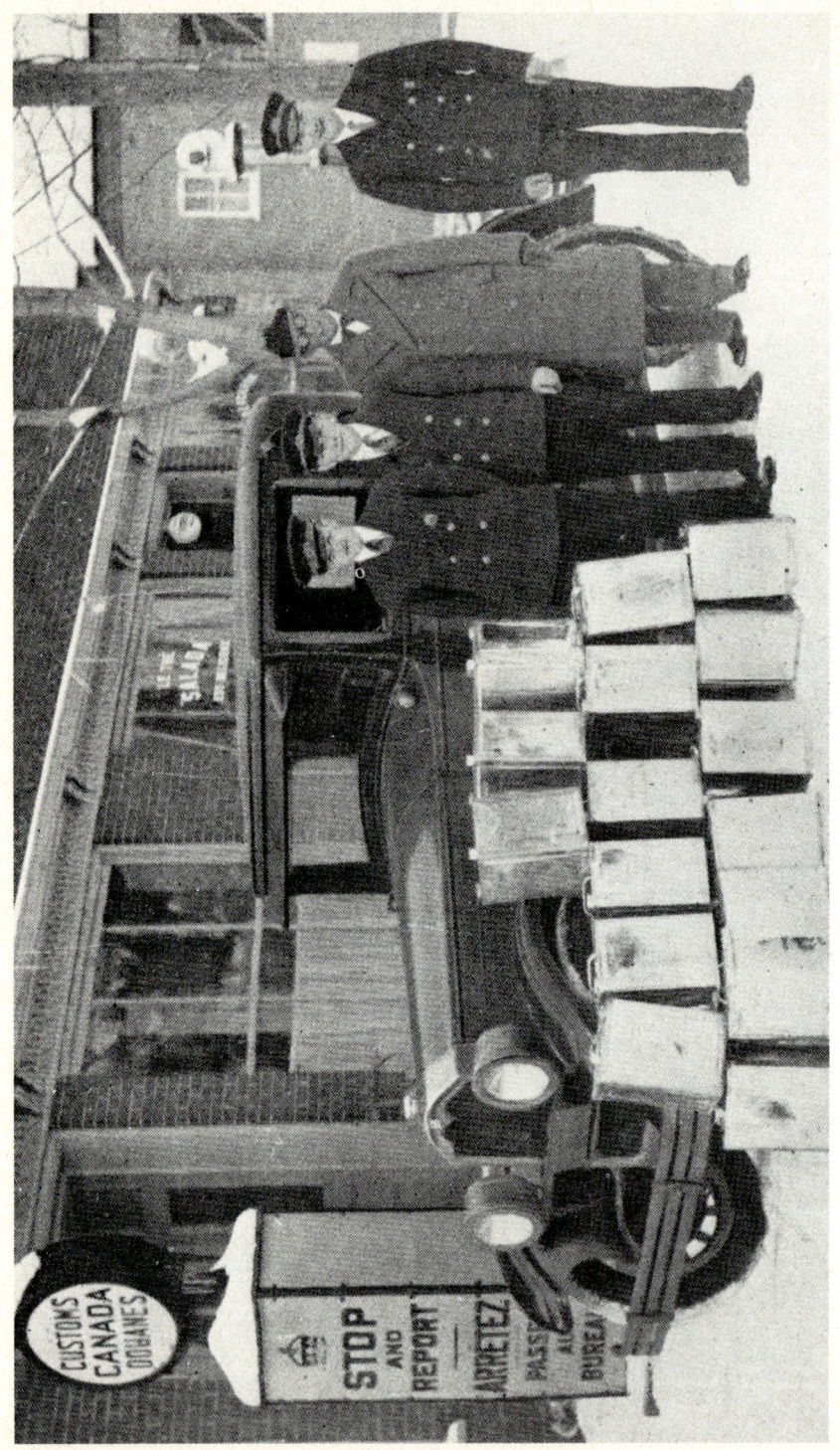

Liquor seizure, five-gallon cans, Hemmingford, Que., 1930 (l. to r.: B. Brault, S.A. Beaudoin, W.O. Orr, Arthur Menard).

Pacific Highway, near Vancouver, 1930.

Chief Mountain, Alta., 1930.

Woodstock Road (Richmond Road), N.B., 1929, boundary marker at corner of Customs House.

Rock Island, Que., 1930; lineup stretches into Derby Line, Vt.; flag is on Customs House.

Peace Bridge, Fort Erie, Ont., 1931.

Forest City, N.B., c. 1950.

Mid-Continent truck terminal, Toronto (Eric Trussler Photography Ltd.).

whale oil, bagatelle tables for army and navy officers and settlers' effects. The entire tariff, with twenty short clauses and five schedules, comprised only fourteen large-print pages. Today's tariff takes up ninety-eight pages in small print and twelve enormous volumes of supporting regulations.

It was in 1879, when Macdonald announced his National Policy, that the list of dutiable goods sprouted to thirteen pages from the original three (of the same size) twelve years earlier. The list included agricultural implements, farm animals, breadstuffs, cement, cotton, earthenware, fish, fruit, furs, furniture, glass, iron, jewelry, leather, meat, opium prepared for smoking ($5 a pound), paint, perfume, quills, salt, ships, soap, steel, sugar, tea, tobacco, vegetables, wood, woollens, zinc — and, of course, liquor in all its forms.

Meanwhile, there were no additions to the duty-free list and it tended to be made up of items most Canadians would consider non-essential, if not unthinkable. For example: alkenet root, bamboo reeds, cat-gut, entomology specimens, fossils, hoofs, lava, leeches, moss, sand, turtles. By 1883 the tariff covered eighteen pages of dutiable items, but the number of duty-free items had also risen, though not, of course, to the same degree. Within a year, the published tariff with amendments had become so encumbered that it required an index for the first time — of fourteen pages, from absinthe to zinc.

By 1908, the tariff was becoming so complicated and lengthy that a Board of Customs was established under the chairmanship of the Commissioner of Customs to interpret the tariff regulations and hear appeals. In effect, it sat in judgment on itself and seldom found itself wanting. This body became the Tariff Board under its own Act of Parliament in 1931, and remained completely independent of Customs and Excise.

Until the turn of the century there was a Schedule E in the Canadian tariff, listing rates of export duties. Though there are no such duties now, there is still statutory provision for application of duty on exports.

In the early years of Customs, little or no attempt was made to supply the public with information on customs laws and regulations. Indeed, customs officers sometimes sold customs information to the newspapers, as shown in the following two letters. The first, June 13, 1849, is by R. Middleton, editor of the *Quebec Gazette*, and is addressed to Commissioner Dunscomb at Montreal:

> I regret to be again under the necessity of calling your attention to a small matter of the publication of the returns of imports and exports from the Custom House at Quebec with regard to which I did myself the honour to wait upon you at Montreal in May last. I need not remind you that you were kind enough to inform me that you entirely disapproved of the system pursued in the Quebec Custom House,

where the publication of the entries in the Manifest book is a source of pecuniary profit to the clerks, and has been sold by them to the Morning Chronicle, to the exclusion of the other Journals of this City, and that in this persuasion you favoured me with a note to H. Jessopp, Collector of Her Majesty's Customs at this port.

The result of an interview I have since had with this Gentleman has been apprizing me that the clerks of H.M. Custom House here have always held the exclusive right of disposal of said privilege — that it has been a perquisite of their office — that they consider themselves entitled, *de officio*, to any profit accruing from the publication of extracts from the manifests — and that having already, for a pecuniary consideration, made over to the Morning Chronicle the exclusive right of copying therefrom, they cannot now extend the same privilege to the Quebec Gazette, or any other periodical. Mr. Jessopp added that he did not feel himself authorized to interfere in the matter. I need not represent to you how seriously the interests of the trade of Quebec are injured by this monopoly, many merchants and others, subscribers to the Quebec Gazette and not to the Morning Chronicle, being thus deprived of much valuable information. I pass over likewise the detriment the proprietors of the Quebec Gazette incur personally, although I might apparently complain of a system which is without parallel in any other station of H.M. Customs throughout the Empire; nor perhaps is it my place to point out to you the manifest impropriety of withholding from the public and making a source of profit to subofficers of H.M. Customs of official documents, which are in reality the most valuable statistics of our commerce, and to which it would seem more liberal and more consistent with a general line of policy of the Directors of H.M. Customs to allow free access to the public.

Aware as I am that you hold these sentiments, I would rather request your interference in the matter, in order to bring about an amicable settlement with the clerks in the department at Quebec. The proprietors of the Quebec Gazette will pay the same price for the information it desires as the Morning Chronicle. All that they request is to share equally with other newspapers in order that their mercantile subscribers may not suffer through the want of necessary information; and for this they will of course afford the same return as the clerks of H.M. Customs now receive from the Morning Chronicle.

Commissioner Dunscomb asked Collector Jessopp for an explanation and got this letter, dated June 18, 1849, in reply:

... Upon Mr. Middleton's first application to which he again alludes, I explained to you the exact position of the matter in question: That long ago (about 30 years) the Gentlemen in the Long Room [Customs' main office] issued under the sanction of the Board of Customs a "Commercial List" for which they subsequently took a Copyright privilege, and have ever since retained it, although from a change of circumstances that right is held by the Morning Chronicle under a special arrangement, made when Mr. Middleton was one of the proprietors of that paper. The Mercury and the Gazette (the latter then under the supervision of the late Mr. Neilson), being aware of the circumstances, offered no remonstrance or complaint, conceiving, it is presumed, that it was not open to objection, as the information obtained gave *extra official trouble*, and took up the *private time* of the parties furnishing it; aware, moreover, that the public was then put in possession of all the information required. Mr. Middleton was afterwards informed, upon stating his willingness to join with the Chronicle in obtaining the information, that every facility would be given to his doing so, but from the present application being made it is supposed he had not effected his object in that way. With these explanations, and again adverting to the still existing sanction of the Honorable Board of Customs, the parties in the Customs to whom it was first given can only leave the matter with you for such Order thereon as may be deemed just and proper.

The surviving Customs file does not tell us what Dunscomb's order was, though it is known that the business community had to continue to rely mainly on the newspapers for official government commercial information until 1856, when John Cameron's massive *The Canadian Tariff* was published.

A later aid was the *Dominion Customs Ready-Reckoner and Importers' Guide*, published in Halifax. Its edition of 1888 recommended:

It will be necessary to bear in mind that the practice of the Customs House is to take the nearest even dollar to the amount in the invoice, viz., from two shillings, one pence, to six shillings, 1 1/2 pence, the Importer will have to pay duty upon one dollar only; but if the sum should be six shillings, two pence, he will be required to pay duty upon two dollars. Again, one pound, six shillings, eight pence is equivalent to $6.49; the 49¢ are thrown off and duty is paid upon $6. But if the amount should be one pound, six shillings, 8 1/2 pence, the value for entry would be $7.

In 1870, no goods or passengers could be carried by water from one port of Canada to another except in British ships. Otherwise, all goods were forfeited "as smuggled" and the master fined $400. However, three years later, Italian ships qualified as British because British ships had been allowed to participate in the coasting trade of Italy. In 1874, ships of The Netherlands, Sweden and Norway were similarly permitted into the Canadian coasting trade.

The law prohibiting the clearance of goods through Customs between sunset and sunrise and on Saturdays and Sundays was still in the act of Parliament up to 1984, though subverted by regulation. An old customs sign found not long ago at North Portal, Saskatchewan, began: "Public notice is hereby given that all importations by land must be between sunrise and sunset."

The excise tradition that Canada inherited from England had come only a hundred years or so earlier, from the Dutch, who taxed everything and everyone in daily use: flour, meal, bread, wine, beer, salt, horses, servants, carriages, cattle, boats and seeds. Of course, there had been some non-customs taxes such as exemption from military service in the reign of Henry II for a knight on payment of a scutage (from the Latin *scutum*, a shield), and Henry VIII's tax on widows who did not remarry within a year. But the first excise tax did not arrive until 1643, when it was imposed on domestic beer, spirits, cider, perry (fermented pear juice) and soap, to raise money to support Parliament's army. The taxable list of goods grew every year and fell most heavily on the poor. There were riots, and the army had to be called out to protect excise officers. One of the strongest opponents of excise was a pamphleteer named William Prynne. He suddenly desisted when given the post of commissioner for collection of excise arrears at £100 a year.

During the plague of 1665, the exciseman in Kent reported: "The plague raged so much that one-third of the receipt of the excise has failed." The first public buildings rebuilt after the great fire of London in 1666 — a special rebuilding tax was not abolished until 1831 — belonged to Customs and Excise. In 1660, Englishmen began paying a "hearth tax" at the rate of two shillings per chimney. It was replaced in 1695 by a window tax, and people began boarding over windows. At the same time, a registration duty began. It was a tax on births, marriages and funerals, graded by social position. A commoner's funeral was taxed four shillings, a duke's £50. In a ten-year period in the mid-1700s there were two thousand prosecutions for use of false witnesses to defraud the excise; two hundred and fifty excise officers were assaulted and six murdered.

Samuel Johnson's 1755 dictionary defined excise thus: "A hateful tax levied upon commodities and adjudged not by the common judges of property, but by wretches hired by those to whom the excise is paid." The attorney-general of Britain advised the commissioners of excise that the definition was libellous and that Johnson should be sued if he did not change it. In the revised 1773 edition, the definition remained unchanged. The commissioners took no action. Poet Robert Burns was an exciseman in Dumfries from 1789 until his death in 1796. He wrote: "I find £50 per annum, which is now our salary, an exceeding good thing. People may talk as they please of the ignominy of the Excise, but what will support my family and keep me independent of the world is to me a very important matter; and I had much rather that my Profession borrowed credit from me, than that I borrowed credit from my Profession."

The distinction between legal and illegal distilling of spirits has everything to do with the collection of excise. In England, armed excisemen had to be protected by soldiers when they smashed illegal stills. In Ireland, in the early 1800s, uniformed and armed revenue police uncovered more than three thousand illicit stills a year. (Canada's history of illicit liquor traffic is described in the chapters of this book on smuggling.)

The imposition of excise in Canada fell early and heavily on liquor, wine, beer and tobacco. The Nova Scotia House of Assembly, for instance, did not hesitate to tax potables right from its first session in 1758. It took five years before it got around to its first taxes on non-potables. Excise duties in the United Province of Canada in 1862 amounted to $475,578, all on malt liquor and spirits.

Upon Confederation, the act of Parliament constituting the department of inland revenue was assented to May 22, 1868, though the department for months had been operating as a separate entity. The department's Circular No. 1 read:

> Department of Inland Revenue
> Ottawa 5th Oct., 1867
>
> To Collectors of Inland Revenue
> I am desired to instruct you to transmit to my address all future communications upon Excise or Inland Revenue business from this date — the Customs and Excise having become separate and distinct Departments.
>
> I remain, sir,
> Your obedient servant,
> Tho. Worthington

By 1874, proceeds of excise amounted to 24 per cent of Canada's total revenue, double that for the British North American colonies in 1866.

Up until the First World War excise duties were confined almost entirely to beer, liquor and tobacco. Excise taxes (as opposed to excise duties) were first imposed in 1915 with the Special War Revenue Act of that year. Even at that, customs and excise levies began accounting for a smaller and smaller share of total revenue. The First World War marked changes which led to increasing reliance for revenue on direct taxes, such as income tax, and less on direct taxes such as customs and excise duties, sales and excise taxes. By 1943, these indirect taxes provided only 40 per cent of total revenue compared with 75 per cent early in the century.

National personal income tax was introduced as a "temporary war measure" in July, 1917. Unfortunately, Canada did not follow an excellent, though discarded, British example: Britain introduced a tax on income in 1798 but, until 1842, used to repeal it in peacetime, which was rare enough. (The first provincial income tax was levied by British Columbia in 1876.) Though direct income tax was found necessary for revenue, governments still preferred commodity taxes because, politically, they were less unpopular than personal income tax, administrative costs were comparatively low and compliance simple and certain.

There are quite specific differences between excise tax and duty, though the differences are mainly in law. Excise duties are levied under the Excise Act. On the other hand, excise taxes, chiefly the sales tax, are imposed under the Excise Tax Act, whose forerunner was the Special War Revenue Act of 1915. Excise duties are levied on commodities which remain in the possession of the crown until duties are paid. Excise taxes are required to be paid by a person on the performance of some action by that person, such as manufacture or sale of goods. Excise duties are specific imposts by weight and volume. Excise taxes generally are at ad valorem (percentage) rates. Excise duties are levied on liquor and tobacco, excise taxes on a wide range of commodities. Excise duties fall on goods of domestic manufacture; excise taxes apply on domestic and imported goods. The evidence of payment of an excise duty usually appears on the dutiable commodity, for example, a stamp on a bottle of liquor. Excise taxes can be considered "hidden" in the sense that the consumer is given no visible indication of the tax.

Excise taxes are used not only to produce revenue but as a fiscal weapon to restrain consumption or reduce foreign trade deficits. This was particularly the case in the post-war periods of 1920 and 1947 when consumer demand was heavy and the government wanted to limit the public's purchasing power so as to control inflation. There are three basic forms of commodity tax: single stage at the manufacturer's, wholesale, or retail level; turnover or cumulative applied at various levels; and value added tax, pioneered by France in 1954, a single-stage tax collected in installments.

The history of excise taxes in Canada is little more than a chronicle of numerous classes of goods being brought into the excise tax net, or let out of it. Capture is more common than escape. In 1915, sales and excise taxes were imposed on a long list of items: telegrams, railway and steamship tickets, cheques, perfumes, patent medicines, bank notes, insurance premiums (except for life and marine insurance), bills of exchange, promissory notes, money orders, postal notes, letters and postcards. Many of these were not withdrawn until 1949, and the excise tax on letters and postcards lasted two years longer.

A tax on corporate profits was introduced with the personal income tax in 1917, but still there was insufficient revenue to support the war effort. So customs duties and excise taxes were increased and expanded to cover: automobiles (ten per cent), gramophones, records, player pianos, jewelry, tea and movies. Stamp taxes were put on matches and playing cards. (The British had had an awkward time with the stamp duty on playing cards in the 19th century: at first the stamp was affixed to the ace of spades, distinguishing the card to touch and therefore leading to cheating. In 1863, the stamp was transferred to the wrapper.) In 1915-1920, 90 per cent of national revenue came from customs and excise, only one per cent from personal income tax.

The end of the war did not bring lower taxes. Instead, the government was determined to try to reduce the $2,000 million war debt. Personal and corporation income taxes were increased, and a sales tax of one per cent was introduced. A stamp tax was put on sales or transfers of stocks or shares; new excise taxes were slapped on candy, chewing gum, firearms, musical instruments, pleasure boats and gas and electric fixtures. Canada's total revenue had been $312 million in 1919. In 1921 it was $436 million, a 40-per-cent increase in two years. For the public, the years 1924 to 1929 were one of the great periods in Canadian tax history: there were no new taxes. The sales tax dropped gradually from six per cent in 1924 to one per cent in 1930.

The depression of the 1930s brought heavy relief expenditures and the need for additional revenue, so the sales tax started up again, to four per cent in 1931, to six per cent in 1932, and to eight per cent in 1936, the year after the Liberal leader, Mackenzie King, denounced the sales tax in the federal election campaign which returned him to office. The sales tax yield increased sevenfold from $20,146,600 to $138,054,536 in 1938, or 30.8 per cent of total tax revenue. By 1939, income was nine per cent below that of 1929, but revenue was 30 per cent higher. The Rowell-Sirois Royal Commission on Dominion-Provincial Relations found, in 1940, that the sales tax weighed more heavily on the poor than the rich, something any poor person could have told them.

The tax story was the same in the Second World War. More revenue was needed because war expenditures soared from $553 million in 1939 to $5,136 million in 1946. Revenue fell farther and farther behind spending: $520 million in 1939; $3,085 million in 1946. New taxes included an excess profits tax in 1940, succession duties in 1941, pay-as-you-go income tax in 1942. The eight-per-cent sales tax remained unchanged so that the government would not break its own established price ceilings (the excise tax on sugar had to be lowered to avoid putting the price through the ceiling) and to discourage demands for wage increases. Before the war, about 30 per cent of federal tax revenue came from taxes on incomes and profits and 70 per cent from taxes on commodities. By 1943, the ratio was 60-40 for incomes and profits.

At the end of the war, Canadians found themselves with a new wealth of resources (oil, gas and iron ore), remarkably expanded industry and experience in technology and research. Combined with a huge backlog of consumer demand for goods and a store of savings, this meant a boom in the economy. The tax system was manipulated to encourage industrial production and consumer spending. Between 1945 and 1949, personal income tax rates for the majority of taxpayers were reduced between 60 and 70 per cent. The standard rate of corporation income tax was reduced to 30 from 40 per cent in 1946. The excess profits tax was revoked in 1947. The ten-per-cent war exchange tax on importations was removed. A great many commodity taxes were repealed, including the eight-per-cent sales tax on capital equipment. The Special War Revenue Act of 1915 was renamed the Excise Tax Act in 1947.

The "radio budget" occurred in 1947. On November 17, Finance Minister Douglas Abbott announced, in a radio speech, a prohibition on the importation of a wide variety of consumer goods, quotas on others, import controls on capital goods, travel restrictions and the imposition of excise taxes on many durable goods. The tax on cars, for example, increased from ten per cent to between 25 and 75 per cent; on cameras, films, radios and tubes from ten to 25 per cent. The increases were withdrawn in 1948 and the old rates restored.

But, apart from this, the trend was to lower taxes in the immediate post-war period. This was rudely interrupted by the Korean war in 1950 when defence expenditures went from $300 million a year to $2,000 million. Personal income taxes increased by one-fifth and corporation income taxes by two-fifths. The sales tax went from eight to ten per cent. Special excise tax rates increased from 15 to 25 per cent. In 1950, customs duties produced only eight per cent of $900 million revenue, while sales and other excise taxes brought in 23 per cent. In 1952, the sales tax reverted to eight per cent. But the two-point difference was not restored to the taxpayer. Instead, it became the old-age security tax. The sales tax went to 11 per cent in 1959, 12 per cent in 1967, down to nine per cent in 1978 (except for wine, alcohol and tobacco), and was back at 12 per cent in 1981.

Until 1961, the collection of sales taxes was the responsibility of collectors at customs and excise ports. After that time, taxes payable on domestic goods were collected by new district excise tax offices. The excise tax division was completely decentralized in 1966, and headquarters staff became primarily concerned with planning, research and quality control.

Some of the history of the excise can be traced in revenue stamps; the department of National Revenue has placed a unique collection of these stamps in the postal museum at Ottawa. Excise stamps on tobacco were used from 1864 until 1974. The first set of tobacco stamps was printed on

4-inch diamond-shaped paper. The design of the stamps changed, over the years, but strict control was maintained on the engravings to prevent counterfeiting. Some stamps were very elaborate, more to prevent duplication than to provide decoration. The 1897 issue even gave the number of cigars in each package and depicted such scenes as the Parliament Buildings, Rideau Canal locks and outdoor life. In the early days, all tobacco stamps were numbered serially, but this became impossible with the huge increase in tobacco production.

Audit supervision eventually replaced the stamps. But the excise stamp on liquor bottles remains, mostly because it is widely regarded as a guarantee of proper bottling and aging. The stamp, called an age-strip, certifies the year when the spirits, or a major portion of them if blended, were manufactured. There are 48 breweries and 49 distilleries in Canada, and 400 other companies, such as manufacturers of vinegar, perfume, cosmetics, detergents, toothpaste, explosives, household extracts, pharmaceutical preparations, wine and soap which use some form of alcohol in their manufacturing processes. All are licensed or operate under a permit. An excise officer could be fairly asked, when he goes home at night, "Hard day at the brewery?" Excise personnel work right at some breweries, distilleries and tobacco factories or pay visits to them regularly. The officer is a combination of policeman, accountant and chemist.

Excise duty, by the way, is one tax which can be avoided: that is, if you don't drink or smoke.

Customs and Excise has a laboratory and scientific services division which analyzes imported products and develops test procedures. The work it does for Excise centres mainly on alcohol and the control and use of materials containing alcohol. Decades ago, the rough-and-ready test for the measurement of alcoholic content was the gunpowder test. The spirits were saturated with gunpowder and ignited. If a flash was produced, the spirit was overproof; if not, underproof. In those far-off days, precise measurement was not considered necessary because only nominal rates of duty were in force. In the modern laboratory, measurement is considerably more accurate. In 1979, a new system of measurement, or alcoholmetry, based on metric units, was devised by the department's laboratory. Alcoholic strength is expressed as the percentage of absolute ethyl alcohol in the total volume of the spirit, a method which should be more readily understood by the public than the proof system.

For a department of long tenure and tradition, Customs and Excise has shown a perhaps surprising ability to adapt quickly to new social and technological circumstances. It is true that change sometimes has had to be forced upon it, but often the department was in step with the times and, now and then, helped lead the way. In the tourist trade and aviation, for example, Customs and Excise both accommodated itself to them and helped in their development.

Courting the tourist trade goes back to the start of Confederation. Here are the regulations issued by Customs Commissioner R.S.M. Bouchette in March, 1869:

> 1st — Regular stages and hacks, when the owners or the drivers are known to the officers, may be allowed to cross the frontier and return, within two days, without being required to make an entry at the Customs House, subject only to the ordinary examination, search and inspection.
>
> 2nd — Travellers intending to remain within the Dominion for a longer period than two days are required in all cases to report and enter their horses, carriages and travelling equipage; and in cases where they do not intend to leave at the same port at which they enter, or are uncertain on that point, they must deposit with the Collector the full amount of duty on such horses, carriages and other dutiable articles, to be returned only on their furnishing satisfactory evidence that the same articles have been returned unchanged to the United States. Travellers intending to leave at the port of entry may be allowed to enter as above, and in lieu of cash, to give a bond, with an approved resident surety, covering the amount of duty, and with the additional condition that such bond shall be enforced if the time specified therein is exceeded.
>
> 3rd — The time to be allowed travellers in either case shall not exceed one calendar month; and if that term be exceeded, the entries shall be considered bona fide entries for duty, and be included in the accounts of the port.

In 1891, "summer residence equipment," as tents were called in the regulations, was allowed in on deposit with a refund of 90 per cent of the duty. In 1897 the same provision was applied to sportsmen's guns; and teams, carriages, stages and hacks could be admitted under bond. In 1898, bicycles were admitted on deposit and non-resident members of organized shooting and fishing clubs were allowed to bring in their sportsmen's outfits.

On December 27, 1901, the Automobile Club of America wrote from New York to ask for a copy of Canadian regulations governing admission of tourists' automobiles, or, as they were sometimes known then, horseless carriages. The customs department had no regulations for automobiles at that time but replied that, though the ordinary duty on cars was 25 per cent, instructions could be given in this case to accept a deposit of the duty subject to refund if the cars returned to the United States within six months.

In 1902, more than fifty inquiries were received, and the department decided that there was something in the automobile after all and scrambled to prepare some regulations, which it issued in 1903. All applications came from the rich (as was noted at the time): wealthy businessmen, bankers, manufacturers, congressmen, consuls and high railway officials. Many of the inquiries related to shipping cars into Canada by boat or railway, indicating that trans-border roads were poor or non-existent.

As of July, 1903, regulations asked only for a deposit of five per cent of the value of the automobile and a bond for double the estimated duties. By 1916 no deposit or bond was required for a stay of thirty days. As early as 1904, a political candidate in Ontario's Essex County imported automobiles from nearby Detroit for conveying voters to the polls. In 1907, provision was made for a refund of duty on tires brought in to replace damaged tires on tourist automobiles (tires were not then manufactured in Canada).

Up to 1920, customs officers who had to stay on duty after regular hours at frontier posts collected a fee of fifty cents for clearing each car. This was discontinued that year. In 1930, not even a permit was required for a 24-hour stay; in 1935 this period was extended to 48 hours with no bond or deposit needed for a stay of up to six months.

Customs records show that the first resort in Canada to see the big possibilities of tourist business by car was Baddeck, Nova Scotia, whose board of trade, in 1906, wrote to Finance Minister Fielding, a Nova Scotian, to ask that importation of cars by tourists be made as convenient as possible. By 1937, though it was a depression year, the tourist business brought $300 million into Canada. Meanwhile, at ocean terminals, efforts were being made to speed up clearance time. The early decades of the 20th century were the era of the ocean liner and settlers' trains, and most customs officers worked the big ships and the long train sheds. Up to 1928, relatives, friends, greeters, other well-wishers and members of the general public mingled with the disembarking ocean passengers in an uproarious melee of joyful tears and lost children. The only outsiders in this exuberant scene were the customs inspectors who had to sort out arrivers and greeters for immigration purposes, not to mention the ownership of baggage awaiting examination. A system had to be worked out requiring permits for those meeting relatives and friends at the steamship sheds, especially in Montreal, the busiest port in summer. It reduced the confusion and brought some degree of order to the formalities of clearing customs and immigration. Most passengers cleared customs faster than before, though not, perhaps, immigrant settlers who spoke neither French nor English.

Early air transportation in Canada differed from that in most other countries, where the primary focus had been on air traffic between the chief centres of population. In Canada, the first practical use of aircraft was for surveying and forest reconnaissance, and for transportation to otherwise inaccessible areas.

Forest protection and survey flights were first made in Quebec in the summer of 1919. In 1920 and 1921, the Air Board established bases at various points in Canada from which forest and survey patrols could be flown. The first large-scale attempt to establish air transportation in the far north followed the discovery of oil at Fort Norman on the Mackenzie River in the fall of 1921. The first regular freight and passenger air service in Canada was inaugurated in 1924 at Rouyn, centre of the northwestern Quebec mining district.

The St. Hubert air harbor, or *champs d'aviation*, twelve miles south of Montreal, was officially opened October 1, 1928, and National Revenue opened an office there the very same day. Fortunately, some reports from the customs officer at St. Hubert have survived. Some are simple listings of arrivals and departures and the number of pieces of baggage, but some are chatty letters to headquarters in Ottawa about new air services coming into being, types of planes, smuggling by air, and the thrill of flying. The first customs officer at St. Hubert — it was a one-man station — was Paul Ejlert-Jensen; he himself ignored his double-barreled name and signed himself Paul Jensen. His first quarterly report, to January 1, 1929, noted that one hundred and sixty-six passengers had arrived or departed in the three months and that he had examined one hundred and twenty-three pieces of baggage. The total number of planes was one hundred and ninety-one, both Canadian and foreign, carrying eleven hundred bags of mail. Obviously keen about working at a new air harbor, and curious about aviation in general, Jensen also provided this information: six companies had established field headquarters at St. Hubert (Canadian Colonial Airways Limited, Canadian Airways Limited, Canadian Transcontinental Airways Limited, Continental Aero Corporation, Commercial Air Transport and Montreal Light Airplane Club); all international business was performed by Canadian Colonial Airways, which had a contract to carry mail between Montreal and Albany and carried passengers and express and postal parcels. This company was operating two Fairchild cabin monoplanes powered by Pratt and Whitney Wasp engines, and proposed to acquire a Pitcairn Super Tailwing powered by a Wright Whirlwind motor. Pilots' log books (open to customs inspection) showed only three forced landings in Canada in the quarter.

Most of the customs revenue at St. Hubert came, not from duty on articles carried by passengers, but on imported planes, engines and airplane parts. Jensen reported for May, 1929, that he had collected $97,782.70 from such duties, and $25.73 on passengers' baggage. He also noted that eighteen different makes of aircraft had been shown at a St. Hubert exhibition. Canadian Colonial Airways had informed him that a new passenger service with Sikorsky amphibians would begin within a week, the first flight carrying directors of American aviation companies to a landing in Montreal Harbor at the foot of McGill Street. (The seaplane base was at Longueuil, and Jensen advised headquarters that the customs officer there should be able to swim.) In late 1929, Jensen wrote an article for the *National Revenue Review* in which he extolled the wonders of flying:

> The mail and passenger planes travel as the crow flies. You are making over a hundred miles an hour, yet you have very little sensation of speed; rather, you seem to be stationary and the country beneath you unrolling like a strip of map. The beautiful St. Lawrence, numerous lakes, small streams, woods, towns, trains and railroads are all seen from such an unusual aspect that it fills the flight with intense interest.

Jensen said that there had been a brief flurry of excitement over a report that parcels of goods were being dropped near the air harbor from the regular New York mail plane and whisked into Montreal. The parcels turned out to be cartons six inches deep and four inches wide provided for airsickness. Many airsick passengers declined to observe the rule that they carry these cartons away with them, and chucked them out a window of the plane. Such cartons littered the countryside between Montreal and New York. Jensen noted that U.S. Customs had started an air border patrol and suggested Canada would soon have to do the same: "Smuggling by air will in the future be one of the worst enemies of the Department as it is so very hard to obtain evidence and actually seize an aircraft flying at from five to ten thousand feet altitude with no apparent regular landing point."

The British dirigible R-100, with a crew of thirty-eight and six passengers, moored at the St. Hubert mast August 1, 1930, and the first Canadian aboard was customs officer Jensen. Nothing was left to chance. These instructions had been sent from Ottawa:

> In view of the limited number of passengers which will be carried on the R-100 on her initial trip to St. Hubert, and in order to co-operate to the fullest extent with the Department of National Defence, the details of Customs examination are being curtailed to an absolute minimum. There are, however, certain formalities which are absolutely essential in connection with any vessel arriving from a foreign port by sea or by air, and in order that this work should be carried out expeditiously, the following routine has been suggested and tentatively approved by Mr. J. A. Wilson, Controller of Civil Aviation:
>
> As soon as the R-100 has been satisfactorily berthed at the mooring tower and before anyone disembarks, a single Customs Officer

should go on board and receive from the Commander, or the Officer who corresponds to a Purser on an ocean liner, the usual report Inward which is required in every case no matter whether the vessel is a commercial one, a pleasurecraft or a Government ship. A second officer will be stationed inside the tower at the head of the stairs leading from the landing platform to the elevator. This officer will examine any hand baggage which may be carried off the vessel either by the officials or the crew, and if no dutiable articles are found, will pass same at once. If, however, there is any question in this regard, the individual piece of baggage will be set aside for further examination, to be returned to the owner at a convenient time. This Guard will be maintained until the ship has been re-ballasted and is ready for search by Customs Officers. As soon as this inspection has been completed, the Guard will be withdrawn and no other formalities will be required except clearance which is necessary when leaving Canada.

A suggestion that the Customs examination of passengers and baggage should take place in the upper storey of the house surrounding the Base of the tower is not approved as it is understood that part of this space is to be used as living quarters for the landing crew and that the remainder of the space on the day of arrival has been placed at the disposal of the reception committee and the press. It would be utterly impossible to transact business satisfactorily in the confusion and congestion which would exist in this particular space.

This suggested arrangement only refers to the present visit of the R-100 and in agreeing to same it must be distinctly understood that in the case of future commercial transports, additional facilities and safeguards will be required. Unless otherwise advised the proposed examination of the R-100 will be carried out as noted above.

The instructions were signed by G.N. Bunker, chief inspector of Customs and Excise and one of only two men (the other was David Sim) whose mastery of detail struck terror throughout the department.

So fast did aviation grow that, as early as February, 1932, Jensen was raising the possibility that St. Hubert would soon be too small to accommodate the growing traffic. He suggested that the seaplane base at Longueuil could be used for land planes as well. He had picked up a rumor that the military might take over St. Hubert. (By 1937, two Royal Canadian Air Force squadrons were based there: No. 18 bomber squadron was a French-speaking unit, No. 15 fighter squadron English-speaking. Each squadron had three planes.) Hector Fortier, who replaced Jensen in 1936, later recalled that he often had to wear "a real and true smile" because many of the air passengers were rich American tourists. Because the customs inspector was also the immigration officer, immigration headquarters and the Canadian and American justice departments regularly sent him photographs of gangsters who might pass through the airport.

Fortier reported extensively on operations in winter, when planes swapped wheels for skis. A "special feature" of the 1936-37 winter was inauguration of a Montreal-Ottawa flight. A trial run was being planned from Newark direct to Montreal with a Douglas DC-3 carrying twenty-one passengers. "These planes are of the finest type, ultra modern, completely equipped for night flying, restaurant services, etc.," Fortier reported. In November, 1936, Clyde Pangborn had flown the new Burnelli transport plane into St. Hubert with the designer, Mr. Burnelli, aboard. Another visitor was J.F. Vultee, designer of the Vultee airplane. C.D. Howe, minister of transport, had made St. Hubert his embarkation point for a flying trip to the United States and Vancouver. Fortier added: "Mr. Howe has shown impressively that he believes in air transportation by using it. His example should commend itself to others who seldom travel by air." Between April 1 and September 30, 1937, five hundred and thirty-three planes landed at St. Hubert with twenty-two hundred and twenty travellers. Passengers had to wait for clearance until the customs officer had searched the plane.

On March 4, 1939, Fortier received a copy of a letter sent from Ottawa to Canadian Associated Aircraft Limited of Montreal saying the company would be exempted from sales tax for parts used in manufacture at St. Hubert and Malton, Ontario, of "large bomber aircraft" for the Royal Air Force. On May 13, 1941, Fortier reported that air traffic was expanding so rapidly that the transport department had torn down the fence in front of Customs to make more room for arriving planes. As a result, greeters were going right out to the planes to meet disembarking passengers, many of whom disregarded customs and immigration and simply walked away. He had gone to the transport department for a new fence, but Transport had said it was up to the air force. The air force had said it was Transport's responsibility. Would somebody please help? Somebody eventually did, by moving civilian air operations from St. Hubert to Dorval later in 1941, the same year that Trans-Canada Air Lines operated its first international flight to New York.

There was administrative conflict from the outset at Dorval. Bunker himself reported December 23, 1941, that a storm window had been placed right over the window through which baggage from international flights had to be passed to the customs room. He instructed that the Dorval manager, Mr. Banghart, have the storm window removed. Then there was the problem of the drinking cups. On May 29, 1942, Fortier received this directive from Bunker: "With reference to the drinking cups for the Waiting Room, since the Department of Transport has decided to do away with this service in lieu of the drinking fountain in the main waiting room, I can see no reason why this Department should provide the required cups. It will, therefore, be necessary for passengers to wait for drinking water either until they have cleared Customs or until they board the plane." And thus were federal budgets balanced.

Between August 1, 1928, and March 31, 1929, Winnipeg Customs reported fifteen planes in and six out. But between April 1 and October 1, 1929, there was a "marked increase in what is known as aeroplane traffic": ninety-eight planes in, eighty-five out. In November, 1929, Customs noted: "Recently a daily passenger air service has been inaugurated between Winnipeg and Minneapolis, each aeroplane capable of accommodating seven people."

For fiscal year 1935-36, Saint John, New Brunswick, reported thirty foreign plane arrivals, thirty departures, a total of seventy-one passengers and one hundred and ninety-four pieces of baggage examined. Fiscal 1936-37 figures were fifty-five foreign planes in, fifty-four out, one hundred and nineteen passengers and two hundred and ninety-seven pieces of baggage. In addition, a passenger service to Halifax operated twice a day in summer. The service employed a five-passenger Stinson with an average number of passengers of three. Another airline was preparing to operate its fleet of five four-seat planes to Moncton, Charlottetown, Sydney, Halifax and Saint John. Still another was already operating from Moncton to Charlottetown to Halifax, carrying mail as well as passengers. In July, 1933, a special customs staff met Genenal Balbo's twenty-four-plane Italian air fleet at the Royal Canadian Air Force seaplane base at Shediac, New Brunswick. Balbo was en route from Rome to Chicago.

After the First World War, the administration of Customs and Excise hit a very bad patch, mainly because of loose and weak control at the top. The attitude of a large part of the Canadian population — that some customs and excise laws were ridiculous, especially as applied to liquor — infected members of the department itself. The department grew lax during the long period when the United States was attempting to enforce prohibition. Widescale smuggling of liquor into the United States led to extensive smuggling back across the border, especially of cigarettes and textiles. The political result was the customs scandal of 1926, which brought down the government. The scandal is described in the chapters on smuggling; we deal here with the administrative aftermath.

Euler and Sim

Oddly, the customs scandal left few scars on the department. Its recovery was rapid, not to say miraculous, mostly because of two men, W.D. Euler (pronounced aye-ler, though he was no "yes man"), the minister of National Revenue, and David Sim, the minister's assistant and later a deputy minister in the department for thirty-five years, from 1930 to 1965.

Euler's appointment by Prime Minister Mackenzie King in 1926 was astonishing in itself. Both had attended Berlin (Kitchener) Collegiate Institute and had disliked each other. Euler was working class (his father was a German laborer who spoke little English and who made his son pay back every cent spent on his education), while King was upper middle class. King did not relish Euler's style or his antecedents (Canada's first war against Germany had ended only eight years earlier), but he was astute enough to see that Euler was the strong, honest man needed to clean up the department and ensure that it remained cleaned up. Euler thus became the rookie minister of a customs department which had been harboring crooks for a good many years.

Euler's choice of Sim as his assistant is perhaps equally astonishing, because Sim had no political experience in Ottawa — or anywhere else. But he had three attributes that Euler needed: he was Anglo, he was army, and he could administer. Sim had joined the army when he was only sixteen and had been wounded at Passchendaele in 1917. He returned to Kitchener to work in the Bank of Nova Scotia and then become secretary of the Kitchener-Waterloo Trust and Savings Company.

It is impressive to reflect upon, now, how an administrative team could restore confidence in the department, within and without, and cause the customs scandal to fade quickly from public consciousness.

"The credit must go to Euler," Sim said during a series of talks with the writer in 1981 in his Ottawa apartment overlooking the Rideau River. "He could make up his mind and then stick to his decision. The most important quality in government is not to hesitate to take responsibility and to make decisions and then stick to them. Euler had this quality. And he was obstinate. He didn't waste time haggling with the opposition — or with his own Liberals, for that matter — but just went ahead and did what had to be done. I guess that is what made him an easy man to work for. You knew he wasn't going to change his mind the next day. The public — and the government — wanted a strong administration in Revenue and a clean one, and that is what we gave them. Really, it was a honeymoon period for us, though there was no love lost between King and Euler."

Euler did not bring in new people, except for Sim. He worked with the material at hand. The first thing he did was to eliminte the post of the single deputy minister and establish a triumvirate immediately below him: a commissioner for income tax, a commissioner for customs and a commissioner for excise, each with the rank of deputy. This did away with the cosy arrangement by which the two previous ministers had so dominated a weak deputy that favors for political friends became the department's ruling — some said only — passion.

The customs commissioner, R.W. Breadner, had been secretary of the Canadian Manufacturers' Association and was a staunch believer in tariff protection for Canadian industry. This suited Euler, a Liberal protectionist. Sim recalled: "Breadner used to come to work in the morning and ring every bell on his desk to summon all his chiefs. Then he'd give them all hell for not doing enough in the interests of protection for industry."

Sim earned a reputation for loyalty very early in his government career. Once Euler and a friend were having an argument about the meaning of a word and made a small wager. Sim was sent to fetch a dictionary. As he returned with it, the friend paid the wager to Euler before the minister could even open the dictionary, and said: "If you'd been wrong, Dave wouldn't have been able to find a dictionary anywhere." Sim says now: "Isn't that a hell of a reputation to have when you're that young?"

Sim explained how he learned when not to speak. Euler was inspecting Customs' marine service and was en route from Quebec to Pictou aboard the patrol boat *Margaret*, whose master was the famous one-legged Captain Alfred La Couvée. One fine day in the Gulf of St. Lawrence, Sim mentioned it would be a grand day for a swim. "I had in mind some warm, secluded cove near Pictou somewhere. But Euler said he was sure Captain La Couvée could arrange it. The captain stopped the *Margaret* and I had to swim around the ship. It was freezing cold out in the open ocean and I barely made it. That's when I learned to keep my mouth shut."

The government changed in 1930, and Sim got ready to go home to Kitchener. But the new Conservative minister, E.B. Ryckman, asked him to stay: "I came with a Liberal minister and stayed with a Tory." He was named commissioner of excise at thirty years of age. He is a mine of recollection:

> The name of the department kept changing and the names of the senior officers kept changing, from commissioners to deputy ministers, for example, because as the need for new revenue increased in a growing country, new official positions had to be created. Just think, before the First World War there was no income tax and no sales tax. Because Customs was the main source of revenue then, a great deal of importance automatically went with the office of customs collector. The king wanted his revenue, and consequently the collector was free from some of the ordinary restrictions placed on most people. The collector had the power of search. He did go through the bedrooms of the nation.

Creation of a Department   147

The deputy minister was always named in the Customs Act as the chief officer rather than the minister because the buck stopped with the deputy minister. When you deal with a lot of unfavorable decisions — politically unfavorable, that is — as Customs and Excise does, it is the deputy minister who should make the announcements. And that's the way it should be. Deputy ministers don't have to get elected. There are few kudos to be won in the department. When there are any, the minister should be the one to take the credit. Things like seizures, search and entry are not popular. In fact, they invite only criticism. And there are bound to be whispers about any organization which collects money. Any deputy minister who starts his job with the hope of making a favorable impression publicly is not going to do a very good job.

I found that the title deputy minister helped me in my work. Above my chair was a framed certificate announcing my position, and every visitor saw it. I once — foolishly — stepped out of my office to discuss an important customs matter. I was out of my element. It is not the individual who is important, but the office itself. The office, not the person, carries the authority, though a lot of civil servants seem to forget that. Of course, you don't want dummies in those types of jobs. One of the hardest things in the civil service is to avoid another department palming off a dummy on you with extravagant, and false, praise.

I thought at one time I might try to get elected to Parliament. But I gave up that idea when I discovered I really liked what I was doing. At the start I was a young buckaroo with no technical knowledge. But I learned to settle things by common sense.

In 1930, the outgoing deputy gave me quite a talk. He had a handsome lot of books in handsome bookcases in his office. He said I would need to know a lot about chemistry and I thought, good God, what am I getting into? When I came to look at the books after he had gone, I found all the pages were uncut. The books were pure swank and had never been read.

His visitors might have seen Sim's certificate of office, but they missed other things: "In the deputy minister's office hang pictures of deputies back to Confederation. One day I took mine down and replaced it with a picture of me when I was one year old. Nobody ever noticed."

"Though I stayed in the same place for 35 years, I now advise others to change jobs. I was offered other jobs. Some I didn't like. Mackenzie King called me before Cabinet and wanted me to take the job of director-general of the civil service. C.D. Howe had told me it was a man-trap, so I made a couple of suggestions of my own: Watson Sellar, who later became auditor-general, and Arnold Heeney of external affairs. King turned down both suggestions. He said Heeney was too close to him — in other words, it was a miserable job and he didn't want any dirt near him (King). I said that if Sellar and Heeney weren't qualified, I didn't feel qualified either. I was able to turn down the prime minister. I don't think that could be done today. Later I was asked to go to New Zealand as high commissioner. That would have been nice because there's not much trouble between Canada and New Zealand. But George Nowlan, the minister, said, 'Don't go.' One thing always sustained me: I felt that what I was doing was important."

Sim had a direct hand in one of the most vital decisions in the history of Canadian customs service: the transfer of the Preventive Service (the name refers to the prevention of smuggling) to the Royal Canadian Mounted Police in 1932. An investigation branch was retained in Customs and Excise.

The Preventive Service had been founded in 1897, with five land officers and seven vessels, and made its first strike on March 27 that year when Captain George May, in the cruiser *Constance*, seized three barrels and five kegs of spirits valued at $400. The parliamentary inquiry into Customs recommended in its final report, dated June 18, 1926, that the Preventive Service be reorganized and strengthened, and include a secret service for criminal investigation. The subsequent royal commission urged that the service be decentralized, with regional officers having jurisdiction over defined, compact territories. As a result, the Preventive Service was expanded and by 1932 it numbered three hundred and fifty land officers, thirty-five cruisers and patrol boats, fifty "high-powered" cars, and an air wing.

At the parliamentary inquiry, Commissioner Cortlandt Starnes of the Royal Canadian Mounted Police had proposed that his force take over the Preventive Service, which he dismissed as ineffectual under customs administration. "There are, of course, Customs Houses, but most of these can be avoided so easily that they cannot in themselves be taken seriously as preventive measures," Starnes testified. These offices were "reported to by the honest, avoided by the dishonest at will." He noted that the hundred and fifty mile stretch of frontier between Hereford, Quebec, and the St. Lawrence River was crossed by no fewer than sixty-three roads. The prevalence of smuggling on the frontier was a comparatively recent development "due in part to inventions like the motor car." The parliamentary inquiry and the royal commission both ignored Starnes' proposal. Six years later, under Sim, the transfer of the Preventive Service to the RCMP was accomplished in less than two months. The order-in-council making the transfer, effective April 1, 1932, was signed by Prime Minister R.B. Bennett. During its thirty-five-year term in Customs, the Preventive Service made 35,808 customs and excise seizures of everything from airplanes to false teeth, and collected revenue of $7,441,603 as a result.

There is little documentation on how the transfer decision was reached. Today, myriad options would have worked their way up through the bureaucracy to the cabinet, accompanied by the usual river of paper. In 1932, ministers simply made a decision and told their officials to work it out. Sim explains:

> In those days, all members of the Preventive Service were appointed by the minister of Customs as part of the spoils of office. It was part of my job to find these people. You can imagine what this meant in all the small towns and villages. The preventive officer couldn't be expected to inform on his brother or cousin for running rum and that kind of thing. Our whole Preventive Service was just too close to home, so to speak.
>
> Let me give you another example. La Couvée was fearless and always businesslike. But his ship, the *Margaret*, was far too big and expensive to keep track of all the little fishing boats carrying liquor from St. Pierre and Miquelon to Canada and the United States. It was almost impossible for us to run a marine service from Ottawa, as we were trying to do. It was hopeless to try to find seamen who would take action against fellow seamen from the same port or coast and arrest them for running rum in small fishing vessels.
>
> Well, about this time, Sir James MacBrien took over as Commissioner of the RCMP. He didn't seek the job. The government asked him to take it. In these circumstances, MacBrien could ask for anything he wanted and get it. One of the things he wanted was our Preventive Service. His wish coincided with our reasoning that we should put the service somewhere else. I was asked to transfer the preventive staff. I talked to MacBrien and between us we worked out a scheme of transfer. The Mounted Police took in nearly all our people and treated them very well indeed.
>
> By and large, it was a good thing to transfer this responsibility to a police organization. We had to close at least two hundred small preventive stations and that was difficult. It's true that the transfer took a lot of the glamor out of Customs but I still think it was right.

Here is the text of the order of April 16, 1932:

> His Excellency the Governor General in Council, on the joint recommendation of the Minister of National Revenue and the Minister of Justice, and under the authority of Chapter 165 of the Revised Statutes of Canada, 1927, is pleased to order the Preventive Service of the Department of National Revenue be, and it is hereby, transferred to the Royal Canadian Mounted Police from the 1st of April, 1932, with the exception of Special Investigation Branch of that Service, which is to remain with the Department of National Revenue:
>
> His Excellency in Council is further pleased to order that the following principles and orders be, and they are, hereby laid down for the information and guidance of the Departments affected:-
>
> (1) The Minister of National Revenue will be responsible for the policy to be adopted by the Preventive Service.

> (2) The Minister in control of the Royal Canadian Mounted Police will be responsible for the administration of the personnel of the Preventive Service, and of the duties and interior economy of that service.
>
> (3) As from the 1st of April, 1932, the amounts appropriated by Parliament for the Preventive Service of the Department of National Revenue for the Fiscal Year 1932-33, under Vote No. 277, will be transferred to the appropriation of the Royal Canadian Mounted Police, upon the understanding that such amounts as may be required for the Special Investigation Branch of that Service, which is to remain with the Department of National Revenue, and those members of the Preventive Service who are entitled to and are to be granted leave of absence, with pay, and who were not taken over by the R.C.M. Police on the 1st of April, 1932, be the subject of arrangement between the two Departments concerned, namely, the Department of National Revenue and the Department of the R.C.M. Police, it being further understood that a Supplementary Estimate will be submitted at the first opportunity for any further amount which may be required by the R.C.M. Police. Appropriate action to be taken in the Supplementary Estimates.

Rum-running has been a favorite source of stories among customs officers for years, of course. One of Sim's favorites, in which he was involved, is about a prominent senator from the Maritimes who often represented smugglers in court, and was probably a director of extensive smuggling operations himself. "He was the type that when he came out of church and somebody asked him if he had looked in his cellar lately he knew right away the rum-runners had put more of their goods at his disposal. Anyway, he tried to sell to us a boat known as *One-Seven-Four* so that we could use it to catch rum-runners. She was reputed to have three power systems, one for normal speed, one for very fast, and a third for go like hell. He wanted forty-two thousand dollars, I think it was. He even told me — in writing — that if the department would buy it there would be something in it for me. I gave him a short, snappy reply on that. One day one of our patrol boats came across *One-Seven-Four* inside the twelve-mile rum limit. The crew was all drunk and the boat had drifted inside the limit. The boat was carrying rum so we seized it and got it for nothing."

Sim is proudest of all about a story set in Saskatchewan, perhaps because of his belief that common sense conquers all:

> One day in the 'thirties I got a letter from a teacher in a Saskatchewan country school telling me that the Mounties had gone out to this farm and shot the family horse right in front of the children and what was I going to do about it. Well, I looked up the file and the teacher was right. This is what had happened: Old Ned and a buggy were the only transportation this family had. The farmer had a still on the farm and used to deliver his moonshine with Ned and the buggy. He was caught one day and sent to jail.

The family had no income, so the farmer's wife got the still going again, or made a new one, and began making deliveries with Ned and the buggy. The Mounties caught her on a back road one day and the horse and buggy, along with the moonshine, were seized. The next thing in the procedure is to sell the seized goods, that is, the horse and buggy. The horse remained on the farm for ninety days while we tried to sell it. Naturally, the neighbors weren't going to buy the horse. Now, goods that can't be sold are destroyed. So after ninety days don't the RCMP go out to the farm and shoot Old Ned, in front of the kids, just like the teacher said. Well, what was I going to do about it? I figured out that it cost $1 a day to keep a government horse, which Ned was after we seized him. Ninety days' keep was $90. So we sent the wife a cheque for $90. She bought a new horse for $60 and had $30 to spend foolishly. And it was all perfectly legal.

Another victory for common sense:

> When governments changed in the 1920s and 1930s, there were a lot of changes in jobs. If a Member of Parliament said in a letter to the minister that some civil servant was guilty of political partisanship, his word had to be accepted and the employee dismissed. An MP in the Eastern Townships of Quebec was being harassed by a man for a job in Customs, so he had to create a vacancy. He accused a customs man (at Armstrong, I think it was) with twenty-five years' experience of political partisanship, and we had to dismiss him. R.S. White of the *Montreal Star* brought the matter to our attention. I read the file and the more I read the more horrified I became that the man had been fired. This employee used to have a few beers in the evening and go to political meetings, where he would cheer on the *rouges* at a Liberal meeting and the *bleus* at a Conservative meeting. He was being as non-partisan as possible, but a *bleu* could complain the man was a *rouge*, or vice versa. Well, we couldn't reinstate the man because an order-in-council dismissing him had already been passed. But we put the amount of his salary in the blue book of estimates so that hiring would be official. Then we advertized for a man with 25 years' experience in Customs. He got the job. . . .

> After one election, 1926, Postmaster-General [Peter John] Veniot dismissed three hundred and fifty postmasters across the country and replaced them with Liberal appointees. The Tories naturally raised quite a rumpus in the House of Commons. Veniot replied in this way: it was true he had dismissed quite a few postmasters. He himself had been in the civil service, a deputy customs collector at Woodstock, New Brunswick. One of the first things the Tories had done when they had come to office was to dismiss him. He wanted to thank the Conservatives because if they hadn't fired him, he'd probably still be in customs at Woodstock. That ended that.

Sim as an exciseman knew the Bronfman family well, especially the king of the liquor dynasty, Sam Bronfman. The family fortune was based on early rum-running on the prairies, especially Saskatchewan.

During the Second World War, I was administrator of alcoholic beverages, and tobacco, too. We were always trying to get $1-a-year men from industry. We would set up advisory boards to deal with various products, textiles, for instance, or liquor. These boards had access to all the information of all the companies in each group, that is, lists of costs, customers, sales methods and so on. The advisers had to have all the pertinent information about an industry or they really couldn't function properly. We gave them all medals after the war for being good citizens. Neither Sam Bronfman nor Harry Hatch would agree to the other becoming the chairman of the advisory board on alcoholic beverages. Neither wanted the other to have access to his books. [Harry C. Hatch became H. Clifford Hatch when he became president of Hiram Walker-Gooderham & Worts.]

Sam Bronfman had all the money he wanted. What he wanted was respectability. So he always readily agreed with all the excise measures we imposed on liquor production and distribution. Harry Bronfman could read a balance sheet and knew how to market a product. Allan was a lawyer dilettante. Abe, the eldest, spent most of his time drinking with rum-runners and making deals to run liquor into the United States and sometimes back into Canada. But Sam tried to play it straight. Nobody was more severe in making sure that his reputation, whatever it was before, was impeccable. He insisted on it.

It is well known that Sam Bronfman devoted a lot of time and energy and money trying to get himself appointed to the Senate by Prime Ministers King and St. Laurent. It is not as well known that he kept up the same campaign when Prime Minister Diefenbaker came to power in 1957. Alvin Hamilton, Diefenbaker's minister of northern affairs and national resources (and later agriculture), recalled in 1981: "One day the subject of Senate appointments came up in cabinet. Many ministers wanted Bronfman appointed on the grounds that the party would never have to worry again about campaign funds, or at least as long as Bronfman lived. At that point, I had to bring up the fact that Mr. Diefenbaker had acted as counsel to the Saskatchewan royal commission which investigated the liquor traffic — and the Bronfmans — in the 1930s. I said it wouldn't look very good if Mr. Diefenbaker were now to appoint Sam Bronfman to the Senate. Mr. Diefenbaker didn't say anything except, 'Shall we go to the next name on our list?'"

David Sim poked fun at himself and the department for its campaign in the 1930s to try to stem the flow of pornography, or what passed for pornography in those days: "There had always been on the statute books the customs law banning importation of indecent publications. We wanted to show that we were right up to the mark in protecting the public and we used to publish a list of all the books and magazines we banned — and kept it up to date every month. Then we started getting requests for the list, especially from the newspapers. All I was doing was keeping the press

Creation of a Department 153

gallery up to date on its light reading. We finally got wise that we were promoting the very books which we were trying to stop coming into the country and we stopped publishing the list. The material then was most innocent by today's standards. But how does one judge what is immoral?

I used to get around the issue sometimes by referring cases to the Tariff Board for independent judgment when there was a rumpus about some particular book being banned. The beauty about a Tariff Board hearing was that it gave everybody who wanted to sound off a chance to sound off. I remember when the novel, *Peyton Place*, came out. I had had a lot of representations from clergymen urging that the book be banned in Canada, so I decided to refer it to the Tariff Board and I notified all the churchmen that this was their chance to be heard. One of those appearing was Dr. J.R. Mutchmor of the United Church. I asked him if he had read *Peyton Place*. 'Twice,' he said.''

Only two classes of goods were banned outright in the original 1867 customs legislation: counterfeit money and "books, drawings, paintings and prints of an immoral or indecent character." The definition in today's customs tariff is little changed: "books, printed paper, drawings, paintings, prints, photographs or representations of any kind of a treasonable or seditious or of an immoral or indecent character." The definition of obscenity is in the Criminal Code: "any publication a dominant characteristic of which is the undue exploitation of sex, or of sex and any one or more of the following subjects, namely, crime, horror, cruelty and violence, shall be deemed to be obscene."

Thrusting Customs into the role of moral vigilante seems to have started in Britain in 1846 when Customs was given the task of seizing and destroying obscene paintings, prints and books. In any case, Canada quickly assigned its customs officers the same task. The first case of pornography in the customs file seems to be a letter written November 24, 1853, by Marcus Fayette Whitehead, collector at Port Hope, to Commissioner Bouchette:

> I beg to report to you that I seized a number of pamphlets and small books of a most obscene, immoral and disgusting description, not fit for the gaze of the most licentious or accomplished libertine, much less to be circulated in a civilized community, and in the event of my own modesty and taste being questioned, I have called to my aid and counsel a very virtuous and pious old Baptist who has pronounced the whole "too abominable to be even looked at." I have therefore placed them under lock and key and await your instructions.

Bouchette ordered Whitehead to destroy them immediately. Nowhere in this correspondence is there any mention of the titles of the books and pamphlets.

On September 9, 1857, Benjamin Seaton, collector at Sutton, Canada East (Quebec), told Bouchette that jewelry had been seized from Lewis Oberndorffer of Clarenceville, Canada East, and:
> among other trinkets was found a small box containing 16 Bawdy, Indecent and abominable pictures, indeed too disgraceful for exposure, evidently of foreign manufacture and calculated to do much mischief in the hands of the pedlar by corrupting the morals of youth. . . . Oberndorffer deserves punishment for having in his possession such beastly productions.

Oberndorffer had to forfeit the pictures, which were destroyed, and was fined £5.

Customs Commissioner James Johnson issued this memorandum to collectors May 22, 1877: "It is stated in some of the public prints that such publications as the *Policy News*, *National Police Gazette*, *The Days Doings* and other similar filthy and obscene literature are freely imported into Canada. You are hereby reminded that such publications are absolutely prohibited and when found should in every case be seized and destroyed." In 1911, Canada acceded, along with fourteen other countries, to an international agreement for the suppression of obscene publications.

Some book bannings were far from funny. On April 27, 1917, Customs banned a book by Arthur Mee and J. Stuart Holden called *Defeat? The Truth About the Betrayal of Britain* and noted that under Order-in-Council PC 146 dated January 17, 1917, adopted under the umbrella of the War Measures Act of 1914, "no person in Canada is now permitted to be in possession of this book or of any issue thereof already published or hereafter to be published and any person in possession of such book is liable to a fine not exceeding $5,000 or imprisonment for a term not exceeding five years, or to both fine and imprisonment."

The campaign conducted against purported licentiousness in the 1930s can appear only ludicrous now. Some of the books banned in that decade were *Lady Chatterley's Lover* by D.H. Lawrence in 1930 (it became a famous test case); *Sanctuary* by William Faulkner, *Nothing in Common but Sex* by Mollie Panter-Downes and *Girl on the Make* by Faith Baldwin and Achmed Abdullah in 1932; *The Gentle Libertine* by Colette in 1933; *Tobacco Road* by Erskine Caldwell, *She Done Him Wrong* by Mae West, *The Pure and Impure* by Colette, *The Postman Always Rings Twice* by James M. Cain and *The Thin Man* by Dashiell Hammett in 1934. The book of customs seizures for Dawson, Yukon Territory, shows that *Lady Chatterley's Lover*, appraised value $1, was seized from one John Day on June 19, 1937, and that four books were seized from the Dawson Free Public Library April 30, 1942. They were: *Avalanche* by Gordon Hayward, *In Praise of Life* by

Walter Schoenstedt, *Highland River* by Neil M. Gunn and *Time Piece* by Naomi Jacob. The offending literature was destroyed, as duly attested: "We the undersigned Customs Officers hereby certify that the four books covered by the above mentioned seizure were this date destroyed by fire, Dawson, Y.T., November 5, 1942, Sgd. F. Cederberg, John Williams." *Lady Chatterley's Lover* had also been burned.

The peak year for banning in the 1930s was 1935 when 95 titles were outlawed out of 1,380 books and periodicals examined. A few of the periodicals banned: *Parisien Life, Paris Magazine, La Paree Stories, Gay Parisienne, Paris Art, Allo-Paris, Spicy Stories, Spicy Detective Stories, Pep Stories, Snappy Stories, True Confessions, Tattle Tales, Stolen Sweets, Bedtime Stories for Grownups Only* and *Nus Fantastiques*; and these books (authors forgotten): *Synthetic Virgin, Professional Virgin, Impatient Virgin, The Virgin's Progress, Hotel Wife, Gin Wife, Rented Wife, Here is My Body, The Way of Some Flesh, What Price Virtue?, No Bed of her Own, Early to Bed, Three in a Bed, Let's Go Naked, On Going Naked, Naked Glory, Lady Chatterley's Husbands, Lady Chatterley's Friends* and *Anecdota Americana* (*"500 jokes for the smoker and those too timid to enter one"*).

The Toronto Globe, among other newspapers, annually commended the department for keeping "filthy literature" out of Canada. In December, 1932, collectors were warned that some prohibited books were getting into the country under false jackets. The Toronto collector had seized a banned book camouflaged under a paper cover titled *Rats and How to Destroy Them*.

The number of prohibited books rose to 124 in 1955 and this number was also reached in 1961 when those banned included *Candy, Passion Shack, Luxure et Tortures, Whips Incorporated* and *The Wife Swappers*. The revenue department gave the Library of Parliament a list with the instruction: "Confidential — not to be communicated to the press." This list carries triumphant, hand-written notes beside a few of the titles, such as "We have it!" Lately, the department has concentrated on trying to stem the flow of child pornography and its banned list (Schedule "C") now includes films and cassettes as well as books and periodicals.

Before formation of the department of industry, trade and commerce, Sim was one of the government's main advisers on export trade and was usually a member of Canadian delegations sent abroad. He was assistant to Euler when he made one of his first trips, to the League of Nations at Geneva, about 1929. Agnes Macphail, first woman Member of Parliament, was a member of the delegation. "We were booked at the Hotel de la Paix and, like a good secretary, I wanted to make sure Euler's room was in order. I found a woman in his bed, backed out hurriedly, and then thought, that looked like Agnes Macphail. It was Agnes Macphail. She had been given the room when Mr. and Mrs. Massey arrived unexpectedly from London and Mrs. Massey wanted a room overlooking the lake. Agnes was a school teacher and she had been in Paris a few weeks before and bought some clothes. I had the pleasure of escorting her to dances where, in her Parisian clothes, she didn't fit everybody's description at that time of a school teacher."

Sim said he received another lesson from Euler on the same trip: "When we travelled then, we had letters of credit. On that trip we had a $5,000 letter of credit from the Bank of Montreal (for the entire delegation of seven) and Euler made me look after the money, including all foreign currency. The letter was a beautiful document with seals. It went missing (I was carrying it in my hip pocket) and I thought it was the end of my career in government service. But Euler had it. He had picked it out of my pocket as a test on how well I looked after the public purse."

As deputy minister of national revenue, Sim was, by definition, an expert on the tariff. He said that Prime Minister Bennett at one time talked about a ten per cent reduction in the tariff and the British jumped to the assumption that Bennett was talking about reducing the Canadian tariff to five per cent from 15 per cent. They were furious when they discovered he was talking about a reduction of one tenth of 15 per cent.

Sim served five prime ministers — Bennett, King, St. Laurent, Diefenbaker and Pearson — and of them all preferred St. Laurent: "He was the most outgoing, the most honest and once he gave you his trust it was for good." Sim served twelve revenue ministers, finding J.L. Ilsley (1935-40) the most brilliant — and fearless.

"All our ministers were good. If they weren't when they arrived they were when they left. Ministers generally try to live up to your good opinion of them."

"If you give good government, it has a way of coming through to the public."

CHAPTER X

Customs and Excise in the West

The Governor and Company of Adventurers of England trading into Hudson's Bay" began operations in 1670. The company clung mainly to the shore of the bay — a rigorous enough task in itself — and was content to allow the Indians to come to its posts with their furs. It did not venture far inland until La Vérendrye and his two sons penetrated overland from Montreal, establishing Fort Rouge at the confluence of the Red and the Assiniboine in 1738. From there and from Fort La Reine (present-day Portage la Prairie) the Canadian traders pushed west along the Saskatchewan starting in 1742.

The pursuit of the fur trade from Montreal did not end with the death of New France. The North-West Company and others simply took up where the old charter French companies had left off. And though the Nor-Westers were soon engaged in bloody frontier warfare with an alarmed Hudson's Bay Company, by 1821 the two companies had buried the hatchet and amalgamated. Not long before, in 1812, Lord Selkirk had established his settlement on the Red River on a land grant obtained from the Hudson's Bay Company despite a view toward settlers that all the fur companies were agreed on: they didn't want permanent settlements dotting the plains. Settlements interfered with wide-ranging hunting and trapping. Here again was the old problem of New France: colonization detracted from the main pursuit, seeking furs.

Professor H.Y. Hind visited the Red River colony and afterward gave a lecture on the subject at the Mechanics Institute in Montreal. He was reported thus in the *Montreal Journal of Education*, December, 1858:

> Who would think of bringing soap from England through Hudson Bay, over 700 miles of barren, rocky country, to a country where tallow and ashes are thrown away? Why, it will be asked, has simple machinery not been introduced to work up the wool which is so easily produced? The answer is clear. A settled industrious life is incompatible with the pursuits of the hunter. A hunter's home is the prairie or the woods, and he can never afford to remain long in one spot. The necessities of the fur trade require pemmican and buffalo meat as well as the skins of the fur-bearing animals. And the buffalo require grazing grounds. To convert the brave and daring half-breed (Métis) hunters into quiet agriculturists or contented artisans might lay the

foundation of a great province; but it would endanger a most lucrative monopoly, and therefore it cannot be wondered that those who enjoy that monopoly should have endeavored to keep the settlement at Red River as the entrepot or station of a hunting establishment on the grandest scale, to which their employees might repair during the seasons when their services were not required in the field.

When Selkirk's venture collapsed, the Hudson's Bay Company repurchased all his rights, selling the land to the settlers if they would agree, among other things, not to traffic in furs. The Council of Assiniboia, administering an area within a 50-mile radius of Fort Garry (earlier known as Fort Rouge, The Forks, and Fort Gibraltar, and ultimately called Winnipeg) presided over the settlement, under a governor appointed by the company as early as 1814. The president of the council was George Simpson, Governor of Rupert's Land, that is, the vast territory of the Hudson's Bay Company from Labrador to the mouth of the Columbia. The council was the company, and the company was the council. We have already seen how the French charter companies operated the fur trade of New France with the assistance and backing of law *fabriqué en France*. But the Hudson's Bay Company wrote its own criminal and civil law. The laws were designed to support the fur trade and were enforced by a private army. After all, didn't the preamble to the English statute establishing the company declaim against the "evils" of any competition in the fur trade?

While there had been meetings of the council at Fort Garry devoted, in part at least, to empowering citizens to seize "unfenced" or "unringed" pigs and sell them, Governor Simpson's "preparatory address" of February 12, 1835 — a sort of throne speech — spoke of matters closer to the heart of Hudson's Bay Company interest. His own personal influence and that of the council were no longer sufficient, it seemed, to maintain the tranquillity and good government of the settlement. Therefore:

> In order to raise funds for defraying expenses as it may be necessary to incur towards the maintenance of tranquillity and enforcing due respect and obedience to the laws, rules and regulations which are at present in existence or which may be hereafter framed for the good government of the Settlement it is Resolved, 1st, that an import duty be levied at York on all goods, stores and Merchandise, of foreign produce or Manufacture which may be forwarded to Red River, either for sale or private use, except made up Clothes, books or other private personal baggage in use, of 7 1/2 per cent on the amount of Invoice, the Gentleman in charge of York Factory taking payment of the same forthwith or such guarantee or Security for the due payment thereof as he may consider necessary for the protection of the fur trade which will have to account for or pay over the said duty on the arrival of the goods at Red River to a Receiver to be hereafter appointed.

Duty was to be paid before delivery of the goods. Furthermore, there was to be an export duty of 7 1/2 per cent as well on all goods, stores and supplies produced or manufactured by the settlement.

In short, a private company had established a customs tariff for imports and exports, albeit in a territory over which it had been granted monopolistic trading rights. James Bird, a member of the council, was appointed receiver of import and export duties at £15 a year. A "military corps" of sixty officers and privates (one commanding officer, one sergeant-major, four sergeants and fifty-four privates, total annual pay £400) was established as a customs branch, primarily to stop smuggling, or, as the council put it, "supporting and enforcing laws, rules and regulations." Sixty customs officers for a population of 5,000 indicated that smuggling was widespread, not to say pervasive.

As a rule, the minutes of the Council of Assiniboia set out only actions taken, acknowledging few if any problems, and congratulating the parent Hudson's Bay Company for every purported favor granted. But smuggling became so prevalent that in 1836 the council lowered the import tariff to five per cent, just one year after imposing a 7 1/2-per-cent rate.

The company and council were nothing if not resourceful. When the smuggling of liquor into Assiniboia and the making of home brew both reached epidemic proportions in 1837, Governor Simpson announced that the company would build its own distillery. Then, to check the abuse of spiritous liquors produced by the company distillery, the council decided that there would be an excise duty of two shillings per gallon on top of the selling price of six shillings. In other words, customs revenue lost through smuggling was being neatly replaced by excise duty on liquor the company produced in the settlement. The revenue would go to the military corps, jail, court house, other public works and institutions. The tariffs on imports and exports were reduced to four per cent and Governor Simpson was to purchase twenty-five "well-finished" guns for the military corps.

In 1839, another twenty-five "well-finished" guns were ordered for the military corps, and there was a crackdown on home brew:

> No individual or individuals whatever other than the authorized servants of the Honourable Hudson's Bay Company shall distil or attempt to distil whisky or any other spirit out of malt or any other substance whether for his, her or their use, or for sale, or shall have in his, her or their possession any instrument, pipe or utensil specially adapted to distillation or actually employed in it by such individual or individuals under a penalty of ten pounds for each offence and the forfeiture of all such whisky or other spirit, all such malt and other substance and of every such instrument, pipe or utensil, half of the penalty to go to the informer.

For selling beer or liquor to the Indians, the penalty was £2 without appeal or, alternatively, imprisonment until the fine was paid. Apart from what was kept to board the offender in jail, the fine went to the informer, who was guaranteed at least half. In 1841, Collector Bird (his title had been changed from "receiver") was empowered to forbid any freighter at York Factory to land imports for any individual that he considered might delay or default in payment of import duty. Bird was also a magistrate. Nobody was allowed to plead ignorance of the law before him after eight copies of these regulations were fixed on pasteboard for distribution throughout the settlement.

By 1843, the number of protests and petitions against the company began to mount: the price of company liquor was too high; there were too many armed company police searching settlers' houses for furs; the trunks of merchants en route to Minnesota on business were being broken into by the police; marriage licences, which cost 20 shillings, now required an oath that neither partner was already married. Besides, in 1844, a competitor went into business at Pembina where the Hudson's Bay Company had been since 1801: Norman W. Kittson opened a trading post for the American Fur Company. Now the Métis and Selkirk colonists could sell their packages of contraband furs without travelling hundreds of miles to meet U.S. traders on the Missouri and Mississippi. Pembina was on the U.S. border less than a hundred miles from the Red River Settlement. Chief Factor Alexander Christie, Governor of Assiniboia, retaliated against the competition with a proclamation that the Hudson's Bay Company would no longer transport supplies from England to any settler unless he signed an oath that he had neither "directly nor indirectly trafficked in furs," that is, sold them to another company.

But disregard grew for the dictates of the Council of Assiniboia. It was suspected that most of the military corps was conniving at non-company trading in furs and smuggling of liquor and other goods. The corps was at first reduced in numbers, then disbanded altogether, being replaced by fifteen constables. There were complaints especially about import duties on goods from the United States because many types of farm implements brought in by the settlers were not then even manufactured in England. (In 1858, the company itself began importing goods through Minnesota as well as York Factory). A special meeting of the council was called at James Bird's request to consider what to do about importers who refused to pay duty on American goods. The minute records: "The Council declined sharing with the collector any part of the responsibility." Bird resigned soon after and was replaced by Alexander Ross, the governor of the jail, who held both jobs concurrently. The company was able to persuade the British government to send troops to Red River on the vague pretext of some external threat. The only threat to the company was internal: the soldiery themselves created problems and on January 15, 1847, the council decreed a fine for any person encouraging a soldier to be absent from barracks. The fine was £5 plus five shillings for each hour the soldier was absent and for each mile between absent soldier and barracks. There was also a £5 fine for selling liquor to a soldier.

The council then tried some relaxation in customs duties. Residents were allowed to import £50 worth of goods duty-free once a year for their own use and export duty-free up to £10 worth. Farm implements were made exempt from duty. But fines were increased for making or having illicit (that is, non-company) spirits. The company tinged its liquor with "a peculiar hue not easily imitated," according to the council, to try to block facsimiles. The governor would grant retail liquor licences providing the licensees did not allow their premises "to become common nuisances in the way of tippling." The customs collector was to be paid at new rates: four per cent of duties collected, 12 per cent of fines imposed for not paying duty. A petition for lower duties on American goods was dismissed on the grounds that it "abounds in imputations and opinions which are equally irrelevant and erroneous."

The Council of Assiniboia vacillated from one extreme to another. On May 20, 1847, it approved importation of liquor from the United States on payment of duty of two shillings a gallon on top of the regular tariff of four per cent of cost plus one shilling a gallon. On November 18, 1847, it banned any liquor imports from the States. Ross resigned as the collector and the council gave him a pat on the back in these words: "He is entitled to the best thanks of this Council and of the community in general for the polite and considerate mode in which he has performed his occasionally difficult and invidious duties." Then it jacked up the duty on American imports to ten per cent from four. The next year, it put it back at four per cent. The privilege of importing a stove free of duty was made contingent on a declaration that the importer had never encouraged a soldier to be absent from barracks without a pass. The English traveller H.J. Warre recorded in his journal from Fort Garry: "The Company are the Complete Lords of the Manor, set the prices, issue their own money and make their own profits upon all imports, receiving skins and peltries from the Indians and Half Breeds at a regulated price which is such as to afford them larger returns on their imports . . . I fear the Settlement never can flourish as long as the Company have completely the sway and regulation of everything."

The charter of the Hudson's Bay Company had had, of course, to be renewed by the British Parliament from time to time. The British Commons had held an inquiry in 1749 at which all the company witnesses testified that yes, the Indians had been treated well, had been given medicine and food, had been sheltered in the factories (trading posts — the factory was the residence of the factor) and no, there had been no complaints from the Indians about trade items, which included guns, powder, hatchets, knives, kettles, tobacco, coats and blankets. There was scant information, however, on company profits. For instance, a Mr. Hayes, a company clerk for four years, was called before the special Commons committee. Question: "Have [you] not taken an oath to keep the secrets of the company?" Answer: "Yes." That ended Hayes' testimony.

In 1846, at the time of the British-American dispute over the Oregon Territory, some Red River settlers, disgusted with the heavy-handed rule of the Hudson's Bay Company, sent a petition to the United States seeking annexation of their community. On May 31, Major William B. Caldwell, Governor of Assiniboia, (a man who may be remembered by auditors of the world for his financial statement of December 9, 1852, in which he said the books showing revenue and expenses of the Red River Settlement were "pretty nearly balanced") called a special meeting to deal with the complaints of the Red River settlers. These complaints now went far beyond those concerning customs duties, the fur trade and liquor traffic. They had to do with lawful assembly, with language rights in the court house and in the council, and with the need for Métis representation on the council. Now, with the company charter coming up for renewal again in 1858, the settlers saw another opportunity. In 1857, they sent a petition, signed by 575 persons, to the Legislative Assembly of Canada, accusing the company of usurpation of authority and seeking protection of the Canadian law and "the same liberty and freedom of commerce" enjoyed by other British subjects.

The company's reaction was to ask for more troops and to manufacture an external threat. Simpson told London that one hundred U.S. soldiers had arrived at Pembina on the frontier, and were making preparations for a permanent garrison to prevent Red River Métis and settlers from hunting buffalo and trapping furs south of the border. The company offered to pay for transporting the troops to Red River. A 120-man contingent of the Royal Canadian Rifles was sent, by sailing ship to York Factory and by open boat to Fort Garry. Major George Seton of the Rifles went immediately to Pembina. He found that the U.S. detachment had numbered only forty and that it had returned after a month to Fort Ripley, 400 miles from Pembina, and had never come back. Rather than having had to deal with any supposed U.S. incursion, the Hudson's Bay Company had obviously seized on the pretext of a small reconnoitering party of U.S. troops making its first visit to the frontier, in order to get a military force to the Red River to quell a possible internal uprising. Once arrived, the Canadian contingent stayed for four years.

Meanwhile, the legislature of the United Province of Canada struck a special committee to collect information on the charter rights of the Hudson's Bay Company, and the government sent two parties under S.J. Dawson and Professor Hind to the North West. Both reported widespread discontent among the Red River inhabitants resulting from company mismanagement of public affairs. Witnesses before the special committee testified that despite efforts of the company to enforce an exclusive trade monopoly, some 1,200 Red River carts were expected to carry $100,000 worth of furs to St. Paul in the summer of 1857. George Gladman, born at a company post on the Moose River in 1802 and in the company's service for thirty-one years, said that there was no fixed or regular tariff for trading with the Indians. The success of trade and the welfare of the Indians depended almost entirely on the judgment and management of the individual factors. The company had, in effect, three prices: one where there was no competition, one where competition was possible, and one where competition existed. For instance, in 1829, on the west coast, the company had traded one gun for 18 skins and one blanket for five skins. But when two American vessels showed up at Fort George on the Columbia, offering a gun for six skins and a blanket for two, the company immediately reduced its rate to that of the Americans — and sent parties far inland to buy furs at its old rate before the Indians heard of the American offer.

There were varied political forces at play on the Red River in the mid-eighteen-hundreds: the movement to join Canada; a desire to be a separate British colony; advocacy for annexation by the United States; and the passionate movement, with a heavy lacing of racial, religious and language aspiration, for a Métis republic. Before the Métis leader, Louis Riel, had done more than set up his provisional government, the Canadian government felt obliged to acquire the territory and put it under its own jurisdiction. Assiniboia, for more than two hundred years the property and trading monopoly of the Hudson's Bay Company, became, in 1870, (at a price) the property of Canada and the province of Manitoba.

To central and eastern Canadians of the 1870s, western Canada, or the North West as it was then called, stretched vaguely from the Great Lakes to the Rockies, a terra incognita of Indians, Métis and some whites, mainly fur traders and dirt farmers in the Selkirk Settlement on the Red River. Manitoba, tiny in extent compared with today's province, was politically as well as geographically central to the future of Canada as a nation stretching from sea to sea. When it came into Confederation, Manitoba was excused the Canadian customs tariff for four years; in the meantime, the lower rates set by the Council of Assiniboia applied. (Assiniboia's revenues in 1867-68 amounted to £1,816 of which £708 came from the Hudson's Bay Company itself as the chief importer.) After thirty-five years of grumbling about the Hudson's Bay Company customs duties, the territory that was now Manitoba was glad to submit to them for a while longer.

Imposition of customs tariffs there had not only been assumed by private companies; private individuals had tried a hand at it, too. In January, 1868, Thomas Spence had declared establishment of the Republic of Manitoba with himself as president and the seat of government at Portage la Prairie. He needed revenue, of course, so he established a customs tariff. Unfortunately, his largest potential taxpayer, the Hudson's Bay Company, refused to pay. Spence's republic collapsed after a few weeks, when a man accused of treason for protesting against the customs duties was rescued forcibly from jail by friends. Spence went into the salt business on the shores of Lake Manitoba.

The first Canadian government customs collector at Winnipeg was G.B. Spencer, a native of Cobourg, Ontario, appointed December 1, 1870, who managed in his first year to get his monthly office rent down to $9.73 from $19.46.

With a base for authority on the prairies in the form of the new province of Manitoba, Canada began to assert itself across the plains to the distant Rockies. It was a slow and painful process whose outcome sometimes appeared doubtful in the face of the American menace of Manifest Destiny, or subjugation of all North America. The authority of the government of Canada gained its significance from its being the first acknowledgeable authority of any kind on the plains, in conditions, moreover, which might seem to have begged for it. There was an untrammelled trade in liquor, run by Americans, but operating in what might be considered Canadian territory, and with certain tragic results. The Indians were losing their last wealth, the buffalo robe, while being debauched by whisky runners from the Dakotas and Montana — a camp of thirty Assiniboines was butchered in the Cypress Hills by a gang of brigands operating out of Fort Benton on the Upper Missouri. Seven miles from today's Lethbridge, Alberta, Fort Hamilton, named for its original American founder, was renamed Fort Whoop-up in 1869 because of its carousing. There were other American-built liquor posts, as they were called, at Spitzee, Stand-Off, Slide-Out, Kipp, High River, and Sheep Creek. (Stand-Off, built in 1871 at the junction of the Belly and Waterton Rivers, was named by its builders for standing off a U.S. marshal who tried to seize their whisky in Montana.)

Conceived as a remedy for these conditions, a bill was presented in

Parliament by Prime Minister John A. Macdonald, on April 23, 1873, establishing a police force in the North West Territories. In late October, three 50-man troops of the North West Mounted Police reached Red River after a trip over the Dawson Route from the head of Lake Superior. The three troops trained at Lower Fort Garry during the winter and in the spring were joined by three more. On July 8, 1874, 274 men set out across the plains from Dufferin (Emerson), headquarters of the International Boundary Commission, with oxcarts, cattle for slaughter, two field pieces, two mortars, portable forges, wheeled kitchens and mowing machines. Three troops made a round trip of 1,959 miles in four months without the loss of a man. The other three pushed on to Fort Whoop-Up, which was flying the U.S. flag but was almost deserted because word of the redcoats had preceded them, and by mid-October were building Fort Macleod, so named for the commander, Assistant Commissioner James F. Macleod, on Old Man's River within sight of the Rockies.

The Boundary Commission had marked out the 49th parallel on the prairies in 1872-74. But the rude border marks, some of them mounds of dirt, did not in themselves halt or restrain the casual crossings of the Indian, explorer, missionary, fur trader or whisky runner who came and went as he pleased. The arrival of the North West Mounted Police changed all that, and more swiftly than perhaps even the prime minister had thought possible.

The Mounties were not the first prairie frontier force on the 49th parallel. British and Canadian troops, as we have seen, were twice stationed in the Selkirk Settlement in the mid-eighteen-hundreds and in 1870 a company of the 1st Ontario Rifles was sent to Pembina because Lieutenant-Governor Adams G. Archibald of Manitoba expressed some anxiety that the Americans might interfere with steamships and other supply boats coming down the Red River to Fort Garry. These fears proved groundless, and the unit was soon withdrawn.

The first collector at Emerson was F.T. Bradley, a young adventurer from Ontario. He bought up 200 acres north of the new townsite and was not averse to advising businessmen and home buyers arriving by the Red River, as nearly all immigrants did then, about good available land. He also became a director of the Emerson and Northwestern Railroad and was on the board of the Southern Manitoba Loan Company. His promising career was cut short in 1883 when he was arrested for embezzling $4,000 from Customs. There was considerable evidence the theft was committed by two of Bradley's staff, who fled to the United States. Bradley shot himself to death in 1884 as his case came to trial. His wife and four sons had been carried off in an epidemic five years before.

The immediate objective given the NWMP by the government in 1874 was to destroy the liquor traffic, gain the respect and confidence of the Indians, collect customs duties, and carry out all regular police duties. It might be said that the first duty ever carried out by the NWMP from their first permanent post on the prairies was taking charge of Customs and Excise. For evidence, we have Assistant Commissioner Macleod's letter sent October 30, 1874, from Fort Macleod to Commissioner G.A. French at Fort Garry: "Sir, I am happy to be enabled to inform you that although we have all been very busy in the construction of our winter quarters, we have been able to carry on some police duty as well, and have struck a first blow at the liquor traffic in this country."

Macleod went on to describe in some detail this "first blow": an Indian named Three Bulls had tipped him off that an American, William Bond, had traded a couple of gallons of whisky for two horses at Pine Coulé about fifty miles from the fort. Macleod had selected his ten best men and horses and sent them out with Jerry Potts, guide and interpreter, with orders to seize all robes and furs believed to have been traded for liquor and enough goods and chattels "to satisfy the fine which in each case might be imposed." Macleod added that he didn't see any other way to collect fines in event of a guilty conviction. The patrol returned after a two-day ride, bringing in Bond and four others who had had in their possession two wagons, each containing cases of alcohol, and sixteen horses, five Henry rifles, five revolvers and one hundred and sixteen buffalo robes.

"I confiscated the robes and tried each of the prisoners for having intoxicating liquors in their possession," the commander wrote. He fined Bond and two others $200 each and the other two $50 each. The next day a Fort Benton businessman, J.B. (Waxey) Weatherwax, paid all the fines except Bond's. Bond was also charged for trading liquor to Macleod's informant, Three Bulls. He couldn't raise the fine money so Macleod held his horse, rifle and revolver although "they will of course not realize the full amount of the fine so Bond will undergo imprisonment." Macleod also reported that Three Bulls brought him a horse as a present: "I of course refused to take the horse, telling him that it was not considered right for a judge to take any presents from a party who had a case before him. He was in great distress at my refusal." He concluded: "I have got word today of some concealed liquor which I expect to get hold of and only hope I may be able to get hold of the owners too. The place where liquors are concealed is called in the slang of the country a 'Cache.' If I happen to use this word hereafter you'll know what I mean. I have the honor to be, Sir, Your obedient servant, James F. Macleod, Assistant Commissioner."

In the very next letter, December 4, Macleod reported good reason to believe that a large quantity of whisky was "cached" near Fort Kipp. Thirteen men had been sent there to get hay and to uncover the liquor. Later in the same letter (letters were infrequent and sometimes composed in fits and starts over a period of days or weeks, with plenty of time for afterthoughts) Macleod declared, perhaps a little prematurely:

> I am happy to be able to report the complete stoppage of the whisky trade throughout the whole of this section of the country, and that the drunken riots, which in former years were almost of a daily occurrence, are now entirely at an end; in fact, a more peaceable community than this, with a very large number of Indians camped along the river, could not be found anywhere. Everyone united in saying how wonderful the change is. People never lock their doors at night, and have no fear of anything being stolen, which is left lying about outside, whereas just before our arrival gates and doors were all fastened at night and nothing could be left out of sight. So strong was the Indian's passion for whisky, they could not be kept out of traders' houses by locks and bars; they have been known to climb up on the roofs and endeavor to make their way through the earth with which the houses are covered, and in some instances they slid down through the chimneys. The Rev. Mr. McDougall has been paying us a visit. He is delighted at the change that has been effected. He tells me that he believes there are some traders still on Bow River. If Walsh brings back the horses I asked the Government to allow me, I shall pay them a visit before many weeks pass.

In another letter dated the same day, December 4, Macleod regretted extremely to report that the whisky trader, Bond, had escaped. A sentry had fired at him but missed. The two men responsible for guarding Bond were reduced in rank.

A sober account of the darker side of the NWMP role is given in a letter sent by Dr. R.B. Nevitt, assistant surgeon to the force, from Belly River, October 11, 1874: "This is a wild, wild region. We are right up in the country of the Blackfeet Indians, surrounded on various sides by the forts of the whisky traders, against whom we have come — men of the most degraded and desperate character, who make their money by selling the rankest poison to the poor Indian."

Five months later, on March 2, Nevitt reported home: "Two wagons from High River came in this evening with the news of a murder and brought the body of the murdered man — struck on the head with a bar of iron and died after three or four days' suffering. The murderer is not to be found. Another whisky trader has also been routed out of the place and his stock seized, so we are doing some good."

Not everybody had as keen an appreciation of Fort Macleod as the police did. Charles John Brydges, land commissioner of the Hudson's Bay Company, visited the fort in 1882 and wrote: "This is a Mounted

Police station and one of the most wretched places I have seen. It is on a spit of sand, where the wind appears to be perpetually blowing a hurricane. The condition of the atmosphere is consequently almost unbearable." Brydges also said that the bulk of goods came from Montreal because the cost of transportation (4 1/2 cents a pound) was cheaper than the tariff on imported U.S. supplies.

Near the end of 1874, Macleod reported receipt of his first dispatch from his superiors. It was from the Department of Justice in Ottawa, informing him he had been appointed a preventive officer in Her Majesty's Customs. Macleod added: "I have already taken inventories of the stocks at several posts about here, and intend tomorrow to proceed to Forts Kipp and Hamilton to do the same there, and to enter a lot of goods which are arriving." In other words, all merchandise arriving from Montana was going to be subjected to the Canadian tariff. "Waxey" Weatherwax himself was caught by the Mounties in February, 1875, for trading whisky for Indian buffalo robes and went to jail for six months. He was brought in by a patrol which had spent eighteen days on the prairie, converting its wagon to a sleigh when it was caught in a blizzard and telling time by the sun because all watches had been sent to Helena, Montana, for cleaning after the dusty summer trip on horseback from Manitoba.

Fort Benton was the most westerly point on the Missouri River reached by steamer and therefore a centre for the trade in furs and buffalo hides. The .240-mile trail from Fort Benton to Fort Whoop-Up and Fort Macleod served until 1885 when the railway was completed from Medicine Hat to Coal Banks (Lethbridge). Most of the supplies for the ranchers, storekeepers and police went over the trail by ox and mule team. A bull train took fourteen to twenty days to travel from Fort Benton to Fort Macleod. A train comprised eight to ten teams, each team with six to twelve yokes (pairs) of oxen pulling three wagons.

John Peter Turner, the RCMP's historian from 1939 until his death in 1948, said this of the NWMP's ability to do police work while checking smuggling, collecting Customs, delivering the mail, issuing marriage licences and death certificates, and acting as justices of the peace: it had raised the West from infancy to adulthood, and done so with "no great generals, no regiments of soldiery, no merciless cavalry, no prodigious munitions of war, no armed suppression." The allusion to American methods couldn't have been clearer.

The whisky running might not have been completely stamped out as Macleod claimed in his 1874 letter to headquarters, but we have early testimony about how effective the NWMP was as a customs service. John George (Kootenai) Brown, soldier, scout, rancher, prospector (gold and oil), game warden, lawman, buffalo hunter, mail rider and founder of Waterton Lakes National Park, was a trader on Lower Waterton in 1876. He recalled in later life: "Our customers were Indians, mostly Kootenais, Nez Percés and Flatheads from the Flathead Reservation in Montana. Customs regulations didn't bother them but we didn't sell much whisky to the Indians although a good deal of it was consumed on the premises. To sell to the Indians was too risky a proposition though it yielded much profit."

Fort Walsh, built by and named for James M. Walsh, Macleod's righthand man, was put up in 1875 in the Cypress Hills 160 miles east of Fort Macleod and near the site of the Assiniboine massacre by the Hardwick gang. Fort Calgary, named for Macleod's birthplace in Scotland, was built in the same year. (Macleod had rejected the first name, Brisebois, chosen by Inspector E.A. Brisebois.)

The most famous immigrants of the time were Chief Sitting Bull and his four thosand Sioux followers who arrived in what is now southern Saskatchewan after wiping out General George Custer and his U.S. cavalrymen at the Battle of the Little Big Horn in 1876. The Mounties watched over the Sioux until Sitting Bull gave himself up to U.S. authorities in 1881. The Mounties had had good relations with the prairie Indians since the solemn hand-shaking, December 1, 1874, between Chief Crowfoot of the Blackfoot Confederacy and Assistant Commissioner Macleod.

From NWMP annual reports we have an account of customs collections by the Mounties in their early years on the prairies. In the first ten months of 1876, for example, revenue collected at Fort Macleod amounted to $16,324; in the first nine months at Fort Walsh, $5,584. In that year more than 40,000 buffalo robes were shipped south. The revenue at Fort Walsh in 1880 was $17,233, but it plunged to $6,870 the following year when I.G. Baker and Company of Fort Benton closed its business at the fort. Exports were nil: the plains buffalo had been decimated. Fort Walsh was torn down in 1884, to be rebuilt in 1944. Fort Macleod collected $33,526 in 1882 and Qu'appelle $1,076. The next year, $50,501 was collected at Fort Macleod, where the customs department took over in 1886, and $27,417 at Maple Creek. It was a measure of how the west was growing.

For their services as customs and excise collectors, the Mounties were paid commissions of ten per cent by Customs. On a small, one-man post, this could mean an annual nest-egg of about $250. Macleod's salary was $1,600 a year and a constable's one dollar a day. The NWMP also issued a "let pass" for any Canadian wishing to go to the United States and to get back into Canada. The Wood Mountain, Saskatchewan, detachment, for instance, issued 110 "let passes" covering 172 persons in the summer of 1912. (Eventually, when the telegraph line reached Wood Mountain from Moose Jaw in 1885, telegraph operator Jim Thompson also filled in as customs officer and Indian agent. This permitted the Mounties in that district to get back to their main job of catching horse thieves and cattle rustlers.)

There is a saying that "work flows to the competent man until he submerges." That nearly happened to the NWMP, as one federal department after another found work for the Mounties to do on the western plains. The department of Indian affairs required an escort for treaty payments and patrols of Indian reserves; the department of the Interior asked help in the prevention and reporting of forest and prairie fires; the department of Railways and Canals needed protection for the railway builders against sabotage and looting; the department of Agriculture in 1893 charged the force with supervision of livestock quarantine regulations. This last duty entailed not only the establishment of quarantine stations across the prairies but driving thousands of head of American stock back across the border to prevent them from spreading anthrax, glanders and scab. And then there were the onerous duties for the department of Inland Revenue.

Some policemen were annoyed that they were assigned to border points mainly to collect money. Some NWMP outposts were established as customs preventive stations and later became regular customs houses manned primarily in the early years by members of the force. For instance, the Saskatchewan detachment at Marienthal (earlier at nearby Dupuis and today at Torquay) found itself opposite the frontier town of Ambrose, North Dakota, one of the largest grain-shipping points in the world in the early 1900s. Superintendent G.E. Sanders at Regina reported in 1909: "Cpl. S. Church at Marienthal reports that his detachment is more of a Customs office than a police department, and I would strongly recommend that arrangements be made for the Customs to take over this office with their own men as soon as possible." Customs took over in March, 1910. The force — which was granted the prefix "Royal" in 1904 and became the Royal Canadian Mounted Police in 1920 — was still manning some customs houses on the prairies as late as the First World War when many Mounties were sent overseas, leaving Customs the choice of staffing the posts or abandoning them. To this day, the RCMP still acts as the customs and immigration service in many settlements in the Arctic.

In its early days on the prairies, the Mounties received most of their supplies from I.G. Baker through Fort Benton — as well as their mail and their pay. The orders were placed by the Department of the Interior. A typical 1880 order covering Forts Macleod, Walsh and Saskatchewan and

Wood Mountain, Battleford and Qu'Appelle carried these prices: beef 4 3/4 cents a pound, bacon 13 1/2, flour 6, tea 50, coffee 23, sugar 14 1/2, beans 6 1/2, rice 8, salt 4 1/4, pepper 25, potatoes 3 1/4, oatmeal 6 1/2, coal oil 48 cents a gallon, oats $3.74 per 100 pounds, hay $10.75 a ton, and bran 3 3/4 cents a pound. The delivery price depended on the length of the haul by bull train.

Customs posts were not static. They were moved around as developments warranted. Some were established to assist the pioneers: as one district was settled, the customs office would be closed and transferred to another where settlement was beginning. The border posts also changed to fit trans-frontier railway and road construction. The first international train service was between Montreal and Portland, Maine, in the 1840s but it was 1877 before international trains were required to report to Customs like vessels and carriages. The Canadian Pacific and the St. Paul and Pacific began between St. Paul and Winnipeg in 1878; the main line of the Canadian Pacific reached Winnipeg from Thunder Bay in 1882 and the Pacific coast in 1885; the Northern Pacific began operating from Emerson to Winnipeg in 1888 with branches to Portage La Prairie and Brandon. Customs houses changed location accordingly. In 1906, there was a customs office at Bannerman, Manitoba — in the railway station — to serve the Brandon, Saskatchewan and Hudson's Bay Railway Company from St. John, North Dakota, to Brandon. It closed in 1936 when the railway tracks were torn up. In 1908, Big Muddy, Saskatchewan, was a border animal quarantine station where the customs collectors were veterinarians. It closed in 1936 when the quarantine station was abandoned. The customs office at Blairmore, Alberta, served the coal mining community there from 1913. It was closed in 1958 as the mines gradually shut down. The customs office at Bridesville, British Columbia, also in the railway station, operated from 1907 to 1939 to serve the Vancouver, Victoria and Eastern, and the Washington and Great Northern Railways. The station was destroyed by fire and all the customs records were lost, a common occurrence in Canadian customs history. Chesterfield Inlet on the west side of Hudson Bay was a customs post from 1926 until 1939. It closed with the opening of Port Churchill, but was reopened in 1953 with construction of the distant early warning radar line in the Canadian Arctic.

In 1890, when the railway arrived at Coutts, on the border sixty miles south of Lethbridge, Fort Macleod was still the only major customs port on the western prairies. Seven miles east of the old Whoop-Up Trail, Coutts was made an outport that year. The town is named after Baroness Angela Burdett-Coutts, philanthropist, friend of Charles Dickens and substantial stockholder in the Alberta Railway and Coal Company which laid the rail to carry coal from the Galt Mines at Lethbridge to Great Falls, Montana. (Burdett, Alberta, took its name from the first barrel of her family name). The railway station at Coutts straddled the boundary and housed both Canada and U.S. Customs and Immigration.

The station itself caused one of the first customs problems at Coutts. The customs officer in charge, Edwin Allen, reported in October, 1890, that ninety-six feet of the station was on the Canadian side and twenty-five feet on the American, and that the builder was seeking a refund of $62.93 duty paid to Canada on $478.90 worth of American materials used for construction on the American side. Canada kept the duty and the railway reimbursed the builder.

The next month, Allen was writing to E.T. Galt, manager of the company, to complain that railway employees were smuggling liquor into Canada and selling it in Lethbridge. He had found ten gallons of whisky in the tool box of engine No. 17 (engineer, William O'Neil) and was compelled to recommend a $400 fine against the company. However, he would reduce the fine to $100 if Galt would agree to crack down on smuggling by his employees. The company accepted and the fine came out of O'Neil's pay.

Much of Allen's work, and that of his successors, was taken up trying to keep track of enormous American cattle herds grazing in Canada. Allen reported January 2, 1891, that he had ridden twenty-five miles west on a Sunday (there were no trains that day) to visit a "camp of cowboys" attending a U.S. herd on what he believed was the Canadian side of the border. He judged the camp itself to be one mile south of the boundary, though he couldn't say for certain because he couldn't locate any mounds, a reference to the earthen mounds which were supposed to mark the frontier. Another camp sixty-five miles farther west was rounding up 20,000 cattle, at least half of which were in Canada. And east of Coutts, the St. Louis Cattle Company had 10,000 head, all in Canada north of the Sweetgrass Hills.

On February 24, 1891, Allen seized thirty gallons of liquor on car No. 288 of the Alberta Railway and Coal Company. On April 18, he found four bottles of liquor in the water tank in the caboose of Train No. 6. In August, he exchanged posts with W.J. Cooper of Killarney, Manitoba, because there was no school for his children in Coutts.

Henry Tennant took over as customs collector in 1893. He was former Conservative MP for West Lynne, Manitoba, and was also the postmaster, keeping the mail in an apple box beside his customs desk. The Americans in adjoining Sweetgrass, Montana, Coutts' U.S. counterpart, also picked up their mail from Tennant. Tennant had even more trouble than Allen with living conditions. In December, 1895, he reported that the wind blew through and under his rented house. He blamed the draughty house for his wife's illness and sent her to Winnipeg for treatment. He sent the rest of his family to Lethbridge to live.

On April 28, 1896, Tennant reported to George H. Young, inspector of ports at Winnipeg, that he had ridden to the south fork of the Milk River to collect duty on cattle and horses belonging to Mormons James Cunningham and William McIntyre who had bought one and a third townships on the north side of the Milk for ranching. The two Americans had 3,089 head of cattle and forty-two horses. He had allowed them thirty-two head duty-free as settlers and collected $6,319.70, accepting a cheque drawn on the Union Bank, Lethbridge, which he had immediately sent to the collector at Calgary.

On August 6, Tennant reported the arrival of another party of "refugee Canadian Indians" under an escort of one troop of the 10th U.S. cavalry. There were several cases of measles among the Indians and he had telegraphed for a doctor. "This makes the fifth party of Indian refugees, 526 all told, brought home by U.S. troops," Tennant wrote.

Later that month Tennant said 100,000 head of U.S. cattle were roaming in Canada: "The whole country seemed to be alive with cattle." The NWMP were driving them back across the border but they had difficulty getting enough horses, and Canadian settlers' cattle had to be cut out of the herd. The police were taking a man from each detachment along the border as range riders. On April 27, 1897, Tennant said a line rider named Thompson stationed at Writing-on-Stone had just resigned: "He got the winter through very easy and now the actual work begins he leaves."

An appointment to Coutts could present its incumbent with the drawbacks of the frontier well into this century: on November 4, 1921, W.B. Rose, inspector-in-charge at Coutts, wrote to his superior in Winnipeg: "I presume nothing has been done yet in the way of having a lavatory installed. I built a temporary one, myself, which blows over every time we have a windstorm, which is often in this part of the country. There was no lavatory of any kind on the premises when I came here. Will you please give me authority to purchase a Sanitary Chemical Closet, at a cost of about $12, which may be connected to the chimney flue leading from the furnace." The request was granted.

Coutts and Sweetgrass, like so many other border communities, have been close to each other by inclination as well as geography. The first private dwelling in Coutts was occupied by a U.S. customs officer. The water tank for both communities was in Sweetgrass. The first school in Sweetgrass had Alberta pupils and the hospital, Alberta patients. Once, when a U.S. president died, the Stars and Stripes was flown at half-mast at Canadian Customs because the U.S. customs house had no flag pole. There have been or still are an international service club, international oilfield male chorus, international study club, international Campfire Girls and international drum and bugle corps. Oil refineries were built in Coutts in the early 1920s but vanished in the depression of the 1930s. Families moved — and had their houses moved with them. But Coutts became an important port of entry when the Alaska Highway was built in 1942 and the modern highway between Coutts and Lethbridge is part of the Alaska system. A new Canadian customs house was opened in 1952. There is also an air strip right on the border immediately west of town. Coutts is now the centre of a prosperous ranching area in the short-grass country of southern Alberta. Fort Macleod has been restored. The most-used border crossing in the long stretch between Coutts and Emerson is North Portal, Saskatchewan. It originated as a customs station in 1893 mainly to service railway traffic. Pre-clearance of passengers became standard practice: the Canadian customs inspector boarded Canada-bound trains at Minot, North Dakota, the American inspector boarded U.S.-bound trains at Weyburn, Saskatchewan.

But many of the border points on the prairies are still almost as lonely as the plains were when the Mounties rode west in 1874. A complaint came in from a member of the public in 1980 about the length of time it was taking travellers to clear one remote, one-person frontier point. It turned out that the customs officer was detaining the infrequent travellers as long as he decently could just so that he had someone to talk to.

It used to be a requirement on lonely posts that the customs officer keep a diary. Unfortunately, very few of these have survived; most of them rotted away with the log cabins in which they were laboriously written by candlelight or kerosene lamp. The diaries were mainly a record of the weather and the goings and comings of people across the border. One diary which miraculously survived, thanks to Herbert Legg, who wrote a history of customs service in western Canada, is that of Frederick Davis Shaw. Some excerpts follow from Shaw's diary kept at St. Mary's, near Cardston, Alberta, in 1896:

> January 2. Cold still, 12 below last night. Posted notice for sale of seized horse branded DE left shoulder on December 26th. Auction took place this 2 p.m. No one at auction so bid animal in for amount of duty. Couldn't destroy him and could not be responsible for him longer and I have ridden over 50 miles after him.
>
> May 18. Returned at 6:30 p.m. and still storming. Met parties from the north going out said they might have known what kind of a country they were coming to by the poverty-stricken government officials at the line.

August 20. No money to be had in Cardston to cash cheque in Union Bank. Will send cheque to Calgary.

December 31. Party reported to me that Mr. Lee of Cardston had gone into the States about September last and returned to Cardston a few days ago with a new saddle. At once I notified the police to have this man brought before me to answer questions.

Shaw, born in 1856, at Kentville, Nova Scotia, was a dentist but joined the North West Mounted Police as a constable in 1880 and pulled a tooth for Sitting Bull. He was a travelling civilian dentist for ten years in Macleod, Lethbridge and Pincher Creek. He joined the customs service in 1895, was at St. Mary's until 1902, at Cardston until 1908, and was promoted from there to collector at Lethbridge, where he died in 1926.

Often only one customs officer and one Mountie covered the entire border from Coutts to Newgate, British Columbia. The frontier customs building was a combined office and residence, the latter consisting of a living room, kitchen and two bedrooms — and usually a small barn for the government horse. The office had direct access from outside. At Whisky Gap, Alberta, named for an old smuggling trail through a coulee, the first customs office was in a windowless storage room in a lumber yard. At night, what traffic there was stopped at the farm four miles away where Collector Frank Freeman stayed. The office was moved to a tent at Del Bonita in 1939 until a building could be put up. Whisky Gap, twenty miles southeast of Cardston, was opened to accommodate wheat growers in northern Montana. It cut their delivery mileage to a grain elevator from forty to fifteen miles. (There is a modern parallel. Customs offices are kept open along the remote Quebec-Maine border to accommodate American loggers taking their timber out of Maine through Canada.)

In the southeastern corner of Alberta, at Wild Horse, the customs service dates from 1904 when NWMP constables lived under canvas in summer and boarded with a rancher in winter. Customs officer Jesse Jarman recalled in later years that there was only one house between Wild Horse and Pendant d'Oreille, a distance of twenty-five miles, and that in 1908 the two detachments met at that house on horseback every Saturday to exchange mail. Pinhorn, Alberta, fifty miles east of Coutts, was regarded as the most isolated customs post on the prairies. The nearest post office was in Laird, Montana, ten miles away, and the nearest Canadian village was Foremost, forty miles away. A customs house was established there in 1913 but it was finally closed in 1929 when the officer, presumably out of loneliness, simply moved out and set up office on a farm where at least there was some company. The office was then re-established at nearby Aden, which wasn't much better. The first man lasted ten months. A farmer filled in for nearly two years, operating out of his farm at Grassy

Butte. The next man could endure only five months and the office was closed. The son of the postmistress at Aden was persuaded to take the job and he lasted a year. In 1934 a combined office and residence was built.

Another isolated post was Flathead, British Columbia. The log-cabin customs house was opened in 1904, closed in 1905, and re-opened in 1914. T.F. Fitzgerald, not long out of eastern Canada, couldn't stand the loneliness and left in one week. A new three-room cabin was built and William Roberts and his wife stayed for nine years until 1923 — and left only because their son needed schooling. Roberts walked in summer and snow-shoed in winter 102 miles to Belton, Montana, to mail his customs reports. In 1920, a new rural mail route in Montana brought Flathead within easy nine-mile reach. Groceries came in by wagon road from Corbin, British Columbia, and Roberts had to order enough in the fall to do him until the following July. He shot game and trapped and fished.

Trading into or through the Canadian north goes back more than three hundred years, when the Hudson's Bay Company built Moose Factory on James Bay in 1673. The company factor there was the customs collector from 1874 until service ended in 1939. From the outset, York Factory had been the great coastal depot of the company's fur trade. Goods received for trading in 1684 at York comprised: 300 guns, 185 barrels of shot, 29 1/2 dozen powder horns, 3,000 jack knives, 2,000 hatchets, 3,000 large knives, 2,000 small knives, 15 gross of tobacco pipes, 5,000 rolls of tobacco, 247 hogsheads of leaf tobacco, two gross of scissors, 252 brass kettles, 20 pieces of calico, two gross of lace, eight pieces of canvas, 350 yards of cloth, 390 blankets, 543 coats, two dozen shoes, 80 caps, 10 pounds of paint, three gross of ivory combs. The last season of any importance at York Factory was 1873 because from that time on the Hudson's Bay Company switched to inland railway and steamship for transporting goods.

After Manitoba became part of Confederation in 1870, the first Canadian customs officer in the north was James Fortescue, the Hudson's Bay Company's chief factor at York Factory. This led to a situation where Fortescue's duties as a company trader and as a customs collector neatly dovetailed. In 1881, he informed Hudson's Bay House in London from York Factory that American whalers in Hudson Bay were trading with the Eskimos without paying customs duties on the goods they were selling or trading to the natives. He suggested on the one hand that the company send out a ship to garner at least part of this trade, and on the other that masters of company vessels be deputized by Ottawa as customs collectors to take in revenue from the American whalers. William Armit, secretary of the company, said the whole thing appeared impractical. He also noted complaints about smuggling by Alaska fur traders on the Yukon River —

the company had had a post on the river since 1847 — but said no remedy appeared in sight.

No remedy was provided until 1894 when Inspector Charles Constantine of the North West Mounted Police arrived at Fort Cudahy at the junction of the Yukon and Forty Mile Rivers near the Alaska border and fifty-two miles below Dawson. This was the first customs post in the Yukon Territory, known variously by the names Fort Cudahy, Forty Mile (name of the townsite) and Fort Constantine. Inspector Constantine said he found customs work "distasteful" but nonetheless he brought out $3,248.82 in cheques and drafts after his first season of collecting customs revenue. He was one of twenty Mounties who had sailed from Seattle on June 5, 1894, arriving at Cudahy July 24 after an ocean voyage to the mouth of the Yukon River and by river boat from there. The exact location of the Yukon-Alaska border was a little hazy at the time and some mining claims made near Forty Mile were issued by Alaskan authorities when, as it turned out, the claims were actually in Canada. The first steamship had arrived at Forty Mile in 1887, when there was already a settlement of some eighty-five men. Constantine, who could look after himself in a bare-knuckle fight, soon tamed brawling Forty Mile. He referred to himself as chief magistrate, commander-in-chief, and home and foreign secretary of Forty Mile. He also collected excise taxes on liquor. Some of Constantine's constables staked fortunes in the Yukon but he himself believed that no public servant should use his position for private gain and all he took with him out of the Yukon years later was his police salary.

Constantine's successor at Fort Cudahy was the colorful Donald Watson Davis, always known as D.W., born in Vermont in 1845 and wounded at Gettysburg fighting for the Union Army in the American civil war. Later, he served at various Army posts in the Montana Territory and then became a trader with the I.G. Baker Company at Fort Benton, the outfit which supplied the NWMP north of the border. He went to the Lethbridge area in 1869 or 1870 and was at one time in charge of Fort Whoop-Up. When the Mounties arrived in 1874, he helped to build Fort Macleod and established Baker enterprises there. He went on to Fort Calgary with the redcoats the following year, again establishing a Baker supply centre, and was general manager for Baker in Alberta until 1890 when the company was sold to the Hudson's Bay Company. Fort Macleod was his head office. Once his warehouse there was over-run with mice and D.W. traded a horse for a cat.

Davis became a British subject in 1886, and was nominated Conservative candidate in the first election of a Member of Parliament for the Alberta district. The nomination meeting was in February in Calgary, and it took Davis and his wife four sub-zero days to reach there by sleigh from Macleod. The meeting endorsed Davis over Richard Hardisty, chief factor of the Hudson's Bay Company at Edmonton who was backed in those days of open partisanship by employees of the Dominion government, by officers of the NWMP, and of course by the company. Davis' wife said it was hard to watch a whole detachment of Mounties, acting under orders, march up and vote against her husband. Nevertheless, Davis won, and Hardisty, the loser, was appointed to the Senate. Davis beat Dr. J.D. Lafferty, the Liberal, in the 1887 election and was re-elected in 1891. He declined to run for a third term in 1896 and was appointed collector of customs in the Yukon Territory at an annual salary of $3,000.

When Davis left for the Yukon it was with a gold-headed cane presented to him by Alberta admirers and inscribed "the most popular merchant in Macleod." He travelled with a Mountie detachment and took over from Constantine at Forty Mile. Davis left two hand-written diaries, now in the possession of the Glenbow Museum in Calgary. They are cryptic and therefore tantalizing. The brief entries are in pencil, many illegible, and often leave the reader high and dry. For instance, "First news from Walsh by messenger" but the entry doesn't say what the news was. Other entries: "20 below. Snowing. Sent mail to Comm. Ottawa by govt dog team"; "Seized outfit from C.C. & Co.,"; "Suicide by Mrs. Jesrophy or accidentally shot by husband." "No good" was a fairly frequent entry, but there is no indication whether the reference is to the weather or customs business.

With George Carmack's registration at Forty Mile, August 21, 1896, of his Klondike gold strike, Davis' old entrepreneurial instincts surfaced, and he began staking mining claims and buying property. Without permission from Ottawa, he moved his office to Dawson to be nearer the gold rush. His self-transfer was confirmed in May, 1898, and Constantine was told to return to Forty Mile, which remained a customs post until 1929. There is no evidence that Davis was slack in his customs duties; as the first collector in Dawson, he took in $237,447 in the 1898-99 fiscal year and supervised operations at six other customs points. He also organized the Dawson fire brigade and put up some of his own money to help buy a fire engine. But he couldn't resist getting into the search for gold himself, and was repeatedly warned by Ottawa to give up his prospecting or leave the civil service.

Davis himself defined the conflict of interest in his letter of resignation on June 20, 1902:

> I beg leave to submit my resignation as Collector of Customs at the Port of Dawson, Yukon Territory, Canada, to take effect immediately.
>
> My resignation is presented for the reason that I understand the Government insists that my wife and myself either sacrifice our mining interests in the Yukon Territory or that I quit the Service.
>
> I have always been fully aware that the mining regulations in force in the Yukon Territory provide that persons in the Government employ should not acquire mining interests, but my understanding has been that this did not apply to the wives of the Customs Department, but only to Territorial Officials; more especially as the Department of the Interior has always accepted the annual fees of both my wife and myself for miner's certificates and renewals of our claims.
>
> At the time that I accepted this office at the small remuneration provided by the Government, there was no such regulation in force, and as my remuneration as Collector, in comparison with the mining interests of my wife and myself, is so insignificant, I have decided to quit the Service rather than sacrifice our interests at a forced sale.

Davis remained in mining and in the Yukon until his death in 1906.

The Klondike gold rush and the Trail of Ninety-Eight brought scores of Mounties and customs officers to the Canada-Alaska frontier. The border was still in doubt at that time, and the early police stations and customs posts were well back from the present border, at places like Lake Tagish. But they were soon moved forward to the very summits of the adjacent Chilkoot and White Passes overlooking Skagway, Alaska. (A detailed account of Customs' role here will be found in the section of the book on the frontier.) In February, 1898, two detachments under Inspectors D'Arcy Strickland and Robert Belcher hoisted the flag at the two passes and set up customs posts. The legendary Superintendent Sam Steele decreed that no one could enter the Yukon without a year's supply of food — about 1,100 pounds, including tent, cooking utensils and tools. For a miner working on his own, this meant twenty trips up the 3,739-foot Chilkoot Pass, humping a 60-pound pack on his back. But also, as it was intended to, Steele's order kept the Yukon free of the gamblers, claim-jumpers, petty thieves, card sharps and grifters who afflicted Skagway. (Steele's advice endured. The 1954, and subsequent, Canadian customs requirements for the Alaska Highway state: "Everyone entering Canada either from Alaska or from any part of the United States and intending to drive over the Alaska Highway should have in his possession at time of entry into Canada a sufficient sum of money for the trip, or should be able to prove to the satisfaction of frontier officers that he can obtain in Canada any additional funds required.")

Customs duties at the Chilkoot and White Passes were not light. *The Chicago Record's* book in 1898 for Klondike gold-seekers, one of scores of such publications printed at the time, listed these items which carried a Canadian customs levy of 25 per cent: shovels, spades, picks, axes, hatchets, adzes, sails, boots, fishhooks and lines, fur caps and coats, dried fruits, canned meat; at 30 per cent were cartridges, coffee, galvanized iron, tinware, harness, oilcloth and portable sawmills; at 35 per cent, knitted goods, waterproof clothing, crowbars, cutlery, edge tools; and these: horses 20 per cent, blasting powder two cents a pound, baking powder six cents a pound, potatoes 15 cents a bushel, maps and charts 20 per cent, blankets five cents a pound plus 25 per cent, breadstuffs 20 per cent, butter four cents a pound, candles 28 per cent, cheese three cents a pound, cigars and cigarettes $2 a pound plus 26 per cent, tobacco 42 cents a pound plus 12 1/2 per cent, tents 32 1/2 per cent, rice 1 1/4 cents a pound, sugar 64/100 cents a pound, socks 10 cents per dozen pairs plus 35 per cent, condensed milk three cents a pound, firearms 20 per cent, wheat flour 75 cents a barrel, lard two cents a pound, oatmeal 20 per cent.

Dawson in its boom days was the biggest town west of Winnipeg and revenue returns were the fifth largest in Canada. It had 40 bonded warehouses, five excise warehouses and a brewery. In 1900, the population was 30,000. The NWMP, in 1898, had 12 officers and 254 men in the Yukon, though the total force numbered fewer than 750.

By the late spring of 1898, the Mounties had collected $150,000 at the Chilkoot and White Passes. They required that every boat heading for Dawson had to carry a serial number, and that the name of every occupant must be taken. The cash piled up in the customs huts, so Inspector Z.T. Wood lugged it in several kit bags to Victoria, getting special protection through Skagway. At the end of June, 1898, J.A. McMartin and F. Charman of the customs department took over from the Mounties; in July they moved the Chilkoot customs post back to Log Cabin near the point where the Chilkoot and White Passes converge, but the White Pass post remained open. The first regular train from Skagway to Whitehorse ran in June, 1900, and cleared Customs at White Pass. Much later, in 1950, the customs house at White Pass burned down and all documents were destroyed. Canadian Customs operated out of Skagway until July, 1951, when Carcross (originally Caribou Crossing) replaced White Pass. But in 1979, with the inauguration of the summer highway between Skagway and Carcross, White Pass was re-opened, under the name Fraser. Another Canadian customs post established for the Klondike rush was Wells, about twenty miles from Haines, Alaska. It operated from 1901 until 1903, when it was found to be situated in Alaska. Whitehorse, the present capital, was created a customs port in 1901.

A lot of customs work in the Yukon involved steamship traffic. In the early 1900s many river boats operated between Whitehorse and Dawson, including the *Selkirk, Dawson, Whitehorse, Yukoner, Bonanza King, Auro, Flora, Eldorado, La France, Videtto, Zelandian, Joseph Closset, A.H. Goddard* and *Thistle*. Up to 1955, the *Keno, Whitehorse, Casca, Klondike, Tutshi* and *Alaska* were operating between Whitehorse, Dawson and Mayo. The customs collector in the Yukon was also the registrar of shipping for the Territory.

During the Second World War, a Canadian fighter squadron served in Alaska. The American collector of customs in Alaska tried to make members of the Royal Canadian Air Force pay duty on equipment they were taking in for the common defence in 1942. Cordell Hull, U.S. Secretary of State, had to circumvent the regulations by declaring the Canadian airmen "distinguished visitors," entitled to enter the United States without customs examination.

In the early 1940s nearly all the imports for the Yukon went over the White Pass and Yukon Railroad. With construction of the 1,520-mile Alaska Highway in 1942, much of the Yukon trade was diverted to Edmonton and to Dawson Creek, British Columbia. Equipment used in Canada on construction of the highway was imported duty-free by special arrangement with the United States. But the law said that any goods diverted to use other than construction of the highway would be subject to customs duty. It would not have been worth the cost to return the equipment to the States after the highway was built, so it was dumped in the Yukon. People who grabbed this equipment — a refrigerator from a construction camp, for instance — were immediately charged duty. This made people madder at Customs than at any time since the prospector stood in the biting wind at the summit of the Chilkoot Pass and found that he had to pay 20 per cent customs duty on the map that had got him that far.

At the start of the century, the farthest-north customs post in Canada was on Herschel Island off the Arctic coast northwest of the Mackenzie River delta. It had been used as a U.S. whaling base in the 18th and 19th centuries. A detachment of the NWMP arrived in 1903, but the man in charge, Sergeant T.F. Fitzgerald, was obliged to write on August 21 that year: "I could not collect anything as I have not yet received the tariff, which I suppose will come with the next load of supplies in the fall." (Fitzgerald starved to death with four others on a Dawson-McPherson patrol in 1911). Herschel Island later became police headquarters for the western Arctic, but the headquarters was moved in 1931 to Aklavik. No customs officer was ever stationed at Herschel so the RCMP always had to act on behalf of National Revenue. No money was collected at Herschel Island from traders; entries were sent to Edmonton, (where they were received in March for transactions the previous year), together with blank drafts, and invoices were sent out from there to the trading companies. An invoice could amount to as much as $40,000. There is no record of any losses in revenue at Herschel. The ten-per-cent commission paid to the Mounties for collecting the revenue went to the policemen personally until 1932, when the money was paid by National Revenue into the RCMP benevolent fund.

After the flurry of customs activity occasioned by the building of the Alaska Highway during the Second World War, matters were more or less dormant in the Arctic until construction of the distant early warning radar line began in 1953. In that year, the department of External Affairs noted a large increase in the number of people visiting the Canadian north. Many of these people were not Canadian citizens and were travelling directly to the north from the United States; as well, many goods were moving directly from the States into northern Canada without benefit of Customs. The Canadian government decided to establish customs and immigration offices at twenty-two locations: Baker Lake, Cambridge Bay, Cape Herschel (Ellesmere Island), Chesterfield Inlet, Clyde River, Coppermine, Craig Harbor, Eskimo Point, Fort Chimo, Frobisher, Herschel Island, Lake Harbor, Pangnirtung, Pond Inlet, Resolute Bay, Sachs Harbor, Spence Bay, Tuktoyaktuk and the four weather stations in the high Arctic, Alert, Eureka, Isachsen and Mould Bay.

The customs and immigration officers were all deputized from other federal departments and agencies. For instance, on September 21, 1953, Revenue Minister James J. McCann issued an order designating the meteorological officer at Alert, the most northern habitation in Canada, to be "Acting Customs Excise Enforcement Officer" without salary from National Revenue but with authority to seize goods for infractions of the Customs and Excise Acts. Other appointees were from the RCMP, Royal Canadian Air Force and department of Transport. In 1956, the airport maintenance foreman at Coral Harbor was appointed customs officer there. In the next several years, cheap goods became available at American military bases in Greenland and Alaska. In 1969, a customs post had to be established at Cape Dyer to handle travellers and goods from Thule and Sondrestrom in Greenland, the goods being mainly radios, television sets, record players and cameras. The nearest RCMP post was at Igloolik, hundreds of miles to the west. The air traffic in the north has grown tremendously — to the point where there are as many as four or five hundred flights a year into and out of Alert. Oil drilling rigs are off the Arctic coast and more than $50 million worth of lead and zinc concentrates were shipped out of Nanisivik at the northern tip of Baffin Island in 1981 alone. But in 1982 there were still only two customs inspectors in the north — at Frobisher and Inuvik.

SECTION II

Development of the Canada-United States Border

CHAPTER I

Sea to Sea, Acrimoniously

For at least a century, Canadians have been taught that their frontier with the United States is unguarded. But we *are* defended at our border, against illegal importation of firearms and narcotics, diseased plants and foreign criminals, professional and amateur smugglers, and other artful dodgers who would cheat that venerable Canadian institution, the Consolidated Revenue Fund. From Campobello, New Brunswick, to Little Gold Creek, Yukon Territory, watch is kept on the frontier by hundreds of customs officers at such frenetic places as the Windsor tunnel or at lonely prairie crossings where one may wait and wait for travellers who never come. (It is the land frontier which concerns us here, although it is worth noting that, in effect, Canada's international boundary was extended with the advent of air travel to every international airport in the country.)

The Canada-U.S. border, crossed by tens of millions of people each year, developed mainly out of the competition — geographic, political, military, economic — between, first, England and France, and, later, between Britain and the United States. In every border dispute with the United States, Canada lost: a wedge of Maine, a corner of New Hampshire, the Illinois country, the Oregon Territory, San Juan Island, tidewater ports in Alaska. If it is any consolation, it can be said that Canada as a nation never negotiated for itself in any of these settlements. Only in the last, the Alaska agreement, was it even represented, and then in a minority position. One might blame Britain for these losses (assuming one could get worked up over such an issue today), but in most or all of these territorial disputes, the British government, in losing another piece of Canada, was winning some geopolitical or economic advantage in some other faraway corner of its empire. Now that empire has vanished, and Canada is stuck with the territorial quirks of its frontier with the United States, 5,526 miles (8,893 kilometres) long, 3,145 miles on land, 2,381 miles on water.

The border has often been so vague that it led to financial embarrassment: the United States built Fort Montgomery at Rouse's Point on Lake Champlain at a cost of one million dollars and later found it was in Canada. Surveyors found the Canadian customs post at Emerson, Manitoba, was in the States. Plainsman Kootenai Brown, the founder of Waterton Lakes National Park, once remarked that people on the prairies didn't know where the boundary was any more than the buffalo did.

In the four centuries of its history, our border developed more by happenstance than by planning. And always, (this will be seen as well in the chapter on smuggling) it was difficult to collect the revenue.

It is perhaps worth repeating that, up to modern times, the main source, and sometimes practically the only source, of national revenue was customs duties. With nothing like today's income and sales taxes, the well-being, even the survival, of the nation depended on thorough collection of duties. Often this was not possible. Upper Canada, for instance, shied away as long as possible (until 1801) from the establishment of customs houses along the U.S. border because it correctly foresaw the enormous difficulties of maintaining such posts on a largely wilderness frontier. Lower Canada preferred customs for revenue because it had a seaport, but Upper Canada favored property taxes. Upper Canada's border was water and, although one might think it comparatively easy to police at the land bottlenecks such as Niagara, a shoreline presents a great variety of landing sites for contraband-laden boats, and winter turns water into ice bridges. Canada's geography, from the coves of Nova Scotia to the Chilkoot Pass, has made the administration of government, and particularly of Customs, a difficult problem from the earliest times. New France had much the same trouble controlling the smuggling of furs by the coureurs de bois that Canada had two centuries later trying to stop the rum-runners.

A series of wars fought between New France and England's thirteen colonies in the 17th and 18th centuries and between British Canada and the U.S. republic in 1775-83 and 1812-14 had much to do with the development of the land frontier. The Rush-Bagot agreement of 1817 severely limited the number of warships on the Great Lakes, but construction of fortifications on both sides of the border continued until 1872, the last Canadian works being built at Lévis opposite Quebec. War came close several times: American border raids in 1837 which followed the rebellions in Upper and Lower Canada; the bloodless "Aroostook War" in 1839 between New Brunswick and Maine; the Oregon boundary dispute of 1846; the San Juan affair of 1859; the raid on St. Albans, Vermont, carried out by U.S. Confederate soldiers from Canada in 1864; and attacks by the Irish-American Fenian Brotherhood, beginning in 1866. The era of genuine peace between the two neighbors did not begin until the Treaty of Washington in 1871. The Alaska boundary dispute which accompanied the Klondike gold rush in 1898 caused bad feelings but no threats of war. In 1940, Canada and the United States established a Permanent Joint Board on Defence and, in 1949 and 1957, respectively, became formal military partners under the North Atlantic Treaty Organization and North American Air Defence Command.

After this capsule of frontier history, let us go back to the beginnings.

In 1603, Henry IV of France granted a trading charter to Pierre de Gua, Sieur de Monts, for the Atlantic seacoast and territory between parallels 40 and 46 — Cape Cod to Cape Breton — under the name Acadia. Three years later, in 1606, James I of England granted the Plymouth Company the right to form settlements a hundred miles square between parallels 38 and 45. The 45th parallel forms part of the boundary to this day.

There was considerable overlapping in grants so, from that time, every boundary treaty only paved the way for a series of new boundary disputes, right into the present century.

The wilderness frontier between New France and the British colonies of New England was, as one might imagine, very ill-defined. Sometimes it was hard to tell which came first, the border or the customs officer. The Swedish naturalist, Peter Kalm, was en route to Montreal from Albany in 1750 when he arrived at Fort St. Frédéric at the southern extremity of Lake Champlain. (It was called Crown Point by the English.) "The Englishmen insist that this [French] fort is built on their territory," he wrote, "and that the boundary between the French and English colonies in this locality lies between Fort St. Jean and the Prairie de la Madeleine [on the south shore of the St. Lawrence River]. On the other hand, the French maintain that the boundary runs through the woods between Lake St. Sacrament and Fort Nicholson [farther south than Fort St. Frédéric]." That's a hundred-mile argument.

In 1763, France ceded Canada and Acadia to England. Up to that time, England had maintained that the province of Massachusetts extended all the way north to the St. Lawrence River. But with both territories, Quebec and Massachusetts, now in British hands, it made little difference exactly where the border was drawn between the two colonies. Or so it was thought at the time. By royal proclamation in 1763, the new province of Quebec took in the entire south bank of the St. Lawrence up to the point (near present-day Cornwall) where the 45th parallel met the river. To the east, however, the border of Quebec vaguely followed the highlands south of the St. Lawrence.

The War of the American Revolution was ended by the Treaty of Paris in 1783, and Canada lost all the western Illinois country assigned to Quebec under the 1774 Quebec Act. The treaty left poorly defined the boundary between Quebec and New Brunswick on the one side (the latter was created out of Nova Scotia in 1784) and what now are Maine and New Hampshire on the other. The Americans had the effrontery to claim as U.S. territory the town of St. Andrews, New Brunswick, founded by Loyalists. In 1807, the New Brunswick House of Assembly protested that the United States had usurped Moose, Dudley and Frederick Islands in Passamaquoddy Bay though they were part of the province's parish of West Isles in Charlotte County. The Americans used the islands in the way that disputed boundary islands are generally used: to smuggle contraband. (The same thing happened at San Juan in Georgia Strait a half-century later.) In the war of 1812-14, St. Andrews and Calais, Maine, sensibly agreed to abstain from mutual hostilities, and this agreement was strictly observed.

It is a wonder that Canada survived at all in 1783. The chief British negotiator, the elderly Richard Oswald, was willing to surrender all the mainland of British North America to the United States to placate the former colony. And he would be giving away, he believed, land occupied by only a few Frenchmen on the lower St. Lawrence and even fewer Englishmen on the St. Lawrence and in Nova Scotia. In the east, the border was considered to be the Ste. Croix River, but this name had not been used since Champlain's day. In the west (today's central Canada, that is), there was some thought given to making the 45th parallel the frontier all the way, which would have put southern Ontario in the United States and northern Michigan, Wisconsin and Minnesota in Canada. A judgment was passed on the new border agreement by Robert Hunter, Jr., travelling from Quebec to the Carolinas in 1785, who wrote scathingly about "the stupid Oswald" who had given up British forts on the south side of Lake Ontario "through his ignorance of geography."

We have several detailed accounts of what it was like to cross the border in the early 1800s. One is contained in John Lambert's two-volume work, *Travels through Canada and the United States in the Years 1806, 1807, 1808.* In the "miserable village" of St. John's (St. Jean), Lambert tells us, there was a customs house where exports to and imports from the States were registered and duties paid. The customs house was inside the fort, about two hundred yards from the village, along with a powder magazine, a few pieces of cannon and a detachment of soldiers.

The boundary was eighteen miles from St. John's and cut across the Richelieu River within a few miles of Lake Champlain. "Hence the Canadians are completely shut out from the lake in case of war," Lambert wrote, "and even from the water communication with their own territory in Missisquoi Bay. The greatest part of this bay lies in Canada and is thus cut off by this line of demarcation, so ignorantly and pusillanimously allowed by the English negotiators in the treaty of peace with the American States in 1783. In case of war, the Americans have every advantage over the Canadians by confining them to the narrow channel of the Richelieu river, and the ill effects of it have been already experienced since the embargo, as the rafts of timber were not permitted to come out of Missisquoi Bay for the purpose of passing down the Richelieu river. The laws however were broken in several instances; but the parties were liable to fine and imprisonment. If the line had been drawn across the wide part of Lake Champlain, the Americans could never have stationed their gun-boats with such effect as they did in 1807 in the Richelieu river, by which means they interrupted the communication between the two countries by water, and seized great quantities of goods." The reference to the embargo was the temporary U.S. trade embargo against Britain during the Napoleonic War.

Lambert went up the Richelieu and into Lake Champlain by leaky boat. He noted the remains of fortifications on Ile-aux-Noix in the river, the island having been successively occupied by French, English and American armies during various wars. It was to be fortified again beginning in 1819, as the British naval base for Lake Champlain.

Lambert later returned to Canada by the same Champlain route — but mainly by land. He went by stagecoach and wagon to Burlington and St. Albans, Vermont, by wagon to Swanton Falls, where mail for Canada was delivered to a courier from St. John's, then by horseback, canoe and rowboat and on foot to Choisy within four miles of the border. There he met Judge Hicks, the American customs officer and also the local tavern-keeper. Hicks declined to look into Lambert's cases and Lambert comments: "He doubtless thought if he pried too closely into the baggage of his customers his tavern would soon be deserted. He therefore suffered private interest to get the better of public spirit." At St. John's, Lambert dined with Mr. Linger, the customs collector there, at Cheeseman's tavern. If there was a baggage inspection this time, Lambert doesn't mention it.

In 1794, provision had finally been made for survey of the boundary by an international commission, and excavations on Ste. Croix (now Dochet) Island proved that the Ste. Croix was the river of Champlain's published 1613 map and therefore the dividing line between New Brunswick and Maine. The boundary was to run due north from the source of the Ste. Croix to "the highlands which divide the rivers that fall into the Atlantic Ocean from those which fall into the St. Lawrence." But where was this watershed? The Americans wanted the line to run north to a point which the Canadians calculated would be only nine and a half miles from the St. Lawrence River. The Canadians claimed the "highlands" were Mars Hill, a promontory only forty miles north of the source of the Ste. Croix.

Now it became apparent how slipshod it had been in 1763 not to delimit the border between Massachusetts and Quebec and Nova Scotia. After the United States became independent, Britain needed territory for communication between Quebec and Nova Scotia: in the winter, it was the only means of communication. That territory was the disputed northeastern wedge of Maine, created out of northern Massachusetts in 1820.

The arbitrator in the dispute, King William of the Netherlands, awarded the United States two-thirds of the disputed territory in 1831, but Maine rejected the award, and the dispute simmered until 1839 when the "Aroostook War" occurred in the border area between Woodstock, New Brunswick, and Houlton, Maine. There was a lot of military to-ing and fro-ing but, fortunately, no actual fighting. When Maine authorities arrested some New Brunswick lumbermen for alleged trespassing the lumbermen carried out a counter-raid, and Maine mobilized 10,000 militiamen with such martial songs as:

> We'll feed them well with ball and shot,
> We'll cut those redcoats down
> Before we yield to them an inch
> Or title to our ground.

British troops were sent from Quebec and Halifax. New Brunswick volunteers rushed to the militia. There was a lot of drilling and shouting in Woodstock and Houlton. Then the situation was defused in March, 1839, by General Winfield Scott of the United States and Sir John Harvey, Lieutenant-Governor of New Brunswick, who had fought against each other in the Niagara Peninsula in the war of 1812-14. Scott was President Van Buren's special emissary, and was to play the role of peacemaker again, twenty years later, in the San Juan dispute.

The big setback for the Canadians was that the Americans managed to build, unchallenged, a blockhouse, now Fort Kent, where the Fish River empties into the St. John. Indeed, the American garrison at Fort Kent was sustained by supplies ordered and delivered from Quebec over the Temiscouata route patrolled by British troops.

Time produced more conciliatory governments in Britain and the United States and in 1842 the frontier was settled in private talks between Daniel Webster, American Secretary of State, and special envoy Lord Ashburton of Britain, married to the daughter of an American senator. The resulting treaty, signed August 9, 1842, gave less to Maine than King William's award of 1831 which Maine had rejected. New Brunswick thought itself swindled by the treaty, too. In 1890, Lieutenant-Colonel William T. Baird in his book, *Seventy Years of New Brunswick Life,* wrote: "The astute lawyer, Daniel Webster, wound the subtle web of diplomacy and prevarication, which is said to be worse than lying, around his victims." Quebec was preserved practically intact despite forty-year-old U.S. claims to parts of nine of its southeastern counties. But it lost some small pieces to New Hampshire and New York. Fort Montgomery, the million-dollar American embarrassment at Rouse's Point, was restored to the United States.

The boundary was marked in 1843-45. The British commissioner of the survey was Lieutenant-Colonel James Bucknell Estcourt, after whom a Maine border village was named. The American commissioner was Al Smith. Each had a staff of astronomers, surveyors, axemen and others totalling nearly five hundred. A thirty-foot strip, or vista, was cut through the forest. The boundary from the Ste. Croix to the St. Lawrence is 670 miles long, 179 miles of it formed by rivers. The cast-iron monuments marking the frontier were made in the United States.

The International Waterways Commission marked the boundary from St. Regis on the St. Lawrence to Lake of the Woods. Only 4,000 feet of this section of the frontier is on land — old portages between Lake Superior and Lake of the Woods. Some bargaining went on in surveying this border. For example, Canada got Wolfe Island near Kingston in exchange for the Long Sault Islands, including Barnhart. Some business interests in Upper Canada complained about the loss of Barnhart, possibly because it was a prime smuggling depot.

The fur traders, south from Hudson Bay and west from New France, were partly responsible for fixing the western border. There was no formal, agreed frontier between New France and the Hudson's Bay Company territory. In the first half of the 18th century, the company claimed a boundary running from the Labrador coast, between 58 1/2 and 59 1/2 degrees north, to the southwest through Lake Mistassini to the 49th parallel and then due west along the 49th. New France claimed a boundary farther northwest which would have confined the Hudson's Bay Company to a coastal strip around Hudson Bay; between 1731 and 1748 La Vérendrye and his sons established trading posts from Grand Portage to the forks of the Saskatchewan. The Conquest of 1759 laid this matter to rest. Though there had never been anything official about the company's claim to the 49th parallel, British geographers adopted it as the western border between British North America and the United States.

The Treaty of Paris of 1783, which had given rise to so much squabbling over the New Brunswick-Maine frontier, determined that the prairie border would be drawn due west from Lake of the Woods to the source of the Mississippi at 47 degrees, 39 minutes of latitude. A line drawn due west from Lake of the Woods would not intersect with the source of the Missisipi at 47 degrees, 39 minutes of latitude. A line drawn due west from Lake of the Woods would not intersect with the Mississippi. In 1803, the United States bought the Louisiana Territory from France for $27,000,000 when it extended as far north as the Mississippi watershed. The States claimed that the northern boundary of the Louisiana Territory west of the Mississippi was the 49th parallel. Britain, relieved that the claim was no larger, accepted and, in 1818, the 49th parallel became the boundary from Lake of the Woods to the crest of the "Stony Mountains."

Meanwhile, there had been problems where the boundary left Lake Superior and went up the Pigeon River, beginning at Grand Portage. From the earliest days of the western fur trade, Grand Portage had been the great rendezvous for factors, traders, guides, canoemen, interpreters and clerks. As many as a thousand men ate in the large hall, one hundred at a sitting, on bread, salt pork, beef, ham, fish, venison, peas, Indian corn, potatoes, tea, spirits, wine, milk and butter (there were cows on the premises). Once outside the door, the hard work began, the long canoe haul back to Montreal, or the even more difficult trip to the western interior, starting with a nine-mile portage on the Pigeon river.

In 1804, the United States imposed a duty of 20 to 25 per cent on all goods carried over the portage, which was on the south (American) side of Pigeon River. This compelled the North-West Company to transfer its post to Kaministiquia, now Thunder Bay, and to adopt the inferior Dog River route to Lake of the Woods. This route was 381 miles compared with 325 miles by Pigeon River. It was 1842 before this dispute was settled and all portages made free to the traders of both nations.

John J. Bigsby, the Englishman who was secretary and doctor to the boundary commission responsible for demarcation of the frontier from St. Regis to Lake of the Woods, said that islands unequally divided by the border were usually given to the country entitled to the larger share. "The inconvenience of two nationalities on one small island was not to be endured," he wrote. In his two-volume *The Shoe and Canoe, or Pictures of Travel in the Canadas*, published in 1850, Bigsby warned that the country between Lake Superior and Lake of the Woods was a drowned land of ferocious mosquitoes, and quoted William Cullen Bryant, a popular American poet of the time:

> Try some plump alderman, and seek the blood
> Enriched with generous wine and costly meat;
> On well-filled skins fix thy light pump,
> And press thy freckled feet.

There was also a problem about the northwest angle, that is, the northwestern point in Lake of the Woods where the 49th parallel was supposed to start on its long way west. The boundary commission found that this point was not at 49 degrees but instead at 49 degrees, 23 minutes, 55 seconds north latitude. So a line had to be drawn straight south from that point to the 49th parallel, leaving the United States with a peninsula whose only approach, except by boat, is through Canada. The Canadian government offered $25,000 for the peninsula because it had a landing stage but Hamilton Fish, the American Secretary of State, was quoted by Sir Edward Thornton, British minister in Washington, as saying: "The American people would not support the loss of even a small piece of land; this is a matter upon which the Americans are very touchy."

The prairie frontier was marked in 1872-74. The Canadian contingent comprised 270 astronomers, surveyors, topographers, engineers, surgeons, veterinarians, naturalists, photographers, cooks, tailors, mule drivers, carpenters, wheelwrights, blacksmiths, bakers and pick-and-shovellers. The American contingent included cavalry besides. Much of the work had to be done in winter when the swamps were frozen; the surveyors lived in tents and the liquid often froze in their surveying instruments. Between Lake of the Woods and the Red River, the border markers were cast-iron pillars one mile apart. West of the Red, the markers were earthen mounds every three miles.

In 1823, Major Stephen Long had driven an oak post into the west bank of the Red on behalf of the U.S. government, but a new U.S. survey in 1870 for the siting of an American customs house had shown the line to be six hundred feet north of Long's marker. This put the sixty-nine-year-old Hudson's Bay Company post at Pembina right in American territory, and the zealous U.S. customs collector immediately ordered an inventory of the company's goods so that he could apply American duties. He was told by Washington to calm down until the situation could be officially sorted out.

On October 5, 1871, a group of fifteen to twenty Fenians occupied the Hudson's Bay Company post and began looting it. They were arrested by the U.S. 20th Infantry. When the Fenians went on trial at St. Paul, Minnesota, more than a year later, they were acquitted when the court ruled that it had no jurisdiction to deal with an incident which had occurred in Canada. Since the raid, the new survey by the International Boundary Commission had found that the Hudson's Bay Company post was indeed in Canada — but that the nearby Canadian customs house was in the United States. Despite this, Canada Customs operated from this log building for several years afterwards. The boundary commission arranged that its staff would be protected by the U.S. militia if there were trouble with the Indians, but the only time the militia was called out was to stop a fight among drunken Canadians.

As for the far western border, the crest of the Rockies to the Pacific had been left open for ten years (from 1818) because Britain had claims north and south of the 49th parallel and the United States, Spain and Russia also had territorial demands west of the Rockies. The Hudson's Bay Company had long been on the Columbia River when American missionaries and settlers began arriving in 1834. Britain then claimed the Pacific slope down to the 42nd parallel, and the United States up to the 51st. Britain favored the 49th parallel to the Columbia, and proposed that all land west of the Columbia be British. Washington counter-offered with the 49th all the way. In 1824, the United States and Russia, which then owned Alaska, signed a treaty designating parallel 54 degrees, 40 minutes, as the line separating their spheres of influence west of the Rockies; in 1825, Britain and Russia signed a treaty designating the same line as separating *their* spheres of influence. In 1827, Britain and the United States agreed to disagree for the time being. Though the New Brunswick-Maine border was settled by negotiation in 1842, talks about the far-western border remained fruitless.

In May, 1844, the Democratic presidential campaign had adopted the "54-40 or fight" slogan and, in his inaugural address in March, 1845, President James Polk declared that the United States intended to annex all territory up to 54 degrees, 40 minutes north latitude — that is, to the Alaska panhandle. The two sides huffed and puffed militarily as they had done in the "Aroostook War," this time with ships. Britain proposed the 49th parallel to the middle of Georgia Strait, then south through Juan de Fuca Strait. It made the proposal on June 6, 1846, and by June 15 the Oregon Treaty embodying this proposal was signed and ratified. In 1853, the Oregon Territory was divided into Washington and Oregon.

The job of marking the boundary from the Pacific to the summit of the Rockies was not started until 1857 and took nearly five years. The boundary commission had to open trails for pack trains over at least three-quarters of the route. The demarcation coincided with the Fraser River gold rush and the commission had to pay previously unheard of salaries for axemen, mule drivers and other laborers. The land boundary of 409.4 miles was established by twenty-eight astronomical stations. A forty-ton granite obelisk marks the end of the land frontier on the western shore of Point Roberts. The first forty-five miles from the coast are marked by forty-two iron pillars, the next one hundred and eight miles to the Similkameen River by nineteen stone cairns, the next ninety-five miles to the Columbia by sixty-nine stone cairns and the last one hundred and sixty-two miles to the crest of the Rockies by twenty-seven cairns.

Lieutenant Charles Wilson, secretary of the British section of the commission, kept a diary of his travels up rivers, through forests and swamps and across mountains to Waterton Lakes. In the coastal lowlands, the mosquitoes were so bad that axemen refused to work, mules were blinded, and the surveyors often rowed out to the middle of a lake to sleep in their boats. "If those who talk so much about the pleasure of camping out had only a night like the one we had spent, they would be rather less warm in their praises," Wilson mildly observed when mosquitoes drove him from his tent into a nearby river.

Wilson records that customs men were on duty at the very start of the gold rush. Governor James Douglas of British Columbia had established an entry point in 1860 at Rock Creek, a gold mining town near the border. Of his arrival at Rock Creek, Wilson wrote: "We were at first taken (by the gold miners) for customs house officers or gold collectors, but after we had explained that we had no connection with the colony we were hospitably treated."

Another member of the boundary commission in British Columbia was D.G.F. Macdonald, who went home to Britain to lecture on the subject. His lecture was published in 1863 under the title *British Columbia and Vancouver's Island*. Interior British Columbia was, he said, a dreary land of swamp, eight months of winter, smallpox, and clouds of insects.

> Prairies are few, swampy, and of small extent, and are overhung in summer by clouds of insects; while pestilence exhales from the decaying vegetation and reptiles sport in the stagnant pools, or crawl over piles of mouldering logs, brush and rushes . . . infested by legions of mosquitoes which destroy comfort by day and sleep by night, biting alike through socks and sheets. They have subjected cows and horses to the torture of a lingering death and forced whole families to leave their homes for months together. I have more than once been thrown into a fever by the pestilential vapors which the summer heat had caused to float from the slimy sediment of these flats. . . . The country is in reality a miserable one, adapted neither for grazing nor for corn. The larger portion is an inhospitable wilderness, difficult of access and inhabited only by Indians, a few factors and with rare exceptions the rudest outcasts of society. The state of society at the mines is low in the extreme, and life and property far from secure. Night and day bands of murderous-looking ruffians prowl about and commit the most atrocious robberies. . . . Victoria is by no means a desirable place of residence; the population has been gathered from the ends of the earth. . . . There is no society for ladies, nor indeed for cultivated persons of any description.

This did not do much for the efforts of the two colonies (British Columbia and Vancouver Island were separate colonies then) to attract immigrants from Britain.

Given the results of border-making in New Brunswick, Lake of the Woods, and other points, it could have been taken as a foregone conclusion that there would be something messy about the 1846 agreement so far as the section in Juan de Fuca Strait was concerned. And there was. The Oregon Treaty had failed to define the dividing line between Vancouver Island and the U.S. mainland accurately, and a history of alternating confrontation and concession ensued, with sheep and pigs at the centre of it.

The Hudson's Bay Company had occupied the Island of San Juan in Juan de Fuca Strait in 1845 and, in 1853, Governor Douglas, also a company factor, established a sheep farm there. The U.S. customs collector for Puget Sound, I.N. Ebey, took note of the landing of British sheep on what he understood to be U.S. territory and notified his superiors that he intended to collect duty on imports of British livestock. Douglas took the Victoria customs collector, James Sangster, with him to San Juan. Sangster told Ebey to quit the island. Ebey said he would install a deputy there. Sangster unfurled the Union Jack, Ebey the Stars and Stripes. Ebey swore in Henry Webber as deputy, and left. Sangster tried to evict Webber but Webber had four revolvers hanging from his belt. Sangster left. The quiet, except for the munching of the sheep, resumed.

In 1855, the U.S. sheriff landed on San Juan and demanded eighty dollars in duty, then, failing to get it, carried off thirty-four sheep in payment. The Hudson's Bay Company claimed $1,500 for the lost sheep, unsuccessfully. Washington Territory asked Governor Douglas for firearms to help quell Indian uprisings — in which Ebey had been killed — and he complied quickly, paying for some of the arms out of his own pocket. Again, quiet.

By 1859, there were twenty-two British sheep farmers and about thirty American squatters on San Juan. One of the squatters, Lyman A. Cutler, shot one of the Hudson's Bay Company pigs. Told of the incident, the American General William Harney, inflamed, ordered American military occupation of the island. By August, 1859, the United States had 461 troops on the island, and British warships stood offshore. To the rescue again came General Winfield Scott, who ordered General Harney back east (he refused to go) and arranged co-occupation of the island with the British. The Americans stayed at the south end of the 14-mile-long island, the British at the north. San Juan became a smugglers' haven: there were no customs duties between it and Vancouver Island on account of the claim that it was British, and none between San Juan and Washington Territory because of the claim that it was American.

Not until 1869 was there agreement on arbitration, and not until 1871, the year in which British Columbia joined Confederation, was an arbitrator (Emperor Wilhelm I of Germany) named. When the decision was made in favor of the United States in 1872, Britain withdrew from San Juan.

The arbitrary nature of the establishment of the frontier is called up by the names given by the boundary commission to the seventy astronomical points it used for its survey. Listed, from east to west, English, French and Indian, they present an unassimilated record of human incident, attachment and association: Northwest Angle, Buffalo Point, Pine River,

West Roseau, Red River, Point Michel, East Pembina, West Pembina, Long River, Sleepy Hollow, East Turtle, West Turtle, 1st Souris, South Antler, 2nd Souris, Rivière des Lacs, Short Creek, 3rd Souris, Great Coteau, Mid-Coteau, Big Muddy, Bully Spring, East Poplar (or Porcupine Creek), West Poplar, Little Rocky, Frenchman's Creek, Cottonwood Coulée, 500 Miles West, Goose Lake, East Fork Milk, West Fork Milk, Milk River Lake, Milk River Crossing, East Butte, West Butte, Red Creek, South Branch Milk, North Branch Milk, St. Mary's River, Belly River, Waterton Lake, Akamina, Kishenehu, Wigwam, Kootenay East, Yahk, Mooyie, Kootenay West, Kootenay Mountain, Pend d'Oreille, Fort Shepherd, Columbia, Statapoosten, Inchuintum, Newhoialpitkwm, Osoyoos, Similkameen, Naisnuloh, Pasayten, Roche, Skagit, Chuchchehum, Chiloweyuck, Ensahkwitch, Senehsai, Tummeahai, Sumass, British, Semiahmoo, Initial Point.

The last boundary to be fixed between Canada and the United States was the Alaska frontier. The agreement made in 1825 between Britain and Russia gave Russia a coastal strip of Alaska down to latitude 54 degrees, 40 minutes. The inland depth of this panhandle was a line on the crest of mountains no more than thirty-five miles from the ocean. The boundary between Alaska proper and what came to be the Yukon Territory was the 141st meridian.

The Hudson's Bay Company reached the headwaters of the Stikine River in 1824. Because the Stikine is the biggest river to flow out of British Columbia across the Alaska Panhandle and into the Pacific, it thus presented access to — or egress from — the interior for the fur traders, the Hudson's Bay Company and the Russian-American Company. In 1833-34, the Russians built Redoubt St. Dionysius on an island opposite the mouth of the Stikine to keep the Hudson's Bay Company from ascending the river to build a rival post on British territory. The Hudson's Bay Company's ship, Dryad, arrived at the Stikine June 18, 1834, to find the fourteen-gun Russian brig Chickagoff already on the scene. The Dryad withdrew eleven days later to avert an international incident and, in 1839, Britain and Russia agreed that the Hudson's Bay Company could use the Stikine.

In 1867, the United States bought Alaska from Russia for $7,200,000. At the time, the Americans called Alaska "Seward's Folly" or "Seward's Ice Chest" to denote what they considered the ridiculous purchase arranged by U.S. Secretary of State William Seward. But the British were even more taken aback than the Americans. Britain was the only country in the world with a border with Alaska, and it received no advance warning of the change in ownership.

Buck Choquette, a prospector, had found gold on bars of the Stikine in 1862 and later established a store and tavern on the river at a place which became known as Buck's Landing, some thirty miles upriver from Wrangell, Alaska. Gold-seekers went up and down the steep-banked river for more than a decade but there was no big strike until the Cassiar find in northern British Columbia in 1873. The best means of getting to Cassiar was the Stikine.

The Cassiar rush led to a need to mark the boundary between British Columbia and Alaska, because questions of jurisdiction arose in the courts dealing with criminal cases along the lower Stikine. In 1872, and again in 1874, British Columbia requested a survey — this was at the very time the prairie boundary was being marked — but was told by Ottawa it would be too costly.

With miners pushing up the Stikine by steamer, Canada established a customs post on the river in 1873. Officer Richard Hunter was sent from Victoria and pitched a tent beside Buck's Landing. Many miners on their way to Cassiar bought supplies at Wrangell, and Hunter intercepted the boats and levied duty. U.S. Customs made sure no British goods were dropped off in U.S. territory while in transit up the Stikine. The American officers accomplished this by taking passage in the ships, greatly annoying the passengers by locking the bar during the vessel's time in U.S. territory. The Cassiar field yielded about one million dollars worth of gold annually. There were some three thousand miners in the district, eighty miles above the head of navigation at Glenora and about 215 miles from tidewater.

Buck's Landing was not big enough to permit steamers to unload for customs inspection and reship their cargo. So Hunter moved his operation to Glenora where the steamers unloaded anyway. The Americans, seizing on the move as an indication that Canada Customs had not been sure that Buck's Landing was in Canadian territory, claimed that Choquette's store was in Alaska and said he would have to start paying duty on British goods. Choquette appealed to Ottawa and Victoria for help and the Canadian government commissioned a Canadian Pacific Railway engineer, Joseph Hunter, to survey the lower Stikine (spelled Stickeen in those days — and Wrangell was sometimes spelled Wrangle). In 1878, the United States accepted Hunter's line as a temporary boundary on the Stikine. The line restored Choquette's store and tavern to Canada and the border argument died away for nearly two decades. Richard Hunter remained the customs collector at Glenora until 1890. He was succeeded by George Pritchett. When the minister of the interior, Clifford Sifton, looked at the Stikine in 1897 as a possible route to the Klondike (to get around a U.S. Customs problem at Skagway, Alaska) Canada Customs decided to send a new man to Glenora. R.H. Hall of the Hudson's Bay Company had said that there was considerable smuggling of U.S. goods on the Stikine and added: "I have nothing to say against the present collector, Mr. Geo. Pritchett, except that he is a man of over 70 years of age." Pritchett was paid ten per cent of the duties he collected, or about $100 to $120 a year in commissions. The new man, John Turner, went up the Stikine ice by dog team in 1898 to a new NWMP post on the border, and stayed there for three months until navigation opened in May, 1898, and he was able to get to Glenora on the steamer *Ramona*, one of sixteen plying the Stikine. Canadian Customs later went back to the lower Stikine, abandoned the post in the 1950s but reopened it in 1983. The United States still maintains a customs office at Wrangell.

Donald Cameron, a Canadian serving in the British Army, had been in charge of the Canadian section of the prairie boundary commission and though without any particular expertise he liked to keep his hand in on the subject of border controversies. He had considerable political influence because he was the son-in-law of Conservative Sir Charles Tupper, briefly Canada's prime minister in 1896. Cameron advanced a theory which became known as the Coast Doctrine. Essentially, it would have given Canada many Pacific coastal inlets and thus direct access to British Columbia across the Alaska panhandle. Cameron was in a position to be listened to, and the Canadian department of the interior kept his Coast Doctrine alive by printing it on its maps published after 1887. Unfortunately, the Canadians did not put it before the Americans formally for nearly a decade.

CHAPTER II

Customs Holds the Pass

In August, 1896, George W. Carmack, Skookum Jim and Tagish Charlie struck gold on the Klondike River's Bonanza Creek. The discovery triggered the Klondike rush and re-ignited the border dispute. Most of the men and material bound for the Klondike went through Skagway and Dyea at the head of the Lynn Canal in the Alaska panhandle. The Canadians suddenly discovered that as far back as 1891 the United States had appointed an honorary customs officer at the head of the Lynn Canal. In 1897 complaints started to come into Ottawa that U.S. Customs was refusing Canadian vessels permission to land passengers and goods at Skagway and Dyea. On July 22, 1897, John McDougald, Commissioner of Canadian Customs, asked Washington to bond Canadian goods through the panhandle duty-free if the owners would pay for a U.S. customs officer to accompany the goods. Washington complied — and Canada thereby conceded that the United States had jurisdiction over the head of the Lynn Canal.

But A.R. Milne, the astute collector of Customs at Victoria, saw, at the same time that the Victoria and Vancouver merchants did, what the commercial problem was going to be. Unless Canada collected duty on American goods on the Klondike trail, American goods would flood the Yukon and all miners' supplies would be bought in the States. Milne sent urgent telegrams to Customs Minister William Paterson, who was in Paris at the time (July, 1897). At least $7,000 had been lost in revenue already because there was no Canadian customs man on the boundary, he told Paterson. R.S. Drury, secretary of the Vancouver Liberal Association, sent a telegram to Paterson: "Large meeting of Liberal association passed resolution asking government to hasten appointment of customs officers for Yukon trade." On July 24, 1897, McDougald told Milne to send officers to Dyea and Lake Tagish.

Milne quickly realized the boundary problem as well as the trade problem. As early as August 5, 1897, he was urging McDougald to advise the North West Mounted Police to push forward and station themselves on the boundary, or on what the Canadians maintained was the boundary. Strangely, the Mounties held back, and it was the customs department which carried the sovereignty flag. A single customs officer, John Godson, began collecting duties in territory which the Americans claimed was theirs and, in effect, forced the Mounties to start policing the Chilkoot and White Passes in February, 1898. It can be argued that if it had not been for the unsung Godson, Canada might well have lost more territory in the Alaska boundary settlement than it did. (Documents giving details of Customs' part in the early story of the Klondike, including Godson's letters, are in the Public Archives of Canada.) James M. Walsh, the famed Mountie called out of retirement to be Commissioner of the Yukon, told the customs minister December 22, 1897, that Godson was "a very efficient and capable officer."

As collector of customs, Milne had instructed Godson on July 28, 1897: "A rigid collection of duties must be obtained and no persons are entitled to anything free unless it is their blankets or personal clothing actually in use, or provisions in broken packages, and used cooking utensils." Milne later informed his commissioner that seven men had reached Lake Tagish where the trails through the Chilkoot and White Passes converged; one was at Skagway and another at Dyea. The seven at Tagish were Godson, who was in charge at $100 a month ($43.71 a month more than his Victoria salary), W.W. Hall, F. Hinds, and four British Columbia constables. T.R. McInnes was at Skagway and Fred W. Davey at Dyea. T.R. McInnes was at Skagway and Fred W. Davey at Dyea.

Milne said he picked Godson from his staff of junior clerks at Victoria because he seemed the most dependable with the most initiative. In the end, he had a little too much initiative for Milne. Godson first reported from Tutshi Lake, British Columbia. In his letter of August 11, Godson spelled the name Koochi, then crossed this out and changed it to Toochi. He said he had been on the road six days and still had about fifty miles to go to reach Tagish. He was accompanied by provincial constable McGraw and each carried a pack of sixty to seventy pounds containing: rifle, axe, pail, blankets, tent, sixteen pounds of rice, sugar, bread, tea, chocolate, a dozen onions, four tins of corned beef, eight pounds of bacon, underwear, tins for boiling water, tin cups, hip boots and about one hundred Customs entry forms, pens and ink. Godson added, in his beautiful handwriting:

> On account of the River Skagway being very swollen we had to cross on horseback and even then the water reached the seats of the saddles. We then proceeded to climb the [White] pass, making about 12 miles, camping about halfway to the summit at six in the evening after a very hard day's march.
> The second day, starting at 7 a.m., we made about another 12 miles — passing the summit 18 to 20 miles from Skagway at about noon. Being too tired to proceed further and there being absolutely no wood to make fires or erect the tent, being higher than the timber limit, we passed the night on a moss-covered rock — drawing the tent over us

as well as possible. It rained nearly all night, and starting at six a.m., saturated to the skin, with wet clothing, wet blankets and wet food, we travelled as quickly as possible North, and about nine o'clock came to some dry timber, made a fire and breakfasted. We then found the trail getting somewhat easier and passed the third night as near as I could judge about 32 miles from the starting place. Making a large campfire we managed to dry our blankets, clothing, etc., before going to bed. . . .

I am sorry to inform you that the tents supplied are totally unfit for this climate, and are only suitable for summer outings in British Columbia. They are very small, and made of very light drilling, too light to turn the rain. To add to the difficulties of the situation the woods are alive with mosquitoes and McGraw's hands and face are so swollen that the former were almost useless and he could hardly open his eyes. His feet too were terribly blistered. We had to ford on foot two other streams in the pass, both being very dangerous.

Please do not think that I am complaining. I came on what I believed was a very tough undertaking and will use everything in my way and strain every nerve to accomplish the object the Government has in view. . . .

You will be pleased to hear that by pushing forward as I have succeeded in doing I shall head off and collect duty from people who landed in Alaska several weeks in advance of [me].

Godson was going to make a raft to float down Lake Tagish but was offered a skinboat by 73-year-old Yukon pioneer Billie Moore for one hundred dollars. He asked Milne to pay Moore for the boat: "I might add that the boat is worth at least $250 and the long delay in staying here to make one might entail a loss to the Government of far more."

McInnes reported to Milne from Skagway on August 21 that he had just received the first definite news that Godson had reached Tagish, Yukon Territory. (Actually, it took Godson another twelve days.) Three others were on their way and were already five miles beyond the summit. About seven hundred pounds of provisions had left for Tagish by pack train. Hinds was waiting with a boat at Lake Tutshi to receive them. He had sent Godson a list of boats with the number of passengers and horses which had arrived at Skagway since Godson's departure. Neither Yukon customs collector D.W. Davis nor the Mounties in the Yukon saw the border problem at the summits of the Chilkoot and White Passes. They expected the stampede to come up the Yukon River to Dawson, the route used by prospectors for at least two decades.

Godson wrote to Milne on September 9 from Tagish that he had reached his destination a week earlier:

We had many and serious delays but have pushed through as quickly as possible. If I had been furnished with money sufficient to buy boats, horses, etc., we might have reached here possibly a week earlier. Not having any money whatever at my disposal I have incurred as little expense as possible and, acting under your instructions, I will pay all expenses of the packing, etc., before forwarding any money to Victoria.

The trail from Skagway to the Lakes is in an infamous state. Men are nearly up to their waists in mud and horses and mules with their packs have been buried and lost in the mud daily for the past few weeks. There are upwards of 400 dead horses on this trail and there has been no step taken to remove them (this is in U.S. territory). If no steps are taken before spring the road will be impassable. I can hardly say how very wretched this trail is — but when you hear that strong men working like horses from daybreak to night are taking six to eight weeks to cover about forty miles of country with a few hundred pounds of food, etc., you will be able to conceive in what a deplorable state it is in. I am afraid I shall have to wait for snow and ice before making an attempt to reach the coast.

We commenced making collections on the 3rd of September and have been at work steadily since. Fortunately people do not know the country sufficiently to try to go down this river at night — but Davey and I are up at four in the morning and on Wednesday were at work until nearly eight at night — our takings reaching in all for the day nearly $900. . . .

The water here is very shallow and we wear rubber hip boots all day, wading out over knee-deep to examine each boat and make out entries. It has been raining continually for the whole week and we have been unable to make out entries in ink. We have been using indelible pencil and even then some of the entries are nearly unreadable.

Our tents are so small that we can only get in on hands and knees and when lying at full length, my head at one end against the canvas, my feet are within a few inches of the other end. The tents are just wide enough to cover my blankets. There are two men to each tent and the others are used for groceries. . . .

I am today sending, if the weather allows, two men to Bennett, a distance of fully sixty miles, to see if there are any goods arrived from Skagway. We are very short of provisions, having no meat or bacon of any description, and a very small quantity of rice, oatmeal and sugar. . . .

As these little camp stoves only last a few months at the most, I thought it best to have a permanent stove in our winter quarters — and am asking for a steel range (not cast); a good one I believe would be cheaper than a cheap one as it should be lighter for carriage up here, and with less danger of breakages.

You will be glad to hear that up to the present we are all in perfect health — our bad colds are gone — and if we can get our winter quarters put up within the next three or four weeks we will be prepared to face the Arctic winter. Directly the lakes are frozen we expect a great rush of people and goods from Dyea and Skagway who are now unable to get over the trails.

There has not been a single grunt out of these people. They were talking a great deal in Skagway and Dyea and on the trail of what they were going to do but, on the arrival at our flag, turn in and pay the duties readily and in most cases express surprise at the smallness of the amount of duty. The fact being that there has been so much said and written about the Collection that they expect to have to pay large sums — and when they are presented with the total duty required pay most cheerfully and go away wishing us all good wishes for our winter here. It is just as well though to have the constables here and in case you should see fit to move them I would certainly suggest that they be stationed in B.C. at Lake Bennett as there is much lawlessness and thieving going on between the Coast and the Lake.

I would respectfully urge that the supplies asked for be sent as early as possible to Skagway to care of George Rice [a packer] and I will make the best arrangements possible for their being sent over here on the ice.

On September 13, Godson told Milne that collections in the first eleven days amounted to $4,000. "It is absolutely necessary that we be furnished with a small safe and steam launch, to burn wood only." An inch of snow had fallen and, "my hands are almost too stiff with cold to write." He understood from "people passing" that the Mounted Police might be expected that week.

On September 15, Godson wrote again to Milne from Tagish: "Intend in about two weeks' time to start for the coast, a hundred miles away, with a strong escort and hope to be able to forward to you eight or ten thousand dollars. . . . We are almost out of supplies — we have no stationery whatever and until it is forwarded from Skagway I have to borrow from passersby — and will replace with stores upon arrival with the Mounted Police." The paper on which this letter was written was borrowed: at its head was "Canadian Pacific Railway Co.'s Telegraph, Electrician's Office, Montreal."

On November 3, Milne wrote McDougald in Ottawa that he had just seen Sifton, the minister of the interior, returning from a month-long trip up the coast. Sifton had gone from Dyea to the Tagish customs station where "he mentioned everything was satisfactory and that our customs officers were doing well." Milne told McDougald on November 6 that the Mounties had arrived at Tagish October 4 (the actual date was October 6) and he urged Ottawa to put a customs man on the Dalton Trail, the western route into the Yukon now known as the Haines Road. The NWMP diary kept at Tagish noted on October 19 that the "customs men put ten men to work for one day who failed to pay duty."

A jubilant telegram from Milne to McDougald announced that $20,000 in revenue had been turned over by the Tagish officers to the Commissioner of the Yukon. Customs Minister Paterson immediately informed the cabinet. Milne followed up with a letter written November 27, saying he had just heard from Godson at Bennett Lake, reporting collections of $21,500. The Godson letter, dated November 9, 1897, said he had seen Sifton "and received orders from him to pay all monies to the Mounted Police." He said he had purchased food from people "who were short of money to pay duty" and added: "I might almost as well be in Central Africa as here — I doubt whether communications would be carried on under greater difficulties. Yesterday we towed our boat along for about 16 miles down this lake [Bennett] against a high wind we could not have rowed against and at last worn out with towing over boulders, snow and ice we got into the boat and I and three other men pulled against the wind and in a blinding snowstorm from three in the afternoon until midnight — arriving here wet through and completely fagged out, my clothing almost ruined and boots nil."

Godson apparently began collecting duty at Bennett Lake on his own, without instructions. Inspector Zachary Taylor Wood of the Mounted Police informed his headquarters from Skagway on Christmas Day, 1897, that Godson had attempted to collect duty on steer beef from three men at Bennett Lake. Two had paid but the third, Willis Thorpe, had refused on the grounds that he had documents from U.S. officials at Sitka, Alaska, claiming that the head of Lake Bennett was American territory. (This would have placed the border some twenty miles north of the summits of the Chilkoot and White Passes.) Wood said Godson was claiming that the summit was the boundary.

Wood followed this up with another letter, on January 12, 1898, to Fred White, comptroller of the North West Mounted Police at Ottawa: "Mr. Godson, collector of customs at Tagish, has called on the police for assistance in collecting duty from those who have not so far paid. Mr. Godson asked me to call on Mr. Willis Thorpe and collect duty from him. . . . I am not taking any decisive action as it would only lead to trouble, though [Godson] may have asked me to do so simply to bring the matter to a climax." Godson pressed Wood to take action: "Captain Dillon will give you the names of some parties who have not paid duty assessed by me and fines and amounts due. In case of refusal to pay on demand, please take one or two men and secure goods to cover expenses and advise me."

There is no indication that any police action was taken. Thorpe wrote to Inspector Wood that he would not pay the $480 in duty Godson was demanding because he was an American citizen on territory "firmly claimed by the U.S." Mounted Police Constable Holmes at Bennett Lake told Wood he had refused to follow Godson's instructions and would await orders from Wood. Wood, in turn, was already awaiting orders from Ottawa. If Wood did not see the danger, the collector of customs did, from faraway Victoria. Milne warned McDougald on January 12, 1898, that the police must move up to the summits. He said he had just seen Inspector D'Arcy Strickland, arrived in Victoria from Tagish, and knew that Strickland was training six troopers to do customs work. On January 28, McDougald wired Milne to appoint customs officers at Chilkoot and White Passes. On the same day NWMP Comptroller White informed the customs minister that "Inspector Wood has definite instructions to the effect that the summit is the boundary line." The instructions had come from Sifton.

Milne immediately appointed Inspectors Wood and Robert Belcher to the passes — and Godson to Chilkoot as well — and McDougald approved the appointments. Strickland replaced Wood, and the two posts opened in late February, 1898, collections beginning immediately. Milne again pressed for similar appointments on the Dalton Trail, and on March 26 White said twenty men would leave soon under Inspector A.M. Jarvis, who would also be customs collector. Godson left Tagish on February 4 to collect duty from all the outfits he would intercept between Tagish and Chilkoot. He pursued his duty as arduously as ever, and Superintendent Steele informed Milne by letter: "Mr. Godson is ill suffering from a severe attack of snow blindness caused by travel while collecting duties between Tagish and Lakes Lindemann and Bennett."

In the Mounties' own reports on Klondike Trail duty, Wood wrote of the stations in the passes: "Not a complaint was heard from the thousands that passed." (Tagish was the only customs post from September, 1897, when the collection of duties commenced, until February, 1898, when the NWMP opened their stations in the Chilkoot and White Passes.) This was in marked contrast with the treatment to which people with Canadian goods were subjected at Skagway, Wood said; a convoy to accompany all goods purchased in Canada from Skagway across the boundary at eight dollars a day was "most unjust." U.S. Customs did not recognize Canadian presence on the summits and ordered convoys to accompany goods to Bennett, twenty miles on the Canadian side of the border. "The idea of an American convoy escorting Canadian goods through British territory was too much for the police at the summits," Wood wrote, "and convoys were politely but firmly impressed with the necessity of returning to Skagway or Dyea as soon as they reached our camps."

Wood was referring to J.W. Ivey, the U.S. customs collector for Alaska, who insisted that the border was at Bennett Lake. Ivey was a swashbuckler who found everything British and Canadian distasteful, including the North West Mounted Police. Once the Mounties chased a suspected thief down the Yukon River and into Alaska before they caught him and the $18,000 he had stolen, whereupon, at gunpoint, Ivey took the prisoner and the money away from them, claiming that Alaska was out of their jurisdiction. (The prisoner escaped jail in Eagle, Alaska, but left behind the $18,000 which was eventually restored to the Dawson owners.) Ivey arrived at Skagway on March 12, 1898, less than three weeks after the Mounties had established customs posts at Chilkoot and White Passes, then promptly marched to the summit and demanded of Inspector Belcher that he be permitted to place U.S. customs officers at Lindemann and Bennett Lakes. Belcher refused. Superintendent A.B. Perry of the NWMP detachment at Skagway informed Milne on March 20: "The collector of Customs Alaska will not recognize our right to the summits." This of course did not bother Sam Steele, who issued an order on May 17 that any American flags flying on land claimed by Canada were to be "removed on sight."

Steele reported: "The officers [at White Pass and Chilkoot] found the majority of people so anxious to get in that they gave very little trouble and the result was that when the goods were re-inspected at Tagish it was found that very few had underpaid their duty." He added that Godson, assistant to Belcher at Chilkoot, had gone to Bennett, Lindemann and Log Cabin to collect duties because many people had crossed the passes before the posts at the summits were established and were camped at those three places. Godson had completed this work before the end of May and had gone back to Tagish. Steele took the opportunity to say that members of the NWMP acting as customs men should be paid ten per cent commission on collections, making the point that no customs collector had been appointed in the North West Territories before 1883 and that the NWMP had performed this duty for nine years "with the greatest satisfaction to the department." The ten-per-cent commission for such work became general.

Belcher reported that he had arrived at the Chilkoot summit on February 11, 1898, and had started putting up a 12 x 12-foot building by moonlight, February 13. The planks had come up the pass and were so green that they shrank and the snow drifted through the crevices into the cabin. The nearest firewood was seven miles away. A storm lasted more than ten days, but on February 26, the first fine day, "the Union Jack was hoisted and the collection of Customs began." The cabin was small, unfit, cold and wet. The counter was a rough board a foot wide, and bunks took up much of the space. Belcher said he had no safe, although at times he had as much as $8,000 to $9,000 on hand, principally in gold coin. He and a corporal slept with it. Between February 26 and June 30, when he turned over the post to Customs, he collected $174,470.32. Belcher also reported an avalanche which killed fifty-three Americans, including one woman, on April 3. And at Sheep Camp on the way up the pass "one gentleman, who wished to distinguish himself, wanted volunteers to the number of one thousand to march up and turn us off, but as he did not feel inclined to take the responsibility of leading this gallant band the affair fell through."

Jarvis set up a post on the Dalton Trail on May 4, 1898, and noted that the first person to pay duty was W.M. Thompson of St. Thomas, Ontario, who had come from the western United States where he had lived for twenty years. Jarvis also had a complaint for Customs. He had not been paid as a customs collector: "Had the government sent up customs officers to fill these positions it would have cost them several thousand dollars in salaries, travelling expenses and maintenance."

The most appealing figure among the Klondike Trail Mounties is D'Arcy Strickland at White Pass. He was quick to note in his report that if the NWMP was aiding the customs department, Customs was returning the favor. He had arrived at Tagish October 6, 1897, and found Godson and four assistants collecting duties. "A few days before my arrival at Tagish a brutal murder had been committed at Marsh Lake. A man named Edward Henderson had shot and killed his partner, Thornburg Petersen. Word was sent to Mr. Godson and he dispatched some of his assistants to the scene and arrested the murderer. He was brought to Tagish and kept there until the arrival of Inspector F. Harper who took him to Dawson for trial."

Strickland pinpoints the date when Sifton reached Tagish on his inspection trip. He had arrived October 13 with Commissioner Walsh, stayed one night, and started back for Bennett.

Strickland went out on leave December 26, calling on Milne in Victoria, but was back at Skagway February 9, 1898, and was immediately ordered to the summit of White Pass. He arrived February 13 with twenty men and pitched tents. There was no timber within twelve miles for building or firewood. Some of his men were dispatched for both while a blizzard raged for ten days. "The little house was ready February 27 and at reveille on that date I hoisted the Union Jack on the summit of White Pass and began the collection of Customs duties there."

Strickland does not say so in his report but he nearly died of pneumonia and had to be relieved by Inspector F.L. Cartwright on March 27. Strickland was sent to Tagish, from where he wrote: "The ice went out of Tagish May 28 and then thousands of people who had been camped along the lakes building boats and waiting for navigation to open began to swarm down to Tagish. I had received orders from Col. Steele to examine all boats to see that no intoxicants were being smuggled into the country." Strickland numbered all the boats and took all the names of those who passed. He registered some 28,000 names. Strickland said Godson had already started registering boats at Bennett: Godson's total was 2,344 at Bennett, and his was 4,736 at Tagish.

Strickland said he had answered a couple of hundred of letters from all parts of the world from people anxious about their relatives and friends in the Yukon. There had been such a crush of people he had not been able to register the names in alphabetical order. He added: "Had that been done I would have found the task of finding out names and answering letters much easier. I have sometimes had to look through the whole 28,000 names to find one address."

Meanwhile, Milne, who had started at Customs in Victoria as a clerk in 1875 at $1,000 a year, was becoming exasperated with Godson for failing to keep up with his accounts and send them to Victoria on time. He pressed Godson for this paperwork. Godson, recovered from his snow blindness, wrote Milne March 9: "I have been working Sunday and weekday alike and often from 7 a.m. to 9 p.m. with very little interval for meals. I had no conveniences whatever. It has been hard work and I may not be through with the entries and accounts for three weeks yet. So many people round here have not paid duty yet and I am taking in entries daily." Somebody, presumably Milne, scratched across this part of the letter "nonsense."

Godson wrote of what he could do if he had a dozen men to help him and added: "I have been working single-handed since the middle of October. I have had an immense amount of work to get through. I was under canvas until December 24. The weather in November and December was so severe as to make it impracticable to sit and write for more than a few minutes at a time and since Christmas there have been numbers of persons coming down on the ice and I have been continually interrupted."

On March 25, Milne complained to McDougald about Godson's "lack of discretion." Godson had made no proper arrangements, he said, about who was to receive his salary while he was absent from Victoria. Other customs officers and the four constables had arrived back from Tagish November 10 but Milne still had not received Godson's statements of collections or vouchers for expenditures; Godson must consider himself under the direction of Commissioner Walsh of the Yukon instead of Victoria. He was transferring Godson to Chilkoot to act as a clerk under Belcher, where he would "be required to attend to his clerical duties, and nothing else."

However, Milne himself was rebuked by McDougald on April 14 in these words: "Full allowance must necessarily be made for the difficulties of the situation. Later intelligence as to the loss of life on the Chilkoot Trail, and the partial blindness of officer Godson, indicate that the conditions attaching to travel on that route are surrounded with danger and difficulties." The last we hear of Godson is in a note from Milne to McDougald April 21, 1898. Godson, he said, was working at Chilkoot and "has nearly completed his returns."

But the stand taken at Chilkoot and White Pass by Customs and police was a small, even hollow, victory. Canada was perched up in the mountains while what it wanted — a harbor at tidewater — was far below, firmly in American hands. In late 1898 and early 1899, Canada was represented at British-American talks held at Quebec City and Washington. Canada sought a small port called Pyramid Harbor, south of Skagway, with a strip of territory to connect it with British Columbia. The United States offered a fifty-year lease. Canada asked for a hundred-year lease. While this dickering went on, the proposal for a Canadian port in the Alaska panhandle leaked out and there was a hue and cry up and down the U.S. west coast and in Congress. The conference broke down. There was an exchange of notes later in 1899 which accepted the Chilkoot and White Passes as the temporary boundary. In 1901, there was an international incident at Skagway involving the Canadian flag and a Canadian customs officer, a detailed account of which will be found in the section of this book dealing with the lives and times of customs officers.

At last, in 1903, arbitration was arranged and a six-man tribunal established: three Americans (Secretary of War Elihu Root, Senator Henry Cabot Lodge of Massachusetts, and Senator George Turner of Washington), two Canadians (Sir Louis Jetté, lieutenant-governor of Quebec, and A.B. Aylesworth, a Toronto lawyer) and one Briton (Lord Alverstone, Lord Chief Justice of England).

The best Canada could hope for was a draw, because it was taken for granted that all three Americans would favor the U.S. position and that both Canadians would vote for the Canadian stand, which was the Coast Doctrine with multiple access to the ocean. The key was Alverstone, garrulous and indiscreet all through the negotiations, but a necessary member because Canada had no treaty-making power of its own at that time. Alverstone sided with the Americans in a 4-2 vote, and Canada was excluded from salt water along the entire length of the panhandle. It took ten years to mark the boundary. In the demarcation, three Canadians were killed in avalanches.

Nature herself may one day give Canada a tidewater harbor in the northwestern corner of British Columbia. Ice which once filled Glacier Bay has receded more than sixty miles since it was recorded by Captain George Vancouver in 1794. This ice recession, first noted in 1932, has been opening a deep waterway through the panhandle to Canadian territory.

Today, there are still two customs posts at or very near their original sites on the Trail of Ninety-Eight. One is at Fraser, British Columbia, two miles from the first Mountie post in White Pass; the other is at Pleasant Camp, British Columbia, only a few hundred yards from the original NWMP station on the 305-mile Dalton Trail from Haines, Alaska, to Whitehorse, Yukon Territory. The former is named after a stop on the White Pass and Yukon Railway, built in 1900, and was opened in 1979 with the completion of a new highway from Skagway to Carcross, Yukon Territory, twenty miles from where Godson set up his tent at Tagish in 1897. Pleasant Camp is the original name given the location by the trail blazer Jack Dalton and predates that of 1898, Dalton Trail Post, given it by the Mounties. The customs house was re-established in 1946, three years after construction of the Haines Road connecting Haines to the Alaska Highway. The American office is called Dalton Cache. The Alaska Highway, built in 1942, necessitated a customs house at the point where it crosses the Yukon-Alaska boundary. A station was opened at Snag Creek in 1946 and has since moved to adjacent Beaver Creek, Canada's westernmost community. The most northern border customs point is Little Gold Creek, Yukon Territory, on the Top of the World Highway between Dawson and Tok, Alaska.

In 1908, the International Boundary Commission was established by treaty, which reconfirmed the border throughout its entire length. The commission was made permanent in 1925 by another treaty, the first such negotiated and concluded by Canada itself. The commission still maintains the transcontinental line, which has no curves but 10,311 straight courses, one as short as 23.5 inches (in the Quebec-Maine highlands) and one as long as 647.1 miles (the 141st meridian boundary between the Yukon and Alaska). Approximately 8,100 monuments mark the border. Where the boundary runs through woods, a twenty-foot strip is kept open.

SECTION III

Smuggling

CHAPTER I

The Golden Age

I like a smuggler; he is the only honest thief. He robs nothing but the Revenue, an abstraction I never greatly cared about.
— Charles Lamb

Even in the face of the ugliness of the narcotics traffic, the smuggler has retained some of the aura of a romantic Scarlet Pimpernel. Who could not help laughing at the discomfiture of the law when in 1965 drug runner Lucien Rivard scaled his Montreal prison wall in 45°F weather on a garden hose with which, he had told his guards, he was going to water the rink?

Smuggling flourishes wherever there are high duties or outright prohibition on imports. Examples abound: tea, spirits and silks in 18th-century Britain; coffee and salt in 18th-century France; tea in 19th-century Canada; liquor in the United States in the 1920s; narcotics and firearms today; tobacco almost everywhere ("pernicious weed, abomination of the devil," said James I, tripling the duty).

Joseph Howe, Nova Scotia's reluctant Father of Confederation, said in 1865: "The smuggler is a check upon the extravagance of governments or the increase in taxation ... The only way we can keep out smuggling is to keep our tariff so low as to make it not worth while for any one to smuggle." (At that time, Nova Scotia's import tariff was about ten per cent.)

Writing in 1871, John Banks said in his *Smugglers and Smuggling*: "We may lay it down as an axiom that whenever the duties exceed 30 per cent ad valorem it is impossible to prevent a contraband traffic. The lowering of the import duties in this country [Britain] since 1830 has done more to prevent smuggling than all the Custom-house officers, Coast-blockade, Preventive-men and Coast-guard put together."

The 18th and early 19th centuries in Britain are usually thought of as the Golden Age of Smuggling, though this might be disputed by veteran rum-runners who helped assuage the U.S. national thirst during its prohibition years from 1920 to 1933. A British author, himself a customs officer, wrote in 1892: "The pettifogging attempts of modern times pale into utter insignificance when compared with the gigantic scale in which smuggling operations were conducted in the 'good old times.' The modern smuggler can only be regarded as a contemptible cheat when measured by the heroic standards of other days."

The first great smuggling enterprises involved exports, not imports. The earliest recorded widespread smuggling in England was by the Owlers, so called for their nocturnal activities. To encourage the manufacture of woollen cloth, the English government had banned the export of raw wool and a backlog of three to five years' supply piled up in England while France and Holland were crying for it. Despite the penalty of death on the gallows, wool smuggling by the Owlers and their successors was prevalent from the 13th century until the mid-1700s. When the price of wool fell in Europe, English smugglers turned to other staples such as liquor, wine, tea and silks.

Smuggling provided goods to the poor at much cheaper prices than otherwise possible and, consequently, the populace was the friend of the smugglers and often their abetters. In England, houses, churches and churchyards were convenient hiding places for contraband — tea in the pulpit, brandy in the belfry, gin in the tomb were common — and, even when arrests could be made, convictions by juries were practically unobtainable.

Not only Britons themselves smuggled tea, brandy, wine, silk and tobacco into Britain. Frenchmen did the same. They brazenly sailed their brandy-laden sloops into English ports and sold the liquor on the docks to local innkeepers. The customs men were often helpless. The smugglers worked in gangs of twenty to a hundred men. They had faster and better armed ships and more men than the revenuers, and simply used brute force when stealth did not work. Often, they did not even bother to try to hide their operations.

The basic tool of the smuggler was the cask, or "tub," or "anker," which held eight and one half gallons of spirits and weighed fifty-six pounds when full. A gallon of brandy in France cost four to five shillings. The legal cost in Britain was thirty-six shillings per gallon. Without damage to the contents, the tubs could be buried in the beach sand or tethered underwater offshore for weeks until safe collection could be arranged, or a ship could unload and the supplies be off the beach in three to five minutes. The tubs came equipped with carrying ropes so that porters could trot inland with them quickly. The porters, working at five shillings a night, were protected by batmen equipped with flails and clubs to beat off any revenuers who tried to make an arrest or seizure.

There was a curious inversion of the moral order: the revenuer was cast as the villain, and often the fool. The Reverend R.S. Hawker of Morwenstowe in Cornwall reported that he had tried to make smuggling a moral issue in his parish and had received the unanswerable argument: "But why should the King tax good liquor? If they must have taxes, why can't they tax something else?" (The King of France did — salt.)

Brigand-smugglers held the upper hand over customs officers. A revenuer's life was hazardous in the extreme, even though the penalty for "running uncustomed goods" was death by hanging. In the decade beginning 1723, two hundred and fifty-six officers were killed or wounded by smugglers who had become thugs, thieves, and highwaymen, and terrorized whole districts. One gang successfully raided a customs house and retrieved 3,700 pounds of tea seized earlier; another raided Newgate prison in London and rescued condemned accomplices. Still another gang, comprising 100 smugglers with 210 horses laden with tea, liquor and tobacco, rode calmly by the Wigtown customs house despite the presence of thirty soldiers. In 1755, some smugglers' wives who were signalling to their husbands from atop seashore cliffs pushed to his death a customs officer who was investigating their signal fires. This was a rhyme of the times:

> A beacon gleam on the clifftop edge
> Where no light has ever been
> And the smugglers lurk in their secret cove
> As they flash the lugger in.

(Nearly a century later, a similar system was in use by smugglers' accomplices on the Niagara frontier in Canada to indicate safety or danger. Flags were employed in daytime, fires by night.)

When the smuggling gangs passed through a community, villagers were supposed to turn their backs on them so there could be no recognition and therefore no identification if Customs came around. A rhyme of 1750 went:

> If you wake at midnight and hear a horse's feet,
> Don't go drawing back the blind or looking in the street,
> Them that ask no questions isn't told a lie.
> Watch the wall, my darling, while the gentlemen go by.
>   Five and twenty ponies
>   Trotting through the dark,
>   Brandy for the parson,
>   'Baccy for the clerk,
>   Laces for a lady, letters for a spy,
> And watch the wall, my darling, while the gentlemen pass by.

In 1736, it was estimated that the people of Britain consumed 1,500,000 pounds of tea. The figure had to be guessed at because only 650,000 pounds were legal — with duty paid on it. A century later, Upper Canadians had an even better record as tea smugglers: 917 chests of tea were imported into Canada legally one year but annual consumption was about 10,000 chests.

English smugglers employed resident agents in French, Belgian, and Dutch ports to speed purchases and arrangements for smuggling. They formed the entire clientele of some distilleries on the European coast. Even the Napoleonic Wars hardly interfered with smuggling. Indeed, some smugglers, as in the verse above, increased their profits by selling military information to the French.

By 1787, 1,425 articles were subject to high import duties in Britain. Tax rates prompted Sydney Smith to write, in 1820:

> Taxes are levied on everything that enters the mouth, covers the back or is placed underfoot; taxes upon everything on earth and the waters under the earth; on everything from abroad and grown at home; on raw material and on every fresh value added to it by the industry of man; taxes on the sauce that pampers the rich man's appetite and the drug that restores him to health; on the ermine that decorates the judge and the rope which hangs the criminal; on the poor man's salt and the rich man's spice; on the brass nails of a coffin and the ribbons of a bride.
>
> At bed or board, couchant or levant, we must pay. The schoolboy spins a taxed top; the youth manages a taxed horse with a taxed bridle and taxed saddle on a taxed road. The dying Englishman, pouring his medicine, which has paid 7%, into a spoon that has paid 15%, flings himself back on his chintz bed that has paid 22%, makes his will on an eight pound stamp and expires in the arms of an apothecary who has paid one hundred pounds license for the privilege of putting him to death.

So many people were engaged in smuggling in England's southern counties that farmers could not hire harvest hands, and a bread shortage developed. When Britain tried to crack down on smuggling from the Channel Islands, the smugglers simply moved their seat of operations to Roscoff on the Britanny coast. This led Lord Holland to complain in the Lords that if the necessary consequence of high duties was to be smuggling, better it be carried on by British subjects than by foreigners. Another Member of Parliament, Thomas Benson, a merchant, leased Lundy Island in the Bristol Channel, from which he ran a lucrative smuggling business. When he was placed in charge of transportation of convicts to America, he pocketed the passage money and shipped the convicts to Lundy Island as workers for his smuggling empire.

Smuggling boosted the shipbuilding industry. Hundreds of boats were built for only one purpose: smuggling. (This happened in Canada, as we shall see, though not on quite the same scale, with the running of liquor into the United States in the 1920s.) The history of smuggling and customs in England kept an alternating rythmn of attempts at repression on the part of the customs service and fresh devising on the part of the smugglers. As the English preventive service was gradually increased, the smugglers became so adept at building secret hideaways into ships' beams, keels, knees and masts that Customs had to bring in a regulation that any concealed place in a ship, even empty, was evidence of smuggling and cause for seizure of the ship. Seized ships were sawn in three and their crews sent to prison or impressed into the Royal Navy for five years. Most smugglers chose prison — when given the choice.

The British coast guard introduced a regulation which forbade "mixed marriages" in the service. If a coast guarder married into the family of a suspected smuggler, the officer was dismissed. Yet support for the smugglers was almost universal, and the revenuers even had trouble enlisting the help of other government agencies. Once, in Dorset, the 14th Light Dragoons refused to aid Customs in the roundup of a smuggling gang; the smugglers were supplying the regiment with cognac and tobacco — duty-free of course.

Vessels coming into port with a cargo and afterwards seen riding high in the water with cargo unaccounted for were automatically subject to seizure for smuggling. Some members of Customs hit upon the expedient of training dogs to find contraband liquor buried on beaches: they raised fox terriers from puppyhood on a diet liberally dosed with gin or brandy. The smugglers countered by setting out liquor laced with poison.

Eventually, organized smuggling died away in Britain, as the country turned to free trade and the flow of capital to buy contraband goods dried up. Many persons who had earned their living as porters or batmen were thrown on parish relief and, with the collapse of the smuggling fleets, the training grounds were lost for a certain expert seamanship.

CHAPTER II

The Fur Smugglers of New France

In North America smuggling began almost from the founding of the first coastal settlements in the 16th century. The main reason was that Britain and France had similar restrictive mercantile policies: the colonies could trade only through the mother country and only in ships belonging to the mother country. In 1660, there was an edict from Charles II which said that no sugar, cotton, wool or other products of the English plantations (colonies) in America, Asia or Africa could be traded except with Britain or British possessions. Three years later, the American colonies were barred from importing any goods except those shipped through British ports.

Smuggling became almost universal in the colonies. Most of it was carried on through the Dutch and French West Indies. The Molasses Tax Act was one of the greatest incentives to smuggling ever enacted. Of the 15,000 hogsheads of molasses imported into Massachusetts in 1763, all but 500 were smuggled.

In New France, there was no government customs service as such. The French charter companies which held the trade monopoly provided their own customs officers, known as *Les Commis* (literally, the clerks). The *Commis* wielded considerable power and had the right, for instance, to search ships for contraband or undeclared goods anywhere within the *Domaine*, that is, within the charter territory, which was, in effect, half of present-day Canada. Even explorers Médard Chouart des Groseilliers and Pierre-Esprit Radisson were fined after their expedition to Lake Superior and Hudson Bay in 1661-63 for failing to turn over to the charter company of the day furs they had brought back with them. In resentment, they later went to England and helped establish the Hudson's Bay Company.

There were several motives for smuggling in New France, as there always are everywhere. An important one was the frequent failure of the charter companies to provide sufficient supplies for the fur traders of the St. Lawrence and Acadia. Of necessity, the colonial merchants turned to the British colonies to the south for their provisions. There might have been some customs control by the monopoly-holders at Quebec and at the few other ports, but there was none on the wilderness frontier. The merchants paid for their illegally imported supplies with the only item they had for trading: furs. From there, it was a simple step to smuggling as many furs as possible to the English. This was a severe penalty for the colony because most of its revenue came from the 25-per-cent export tax on beaver skins. Several of the charter fur companies went bankrupt, sometimes because so many furs were being smuggled to the English and Dutch.

Another inducement for smuggling was that the English paid more for pelts than the French monopolists did and, moreover, gave the Indians a better rate of return on trade goods, charging less than the French for guns, ammunition, rum and clothing. For instance, a gun cost five beaver pelts at Montreal but only two at Albany in the British colonies.

The coureurs de bois were naturally attracted by such a favorable pricing system. Not to be confused with the voyageurs, who were the locomotion for the canoes of the charter trading companies, the coureurs de bois were free spirits who ventured farther and farther afield, adopted Indian life, and eventually became the Métis. What revenuer, private or government, could catch a coureur de bois in his own milieu on a wild and ill-defined frontier? Often they worked for the Quebec, Montreal and Trois-Rivières merchants, but, just as often, they went into business — the smuggling business — for themselves. In either case, they were a deep thorn in the side of official France.

The first edict pronounced on smuggling in New France seems to have been one dated April 15, 1676, when an order of the king decreed fines and confiscation of goods for anyone caught selling furs to foreigners. The order noted that some French traders were going deep into the interior (*"la profondeur des bois"*) and trading with the Indian nations farthest away from the colony. This was very prejudicial to the well-being of the colony, said the order, not only because it divided the colonists but because it inhibited the Indians from transporting their furs to the French trading posts. Moreover, the colony's *"vagabonds et libertins,"* the order's epithet for coureurs de bois, were taking their furs to foreigners instead of selling them, as required by law, to the French charter companies. The penalty was seizure of the goods and a fine of 2,000 *livres*, half to be paid to the king, half to the poor in hospital. The order was to be read, published and posted throughout New France so that no one could plead ignorance of the law.

Later, the penalty for smuggling was to be chained to an oar in the French galleys and, later still, it was death by hanging. We might pause here to note some of the penalties in the law of royal France, which also applied, of course, in Canada. The *Coûtume de Paris* was the civil code of some 400 articles which covered marriage, wills, dowry, debt, and so on.

Then there was the criminal law or, as codified by Louis XIV, August 26, 1670, *La grande Ordonnance criminelle*. There was a wide range of corporal punishment, including torture, and execution by various grisly methods, for a host of crimes from theft, adultery, sorcery and blasphemy to murder, treason and duelling. Sentences were usually carried out in public — punishment was regarded as a deterrent — and on the same day of sentence, except in the case of the hanging of a pregnant woman, when it was deferred until after the birth of the child.

A total of one hundred and eighteen persons, including seventeen women, were executed in New France, mainly for theft, murder, sex crimes and counterfeiting. Hanging was by strangulation, not breaking of the neck. Other methods included burning alive, decapitation and breaking on the wheel — being beaten to death by an iron bar. Other known punishments in New France included ninety-five floggings, the first carried out on Roberval's orders in 1542; fifty-nine brandings on the shoulder or cheek with a red-hot iron; fifty-six banishments from the colony; forty-seven condemnations to the galleys, some of them for life; thirty-one chainings to the stake, sometimes in an iron collar (*le carcan*), or in the pillory; and nineteen incidents of the *chevalet*, a wooden horse with a sharp metal back on which miscreants were placed with heavy cannon balls or other weights attached to their feet and wrists.

Executions and sentences of corporal punishment and torture were carried out by the hangman, called *le bourreau* or *le maître des hautes oeuvres*. The first name is derived from his whip for floggings. The second means literally "the master of high works" and refers, in gallows humor, to the elevated gibbet; to speed strangulation, the hangman usually clung to the person being hanged. Torture was usually by means of *les brodequins*, boots of oak planks into which stakes were driven between leg and board. A form of torture for women was being hanged by the wrists and having one's finger-ends burned with a candle flame. There are thirty known cases of torture being used in New France between 1663 and 1759. In the penal code, torture was referred to as *"la question."*

Public whippings were usually carried out in Quebec or Montreal. The hangman would arrive in a wagon with the condemned person, tie him or her (women were also flogged) to a wagon wheel, and administer one to twelve lashes or, if the number was unspecified, until blood came. Then the condemned person would be bundled back into the wagon for a repeat performance at the next public place. The lash was sixth in order of severity for sentences, being preceded by death, galleys for life, exile for life, torture, and galleys for a given period, such as nine years. Branding was usually done in the form of a fleur de lys, on the right shoulder.

At the founding of Quebec in 1608, Champlain hanged Jean Duval for conspiracy against him. Duval was beheaded and his head stuck on a stake. In 1669, François Blanche was hanged for murder and his hands cut off and nailed to a stake in Place Royale in Quebec's lower town. Less than a month later, Jacques Nourry was hanged for theft and his head put on a stake. Ten of the fourteen official hangmen in New France were criminals; one, Denis Quavillon, aged nineteen, lasted only four months because he himself was hanged for theft.

Despite the harshness of French law, it was less savage at the time than British law, which allowed for little or no discretion by judges and called for the mandatory death penalty for even petty felonies, such as stealing a loaf of bread. In New France, one could often get away with mere time in the stocks for minor offences, and there were avenues for appeal.

In 1647, the affairs of New France were brought forcefully to the attention of Louis XIV by the clash between the Jesuits and *La Compagnie des Habitants* (which held what we would call today a sub-contract from *La Compagnie de la Nouvelle France*) over trading liquor to the Indians for furs. The Jesuits maintained that liquor corrupted the Indians. The fur traders said they needed liquor in their business because the English were using it indiscriminately. Thus began a struggle that lasted more than a century and was never finally resolved.

The king established a council composed of the superior of the Jesuits and important merchants of the colony, that is, the chief fur traders. This council endured, with changes from time to time, from 1647 to 1663. But it did not solve the liquor question. In 1659, Bishop Laval called together what became known as the "brandy parliament" to convince the merchants of the evils of the liquor traffic. When this had no effect, the bishop simply threatened excommunication for anyone defying his proclaimed ban on trading or selling liquor to Indians. Many defied it. In effect, there was a twin smuggling operation — first: selling liquor to the Indians to obtain furs; second: selling furs to the English.

In 1662, when Governor Baron d'Avaugour authorized the use of liquor as a medium of exchange in the fur trade, Bishop Laval managed to have him removed. When the new governor, de Mésy, complained about Laval's encroachment on civil affairs, Laval excommunicated him (though he relented to administer the last rites of the church to him at his death in 1665). Still, although his influence could be felt in the 1666 decree of the death penalty for selling liquor to the Indians, Laval gradually lost ground to Intendant Talon. In 1667, colonists with hunting licences were permitted to carry liquor for (ostensibly) their own use and, the following year, to prevent the entire fur trade gravitating to the English, permission was granted to sell or give liquor to the Indians. Laval tried to counter this civil order by making the sale of liquor to Indians a *cas réservé*, or a matter for which absolution was required, but few people paid any attention.

Enterprising, brave and haughty, Louis de Buade, comte de Palluau et de Frontenac, was appointed to his first term as governor of New France in 1672 but, despite being held in a mixture of fear, awe, respect and affection by the Indians, he could not stop them selling their furs to the English and Dutch. And he had other reasons for concern, like the unofficial trading in furs conducted by Governor Perrot of Montreal, who had cleverly increased his income to fifty times his annual salary of 1,000 crowns by this means. But then, nearly everybody else in New France, including Frontenac, was in the fur trade, too.

Frontenac built a fort at Cataracoui, now Kingston, in 1673, setting fears among the Montreal merchants that the fort would afford Frontenac the opportunity to intercept the Indian traders en route east. Their fears were justified. Frontenac declared that any coureur de bois caught trading without a licence — a licence from Frontenac, as it turned out — would be subject to the death penalty. Montreal was headquarters for the coureurs de bois, so Frontenac ordered Perrot to halt their operations out of Montreal. Perrot had authority to issue his own trading licences — all licences had to be paid for, of course — but Frontenac limited the Montreal governor's jurisdiction to the immediate area of Montreal. But while Perrot cracked down as ordered, arresting coureurs operating in areas not allowed by their licences, only those with licences issued by Frontenac were arrested, while those with licences signed by Perrot went free. An indignant Frontenac ordered Perrot to Quebec and arrested him there. Abbé de Fénelon protested Perrot's arrest from the pulpit, and accused Frontenac of using his official position for private gain. Frontenac charged de Fénelon with sedition and ordered him to return to France. Perrot also returned to France to defend himself, was reprimanded, and was sent to the Bastille for three weeks as token punishment. He was then reinstated as governor of Montreal, and the king told Frontenac to stay out of local affairs.

When Frontenac found the coureurs useful as informants on the movements of Indian tribes, he relaxed trading restrictions against them, but Laval objected because they carried liquor as a trading item. Then, although the king instructed Frontenac not to issue more trading licences, the governor continued to issue "hunting licences" which were, in effect, disguises for illicit trading. In 1678, Sieur Migeon, bailiff at Montreal, arrested several coureurs de bois, whereupon Frontenac sent Migeon to jail for two months. Frontenac was again reprimanded, this time by Finance Minister Jean-Baptiste Colbert, and the prohibition against the coureurs running liquor to the Indians was renewed. It was unenforceable, and the king ordered what today we would call a public opinion poll to be taken among prominent colonists. The churchmen, citing hideous crimes by the Indians when under the influence of liquor, were ignored; most merchants felt liquor was necessary in the fur trade because the English and Dutch were using it. At a special meeting, fifteen of twenty delegates voted for the liquor trade, and the king assented. The clerics continued to press for prohibition and, in 1707, corporal punishment for selling liquor to the Indians was re-introduced. Two coureurs were hanged for the crime. But the argument continued to rage long beyond the time of the French regime, until the North West Mounted Police ran most of the whisky-traders out of the prairies, late in the 19th century.

Orders from Versailles did nothing to stop smuggling in New France, in low places or high. When Governor de la Barre sent a delegation to Albany to negotiate trade and other matters with the English in 1682, one of the delegation, Sieur Salvaye, took the occasion to smuggle 800 beaver pelts to Albany in his bulky luggage. In 1683, coureurs de bois who smuggled furs were described by de la Barre as "miserable French deserters" who would cause the ruin of New France and who deserved hanging. Yet smuggling was carried on almost openly from the forts at Chambly and Frontenac despite special local ordinances prohibiting it. When, for instance, in 1736, Commandant Beauvais at Frontenac learned that two traders, Duplessis and Deneau, were making for Oswego across Lake Ontario with a load of furs, he had their three hundred pounds of beaver seized, four miles off Oswego, and sent them to prison in Montreal for three months.

The royal court both needed and despised the coureurs de bois. They were needed for their contacts, among the Indians and on the frontier beyond the farthest outposts, but were kept away from the colony by threat of fines and punishment, so traded and lived at the English posts. In 1681, the king granted an amnesty to coureurs de bois on condition that they give the conseil the names of Canadien merchants for whom they were running furs to the English. This condition was not insisted upon, however, when it turned out that these merchants included some members of the conseil. Three years later, the king decreed the death penalty for colonists who deserted as traders to the English and Dutch, and one colonist was hanged.

The galleys were the punishment for selling furs to anybody except the French charter companies — and for the ship's captain who transported them; one trading company placed a twenty-four-hour watch on every ship in Quebec harbor. Even at that, the visiting of ships between dusk and dawn was prohibited. (This is one of the sources of the clause in the

Canada Customs Act which says all importations "must be between sunrise and sunset.") Some ships unloaded seven or eight miles below Quebec to evade duties and a royal order in 1702 warned that all goods would be confiscated if full duties were not paid.

Heavy penalties did not curb smuggling. In fact, it increased, drawing a profusion of new ordinances from king, intendants and conseil souverain. There were eight such ordinances between 1707 and 1728, some of them relaxing the penalties in an effort to cajole the coureur de bois into renewed service for New France. In 1707, the order banning beaver trade with the English called for seizure of goods, ships, canoes, and so on and imposed fines, one-third to go to the informer, one-third to the Hotel-Dieu hospital in Quebec, and one-third to the charter fur company. But there was no mention of the galleys or corporal punishment. Rather, in 1716, there was another amnesty for the coureurs de bois if they would undertake military service out of Fort Michilimackinac. This was only one year after Intendant Bégin estimated that beaver furs weighing 50,000 pounds — about one-quarter of the total yield — went to the English every year to evade the 25-per-cent export tax and obtain higher prices than those paid in France. Most of this contraband trade was between Montreal and Albany. An order had to be issued, in 1732, to put a stop to religious institutions which, out of *"un zèle indiscret,"* gave refuge to deserters.

In 1736, Intendant Hocquart wrote Cardinal Fleury in Paris that the English easily attracted the fur trade of the Indians by selling liquor indiscriminately to them. But he also conceded that the English gave more goods in trade and paid a better price for beaver. In passing, he accused the coureurs de bois not only of selling furs to the English ("le commerce étranger") but of spreading pernicious rumors about New France ("mais prennent des impressions chez les Anglois très-pernicieuses à la Colonie"). But Hocquart threw up his hands about what action might be taken: "L'autorité ne peut, quant à présent, apporter d'autre remède à ce désordre qu'en accordant à ces coureurs de bois une amnistie, ainsi qu'il s'est pratiqué cy-devant; il y a apparence qu'ils en profiteront tous; mais pour éviter de tomber en pareil cas par la suite, il est de conséquence de ne laisser monter dans les païs d'en haut, que les voyageurs sur la fidélité et la bonne conduite desquels on pourra raisonnablement compter: cela demande d'estre suivi." (The only remedy we can think of at the moment is an amnesty for the coureurs de bois, as in the past; they will probably take advantage of it; but to avoid falling into the same situation again, it is important that we allow into the interior only travellers on whose loyalty and good conduct we can reasonably rely: this must be followed up.)

The intendant did not offer any suggestions about how travellers to the interior could be selected. Even the Jesuits, after all, were sometimes accused of trafficking in beaver pelts. Governor La Jonquière was one of the accusers. In his case, the Jesuits retaliated by accusing him of making a tidy profit in furs by trading liquor to the Indians.

The French fur trade was also afflicted by widespread fraud. The deception had to do with the condition of beaver skins. The best skins were those which had actually been worn by the Indians and were called *castor gras*, or fat beaver. The inferior ones were *castor sec*, or dry beaver. To give the *castor sec* the appearance of the *castor gras*, the colonists of New France who were in the trade treated them with grease or oil. It was usually not until the pelt reached a Paris hat-maker that the *castor sec* could be detected for what it was, an inferior fur. The Paris furriers naturally declared them second-grade and would not pay the price demanded by the charter company. When Nicolas Oudiette, who held the charter, complained about this, in 1676, a two-price system was installed for fat and dry beaver. But the same thing happened again in 1726. *La Compagnie des Indes en Canada*, the contemporary charter holder, found it was paying a high price for treated skins but hearing complaints from the furriers of Paris that good hats could not be made out of the poor skins they were receiving. Another two-price system was installed: four francs a pound for *castor gras*, 40 sous a pound for *castor sec*.

In the clandestine trade between New France and the British colonies, particularly New York and Massachusetts, the English traders not only offered better prices than the French, they paid for the furs in coined money — English, Spanish and Portuguese. The extent of the contraband trade showed itself in the prevalence of foreign coinage in Canada, so much so that in 1681 the conseil supérieur had to set values upon it and conditions for its circulation in Canada. In the early days of the colony, beaver, moose and other skins were the standards of value and the medium of currency exchange.

Only after the establishment of Montreal in 1642 did the need for regular currency become evident and money replace the barter system. But French coinage was always scarce, and card money was introduced in 1685 as a "temporary measure" (it lasted until the end of the French regime) to pay the troops and purchase military supplies. It was literally card money. Because there was a lack of suitable paper, and because there was no printing press in New France, playing cards were cut up for money and each piece signed by the governor and the intendant, a heavy drain on their time. In 1690, the card money was called in for redemption, but the coinage failed to arrive from France, so that those turning in their card money were given temporary notes — the first recorded issue of treasury notes in Canada as a substitute for other paper obligations of the colonial government.

Counterfeit card money appeared almost as soon as card money. In 1690 Pierre Malidor, a surgeon, was flogged in public in Quebec and given hard labor for three years for counterfeiting. In 1731, François Pelletier was exiled to the French West Indies for the same offence. Five years later, Louis Mallet and his wife, Marie Moore, were sentenced to death and hanged the same day for counterfeiting; they were two of fourteen persons executed in New France for this. Intendant Bigot, referring to a case in which the accused escaped the gallows and was exiled to France, commented drily that banishment from Canada for life was very slight punishment indeed for a rogue who didn't care where he lived.

In all this, the French were proving once more what they themselves and all other countries had already proved over and over again through the centuries: smuggling cannot be legislated out of existence. Now we shall see how the English went through the same vain procedure in their North American colonies.

CHAPTER III

Smuggling in British North America

Smuggling thrived on the Atlantic coast from the earliest days. Near the end of the 18th century it was judged that in the Maritime colonies illicit imports far outweighed legal landings in such products as tea, sailcloth, cordage, anchors, wine, spirits, soap, candles, indigo, starch, mustard, tobacco and cotton. The French islands of St. Pierre and Miquelon off Newfoundland were early smuggling centres, too. The British once assigned two cutters to stop the flow of European goods through the islands to New England, with little success. When, later, Britain had fishing treaties with France and the United States which barred customs inspection of fishing vessels at sea, contraband runners decked out as fishing boats appeared almost immediately.

In 1764, the governor of Newfoundland, Sir Hugh Palliser, tried to crack down on smuggling with new powers of seizure and arrest and a generous bounty for the informer — and himself — in all cases. Palliser fined a captain £60, in 1765, for carrying sixty fishermen and seamen to New England. Most of these were emigrating from Newfoundland to escape debts, and the captain was obliged to pay not only the fine but all his passengers' debts as well. Palliser bore down particularly hard on New England smugglers but, historian D.W. Prowse tells us, "they beat him, as they had beaten all the custom house officers in America; they had an invincible prejudice and objection to the payment of duties of any kind to King George, and they lied like troopers." Many New England vessels were seized, but somehow the Americans got them out of the rapacious clutches of Admiralty Court.

Authorities everywhere openly solicited the services of informers. For instance, the customs house at Quebec placed this advertisement in *The Quebec Gazette* of June 21, 1764, (a "composition" is a false declaration):

ADVERTISEMENTS

The Honourable Commissioners of His Majesty's Customs, having been inform'd that Compositions have been frequently enter'd into for the Duties imposed by the Act of 6 Geo. II, payable to His Majesty at the Ports of America, give this Publick Notice, That whoever will make Discovery of any Person or Persons, who shall have been guilty of entering into, or conniving at such Compositions, to John Temple, Esq; or Peter Randolph, Esq; Surveyors-General of His Majesty's Customs in North-America, or other Principal Officer of His Majesty's Customs, the Collector, or Comptroller, of any Post, except the Post where such Fraud was enter'd into, so that the Parties offending may be convicted thereof, and the Duties recover'd to the Crown, shall receive One Third Part of the Duties so recover'd.

By Order of the Honourable Commissioners of His Majesty's Customs in London.

Custom-House, Quebec,   THOMAS AINSLIE, Collector.
20 June, 1764.

It appears that the Hudson's Bay Company never experienced any major problem with smuggling by its employees, or "servants" as they were called, though it had plenty with the Red River settlers. Edward Umfreville's book, published in 1790, on the state of the company, suggests one reason for this: the company never informed its factors in Canada of the prices fetched for furs in England in the apparent belief that, if the factors were aware of the huge markups added there, over what the Indians received for the skins, they might be inclined to channel pelts to the rival North-West Company.

There are frequent references to smuggling in the books by early travellers to Canada. Hugh Gray, writing in 1809, noted that St. John's was the only legal point of entry in Lower Canada for goods coming from the United States, and added: "We generally have some troops at St. John's, as it is the frontier town. The officer who commands the detachment generally examines those who pass either way; it is a kind of check of evil-disposed subjects, but a very ineffectual one, as experience has proved. Those who do not wish to be known can find many ways of getting from the one country to the other without going by St. John's." Gray said official figures showed legal imports through St. John's of £75,546 in 1806. But the amount of smuggled goods in the same year was at least £100,000, he added.

Another visitor to St. John's, John Lambert, author of *Travels Through Canada and the United States in the Years 1806, 1807, 1808*, said people were so used to smuggling that they even smuggled non-prohibited and low-duty goods: "Great latitude is given to the introduction of goods from the United States, without passing through the custom-house at St. John's. The means of conveying them into Canada, across the extensive boundary line which divides the two countries, are so easy, and require so little exertion to avoid the Argos' eyes of a custom-house officer, that every temptation is offered to introduce articles which are neither prohibited or pay any considerable duty." During the U.S. trade embargo at that time, armed militia assisted American customs officers but imports into Canada doubled in 1807-08. Lambert wrote: "A variety of curious expedients were resorted to by the Americans in smuggling their produce over the line [into Canada]: buildings were erected exactly upon the boundary, one half in Canada, the other half in the States; the goods were put in at night and before morning were safe in Canada." Ingenious Vermonters also built huge rafts, loaded them with goods and awaited storms, when it was impossible for customs officers to board, to carry them swiftly downriver into Canada. They made such a mockery of Customs that President Jefferson declared them in a state of rebellion and ordered out militia reinforcements. The Vermonters were enraged for being classed as rebels just because of a few frays between customs officers and smugglers.

Lord Dalhousie, governor of Lower Canada, noted in his diary this incident at St. John's in 1822: an American steamboat which regularly brought passengers and goods from New York and Lake Champlain was seized by the Canadian customs collector at St. John's because it was carrying contraband. Two soldiers were put on the boat as guards while the captain and the collector went to Montreal to arrange posting of bonds to avoid delay of the ship's departure. However, the mate got up steam, threw the soldiers in the hold, and made off: "an outrage on the laws and an insult to our flag." Dalhousie said the British government was partly to blame for allowing U.S. ships into Canadian harbors. The governor wrote about another border incident in the same year: "outrages" (he does not specify them) had been committed against the newly-established customs house at Sherbrooke where smuggling, counterfeiting and forgery "are matters of trade openly carried on." Dalhousie added that he had sent a detachment of troops to back up the magistrates, and that a circuit court of two judges would follow in a month, presumably to mete out quick justice. At another point in his diary, Dalhousie wrote that "to trade a little" was a Yankee phrase meaning to smuggle and that open barter in tea was "quite common."

"Tea was truly Britain's gift to the smuggler," wrote Gordon Blake in his study, *Customs Administration in Canada*. The law said tea could not be imported except from England. Legal tea was that supplied by the East India Company, which held the monopoly for the British Empire. But in the United States, Chinese tea was about one third of the price of legal tea; a smuggler's net gain, after his purchase, transportation and other costs, was about one shilling a pound. When imports of tea from Britain declined, year by year, it was first believed that Canadians were switching from tea to coffee. Then it was found that the simple reason for the decline was the enormous amount of smuggled tea entering Canada from the

States; three-quarters of the tea drunk in Upper Canada had been smuggled in.

In 1828, John Neilson, a member of the Lower Canada Assembly and star witness before the British parliamentary committee on the civil government of Canada, testified:

> There is an extent of settled frontier between the British provinces and the United States of America of upwards of 1,000 miles, and more than 500 of that is a mere water communication; a broad river and lakes; the settlements are thin along these, and the river may be passed in any direction by night or by day. Anything that can give any profit by smuggling will come in; all the custom-house officers in the world could not prevent people, living as neighbours and friends, relations, brothers and sisters, people who visit one another almost every evening, from bringing in anything that will enable them to make a profit, or exchanging articles for mutual convenience. Then there is another thing to be considered; all over the world the Revenue Laws have been unpopular; people have not considered offending against them in the light that it ought to be considered, as an immoral act, but they have voluntarily violated those laws, thinking that they did not commit a very immoral act; they join in countenancing the smugglers instead of preventing them; every one feels that he has got a kind of interest in getting a thing as cheap as possible, and he does not hesitate when he feels the workings of that interest to violate the law; therefore, you have people on both sides interested in some measure in this system of smuggling and unrestricted intercourse; and when the body of the people on each side the frontier are interested in favour of it, how can you prevent it being done?

Neilson continued:

> There is something so consonant with the character of the people of America in this kind of trading with one another, independently of all regulations, that during the last war [1812-14] our army was supplied through the American army with the greatest part of its provisions. Under these circumstances, I would submit whether it is practicable on such a frontier to prevent smuggling if there is anything to be made by it, and if there is nothing to be made by it, what is the use of the laws and regulations? If a system of custom-houses were established along the frontiers, it would ultimately make the people on both frontiers hostile to the British government, for the acts of the officers of the government are too commonly ascribed to the government, and particularly in America; if anything is done it is in the name of the British government, and if they quarrel with officers they are quarrelling in some measure with the government, so that in reality this kind of nuisance that the people will suffer in consequence of all those custom-house officers collecting a revenue, which will be no revenue, upon the frontiers, will dissatisfy the people with the British government, and consequently, being dissatisfied in that way,

both the Americans on their side and our people on ours, we will run the risk of being overwhelmed.

How do the American States regulate the intercourse between Canada and their territory? There is hardly any regulation or difficulty to the intercourse. I came through that way; I brought all that was necessary with me to this country, books and papers, and other things; when I came to the first [U.S.] custom-house, a gentleman came in to the inn where I stopped and told me that he was a customhouse officer, if I would be so good as to report what I had brought. I told him what I had brought, and he wished me good day and a pleasant journey; that was the whole ceremony; there was nothing to pay; but with us they make them pay for every little thing, permits, and so on.

Neilson outlined the predictable effects of smuggling on regular trade: it was easy to collect customs duties at Quebec, the port of entry for British goods, but it was difficult to collect them along the land frontier. Therefore the Lower Canada Assembly tended to levy heavy duties at Quebec. This drove prices up, and resulted in decreased importation of British goods. The duties at Quebec were, in effect, a bounty for clandestine importations by land from the United States. "It is utterly impossible to prevent smuggling in America; the only way is not to give an inducement to it," Neilson told the investigating committee.

On this point, it might be worth mentioning here that in 1872 the Canadian government, concerned over the possibility of widespread smuggling, repealed the duty on tea and coffee. The United States had reduced its tariff, making American tea and coffee much cheaper than in Canada. Sir Francis Hincks, the finance minister, said: "It would be impossible for the government to guard against American tea on the frontier." (He had before him the example of smuggling forcing repeal of the British tax on salt in 1825.)

In the view of Lieutenant-Governor Sir George Arthur, writing from Toronto in 1839, smugglers spread "disaffection" throughout the country and kept up "treasonable communications" with enemies of Canada in the United States, reminding us of what Intendant Hocquart had said about the coureurs de bois of New France. Robert Gourlay in his *Statistical Account of Upper Canada*, 1822, took a very different view: "To give scope in free trade is noble; to beggar custom-houses is delightful."

Lieutenant E.T. Coke, writing in 1833 of his visit to Canada, described his sojourn at Prescott: "The inn was in so dirty a state, and the whole town presented such an uninviting aspect, that we were induced, in spite of the necessity of subjecting our baggage to the scrutiny of a customhouse officer, to cross the river to Ogdensburgh, immediately opposite, where we found a comfortable bed."

Coke found the next day that Prescott, with 800 to 1,000 inhabitants, did a great deal of business in transportation "and a vast deal more in the smuggling line." He added: "Endless are the disputes and broils on account of the seizure of a steamboat which plies between the two towns every ten minutes for the convenience of passengers who are not unfrequently well supplied with contraband goods."

Coke's book is probably best remembered for his description of a "dirty and uncomfortable" hotel in Niagara and, though it does not directly concern us here, it is worth quoting: "I felt my English blood almost boil in my veins when I found myself sitting in company with two servant women at the table d'hôte, at the same time that their mistress occupied a place at the other end of the table. I could have very well accommodated myself to such neighbors in the States, but never expected to have found the levelling system introduced into the British provinces to such an extent."

Now let us see what smuggling looked like from the point of view of the Commissioners of Customs in London and of their collectors in the British North American colonies. Three commissioners made a special revenue inquiry in the colonies in the years 1812, 1813 and 1814. Their first report dealt with Nova Scotia, where they found illicit trade carried on "to a very considerable extent." Proximity to the United States and excellent American harbors, they saw, afforded opportunities for smuggling "which the utmost vigilance can scarcely counteract." By the 1783 treaty, the United States was authorized to fish the Nova Scotia and New Brunswick coasts and U.S. fishermen permitted to dry their nets on shore. These fishing vessels introduced East India and American goods, and "clandestinely sell all kinds of fishing equipment to British ships." Nova Scotia ships carrying gypsum (plaster of Paris) to the United States brought back contraband goods, including tea and manufactured articles. The U.S. government encouraged this trade because smuggling voyages were insured by companies at rates not much greater than and often less than trans-ocean risks.

John Black, Halifax merchant, was alarmed by the remedy proposed by the commissioners; he told them in testimony at Halifax August 23, 1811, that any British naval ships on smuggling patrol would likely impress seamen from Nova Scotia ships, and they would frighten others into thinking that the same fate might befall them. The colony's coastal trade would be ruined.

Another witness was John Richard Uniacke, attorney-general of Nova Scotia. His summation was that smuggling kept pace with the increase in population, capital investment and the fisheries. He listed smuggled items as tea, spices, East India dry goods, tobacco, gin, brandy, leather, U.S.

distilled spirits, cordage, sailcloth, linen, wrought iron, soap, candles, salted provisions, refined sugar, cotton and wool. Vessels for the gypsum trade brought back all kinds of contraband goods from the United States to the great injury of the fair trader and the colony's revenue. Uniacke's proposals for combatting smuggling included provision of two small vessels, thirty to forty tons with six to eight hands each, to carry customs surveyors everywhere along the coast to check on smuggling. A daily log would have to be kept to make sure the ships were active and diligent in anti-smuggling operations. Every coasting vessel should carry a manifest of every single package and item on board, signed by a customs officer.

William Robertson, a merchant of Sisibou, estimated that at least half of Nova Scotia's trade was in smuggled goods. Most of the fishermen and many farmers were engaged full-time in the contraband trade. Michael Wallace, treasurer of the province's executive council, testified that for years the legislature and the council had enacted laws to repress smuggling but a remedy was very improbable "as long as the inhabitants were not disposed to help in observance of the law."

The commission of inquiry looked into customs affairs at two Nova Scotia outports. At Liverpool, it found that smuggling was so prevalent that the preventive officer didn't dare interfere because there was no revenue cutter or military unit to back him up. Farther down the south shore at Shelburne, it found that the customs establishment should be abolished. Shelburne was founded by United Empire Loyalists in 1783 and it had flourished for a few years, shipping fish and lumber to the West Indies. Its population soared to more than ten thousand, making it bigger than Halifax. But then the United States had started supplying goods more cheaply to the West Indies, and Shelburne had fallen into "extreme and hopeless" decay; the population was down to only four hundred.

At Saint John, the commissioners found the contraband trade "much beyond" even that in Nova Scotia. It was conducted mainly through Moose Island (Eastport, Maine), ceded to Britain in 1783 but "surreptitiously obtained possession of by the Americans in 1786." Moose Island was little more than a mile from Campobello Island which was "distinctly British." American ships anchored in the channel between the two islands on the basis of an agreement allegedly entered into by the U.S. and British customs houses on Moose and Campobello Islands. In the channel, goods were passed from American vessels to New Brunswick and Nova Scotia ships in exchange for gypsum and fish. If there were any customs interruption of these transactions, the ships merely put into Moose Island as a place of refuge. Warehouses on Moose Island were "stuffed" with produce for the contraband trade. The warehouses were larger than any in Saint John. Frequently, there were a hundred sail in the channel, and more business was done in one day off Moose Island than at Saint John in two months.

Another source of contraband was Woodstock, on the St. John River above Fredericton and sixteen miles from the border. Goods were moved across the frontier from Houlton, Maine, and smaller points, and brought down the river from Woodstock in open boats. They were stored in houses, fishing shacks, barns, sheds, and so on, in and around Saint John. The commission of inquiry estimated that in New Brunswick smugglers had monopolized the entire trade in East India goods, brought in fifty times the amount of tea imported legally from England, three-quarters to seven-eighths of all wine, nine-tenths of the gin and brandy, seven-eighths of all soap and candles, the greater part of indigo, tobacco, starch, mustard, dry goods, all sailcloth, cordage and anchors.

Currency was scarce because what was issued to pay the troops disappeared into the pockets of the smugglers. The legitimate trader in East India goods and tea could find no sale for them; but other shops in Saint John were filled with goods not one item of which was imported legally. (There was already evidence of this from another source. Robert Wood, a Saint John tobacconist, complained in a petition to the New Brunswick legislature January 14, 1807, that he was being driven to the wall by smugglers. Very large quantities of smuggled American tobacco were being consumed by "His Majesty's Troops and other Inhabitants of the province." In the previous nine years, twenty-six hogsheads of American leaf tobacco had been legally imported but in the same period at least two hundred hogsheads had been smuggled into New Brunswick. Wood pleaded: "This loyal subject ... in consequence of this illicit traffic has been struggling with difficulties from the first settlement of the province which now threaten him and his family with poverty and ruin unless some remedy is speedily applied for this evil." He proposed that raw tobacco be imported and manufactured by New Brunswickers, thus providing jobs and increasing the revenue. The legislature took no action.)

The commissioners also found that customs officers were so ill paid that some took part in smuggling rather than trying to prevent it. One suggestion was that customs officers visit all stores in Saint John and seize all contraband goods. (Something similar had been done in New France.) This was not acted upon, and probably for a reason which lay between the lines in the testimony of merchant John Robinson: some of the richest people in the province had made all their money through smuggling. Of the customs establishment in general in New Brunswick, the commission said: "There did not appear to us to have been that active zeal and vigilance among the officers of the revenue, particularly at St. Andrews, which the exigency and importance of the case seemed to require of them;" it was quite usual for a New Brunswick shipbuilder to go openly to Moose Island to buy all the sailcloth, anchors, cables, cordage and other articles he needed.

On to the United Province of Canada went the commission of inquiry. There, it all but threw up its hands at the poor administration of Customs. Moreover, the war of 1812-14 was just beginning and the commission did not get much beyond Quebec City where it found, among other things, that the entire "waterside business" at Quebec was "imperfectly attended to." Cargo was landed without inspection, and promissory notes were taken in payment of duty on the basis of unsubstantiated valuation given by the importer. The customs procedure was so complicated that "we cannot detail the practice with any confidence." The outports of Gaspé, New Carlisle and Magdalen Islands, moreover, had apparently never been visited by the Quebec collector or comptroller, nor was there any regular communication with them. In fact, the manner in which the business of the revenue, if any, was conducted could not be ascertained. Considerable quantities of goods were smuggled into Lower Canada simply by being carried through the woods to avoid the customs house at St. Jean. (Official trade between Lower Canada and the United States had been opened in 1788 and all boats, carriages and conveyances were subject to "visitation" by customs officers at St. Jean.) Not least, the consumption of West Indies rum in Upper Canada had "exceedingly diminished" because of smuggled American whisky.

The commission summed up these factors as "open defiance of the law" and concluded: "The extended line of inland-frontier in these provinces certainly opposes great difficulties to the adoption of any measures that would effectually prevent this illicit traffic; and it is a matter of some doubt to us, under the present circumstances of the province, what to propose." These frank commissioners were R.B. Dean, R. Thompson and George Wyke.

Gathering the customs in Newfoundland was a challenge to the wits of officers. On December 6, 1836, customs officer Lorenso Moore at Carbonear, Newfoundland, reported that brandy had been illegally landed from vessels returning from the Labrador fishery where they had met French ships at Hawks Harbor. He had found one thirty-gallon cask in the shop of William Harding, publican. Moore had no place to store seized goods and, fatally, asked Harding to keep the cask until he heard from him. Meanwhile, he had discovered another cask in the house of Francis Ash, took a sample, and accepted Ash's guarantee of security. Later, he checked on Harding's cask "and upon taking out the bung found that water had been substituted for brandy." Brandy in the sample from Ash's cask was "very inferior." Moore would await instructions.

On December 17, Edward Stewart, collector at St. John's, told the subcollector at Harbor Grace to instruct Moore that he had acted contrary to the law in entering Ash's house without a writ of assistance and: "We must express our disapprobation of the conduct of Mr. Moore for not taking of the brandy into his possession after he had seized it."

The thanklessness of trying to collect revenue at great distances from the seat of authority is shown in reports on the customs situation in Labrador. In 1826, the collector at St. John's, having received little or no duty from Labrador, made arrangements with William Langley, the agent for a Labrador fishing firm, to collect such duties as he could. He was to receive no salary at first but was told that if he were successful he might be appointed collector for Labrador. In three years, Langley collected and sent to St. John's several hundred pounds in duties from the fishing fleets. He didn't receive even a thank-you note. He returned to his home in Devon and from there asked compensation for his services. He was granted £150 and was offered the post of collector in Labrador with an allowance of 25 per cent of the duty collected. He refused, and no appointment was made until 1840 when the Newfoundland legislature appointed Elias Rendall. Nothing seems to have happened in the way of collections, and in 1843 the attorney-general of Newfoundland recommended appointment of two customs officers to the Labrador coast for the period June to September. But it was two more years before the government appointed the officers and found a suitable vessel for their patrols.

Customs collection in New Brunswick was confounded by geography and the advantage the smugglers took by virtue of it. J.W. Spearman, the collector at St. Andrews, reported on a visit he made in the fall of 1830 to the outbays over which he had jurisdiction. At Mill Town, Richard Brothers owned mills on both sides of the border (the Ste. Croix River) and it was impossible to determine which boards going through the mills were British and which American. "Hence arise frauds to a considerable amount on the revenue," Spearman wrote to the Board of Customs. "Duty per 1,000 feet is £1-1 and we have no instance on our books of a single foot manufactured at these mills having ever been entered as of foreign production." The lower or St. Stephen mills were also conveniently situated for the purpose of illicit traffic but the breadth of the stream was greater than at the upper mills and consequently "facilities for smuggling are in some degree diminished." Boards "precipitated into the stream become completely intermixed and impossible to distinguish between those manufactured on the one side from those manufactured on the other." Besides, there were three bridges at short distances from each other and it was impossible to check "the system of smuggling which prevails." There were twenty-four unguarded miles of river between St.

Andrews and St. Stephen. Several shipyards were owned or rented by Americans who lived on the U.S. side but had businesses on the Canadian; their workmen were among the inveterate smugglers of flour, meal, pork and timber.

On Campobello Island Spearman found a brisk contraband trade made even brisker by the necessity of catching the outgoing tide to save sea time to Windsor, Nova Scotia, and other ports. Trade was becoming every day more extensive, he said,

> though I am sorry to have to report that smuggling is increasing even in a greater ratio. This I attribute in a great measure to the relative situations of Campobello, Eastport and St. Andrews. The charter vessels arriving from Windsor and other places situated on the Bay of Fundy discharge their cargoes on the wharfs of Welsh Cove or transship them into American craft in the harbor. They then proceed off Eastport or Lubec [Maine] and take on board cargoes of flour in payment for their plaster. These return cargoes they must either enter at St. Andrews or they must smuggle them into Windsor and such is the nature of the tides and the difficulty of the navigation in the Bay of Passamaquoddy that if they proceed to St. Andrews for the purpose of entering their cargoes, thereby legalizing them for exportation to other parts of the province, or with the neighboring parts of Nova Scotia, they lose the opportunity of making a second voyage. This operates in such a manner as to reduce the profits on the carrying trade to the following state: they may either pay the duty and lose the second voyage or they may smuggle in the articles at the risk of seizure and save the voyage. The temptation to smuggle is too great in this case.

Things did not improve. On June 19, 1832, Spearman reported from Campobello: "I am sorry to report that nothwithstanding every exertion on the part of the sub-collector, smuggling to an enormous extent prevails in this neighborhood, both into this province and into Nova Scotia and consequent injury which the revenue sustains." Later, from the outport of Magaquadavick, Spearman noted: "Various facilities for smuggling appeared to me so numerous as to present an almost insurmountable obstacle to the entire suppression of the traffic."

(Insurmountability of obstacles did not hinder would-be recruits to the customs service. The Public Records Office in London has preserved three letters by one such appointee at Campobello. The first reads: "To They Survyors Generil Gentleman Having been appinted as sub colector at Campobolo I give this as a spesymint of my hand riteing. I remain gentleman Your obedent Snt Edward Cooke." Cooke practised. His second letter was correct except for "sepecement." His third letter was faultless. He got the job April 10, 1835, at a salary of £150 a year.)

A smuggling case from Prince Edward Island illustrates how long it took to get charges before the courts. On January 21, 1836, George Goodman, collector at Charlottetown, reported that on September 22, 1834, he had seized liquor, tobacco and tea landed at a nearby cove from the 85-ton schooner *Chart*, Horatio Webster, master, after a voyage from St. Pierre and Miquelon. Webster had been charged in the Supreme Court with making an untrue report to Customs and with giving untrue answers to questions. The case had not come to trial until that month (January, 1836) because of "strenuous exertions at procrastinations and evasions by Webster." Webster was fined £100 on the first charge but "an informality in proceedings in the attorney-general's office prevented the second charge coming to trial." Goodman had also taken court action against Benjamin Webster (relationship to Horatio, if any, not given) for receiving the smuggled goods, but the matter had not yet gone to trial. He had also found that John Moore had landed goods from the *Chart* at Hillsborough Bay before the schooner entered Charlottetown. He had not yet taken proceedings against Moore because of the "well known prejudice existing in the minds of jurors against revenue prosecutions." On February 18, 1841, nearly seven years after the case began, Goodman reported that Benjamin Webster had finally been brought to trial. "The verdict I regret to say was against the Crown." Horatio Webster, who presumably would have been a witness, had died in the meantime.

Goodman gave this general picture of Prince Edward Island smuggling operations: "Goods are run clandestinely on the shores of this colony from the French Islands of St. Pierre and Miquelon, the numerous outbays and creeks with which this Island is indented affording the smuggler an advantage which we fear the utmost vigilance of the officers in this colony may not fully prevent. . . . We have also to express our fears that contraband articles are frequently furnished to the settlers on the remote shores of this Island by the fishermen of the United States whose numerous small craft throng the waters on our northern shores. To convey an idea of the extent of this evil, 160 sail were counted at one time in the outbay of Three Rivers." Sub-collector Hugh Macdonald reported four hundred U.S. vessels at Three Rivers during the fishing season.

One of the most formidable collectors in all of the colonies was Thomas Nicholson Jeffery at Halifax who appears in other sections of this book dealing with the fight for responsible government in Nova Scotia and with the lives and times of customs officers. In this instance, we see Jeffery not in his frequent role as the standard-bearer of imperial authority against the claimed revenue rights of the provinces, but as a champion of the common man. The collector at Sydney, Thomas Dumaresq, had complained to Jeffery that the masters of the schooner *Magdalen* and the shallop *Nancy* were picking up coal along the shores of Cape Breton and carrying it to Halifax without clearing Customs at Sydney. At the time, coal was taxed but there were many bootleg diggings. Jeffery countermanded the complaints against the two masters in a letter to Sydney, written Christmas Eve, 1805, which begins with seasonal transcendence:

> The intention of the government is to encourage and not to harass any set of men and particularly those already in a distressed state and we cannot help feeling for them in many instances as their complaints of the enormous fees taken at many of the ports in North America, and that those vessels who only trade from one island or port to another with coals, fish or lumber are certainly not under the orders of the Commissioners of the Customs liable to be considered foreign vessels but coasters and as such only take coasting fees.

CHAPTER IV
Early Canadian Anti-Smuggling Directives

The mid-1800s are one of the most interesting periods in Canadian customs history, just as they are in the development of Canada itself. It might seem surprising that Upper and Lower Canada, after the rebellions of 1837 and now grappling with each other within the confines of a single new province, could find the energy to deal with customs problems. But of course they had to because customs duties provided the bulk of government revenue.

The Canadians were just as adept at smuggling as their fellow colonists on the Atlantic seaboard. If the Nova Scotians and New Brunswickers were audacious as sailor-smugglers, the Canadians were just as bold on the land frontier. Armed gangs of smugglers were not uncommon on the Eastern Townships border of Lower Canada and on the St. Lawrence and Niagara frontiers of Upper Canada. Assaults on customs officers and deliberate maiming of their horses were almost routine. Smugglers and officers were constantly "presenting" (aiming at point-blank range) their pistols at one another. Luckily, both sides seemed to be very bad shots. There is only one case (1852) in Canada we have found in which anyone was shot and killed: a smuggler who was part of a gang intercepted by Customs on a cold winter's night on the road between Brockville and Smiths Falls. A customs officer was also shot, but the bullet didn't penetrate all the way through the thirteen layers of clothing he was wearing. There was also a case (1862) at Napanee in which a customs officer was badly beaten by a gang. He died a few months later but apparently no direct connection could be made between the assault and the death. The customs department took it all rather casually, partly on the grounds that all frontier life was hard and also in the knowledge that juries nearly always took the side of the smuggler rather than the revenue officer's. About the most a brave officer could expect from headquarters was a commendation from the commissioner or, for particularly dashing feats (one is tempted to say foolhardiness), an award of, perhaps, £25.

Nearly all the smuggled goods were conveyed in horse-drawn wagons or sleighs and the customs officer who ventured away from the customs house had to be on horseback if he were to be effective. Here is an extract from a letter February 24, 1846, by John Verner, collector at Maitland, Canada West, to Commissioner Dunscomb:

> Wheeling round, I rode back as fast as possible and reached the spot about a couple of minutes after they had gained the road. I immediately reined in my horse and asked them civilly if they had not been across the river [St. Lawrence]. To this they made no reply, but said they were on the road to Prescott. I told them that the law required them to report at Maitland and that I would advise them to do so. Instead of answering me, they commenced to whip their horses most furiously, when, seeing their intent, I just managed to spur past them, and at the risk of my life, rode before them, while they endeavoured by all means to run me down. Finding that my horse could not long continue that pace, and that they were every moment closer upon me, so much so indeed that I could not possibly have turned off the road without being placed in imminent danger, while they continued to ply the lash on their horses. As a last recourse, I drew a pistol and, turning in the saddle, fired at the off horse's head, lodging a ball in the blinker. A second shot took effect in his forehead and the shock caused by the blow gave me time to turn off the road. They continued their efforts to avoid me, but by this time the wounded horse began to flag, and I found it easy to ride alongside with a pistol given me by my servant (who had not been able to keep up with us) and placing it to the horse's head I told the man I would surely shoot him if he did not stop. Upon this he pulled up and I required him to return with me to the office, first taking the precaution of placing the reins in the hands of my servant.

Customs officers of course were well aware that they were not regarded fondly in their communities. In 1849, Collector James Botham of Huntingdon, Canada East, remarked phlegmatically to Dunscomb when the inhabitants of the townships of Godmanchester and Hinchinbrook and the parish of St. Anicet got up a petition to have him removed: "I am not aware that popularity is one of the indispensables of my office." In 1865, Customs tried to open a preventive station at Gilman's Corner, Eastern Townships, but none of the three families there would board a customs officer.

Malcom Cameron, special commissioner into customs affairs, reported in 1843 that duty was paid on far fewer goods than were smuggled. He gave as one example the smuggling of tea: 50,000 chests of tea were consumed annually in Upper Canada; 32,000 of them were smuggled. In 1841, one person, employing armed guards, had smuggled 600 chests in one place alone. Cameron added:

> The whole agricultural population is in favor of the smuggler. . . A strong prejudice exists very generally in the country against any law, making articles of food or luxury, contraband; and, with this idea, they have lost sight of the evils and sinfulness of smuggling — forgetting that it leads to falsehood, perjury and sometimes to assaults and

even murder, ... and wholly losing sight of the fact that they are really robbing themselves; as should the Revenue fail from this source direct, taxation must be resorted to. Had a moderate duty been collected on tea during the last year, and had the goods entered during the same period been entered at a fair valuation, there would have been no need of the School or Lunatic Asylum Tax ... The solution is ... a low rate of duty so that the risk of smuggling is not worth taking. High duties yield little or no revenue.

Here are some other examples of assaults during that period. First, John Ford, preventive officer at Barnston, Canada East, in August, 1843:

> About one or two o'clock [a.m.] I was set upon by some six or eight men having their faces blackened and otherwise dressed to avoid detection. They chased me and throwing themselves upon me like so many wolves they tied my legs with rope, when they immediately commenced cutting my hair with curses and execrations and said they would tar and feather. I had once an opportunity to halloo for help [but they] gave me cause to rue it for they dug into my breast and stomach in a most furious manner, clapping their sooted hands on my mouth till they nearly suffocated me. Upon my making a faithful promise to return to my home without ever going on such an errand again, they unbound me and gave me my cap but would not give my whip, saying I could ride fast enough without it ... I have since, until today, been confined to my home from the injuries I received. I have emitted a quantity of blood from my stomach in the forenoon of Sunday but am now much better.

John James Fox, collector on Iles-de-la-Madeleine, October 20, 1858:

> On arriving alongside [the *Eugenie*] I was hailed from the deck by one of the crew (named Dominic Cormier) with *N'approche pas* (keep off) but, as I considered myself duty bound to proceed, I attempted to board the said vessel and was immediately struck down by a blow from a handspike, dealt by the hands of the said Dominic Cormier, which stunned me, causing a very severe wound in my head which bled profusely and the effects of which I shall feel from some time to come. After which, I succeeded in reaching the deck, when the said Dominic Cormier collared me using much violence and did all in his power to throw me overboard, and had he succeeded I should certainly have been drowned.
>
> The captain not being on board I seized the vessel until I saw him and demanded payment of the duties upon his cargo which were immediately paid, amounting to $33.70 after which I released the vessel.

In a much later case (November, 1891) John Bowell, collector at Vancouver, was trying to arrest two Chinese firemen who had beaten one of his officers while attempting to smuggle goods off the liner *Empress of Japan*:

> ... I at once went to the ship and demanded that the ringleaders be given over to me. The master of the ship at once ordered all Chinese firemen mustered, when [officer] Hutton identified the two Chinese

who were the cause of the assault and who pounded him the most. I at once demanded that they be given over to the police, when the rest of the 72 firemen refused to give up the men wanted, drawing bowie knives on me. As I was unarmed and there were 72 of them I retired.

In 1844, a customs directive of the United Province of Canada told inspectors to "exercise forbearance and urbanity" and thereby "enhance the value of your services." Preventive officers were not to make "vexacious" seizures; "collision" with smugglers was to be avoided. But such molly-coddling soon gave way to the establishment of ten new customs houses in the Eastern Townships and stricter regulations (some collectors had always been keen enforcers despite the directives) especially on the distilling, distribution and consumption of liquor. Application of temperance laws was often the duty of Customs and Excise, and a volume of its laws and regulations of 1851 for the United Province included an amendment to the previous year's "Act for the more effectual suppression of intemperance." The amendment contained these paragraphs:

> Every licensed inn, tavern, etc., situated in villages and country parts, shall contain at least three rooms, with at least one good bed in each, for the accommodation of travellers, in addition to those used by the family; and the keeper of every such inn, etc., shall have a stable adjacent or attached to such house, with convenient stalls for at least four horses, and the keeper of such house shall be constantly supplied with a sufficient quantity of provisions, and of hay and oats, for travellers and their cattle, and in default of any or more of the foregoing requirements, the keeper of such house shall be liable to a penalty of five pounds.
>
> The keeper of every licensed inn, etc., shall keep a peaceable, decent and orderly house, and shall not suffer any person resorting thereto to play any game at which money shall be lost or won; nor shall the keeper be at liberty to keep a bar in more than one house, or to vend at any time any such liquors to any intoxicated person, or on Sundays to any person whomsoever, except sick persons or travellers, nor to any soldier, seaman, apprentice or servant, knowing him to be such, on any day after eight o'clock in the afternoon in winter, and nine o'clock in the afternoon in summer, under a penalty of five pounds for each offence.
>
> Whenever any person has drunk spirituous liquors to excess in any inn, etc., sold by permission of the keeper thereof, for the gain of such keeper, and while in a state of intoxication arising out of the use of such spirituous liquors, has come to his death by committing suicide or by drowning, perishing from cold, or by any accident occurring in consequence of his being so intoxicated, the keeper of such inn shall be liable to be indicted and tried before the Court of Queen's Bench sitting in the District in which such person resides, for a misdemeanor, and if convicted thereof, shall be liable to a penalty of not less than fifty pounds, nor more than two hundred and fifty pounds, to be paid to the heirs or legal representatives of the deceased person,

or to be imprisoned for a period not less than one month nor more than six months.

Though liquor flowed freely in Canada from the earliest days until a try at prohibition was made, beginning in 1898, the penalties for operating illegal stills were severe. A Nova Scotia excise law of 1864 called for fines of $2,000 to $6,000 for anyone illegally distilling any alcohol, and declared:

> Places fitted or suspected to be fitted for the distillation of intoxicating liquors, or for the manufacturing or rectifying of alcohol, rum, gin, or other intoxicating liquors or strong waters (porter, ale, beer, cider), may be entered and searched by any revenue officer, or by any person specially authorized by the board of revenue, and who in making such search is authorized to disconnect and remove machinery, vessels, and implements, and remove partitions, raise floors, and otherwise dismantle the premises as far as may be necessary for such search, and who may seize and remove all machinery, vessels, and implements of every kind used in such distillation, manufacture or rectification.

A federal excise directive of April 13, 1869, spelled out what the seizing officer was to do with such equipment:

> Stills, worms, rectifiers and other utensils, made of any description of metal, shall be so cut up and mutilated as to make them unsuitable for any purpose but being sold for old metal; all wooden stills, vessels or utensils capable of being used in any way for the purpose of distillation shall also be destroyed; all tobacco-cutting machines unsuitable for legitimate manufacture shall also be destroyed and sold for old iron; the net proceeds of the sales shall be immediately deposited to the credit of the Receiver General, in the same manner that other deposits of revenue are made.

A June 22, 1877, circular informed collectors:

> It has come to the knowledge of the Department that attempts have been made to use Indian corn meal, sugar, glucose, etc., in the manufacture of beer, as a substitute for malt and without the knowledge of the (excise) officers having the survey of the brewery. You are therefore required to exercise greater vigilance for the prevention of frauds of this nature and you will rigidly require brewers to enter on their stock books whatever grain, meal or other article capable of being used for the production of fermented liquor may be brought into any part of their premises.

The thoroughness of smuggling investigations is shown in the case of an inspection of the port of Quebec in November, 1862. The 143-page handwritten report, on purple paper tied with a purple ribbon, was made nearly two years later. The Quebec collector's reply to it was meant "for the information of the Honourable The Minister of Finance." Collector J.W. Dunscomb, it is clear, did not brook any nonsense from headquarters inspectors. The report said many cargo vessels coming up the St. Lawrence were boarded by market and other boats long before a customs officer ever saw them, sometimes as far downriver as Rivière du Loup, and that this lent itself to smuggling. The report continued:

> No examination is made as to whether there are any other means of communication with the hold than by the hatches, nor does there appear to be any more than the most superficial measures taken to discover concealed contraband goods or to prevent their being easily landed. Neither the hatches nor other communications with the hold are sealed or locked even at night after the vessel has commenced discharging, and although one of the tidal officers sleeps on board there is no pretence of keeping up a night watch on the vessels or on the wharves.

Collector Dunscomb replied:

> But the strictures contained in the paragraph regarding precautions taken to discover contraband goods are probably based upon the fanciful notion that the tide surveyor does not board all the vessels coming into port, and does not place a tidal officer on board of cargo vessels without delay, [and are] entirely imaginative, consequently not meriting any notice.
>
> Every word concerning the hatches, etc., is true with the understanding that if any part of the cargo is left on the wharf, an officer is invariably detailed to watch over it at night, but I may add, before the hatches of ships or other communications with the hold are sealed or locked up, and a second officer placed on board to keep watch while the other sleeps, as proposed by the inspectors, it would be well to obtain an estimate of the probable expense of this sealing, locking up and watching, for consideration in connection with the probable advantage to be derived.

The inspectors remarked further:

> We may here direct attention to the facilities which by this practice are afforded for smuggling, vessels reporting in ballast may have goods concealed in them worth thousands of dollars and will have abundant opportunities for landing them while discharging long before being searched; and every vessel which comes up the river could discharge goods to an indefinite amount by means of market boats long before a Customs officer sees her. Even while discharging and in charge of the Customs House the tidewaiter asleep in his hammock is no guarantee against the landing of contraband goods by night.

The collector, however, had the last word:

> If the final paragraph was written in sober earnestness, charging the tidewaiter with being asleep in his hammock even while the vessel was discharging cargo, I think the inspectors of ports would have felt it their duty to have communicated the information to me, for a whole business season has passed since they made this discovery; if it is meant that the tidal officer sleeps at night in his hammock I fear nature and habits acquired from earliest infancy will cause him to continue so, notwithstanding that it is disapproved of. It is right to

state the fact that special permission is occasionally granted to discharge at night, but in that case an extra tidal officer or two are sent on board at the ships' expense, whose business it is to see that no contraband goods are landed at night.

The implication that the inspectors were drunk when they made their purple report was apparently allowed to stand, perhaps as an acceptable riposte of the time.

In the 1880s, one of her periodic tides of immigration swept across Canada and governments, federal, provincial and sometimes municipal, vied with each other in issuing attractive literature for emigrants or would-be emigrants in Europe and elsewhere.

A hand-book for intending emigrants issued in 1879 by the federal agriculture department — most immigrants became farm laborers — made no mention of Customs, possibly on the very good grounds that the vast majority had few possessions to bring with them and that in any case settlers' effects came in duty-free.

By 1886, the agriculture department was barely alluding to the necessity of going through Customs. In its brochure that year, it said merely that upon arrival in Canada the luggage "will be passed by the customs officers and put into what is called the 'baggage car' of the railway train, where it is 'checked' to its destination."

But hand-books prepared by private companies gave a slightly different picture. For instance, W.B. Macdougall's *Guide to Manitoba and the North-West*, published in 1880, gave this advice:

> Immigrant's baggage is admitted free and includes all household effects, clothing, etc., but not uncut cloth in pieces; therefore, it is as well to be careful to have all clothes cut out at home and made up either there or on the voyage, which will find employment for the women and girls when they will be glad of something to do. It is well, also, to remember that the attempt to smuggle through the Customs House small parcels of dutiable goods might lead to very serious consequences, for although the Canadian Customs officers are very considerate with immigrants and save them as much trouble as possible, they are very severe with would-be smugglers.

The guide books usually contained a goodly batch of statistics, including imports and duties and prices of goods in some major locations. The 1886 guide showed, for instance, that Canadian imports in 1873 amounted to $138,011,281 and duties to $13,017,730. A decade later, in 1883, imports had dropped slightly to $132,254,022 but duties had risen sharply to $23,172,308, a clear indication of Canada's new high tariff policy. In 1886, some prices at Toronto were: bacon 12 to 14 cents a pound, white bread 12 cents a loaf, butter 24 cents a pound, beef 12 cents a pound, beer 10 cents a quart, coffee 30 cents a pound, eggs 15 to 25 cents a dozen, milk five to seven cents a quart, firewood 15 to 18 cents a cord, potatoes 40 cents a bushel, sugar five cents a pound, coal oil 20 cents a gallon, a tweed overcoat $8 to $15 and women's shoes 75 cents to $1.25.

Trains provided new methods of smuggling, of course. Customs Commissioner James Johnson sent this letter to the collector at Niagara Falls in 1881:

> I have to call your special attention to the practice of Pullman car conductors or porters of bringing over in concealment, for traders or others, smuggled goods, especially jewelry and such other valuable goods as can be packed in small compass. One of those men has just recently been convicted in Montreal, and sentenced to heavy fine and imprisonment. I cannot sufficiently enforce upon you the necessity of unwearied vigilance in reference to these cars, and the employees connected with them.

Johnson issued this directive on January 22, 1885, about examination of travellers' baggage arriving by steamer and train:

> It is reported to this department, from many sources, that this duty is very imperfectly performed as a rule, and in many cases quite neglected. It is further alleged that parties, especially women visiting New York and other U.S. cities, are in the habit of returning with full supplies of clothing and other goods, which are passed free for want of examination, to the great detriment of the importers of, and dealers in, such goods. The charge has also been made that such travellers occasionally succeed in smuggling by this means by the criminal device of secretly conveying money to the examining officer when presenting their baggage for examination, while seeking to disarm suspicion by an assumption of unusual frankness and complete willingness to have a full and perfect survey made of their packages. I am to instruct you to keep a vigilant oversight of all officers so engaged, and in case of marked negligence, or finding that any such officer has accepted a gift of money or valuables to any, even the smallest, amount, you are to suspend the offender promptly from office and pay and report the case to this department when, unless under very mitigating circumstances, the suspension will be followed by absolute dismissal from the service.

The more sinister side of smuggling — narcotics — was not seen in a serious light for a long time. Opium, for instance, was widely used in some medical treatments and did not come into general non-medical use in Canada until Chinese laborers were brought to western Canada, especially British Columbia, to work on the railroads in the last quarter of the 19th century. Opium, the juice of the white poppy, was sometimes called the "flower of dreams" and Coleridge wrote of its effect: "Through caverns measureless to man/Down to a sunless sea." It was imported into Canada perfectly legally until 1908 (88,013 pounds that year), though it bore customs duty. In 1879, the duty was five dollars a pound. Later it was set at 25 per cent. In 1867, in Victoria, opium sellers had to pay a licence fee of fifty dollars every six months. Marijuana was free of all duties and restrictions until this century.

Opium-smoking was likely ignored because it was considered confined to the immigrant Chinese whom the British Columbia legislature tried to bar from employment on provincial public works once the transcontinental railway was completed. Yet there was anti-Asiatic rioting in Vancouver in 1907, and opium factories were burned down. Mackenzie King, then deputy minister of labor, was appointed to settle property losses of the Chinese, among whom were two opium merchants who had made substantial claims. King also undertook, on his own, a separate study which he entitled *The Need for Suppression of the Opium Trade in Canada*. He wrote: "To be indifferent to the growth of such an evil in Canada would be inconsistent with those principles of morality which ought to govern the conduct of a Christian nation." His report resulted in the hastily prepared Opium Act of 1908 which prohibited the importation, manufacture and sale of opiates for non-medical purposes. Smuggling of narcotics began at once.

At about the same time, in 1906, Canada acceded to the International Agreement for the Suppression of the White Slave traffic. Article 2 of this convention said "each of the governments undertakes to have a watch kept, especially in railway stations, ports of embarkation and en route, for persons in charge of women and girls destined for an immoral life." Customs was given the job of catching white slavers as well as narcotics smugglers.

The difficulty about controlling or preventing opium smuggling was that though there were penalties for importing and selling the drug, there was none for having it in one's possession. Anyone with opium in his pipe, so to speak, was free to smoke it. Smuggling of opium — and of Chinese — became so prevalent that a royal commission was established in 1910, its work resulting in a new Opium and Drugs Act, a year later, which outlawed opium possession and smoking. But enforcement was weak, even with awards to informers of ten per cent of appraised value of the seized opium, instituted in 1915. The royal commission had found that the quantity of smuggled narcotics more or less met demand, and this continued to be the case — some say it is still the case. In 1914, the United States enacted a comprehensive drug law, and by 1918 was complaining that opium was being smuggled from Canada. One consequence of the ban on opium in this country was an enormous increase in the legal importation of other narcotics for (supposedly) medical prescription. For instance, while in 1912 thirty-five ounces of cocaine were legally imported into Canada, by 1919, the legal importations totalled 12,333 ounces.

Amendments to the Opium Act and a concurrent attempt to stamp out the illicit traffic came in 1920. But in 1921 it was estimated that there were 3,000 narcotics addicts in Vancouver alone. The amount of narcotic drugs sold legally in Canada was valued at $182,484 that year, including 2,416 ounces of cocaine, 5,286 ounces of morphine and 1,440 pounds of opium. But the value of illegal imports was put at $2.2 million. In the year ending March 31, 1922, there were 837 convictions under the federal Opium and Drugs Act. Among those convicted were 23 doctors, 11 druggists, 4 veterinarians, 165 peddlers and 634 Chinese. The maximum penalty was a $500 fine or one year in jail. Fines collected amounted to $127,947. The act was amended again in 1929, and then remained largely unchanged until 1961.

Smuggling of narcotics never slackened. As fast as one method of smuggling was uncovered by Customs, another was ready for testing. In 1920, Customs found narcotics in the mail from England: in clothing, magazines, confectionery and puddings. At Vancouver, a favorite method of smugglers was to drop over the side of an ocean liner nearing harbor weighted sacks containing as many as two hundred cans of opium. Long ropes, sometimes with a buoy, were attached to the sacks and the smuggler's accomplices — or the smuggler himself after landing — grappled for them from small boats. So Customs' preventive service began convoying liners into Pacific ports with fast patrol boats and shadowing the passenger ships between Victoria and Vancouver with seaplanes.

As for Chinese immigrants, the 1910 royal commission found that thousands were entering the country illegally. The simplest method used was stowing away. In August, 1910, the liner *Kumeric* arrived in Vancouver with no fewer than fifty-six Chinese stowaways, most of them trying to join relatives already in Canada. Chinese merchants were allowed into Canada legally. But laundrymen, clerks and peddlers easily posed as merchants. Many bore Chinese passports so fraudulent they were written in English. The official interpreter for Customs and Immigration at Vancouver, Yip On, alias Hing Sam, alias Goon Gee, was making most of the arrangements for the illegal entries. And the official interpreter at Victoria was the ticket agent for a Hong Kong-Vancouver steamship line.

There was a free-and-easy, inoffensive (but illegal) coming and going. A Chinese crew member of a ship would go ashore, change clothes and apply as a resident of Canada to visit China for a year. He would then return as a resident a year later, or sell his residence permit to another Chinese who wanted to go to Canada. Or a crew member would go ashore and be replaced by another Chinese who wanted to return home.

The Chinese paid from fifty to five hundred dollars to be smuggled into the United States from Canada. One smuggler compelled the Chinese to allow themselves to be bound hand and foot on the deck of his boat; if the customs patrol boat came along, the Chinese were tossed over the side like sticks of wood. A retired customs officer at Windsor recalls that, similarly, packing cases in which Chinese were hiding on the decks of smugglers' boats in the Detroit River were dumped overboard at any challenge from the U.S. Coast Guard and the Chinese left to be drowned or, infrequently, rescued.

Ultimately, the royal commission recommended a quota system for the Chinese similar to that already in existence for Japanese immigrants.

CHAPTER V

The Customs Scandal of 1926

The moment the United States enacted prohibition — January 16, 1920 — fleets of foreign vessels laden with liquor set sail for American shores. They were like the Indiamen tea smugglers of the 18th century who anchored in the English Channel and sold over the side to small boats from shore.

The smuggling ships were known as rum-runners, and the lineup just outside the U.S. territorial limit waiting to disgorge precious cargoes to eager motor launches from land was called Rum Row. As many as a hundred vessels at a time comprised this bobbing line, like bottles on a tipsy shelf. Liners arriving in New York and other ports complained that the smugglers were obstructing navigation. It was common for rum-runners, coming from the West Indies, Holland, Britain, Spain, Portugal, Germany, Chile, Cuba, Panama and — mainly — Canada, to carry two sets of papers. If they were caught, they flourished papers showing their cargoes were destined for Mexico or Yokahama or wherever. If they unloaded undetected, they had another set of papers which would allow them to call at a U.S. port for a legal cargo. After all, to send a rum-runner home with empty bottom was economically unsound.

Waxing almost lyrical about Rum Row, A. Hyatt Verrill wrote in 1924: "Just outside the territorial limit they all lie, riding at anchor, great, rust-streaked, iron steamships, once-palatial ocean-going yachts of multi-millionaires, stout, heavily-built, powerfully-engined, deep-water towboats, lofty-sparred, noble, old ships and barks with wide crossed yards, salt-encrusted tramps, and all filled to the hatches, laden to waterline or plimsoll, with their cargoes of liquor from every quarter of the globe — rum from the West Indies, gin from Holland, whisky from Scotland, wines and brandy from Spain, Portugal and France, beer from Panama, Chile and Germany ..."

This cordon of floating warehouses formed almost a bridge from the Delaware Capes to the Gulf of Maine. For every boat taken, a hundred landed in safety. For every dollar's worth of liquor seized, $1,000 from successful sales were pocketed by smugglers; for every man arrested, hundreds snapped their fingers at the law.

In 1924, it was estimated that 5,000,000 gallons of liquor were smuggled into the United States. The main smuggling operations were conducted from Halifax, Windsor (Ontario), Vancouver, St. Pierre and Miquelon, Havana and Nassau. At one time, four-fifths of the illegal liquor entering the States was through Windsor-Detroit. In 1924 U.S. authorities seized 753 American vessels, mainly fast-pickup-and-delivery motor launches, and 39 foreign ships. When the United States got agreement with a dozen countries permitting American searches for liquor within a twelve-mile instead of three-mile limit, rum-running from the sea was reduced, though far from eliminated.

Though Canada provided both the operating base and the raw materials for what was a multi-billion-dollar criminal industry, Canadians generally, and their government particularly, for a long time turned a fairly indifferent eye to what was going on. As Revenue Minister W.D. Euler told the Commons on May 21, 1929, "It is impossible to have wet and dry countries adjacent to each other without a flow from the wet to the dry." Smuggling was pervasive and thriving, for as soon as it proves to be feasible in one product, it spreads rapidly to other goods. And if smuggling is practicable in one direction, it often is in the opposite direction. Liquor was pouring across the border into the United States and, before long, smuggled American cigarettes, textiles and other goods were flooding into Canada.

Excise taxes on legal Canadian liquor amounted to nine dollars a gallon. But the tax did not apply on exported liquor. When the smugglers were not landing their cargo in the United States, they found it less risky and often just as profitable to smuggle the liquor back into Canada — avoiding the $10-a-gallon customs duty as well. U.S. pressure forced Canada to adopt regulations requiring exporters to put up bonds certifying the liquor would be landed at the ticketed destination, usually in Central or South America. But this was no problem for the smugglers. They simply presented fake or forged landing certificates to get their bonds back. A ship groaning under its load would leave Windsor (there were ninety docks in Windsor, most of them catering to the liquor trade) with a manifest showing it was to land its cargo in Havana or Vera Cruz or some obscure Mexican village. But the ship would be back in port a few hours later, empty, having unloaded across the river in Detroit, or perhaps on the Canadian side. A rowboat could obtain official clearance just as easily, even if the destination read Havana.

Meanwhile, twenty-five rum-runners at a time would be waiting off the Nova Scotia coast for the propitious moment when they could safely run into shore or be unburdened by vessels dashing out to them. If in danger of being caught by the Canadian preventive service, they jettisoned their casks, weighted by heavy bags of salt so they would float under the surface. In a few days, after the revenue ship had cleared out, the water would wash away the salt in the bags and the casks of liquor would pop to the surface, ready for retrieval — a 17th-century European *modus operandi* recycled.

In 1927, the Canadian preventive service seized so much liquor there was not enough warehouse space for it. It was often necessary to escort a seized rum-runner hundreds of miles seeking a port with an unfilled warehouse. The number of fishing vessels actually fishing fell drastically as their owners converted them to smuggling. Captains averaged $400 a month, excellent money in those days, not including bonuses for successful delivery. Airplanes of the day, which required only a farmer's field for a runway, flew liquor from central Canada into New England.

Canada was a crazy composition of liquor laws. Some provinces were wet, some dry, some half-and-half. Enforcement varied from severe to loose. In Ontario, medical prescriptions could be obtained to buy liquor, provoking Stephen Leacock to write: "It is necessary to go to a drugstore ... and lean up against the counter and make a gurgling sigh like apoplexy. One often sees these apoplexy cases lined up four deep." Indeed, in Prince Edward Island this system persisted until 1948 with the ultimate absurdity attained by the liquor purchaser filling in the name of a doctor (any doctor) on the purchase form.

Prohibition was part of a crusade for social reform which grew out of the industrialization of North America. The ingredients in this reform movement were the desire to overcome widespread poverty and disease and to improve tenement housing, the fight for the vote for women, disgust with partisan and often corrupt politics, anarchism and trade unionism, and resistance to the power of corporations.

Between 1916 and 1919, all the provinces passed prohibition laws in one form or another (Quebec banned liquor but not beer and wine, for instance). A federal order-in-council of March 11, 1918, outlawed the manufacture of beverage alcohol and its transportation or sale in Canada. But there were exceptions: alcohol could be manufactured and sold if it were for medicinal, scientific, mechanical, industrial and sacramental purposes. These exceptions presented all the loopholes any accomplished smuggler or bootlegger could ask for. The federal order remained in effect until November, 1919, when Parliament passed a Canada Temperance Act making it illegal to ship alcohol into any province which voted to forbid its importation or sale. There was a catch, of course: the legislation required each province to hold a referendum before the act came into force October 25, 1920. The liquor trade was thus thrown wide open for a year — just as prohibition began in the United States. Moreover, the

Temperance Act made export of liquor perfectly legal. Export houses were crammed and ready for business along the Canadian land frontier at the same time as the rum-running ships were weighing anchor for U.S. shores.

Canada and its provinces have held dozens of referendums since 1898. A few of them have concerned such subjects as military conscription, Newfoundland and Confederation, and Quebec partition, but at least two dozen have had to do with the liquor laws. Canadians discarded prohibition much more quickly than the Americans: Quebec, British Columbia and the Yukon in 1921, Manitoba in 1923, Alberta in 1924, Saskatchewan in 1925, Ontario and New Brunswick in 1927, (New Brunswick had tried prohibition earlier, in 1855, and repealed it in less than a year) Nova Scotia in 1930 and Prince Edward Island in 1948. Newfoundland was not dry when it joined Confederation in 1949.

When Clifford Rose was an inspector in New Glasgow for the Nova Scotia Temperance Act he kept a diary of his activities, subsequently published under the title *Four Years with the Demon Rum*. He felt that, despite men like A.T. Logan, chief preventive officer in Nova Scotia for Customs and Excise, who "shook the smuggling racket as a great wind shakes an orchard," anti-smuggling operations were hamstrung by powerful politicians. He wrote that the municipality he worked for wanted enough liquor raids to keep up revenue from fines, but not enough raids to drive the bootleggers and smugglers out of business and destroy revenue altogether. Rose expressed an opinion that was commonly held at the time: the provinces all set themselves up as liquor distributors and retailers when they became fully aware of the enormous revenue sources in liquor.

William Guy Carr in his book *High and Dry* (published in Britain in 1938 but never in Canada, apparently because he named too many names) speaks of visiting the homes of three customs officers at St. Leonard, N.B., in 1921:

> When one considers that these men are very poorly paid, it seems astounding that they could afford the luxurious homes they possessed. Sub-collector [J.J.] Walsh had a beautiful home and he and his wife lived luxuriously. An electric washing-machine using power that was manufactured by a local firm, and sold at a fabulous price, did her washing. Electric polishers kept her matched hardwood floors in perfect condition. Douglas fir sheathing was everywhere. One officer had the entire inside of his beautiful home done in Douglas fir. It was one of the finest decorative creations I have ever seen. Panels of dark-against panels of light-grained wood, surrounded by panels let in at an angle which formed a pleasing mosaic effect. Fir stairways, with maple treads, all highly shellacked and varnished. One kitchen was done in white enamel, with a beautiful cooking range and set tubs

Willow Creek, Sask. (John de Visser)

Yukon-Alaska boundary / La frontière Yukon-Alaska (Paul von Baich)

Sarnia, winter / en hiver (Paul Christopher), all National Film Board / *toutes des productions de l'Office national du Film*

Dundee, Qué. (Michel Lambeth)

Basswood Lake, Quetico Park, northwestern Ontario / Le lac Basswood, Quetico Park, dans le Nord-Ouest ontarien

Little Gold Creek, Y.T. / T.-Y. (Paul von Baich)

Pohénégamook, Qué. (Pierre Gaudard)

Osoyoos, B.C. / C.-B., (John de Visser)

and hand basins. And all this out of incomes ranging from $85 to $125 per month!

Sub-collector Walsh was very hospitable. The finest stout and ale were none too good for the guest who visited his home. But he was one of the hardest men to get to talk I ever met. If he did talk, it was always in a circle, and when he had finished he had said nothing.

Carr informs us later that just as the royal commission into the customs scandal reached New Brunswick, Walsh died of heart failure.

The Canadian government remained aloof from the Americans' prohibition problems while legal Canadian distilleries and breweries pumped out liquor and beer by the millions of gallons for the parched U.S. market. But Canada protested vigorously when the Nova Scotia schooner *I'm Alone* was sunk in 1929. The two-master was built for rum-running in Lunenburg in 1924. She earned her owners some three million dollars in her first four years running from St. Pierre and Miquelon to Rum Row. On her first run to the Gulf of Mexico in March, 1929, with 2,800 cases of liquor, the *I'm Alone* was intercepted and sunk by the U.S. Coast Guard vessels *Wolcott* and *Dexter*. One of the rum-runner's eight-man crew was drowned and Captain John T. Randell, a decorated former naval officer from Newfoundland, was slightly wounded. Randell claimed he was in international waters but the Coast Guard said he was only 10.8 miles out when ordered to heave to. An international furore followed, the United States being accused of piracy and an act of war. In 1935, Canada received an apology from the U.S. and $50,666, against $386,000 claimed. Captain Randell and his crew were exonerated and were awarded $25,666 of which $10,000 went to the widow of the drowned boatswain.

Rum-running by land brought sudden death, too. An Alberta policeman, Steve Lawson, was shot to death at Coleman September 21, 1922, and the bootlegger Emilio Picariello and his girl friend, Florence Lassandro, were executed for the killing. On November 8, 1920, in Windsor, Ontario, the Reverend J.O.L. Spracklin, a Methodist minister and leader of an official Ontario liquor inspection squad, shot and killed bootlegger Beverley (Babe) Trumble in his roadhouse. Spracklin pleaded self-defence and was acquitted of manslaughter.

Parliament passed a resolution demanding that liquor sales to the United States be banned. The government ignored it.

Indeed, Ottawa sat on attempts to enforce the law. Here is an exchange of letters which illustrates the point. Collector C.B. Lockhart at Saint John, N.B., wrote to Deputy Minister Robinson R. Farrow, October 28, 1924:

> I have the honour to enclose herewith a clipping which appeared in the Telegraph Journal newspaper of this city on the 21st instant, stating that the three-masted schooner *Over the Top* from this port,

loaded with alleged whisky and alcohol, had been brought into the port of New London, Conn.

This schooner cleared from here on August 27th last with spiritous liquors, exported by the Security Export Company and the Consolidated Distillers Limited for Havana, and 62 bags of coal for Hamilton, Bermuda, and I enclose copy of the Report Outward.

The bond of the Dominion Gresham Guarantee and Casualty Company was deposited with me for double duties on said shipment, and on September 29th last the certificate of the Administrator and Contador of the Port of Havana was handed me, certifying that the liquors had been duly landed at Havana.

Upon receiving said certificate I gave up the bond to Edward L. Whittaker, Customs Broker, and considered the transactions closed, but as the said schooner, when taken in charge, claimed to be from the Port of Saint John and still had the goods aboard that had been shipped from here, I have decided I should report the matter to you, as it would appear as though the certificate handed me was not genuine.

Lockhart got this reply from Charles P. Blair, general executive assistant in Customs:

You state in your letter that the vessel at the time of capture still had the goods aboard that had been shipped from your port. What evidence have you of this? There is nothing in the newspaper clipping that would identify the goods as being the same goods exported from your port. In fact alcohol is mentioned and I see no alcohol described in the report outward.

There was time between the 27th August when the vessel cleared from your port and the 29th September, the date of the landing certificate, for the vessel to have gone to Havana, and there was time from the 29th September to the 20th October for the vessel to have come back again to the locality in which she was seized by the American authorities.

Please let me know in further detail what reason you have for believing that the goods on the vessel at the time of her seizure by the American authorities were the same goods or part of the same goods as were exported outward from your port on the 27th August.

Lockhart promptly wrote the U.S. customs service and got this reply from New London December 29, 1924:

The vessel's papers show the cargo as follows: 3250 cases of Canadian whisky
 999 cases of Gordons Dry Gin
1049 cases of Johnnie Walker whisky
 211 repacks of Scotch whisky
 360 repacks of Malt whisky
  62 bags of anthracite coal.

No evidence has been discovered that the vessel had been to Havana since clearing from Saint John on August 27. It is understood that part of the cargo had been sold and removed from the schooner. The cargo has been under seal aboard the vessel since her arrival in this port.

Lockhart then wrote to Farrow again, on January 2, 1925, with a copy of the letter from U.S. Customs, and concluded:

> The vessel's papers show the cargo found on board to be the same as that taken on board at this port and that [there is] no evidence ... that the vessel had been to Havana since clearing from Saint John on August 27th.

Lockhart's letter was acknowledged, but no action was ordered to deal with the fraud.

In the meantime, the smuggling into Canada of U.S. goods, mainly cigarettes, clothing and cars, usually stolen, grew by leaps and bounds. The Canadian textile industry complained bitterly and repeatedly that it would go bankrupt if the smuggling were not stopped. Many garment manufacturers did go under.

But Jacques Bureau, minister of Customs and Excise, declined to act, and Prime Minister Mackenzie King backed him up. To be on what he thought was the safe side, King sent Bureau to the Senate two months before the October 29, 1925, general election and appointed George Boivin in his place. Boivin rested on his oars, too, reflecting the attitude of the department's senior officers. Laissez-faire was bad on morale, however. In faroff Wild Horse, Alberta, customs officer Reginald Yates noted in his diary that he was patrolling the border each day by saddle horse but that Ottawa had "decided to help Uncle Sam and ordered hands off liquor being smuggled to the U.S." C.P. Howell, the officer in charge at Roosville, British Columbia, at the same time, recalled afterwards: "It was not the rum-runners who corrupted us, but the Canadian politicians, federal, provincial and municipal." And then there was the case of the incorruptible Inspector Cyril Knowles, assistant preventive officer at Winnipeg, whose efforts, in 1920 and 1922, to dent the smuggling operations of the Bronfman brothers in Saskatchewan brought a reprimand from Farrow, deputy minister of Customs from 1919 to 1926, for his "lack of discretion," and an order to confine his work to Winnipeg. Even after he was able to make public his charges of attempted bribery and tampering with witnesses, in 1927, no federal government action was taken and, when Knowles died in 1932, at the age of 43, he was still under orders to confine his preventive work to Winnipeg.

The textile and other industries formed the Commercial Protective Association to try to get action out of the government, claiming that smuggling represented the country's largest loss in revenue, apart from Canadian National Railways. Finally, the government agreed to go so far as to loan the association the services of Walter Duncan, chief investigator in the department of finance.

Duncan began digging. He did not have to dig very far before he came across one of the slickest "scam" artists in the history of Canadian crime: Joseph Alfred Edgar Bisaillon, chief preventive officer for Customs at Montreal.

Bisaillon seized liquor in the name of the law — and then bootlegged it under the name of a dummy company. He seized a launch in the name of the law and soon the same launch appeared on a Laurentian lake in front of his cottage. He owned a farm which straddled the Canada-U.S. border at Beebe, Quebec; textiles arrived at the American side and exited from the Canadian side without benefit of customs duties. He helped two women in drug-trafficking and then, when they were arrested and charged, he testified in court he had never laid eyes on them. He ran a few stolen cars. When the Quebec Liquor Commission seized a barge laden with 24,000 drums of liquor, Bisaillon took charge of it in the name of what he said was overriding federal law, sold it and deposited $69,000 in his own bank account. He offered to put some of his colleagues on his private payroll.

Investigator Duncan uncovered other interesting items: Walter R. Nursey of Toronto had been hired by Bureau in 1923 as a secret service officer at the age of 79; Albert Reid Raymond had been appointed by Bureau as a chauffeur in his department in the same year though Raymond had been convicted ten times in fourteen years of theft, robbery, burglary, forgery and shopbreaking; in Room 216 in the Connaught Building, the department's headquarters, Duncan found cases of liquor and a $200 bribe — the office was the deputy minister's. In deputy minister Farrow's safe he found a letter dated August 28, 1924, to Farrow from J.H. Ducondu, a Montreal customs officer, saying Ducondu had proof that Bisaillon had falsified his income tax returns to cover $50,000 made from bootlegging. No action had been taken.

R.P. Sparks, chairman of the Commercial Protective Association, laid all this material before Mackenzie King, who said that if the association would make charges against Bisaillon he would appoint a royal commission to investigate them. Without such charges, no action would be taken. As Sparks later told a parliamentary inquiry: "We are unable to find any precedent for the government asking private individuals to institute proceedings against suspected officers of the Crown."

Sparks was so incensed at the government's failure to act — though Bisaillon was fired by order-in-council Dec. 12, 1925 — that he leaked all his information to Conservative Harry Stevens of Vancouver who, in turn, dumped it on the floor of the Commons in a four-hour speech, February 2, 1926. Stevens accused Bureau of destroying incriminating documents filling nine filing cabinets, and Boivin of defrauding the treasury of $200,000 by selling seized liquor cheaply to a bootlegger friend who resold it in the United States at a huge profit. When Boivin accused Duncan of passing information to the Conservatives, Duncan angrily resigned. Stevens said that King and four of his ministers had covered up knowledge of the scandal, and he demanded a parliamentary investigation. King was in a very tight spot. The Conservatives held 116 seats after the 1925 election and the Liberals only 101, King having clung to power with the backing of the twenty-five-member Progressive party. King dithered for three days but finally had to agree to establishment of a special nine-member committee to investigate the administration of the department of Customs and Excise and "alleged serious losses to the public treasury because of inefficiency or corruption on the part of officers of the department and others." Four days later the committee held the first of its 115 sittings and heard the first of 224 witnesses.

The committee rummaged into such items as the disappearance of trainloads of liquor manifested to Mexico and Cuba, how distilleries were allowed to sell liquor classed as unfit for human consumption, how the books of some textile companies were suddenly consumed in mysterious fires. Ledger-burning started at almost the same moment the inquiry began, especially at Rock Island, Quebec, which shares the border with Derby Line, Vermont, where millions of dollars worth of textiles, having arrived in Derby Line, turned up, without customs clearance, in Rock Island clothing factories literally next door. There were no fewer than twenty-five factories in the Rock Island district, which had a population of about 2,000. Nearly all of them were cashing in on the smuggling bonanza.

The parliamentary committee looked into rum-running, of course. At Lunenburg, Nova Scotia, it found that the names of those hired by Customs as watchmen over liquor barrels aboard ship had been proposed to the customs superintendent by the top smuggler, locally, a man who ran a ships' outfitting business, giving him easy access to every vessel in port.

The committee found that Ottawa customs headquarters was sometimes embarrassed by the keenness of the captains of the patrol boats. For instance, Captain Alfred La Couvée, master of the customs cruiser *Margaret*, once stopped, within three miles of Prince Edward Island, a leaky, liquor-laden boat claiming to be bound from St. Pierre to Nassau. Ottawa ordered the ship released on the grounds that if one used land miles instead of the longer nautical miles, the seized vessel was 277 feet outside the territorial limit: customs headquarters never tried to explain to Captain La Couvée why land miles should be used at sea. There were other strange happenings in Ottawa: a customs officer who supplied seized liquor free to members of the Civil Service Commission won a promotion. The liquor was delivered in soap flakes boxes by the ex-convict chauffeur of the revenue department.

The committee's report, made public June 18, 1926, found that the department of Customs and Excise had for a long time been "slowly degenerating." Bureau had failed to discharge the responsibilities of his office properly. Bisaillon should be criminally prosecuted; six Quebec officers were delinquent and should be fired; three other officials, including deputy minister Farrow, should be retired at once. Twenty-five companies should be prosecuted and the records of all distilleries audited. Excise and sales tax should be collected on liquor the moment it left the distillery. The preventive service should be reorganized and strengthened. A secret service for criminal investigation should be established. Buildings within one hundred yards of the border should be removed. (In 1935, the International Boundary Commission found more than a hundred such buildings remaining, and there are still some, particularly at Rock Island.)

The committee's report did not go far enough for the House of Commons, the Conservatives scenting that there was a lot more scandal to be unearthed. They were right. On June 29, 1926, the Commons resolved unanimously to add a paragraph to the committee's report saying: "Since the (parliamentary) inquiry indicates that the smuggling evils are so extensive and their ramifications so far-reaching that only a portion of the illegal practices have been brought to light, your committee recommends the appointment of a judicial commission with full powers to continue and complete investigating the administration of the Department of Customs and Excise and to prosecute all offenders."

Sir François Xavier Lemieux, Chief Justice of the Superior Court of Quebec, was appointed commissioner July 20, but he resigned November 11 before the commission started public hearings, to be replaced by a three-man inquiry under James Thomas Brown, Chief Justice of the Court of King's Bench of Saskatchewan, with the assistance of Ernest Roy, Quebec Superior Court judge, and William Henry Wright, a judge of the Ontario Supreme Court. They held public sessions in every province between November 17, 1926, and September 14, 1927. But the Conservatives were not to enjoy the fruits of the commission's labors.

Mackenzie King, knowing that the Liberals would be beaten in a Commons vote based on the damning disclosures of a customs scandal reaching deep into his ministry, asked Governor-General Byng for dissolution and an election. Byng refused, and asked Conservative Arthur Meighen to form a government, which he did on June 29, 1926. It was to be the unlucky thirteenth administration since Confederation. With King maintaining that the Tories had smuggled themselves into office, the Liberals, with help from third parties, won the next Commons vote 96-95 July 1. Byng then granted Meighen the dissolution he had denied King, and the election campaign was on. The confident Tories had expected that the entire campaign would be fought on the issue of the customs scandal, and they printed, by the thousands, pamphlets carrying voluminous quotes from the parliamentary committee investigation. One such pamphlet on smuggled textiles was entitled: "Canada Flooded with Infected Prison-Made Garments." The sub-heading said: "King Government Permit Canadian Men, Women and Children to be Endangered from Infected Garments from United States Prisons" — the convict-made textiles smuggled into Canada by Liberal politicians held the germs of venereal disease, trachoma and tuberculosis. But King was conducting the campaign on an entirely different plane. To him, the issue was the so-called constitutional crisis: Byng was a high-born Briton deciding on his own, like some old-style colonial governor, when and how elections should be called. And it could only help King's campaign when Boivin, his former Customs minister and prime Conservative target, died in the midst of it, of appendicitis, at the age of forty-three. King won the election on September 14 and Meighen soon gave way to another Conservative leader.

The royal commission, once it got started, operated at high speed. (The newspapers referred to it simply as the commission on customs scandals.) It had been sitting only two weeks when it issued its first interim report. It was to issue nine more before its final finding of extensive smuggling and "grave irregularities." It noted that in the fiscal year ended March 31, 1927, the amount collected by the National Revenue department was $345,241,967.01. This was out of total government revenue of $398,695,776.38.

In its first interim report, dated December 3, 1926, the commission showed, with a particular example, how fraud was commonly perpetrated. The steamship *Chris Moeller* had sailed from Vancouver and Victoria for San Blas, Mexico, with 21,479 cases of liquor. This liquor had been purchased in Britain by Manitoba Refineries, the name given to a British Columbian export liquor company. The liquor had been shipped to Victoria and Vancouver by way of the Panama Canal, passing San Blas, the purported point of final destination. San Blas, it turned out, was a village without a harbor; the consignee, a Mr. Rodriguez, was a fictitious name. Manitoba Refineries had stored the liquor in bond — that is, without paying any customs duties — until it had received large amounts of cash from San Francisco and Los Angeles. No liquor had ever reached San Blas, of course. It had been unloaded from the *Chris Moeller* to smaller boats off the U.S. west coast and smuggled ashore, some of it back into western Canada.

The commission recommended that no clearance document in such cases be issued unless the customs collector had a bond for double the amount of customs duties payable. (This was done by legislation.) The commission's auditors went on to investigate the operations of all 106 distilleries and breweries in Canada, 99 liquor export houses and 207 other commercial concerns. The audit showed "grave irregularities with consequent loss to the revenue of the country."

We will deal first with some of the commission's interim reports which resulted from investigation of individual companies and then look at its summing-up and recommendations.

Interim Report No. 3 found that "enormous quantities" of liquor had been shipped in transit (as in the *Chris Moeller* case) from Vancouver and Victoria, without any duty being paid. "The traffic has been carried on by means of fictitious consignees, clearances on false declarations as to destination, false return clearances and false landing certificates." At the same time, there were "persistent organized attempts to smuggle narcotics into Canada," and docks should be guarded and boundary patrols established by land and sea. The commission found that many roads between British Columbia and the United States had no customs houses.

In its fourth report, the commission gave in detail the case of O'Keefe Beverages Limited which had twice refused to permit accountants from the department of Customs and Excise to examine its books. The accountants were admitted on their third try, December 26, 1926, but by that time all books, vouchers and invoices up to the previous September were missing. "The books are concealed purposely and their whereabouts are known to the officials of the company," the commission said; O'Keefe had been acting in contravention of the War Tax Act and Excise Act and its licence should be suspended. On June 26, 1927, the commission recorded that O'Keefe had agreed to pay $320,000 in gallonage and sales taxes.

In its eighth report, the commission delved into the 1924-26 operations of the Regina Vinegar Company, owned by bootleggers Zisu Natanson and Sam Diamond. The company had acquired 4,000 gallons of alcohol, ostensibly to be used in the manufacture of vinegar. The alcohol had not gone into the vinegar mix but into the bootleg business. The firm had paid twenty-seven cents a gallon excise tax on the alcohol on the basis of its use in vinegar production. But the excise tax on liquor was nine dollars a gallon and the crown had been defrauded of $34,920. There was evidence, the commission said, that an excise officer was implicated in the fraud, but it was insufficient for prosecution.

In its ninth report, the commission recommended removal of the customs collectors at Windsor, Toronto, Vancouver and Regina. At Windsor, there was a "great deal" of smuggling and much undervaluation of goods. Inspectors at the ferry docks were lax. At Toronto, there was also undervaluation, and the commission recommended replacement of the chief appraiser as well as the collector. The commission came down particularly hard on Customs' Regina operations. Without naming names, it referred to such companies as Canada Drugs, Yorkton Distributors, Prairie Drugs, Regina Wine and Spirits, Dominion Distributors and, again, to Regina Vinegar. All of them had "conducted business in persistent and open contravention of the laws and regulations governing excise" and "even the most casual observer could not have failed to detect the irregularities" of the companies owned and controlled by Abe, Harry and Sam Bronfman, Meyer and Moses Chechik, and Harry Rabinovitch as well as Natanson and Diamond, "and yet they were seriously expected to carry on a bona fide 'drug' and 'vinegar' business."

The commission concluded: "That such a condition of affairs could have existed at all, let alone have continued for several years, shows not only lack of intelligent and efficient supervision on the part of the collector of the port [Regina] but serves to demonstrate a breakdown in proper and efficient supervision on the part of the department as a whole."

In its tenth interim report, the commission dealt with 129 firms or individuals. It investigated some firms the parliamentary committee had already inquired into the previous year, and found fraud against the revenue persisting. It found fraud in companies importing flowers, silk, auto parts, tombstones, garments, patent medicines, shoes and salt. In one case, that of a Niagara Falls importer, it conceded it could not even discover the nature of his legitimate business, if any.

But it was in the liquor trade that the commission found the biggest and most widespread cheating of the government:

—Selwyn A. Ernst of Mahone Bay, Nova Scotia, a shipbuilder and part owner of several vessels, ran rum from the West Indies. His ships stood off the Nova Scotia coast while his shore agent took orders and posted the buyers on the positions of the ships. Ernst had evaded $1 million in Customs duties.

—The Great West Wine Company of Saint John, New Brunswick, exported liquor to (it maintained) Havana. It posted a delivery bond. The landing certificate for the delivery was forged. It got another certificate and it was again rejected by Customs as forged. It presented a third. It was accepted and the bond was returned.

—James Ball, owner of the British Columbia Vinegar Company

Limited of Vancouver, left for Seattle just before the arrival of the commission's auditors, taking all company books and records with him.

—W.M. Egan, customs solicitor at Windsor from 1922 to 1926, received personal payments from distilleries and breweries for helping them escape prosecution, and castigated an honest customs officer, L.J. Lafferty, for refusing to accept bribes from smugglers on the Windsor docks and ferries. Egan fled to the United States at the commission's approach.

—Joseph U. Piche, sub-collector at Sandwich, Ontario, accepted money from the British American Brewing Company Limited for clearances of beer shipments. Allan Pearsall, sub-collector at Kingsville, Ontario, accepted money from Hoffman and Dunford, a liquor export warehouse.

—The Mexico Export Company of Windsor closed its bank account, withdrew all cancelled cheques and removed all goods from its warehouses as the commission was about to open its Windsor sittings. All principal partners and officials of the company left Canada, and the books disappeared.

—In the desk of Harry Rabinovitch, manager of Franco-Canadian Import Company Limited of Halifax, 50,000 forged U.S. duty-paid excise strips were found.

—Harry Low, managing director of Carling Export Brewing and Malting Company Limited, used stolen Canadian and U.S. customs seals and shipping documents to divert railway cars of beer to the States camouflaged as other commodities.

—Gooderham & Worts, Toronto, used to its advantage the law that sales tax was not payable on exports. All orders for liquor, no matter what their origin, listed destinations in the United States. Orders by telephone or from any point in Canada were invariably written up as orders from the States. Sometimes the company wired an American telegraph office giving instructions to send it back a telegram as drafted by Gooderham & Worts.

—Joseph E. Seagram and Sons Limited, Waterloo, Ontario, evaded income tax by distributing profits to its three principal shareholders in the guise of loans.

—Hiram Walker and Sons Limited, Walkerville, Ontario, used fictitious consignees and false landing certificates for purported shipments to Central America, Cuba and St. Pierre and Miquelon.

The commission investigated the eight Saskatchewan and Halifax companies controlled by the Bronfman family, and then added a special section on the "Bronfman interests" in which it said:

> We have dealt in this report with the activities of several firms, syn-

dicates or companies owned or controlled by members of the Bronfman family, so far as the scope of our inquiry warrants. It would appear, however, to be incumbent on us to consider matters of a general character not related specially to any one concern, but arising out of the combined concerns. This has special reference to matters concerning income tax and sales tax. The evidence indicates that none of this group ever filed any income tax returns until 1921, when a demand was made by the department.

In answer to this demand, Harry Bronfman made an arrangement with the officials of the Income Tax Branch whereby an arbitrary assessment of $200,000 (including interest and arrears) was levied upon eight members of the Bronfman family in respect of the income obtained or accrued from the various Bronfman interests during the years 1917, 1918, 1919, 1920 and 1921, but in respect to the year 1921, it purported to cover only the profits from dealing in liquor then in stock. So far as it deals or purports to deal with the income for 1921, this arrangement would appear to be without any statutory authority, as the year was not then terminated, and the War Income Tax Act does not appear to provide for or contemplate any assessments or adjustments being made in advance. No further income taxes were paid in respect of the profits earned from the stocks of liquor on hand on September 9, 1921, during 1922 or subsequent years.

It was admitted by Harry Bronfman in his evidence that none of the firms or companies in which this group of individuals was interested had made any returns or payment of taxes under 'The Business Profits War Tax Act, 1916' which was in force during part of the periods during which these concerns operated apparently at a profit. This report is to be read in connection with the reports on the following syndicates or companies with which the Bronfman family are identified, namely: Canada Drug Co., Yorkton Distributors, The Dominion Distributors, Gainsborough Liquors Ltd., Gainsborough Liquor Co., Atlantic Import Co., Atlas Shipping Co. and Regina Wine & Spirit Co. Ltd.

These were the commission findings dealing with the Bronfman companies:

—Canada Drug, Yorkton, Saskatchewan, held a provincial permit to sell alcohol for medicinal or scientific purposes. But it never engaged in the drug business. It acquired 300,000 gallons of alcohol, compounded it (a fancy term for adding water), bottled it, and sold it labelled as scotch.

—Yorkton Distributors exported large quantities of liquor to the United States through branch offices on or near the international boundary. It had 32 carloads (614,400 bottles) on hand the day U.S. prohibition began. It used fictitious names of scotch whisky firms for its labels.

—Dominion Distributors also used unauthorized labels. It was at this firm that customs officer Cyril Knowles seized a large number of labels, only to be rebuked by his superiors.

—Gainsborough Liquors Limited and Gainsborough Liquor Company (they took their names from the town in southeastern Saskatchewan) exported to the United States. Inspector Knowles seized three automobiles leaving Canada loaded with liquor on the grounds that the drivers had not reported to Customs on entry to Canada. Knowles told the commission that Harry Bronfman had more than once tried to bribe him to "disregard his duties and to desist from further interference with the operations of the firms or syndicates with which Bronfman was identified." The commission recommended prosecution of Harry Bronfman for attempted bribery, yet neither the Liberal government in Ottawa nor the Liberal government in Saskatchewan would act.

Two years later, after a Conservative administration had taken over in Saskatchewan, Harry Bronfman was arrested in Montreal and charged with attempted bribery and tampering with witnesses. He was acquitted on both charges. At the bribery trial in Estevan in March, 1930, W.F. Taylor, Commissioner of Excise, and C.E. Blair, assistant commissioner, swore that Knowles had never reported a bribery attempt. This flew in the face of Knowles' testimony that he had written a letter to Farrow reporting the bribe attempt and had personally reported it to Bureau and Farrow in Ottawa. Two other witnesses corroborated Knowles' account of Bronfman's $3,700 bribe offer. The royal commission put on the record Farrow's letter of February 7, 1922, to Knowles:

> As explained to you when in Ottawa recently on official business, the department is unable under present conditions, namely — these caused by your lack of discretion and judgment in connection with recent inland revenue cases at Regina, to continue your assignment to duty in excise work. You are therefore instructed that until otherwise ordered your duties are to be confined to customs work at the port of Winnipeg only and performed under the direction and control of Mr. W.F. Wilson, chief, customs preventive service. For the present the department cannot authorize you to make investigations regarding customs matters outside of the port of Winnipeg except as specially authorized by Mr. Wilson. You are directed to communicate to Mr. A. Code, inspector of customs and excise, any information which may be in your possession or may be communicated to you regarding infractions of the inland revenue laws and regulations so that investigations may be made in respect to these by Mr. Code when he deems it advisable to do so.

—When the commission tried to inspect the books of the Atlantic Import Company, Halifax, the company said its books were in Montreal. The auditors never did see the books. Ships carrying the company's liquor exports to Havana (so the manifest said) and Central American countries "never discharged their cargo at the point of destination named in the entry, but were diverted to other places, presumably chiefly to the

U.S., [pointing] to the conclusion that the landing certificates were not genuine." Although the Atlas Shipping Company, Halifax, was incorporated to take the place of Atlantic Import, the commission found the stand-in firm repeating the pattern.

It should be noted that the commission did not find that every brewery and distillery was defrauding the government. For instance, Molson's Brewery Limited of Montreal overpaid $26,410.25 in sales tax and needed to be reimbursed. Similarly, National Breweries Limited of Montreal had overpaid by an estimated $60,000 and Pelissiers Limited of Winnipeg by $1,515.

The commission filed its final report October 15, 1927. In view of the evidence it had already taken at public sittings, its first finding was not very startling: headquarters administration was weak and out of date: "We discovered that many of the officials in the outside ports were not aware of the existence of regulations which directly concerned the duties imposed on them, resulting in non-observance of such duties, a lack of uniformity in the different ports and in unnecessary correspondence with the department at Ottawa." The commission recommended establishment of an information bureau and publication of a periodical for all officers about changes in regulations, new directives and rulings, court cases affecting the department, smuggling methods and so forth. This was promptly done. Indeed, nearly all recommendations concerning administration were carried out, and the department also hired a management firm to conduct still another investigation.

The commission recommended establishment of a staff of appraisers with expert technical knowledge of commodities, the appointment of consular agents in countries exporting large quantities of goods to Canada, a board of National Revenue to hear appeals against seizures, a new system of disposing of forfeited goods, an overhaul of the audit system, and new methods of dealing with promotions and transfers of staff.

The commission said that it had found smuggling right across the country. Commercial smuggling was "somewhat prevalent" in some parts of Canada while running contraband was an individual effort in other parts. There was no efficient border patrol "and in many instances the customs houses were not located in strategic positions to give the officers reasonable opportunity of detecting or preventing smuggling." A considerable number of officers "appeared to be apathetic to individual smuggling, and made no serious effort to prevent same. Their conduct would indicate that they had a misconception of their duties in that respect. They acted as if their sole duty was to receive entries and payment of duties by those willing to pay same." The commission continued: "Along the Atlantic coast there was a large amount of smuggling by the medium of vessels, mostly schooners. In this region there were no proper means of transportation for the preventive officers. There were not enough boats and the boats that were in the service generally speaking had neither speed nor equipment to properly cope with the situation. Before the completion of our investigation, a special preventive force was in process of organization and we are not in a position to state whether such force is sufficient to meet the situation. The evidence showed that a strong preventive force was needed.'' An investigation branch should be established as well to look into all frauds.

One reason preventive work was weak along the Atlantic coast, the commission found, was that the customs cruiser *Margaret* was constantly being used as a private yacht. As early as July, 1914, only weeks after the ship had been commissioned, J.D. Reid, minister of Customs, took the *Margaret* on a one-month fishing trip with friends. Arthur Meighen took a sight-seeing trip. Bureau, Farrow and others took a ten-day cruise in 1922, and that winter the *Margaret* was berthed at Sorel for installation of new bathrooms for the ministerial and guest rooms. The following summer, the *Margaret* was called off patrol duty to take Bureau and guests on an eleven-day cruise on the St. Lawrence. Captain La Couvée was asked by commission counsel: ''Any patrolling you did during these trips would be incidental?'' The captain replied: ''Incidental.'' The commission produced correspondence from Collector William C. Acker at Halifax and Collector Lockhart at Saint John pleading with Ottawa for high-speed patrol boats. But somehow when a good boat became available it was sold to a rum-runner before Ottawa could act or, if one were acquired, it spent all its time in harbor for ''repairs'' ordered by Ottawa. Despite these hurdles, some effective anti-smuggling work was done by men like Captain John (Machine Gun) Kelly who fired about a thousand rounds a month, usually as warnings but not always. Neither customs officers nor their vehicles now carry arms.

The commission found that the smuggling of cigarettes and liquor was carried on ''on a very extensive scale,'' one reason being the high excise duty on both products and the high customs duty on imported liquor.

> The incentive to the smuggling of liquor is the possibility of very large profits to the smuggler. This is possible because of the great difference in price between liquor legally manufactured or imported and that smuggled. This difference is due to a material degree to the high tariff on imported liquors and the high excise duties on liquors manufactured in Canada — the Customs duty being $10 per gallon while the excise duty is $9 per gallon. It may well be that with the profit to the smuggler substantially reduced, he will be loath to take the risks incidental to his operations. As the sale of liquor in Canada is largely, if not altogether, in the hands of the various liquor boards of the pro-

vinces, the full benefit of a reduction could not be realized unless with the co-operation of the provincial authorities. At present liquors exported to a foreign country are exempt from excise and sales tax, and there has been evidence adduced before us showing that considerable quantities of liquors alleged to be for export to foreign countries were in point of fact smuggled back into Canada. This condition offers another inducement to the smuggler, and we have elsewhere suggested that these taxes be imposed. Another result of the present high price of liquor is seen in the somewhat prevalent practice of illicit manufacture of same.

One can judge how effective this recommendation was by the fact that smuggling continued apace. So did the output of illegal stills.

The commission described a variety of commercial frauds on the revenue: widespread undervaluation to avoid dumping duties; fake description of goods and of quantities of goods; a different user of goods than stated in the entry to avoid higher tariff rates; omission of packing, freight and insurance charges before shipment.

In addition to changes in legislation designed to reduce smuggling and fraud, the commission pleaded for stricter enforcement of the laws and regulations already in existence: "We see no reason why parties committing frauds on the revenue should not be proceeded against with the same degree of promptitude and efficiency as usually characterizes prosecutions for enforcement of provisions of the Criminal Code. This, according to the evidence, has not been so in the past."

Many companies holding licences from the government, such as distilleries, breweries, and drug and vinegar firms, "have been guilty of most flagrant and persistent violation of the laws and regulations which they are supposed to observe. They have in this way abused the special privileges granted to them, and have by improper or deceitful methods defrauded the revenue." Despite the Canada-U.S. 1924 treaty for the suppression of smuggling, the trade in contraband persisted, mainly by companies and individuals exporting liquor. The commission again drew attention to the use of forged landing certificates which purported to show the arrival at points outside the United States of liquor which had actually been smuggled into it; and it recommended that liquor export warehouses along the border — many of them, the commission had been told, were in effect forts armed to ward off hijackers — be closed down.

The government was not swift to crack down on forged landing certificates, possibly because taxes on liquor provided, as they do today, considerable revenue (in 1929, liquor taxes brought in $60 million, twice as much as the personal income tax). In January, 1929, the United States organized an anti-smuggling conference in Ottawa at which it called for Canadian legislation to ban liquor exports to the States. Prime Minister King rejected the proposal, but Canada did offer to allow U.S. customs officers into Canada to report on shipments being cleared; the United States declined. Euler, the revenue minister, went to Windsor himself to observe how serious the Americans were themselves about stopping liquor smuggling. He told the Commons in May he had seen liquor boats from Windsor discharge unmolested within 100 yards of the U.S. customs house. Anyway, it didn't seem consistent for Canada to permit manufacture of liquor and then restrict its sale abroad. Euler added that refusal of clearances for liquor boats would not stop smuggling into the States. It would merely drive the traffic underground, to the corruption of Canadians and even bigger costs for preventive services.

A memorandum from the Canadian embassy in Washington dated June 21, 1929, to Euler — it was signed by the first secretary, Lester B. Pearson — said the Americans were going to make a big drive to halt smuggling on the Detroit River as a challenge to Euler's assertions and in an attempt to win Canadian co-operation to halt the liquor traffic. Seymour Loman, assistant secretary of the U.S. Treasury in charge of prohibition enforcement, said rashly, "I think we can dry up the river." It was not long before Carey D. Ferguson, U.S. collector at Detroit, resigned because his river patrol could not even pretend to stop the flow of liquor from Canda. But continued pressure from the United States and the Conservative opposition — and apprehension of an increase in the U.S. tariff — finally forced the King government just before the 1930 election to place an embargo on liquor shipments from Canada to countries under prohibition law. The Americans put up the tariff a few months later, anyway.

King took no action against the Bronfmans or others found by the commission to have defrauded the government of millions of dollars. When Conservative R.B. Bennett got into power in 1930 (he had been a prominent member of the 1926 parliamentary customs committee) he launched an investigation into liquor smuggling and as a result the four Bronfman brothers (Allan joined Abe, Harry and Sam) and fifty-seven others — thirty-six from Nova Scotia — were charged with conspiracy to avoid payment of customs duties. The six-months trial ended in June, 1935, when the judge threw the case out of court.

In the meantime, Conservative J.T.M. Anderson had taken power in Saskatchewan in 1929, ending two and a half decades of Liberal rule. He set up a royal commission to investigate political interference in the provincial police's enforcement, or lack of enforcement, of the liquor laws. The commission's chief counsel was a future prime minister, John G. Diefenbaker. The general finding was that during the Liberal regime, the police cracked down on liquor violations in Conservative ridings and looked the other way in Liberal constituencies, especially at election time.

During the 1926 federal election campaign, Milton Campbell, Conservative candidate in Mackenzie, was alleged to have told a public meeting at Quill Lake, Saskatchewan, that Senator Bureau, when minister of Customs, had operated "a house of ill fame in the sacred precincts of the House of Parliament" so that he could compromise opposition MPs, and that this was only one-tenth as corrupt as other facets of the customs scandal. Bureau sued for libel and, for gathering evidence on his behalf, (as the Saskatchewan royal commission found) acquired the services of Detective Sergeant Charles Dunnett, a member of the Saskatchewan provincial police, on instructions of the then Liberal attorney-general, T.C. Davis. Dunnett had turned over his evidence to J.N. Fish, Bureau's lawyer, who soon after became a Saskatchewan judge. The commission said: "It is proved beyond doubt that a member of the Saskatchewan Provincial Police Force, namely, Sergeant Dunnett, was used at public expense to assist in a contemplated private civil action of a highly political character for the benefit of one of the parties. It is also proved that a flagrant attempt was made to cover up the transaction by letters and reports which gave an untrue statement of facts bearing on the case."

The commission also looked into operations of the Bronfman liquor export houses at and near Gainsborough in 1921-23, but declined to make any judgment on the grounds that it had not acquired sufficient evidence to do so. The provincial police became involved when American rum-runners arrived in border towns of Saskatchewan to pick up their liquor cargoes and carried out bank robberies to fill in time. The Bronfmans' brother-in-law, Paul Matoff, was murdered at Bienfait in 1922, apparently by hijackers, but the murder was never solved.

The smuggling of liquor into the United States did not end, of course, when Canada embargoed such shipments there. All that did was to remove what had been, in effect, official recognition of smuggling. The driver's seat of smuggling operations merely shifted to St. Pierre and Miquelon, where the American racketeer Al Capone once left a hat, still on display, as a souvenir, and these activities continued after the United States ended prohibition December 5, 1933. The only difference was that Canada had become the smugglers' chief market. Moreover, production of bootleg home brew soared to higher levels per capita than at any time since the early days of the Red River settlement.

Illegal stills were made from old wash boilers and car radiators. One was found in a deconsecrated Methodist church in Ranchville, Saskatchewan, another in a stable at Drumheller, Alberta, and still another in the organ loft of the Calgary Baptist church. Special Squirrel Whisky, the Chivas Regal of its day, sold for $25 a quart against the usual bootleg price of $20. When preventive officers patrolled the roads, bootleggers dragged chains behind their car (a "whisky special" or "whisky six" could carry up to forty cases) to stir up dust which blinded the pursuer — or they took to the open prairie with horses. The biggest items smuggled into the prairies were cars, trucks and tractors. They were usually hidden in straw stacks until an itinerant mechanic could change the registration numbers.

Smuggling stories from the 1920s and 1930s are legion, but even today rum-runners from that period are inclined to be circumspect. There are a few notable exceptions, and some books and other publications containing first-person accounts have been issued in recent years. A common thread in stories by customs officers is the destruction of seized liquor. There is a note of regret in most of them. G. Harold Hopkins, a customs officer at Yarmouth, Nova Scotia, from 1931 to 1966, recalls:

> The storage vault contained one-gallon and five-gallon beautiful oak kegs of rum, bags containing liquors such as whisky, brandy and fancy liquors of various kinds. Some of the fancy liquors were in bottles with a large bulblike container at the bottom and a long neck. These particular bottles were divided into four sections. Now it came time to destroy all of this collection. With axes we smashed the beautiful rum kegs, while the bottles were smashed on the concrete floor and the liquid went down the drain. It seemed a crime to smash those beautiful bottles and also the oak kegs. You see, it would not do just to empty the rum from the kegs and save them for sale to someone, especially were it a bootlegger, as he would just pour pure alcohol into the the kegs, shake them up well, let them stand a while, shake again several times and he would finally obtain a potent drink that would certainly make any man's eyeballs wiggle and would likely floor the amateur drinker with one good swig. After spending about three hours destroying these goods, I found my head wasn't in the right place, or else I was seeing things that were not there. The fumes sure got to me all right and I had to get out of that place and into the open air. Just hope that none of my friends saw me when I came out on the street or they would have said that I was stoned. I guess I was, but soon recovered. Not being a drinking man, it sure had its effect on me.

George Large retired in 1965 after forty-one years with Customs at Windsor, the last four as collector. He recalled in a 1982 interview:

> There was a lot of money made in bootlegging, but I heard of only one bootlegger who kept it. You have to remember that in the twenties the export of liquor from Canada was legal. Our government regarded keeping booze out of the United States as an American problem, not ours. For instance, I would spend whole afternoons signing B-13 forms [export papers] for shipments of liquor and beer. These forms were supposed to go to Ottawa for processing but Ottawa didn't care whether they ever saw them. I remember one morning getting a look into a room in the post office building and it was

stacked, floor to ceiling, with B-13 forms. They were there when the building was torn down and we burned them. As long as you had a B-13 you could ship out of Windsor. The shipments were supposed to go to Central America or places like that but some of those barges loaded with beer were lucky to make it across to Detroit, let alone to Cuba or Central America. You could get a B-13 for a shipment in a rowboat — anything. In the winter, cars took over booze on the ice. This was pretty precarious, of course, because the cars often fell through the ice. But it wasn't a big investment to lose. You could buy an old car for ten dollars then ...

The police had seized a ship called the *Vedas* which was full of beer, thousands of cases. I was instructed to take a gang down to the *Vedas* and destroy the beer. We brought it up from the hold and opened every bottle and poured the beer into the river, then tossed the bottle overboard. Things started to slow down on deck and I found that half my men were lying dead drunk in the hold. It took us a week or more to dump all the beer.

Once Milt Gallup, a senior official still at Customs in 1984, made an inspection trip to a border customs post in Quebec: "The old customs house was being torn down and we had to inspect it to make sure everything was cleared out. We had finished, we thought, when we were asked if we weren't going to look at the basement. I didn't know there was a basement. The trapdoor was hidden by a rug in the office. Down there was a huge vat with a spigot. A pipe into the vat led from the sink upstairs down which our officers had been pouring seized liquor for years with a fierce look to show that the law must be upheld."

Wilfrid Simard, who was customs collector at Armstrong, Quebec, from 1924 to 1936, used to pour the illicit liquor down his bathtub (he and his family lived in part of the customs house). He burned seized cigarettes in his backyard. Soon after one seizure, the smuggler sprayed gasoline all over the customs house and was about to set fire to it when Simard stormed out of the office firing his .45 revolver into the air. The pistol was a hold-over from the First World War in which he had fought. On two occasions, American bank robbers he was about to try to arrest in his role as immigration officer committed suicide right in front of him. "I was attacked several times but never hurt, unless you count the time I was bitten on the hand by a fur smuggler. I weighed 170 to 175 pounds, kept in shape, and I could look after myself. I didn't look for trouble mais si ça arrivait, j'étais là."

At age ninety-three, Arthur Bruce, former collector at Shelburne, Nova Scotia, recounted:

> I made only one seizure at sea that I can recall. A woman informed me that a steamer was transferring liquor to a schooner out in Jordan Bay. I took a provincial policeman with me and we drove over there. The policeman didn't want to come with me so I rowed out to the

steamer, ordered both ships to hand over their papers and seized them. The steamer was foreign and the schooner a Canadian three-master. I ordered the steamer to tow the three-master into Shelburne. On the way, somebody cut the tow line and the schooner made off, but was later seized in Halifax. The crew of the bigger ship I was on threatened to throw me overboard. As you can see, they changed their minds. The rum from the steamer was poured into the ocean, right down here in the harbor.

The *Nellie J. Banks* was one of the longest-lived rum-runners. She spent twelve years in the trade, the last nine almost exclusively carrying liquor from St. Pierre to Prince Edward Island. She was not knocked out of action permanently until 1938. Then the RCMP cutter *Ulna* seized her, eight miles off the east coast of Prince Edward Island, but only because the law had been changed to a twelve-mile from a three-mile limit (August 6, 1938) after the schooner had set sail from St. Pierre with a cargo of liquor. The *Banks'* master, Captain Israel Lillington, in the 1920s a member of the crew of the Newfoundland customs cutter *Daisy*, was unaware of the new legal circumstances. The *Banks* was the centre of a famous case in 1927 when the part-owner, Capt. Edward Dicks, accused the customs department of piracy on the high seas for seizing his ship outside the three-mile limit. Dicks threatened to pump the seizing officer so full of lead it would take seven men to lift him, and he got into a scuffle with the chief preventive officer at Charlottetown. Dicks won hands down. He was acquitted of assault, and the Exchequer Court, in a decision brought down ten months after the seizure, not only returned his ship and its cargo of 300 ten-gallon kegs of rum but awarded him $5,500 in damages and $700 in costs. The *Nellie J. Banks* immediately resumed her position off Prince Edward Island and sold the rum over the side in three days.

There were many cases of piracy on Rum Row. Hopkins recalls that the rum-runner *P.J. McLaughlin*, a schooner, was lying off the New Jersey coast waiting for the "contact" boats to unload her when she was boarded by twenty hijackers. They left the crew bound and locked in the cabins and made off with the full cargo of 4,200 cases of liquor. Many Nova Scotia rum-runners were built with steel-reinforced wheelhouses to protect them from Coast Guard fire and from thugs who boarded them in the guise of friendly liquor traders. Sometimes the hijackers waited until the rum-runners had sold nearly all their cargoes and then boarded them to grab the cash. Piracy became the worst dread of the smugglers. Hopkins also recalls that the schooner *Lucille B* out of Digby, Nova Scotia, was attacked off Boston by fifteen men who hijacked the cargo of a thousand cases. The schooner's captain was ashore doing business in Boston and it was suspected he had double-crossed her owners.

Passenger J.M. Isaacs of Montreal related to the royal commission in 1927 how the *Lutzen*, out of Saint John, New Brunswick, had been coolly hijacked in October, 1923. When the *Lutzen* was forty-eight hours out, bound for Havana (it was said) with a cargo of liquor, she had been quietly boarded by a "Captain Ford" and a small crew. The new crew had locked up the regular crew and disguised the *Lutzen* by effacing her name, painting her black and installing a fake wireless on the mast. For the next ten days, the cargo had been sold over the side to visiting speed boats: as many as 2,300 cases a day to twenty boats. The usurper captain had kept the money in a huge roll of $500 and $1,000 bills in his pocket. One day he had changed to shore clothes, been taken off by a speed boat with his crew, and was never seen again.

In his memoir *I Was a Rum Runner*, Don Miller of Yarmouth recounts that he went on his first rumship in 1923 at the age of fifteen, helping to sail the *Pat and Mike* from Belgium to Montauk Point with 3,140 cases of pure alcohol. It took weeks to unload because pure alcohol was not in great demand on Rum Row. Later, Miller says, the smugglers acquired faster ships with bullet-proof pilot houses and equipped with two-way radio, the shore radio being located usually in a hotel room and easily transportable from place to place. The man on shore informed the rum-runner when and where to meet the contact boats. Identification was usually made at sea by matching the torn halves of a bill, the captain of the rum-runner holding one half and the inshore smuggler the other. The denomination of the bill sometimes showed the quantity to be sold, a system which helped to reduce hijacking. Miller recalls that he was a crew member of the *Shanaliam* carrying 7,000 cases of liquor off Fire Island when it was caught inside the twelve-mile limit by the U.S. Coast Guard. The wireless operator quickly dropped the receiver and transmitter and code book overboard, weighted as they were for just such an emergency. The owner's lawyer had them out of New York jail and home in two weeks, ready to sail again in another rum-runner.

Mystery surrounded the deaths of some smugglers. In the summer of 1931, the 20-ton, two-masted fishing schooner *Catalogue* out of St. John's, Newfoundland, with a crew of four, was carrying 200 kegs of rum and 100 cases of whisky to be landed near Cape North, Nova Scotia. Weeks later, the dismasted, waterlogged wreck of the *Catalogue* was found drifting eighteen miles offshore and was towed into Cheticamp, Nova Scotia. The derelict was beached and pumped dry. Boards had to be torn from the deck to gain access to the cargo. Inside the sealed hold customs and excise preventive officers found the bodies of two crew members and fifteen kegs of rum. No trace of the other two members of the crew or the rest of the cargo was ever found.

286 *Smuggling*

There is little doubt that the parliamentary committee and royal commission investigations into Customs and Excise sent a jolt through the department. In 1926-27, the value of seized goods was only $426,746; in the following fiscal year, it was $3,154,078. In September, 1928, the largest narcotics seizure up to that time was made at Nanaimo, British Columbia, when 1,440 tins of opium were found concealed in packages of peanut oil. The street value, then known as the retail value, was $150,000.

But sometimes the crackdown was very gentle. In 1929, James Ball furnished information to the department which enabled it to collect $33,634 from British Columbia Distillery Co. Ltd. for fraudulent practices. As agreed, Ball received 25 per cent of the settlement, or $8,408, but Gordon Lindsay, a royal commissioner investigating a related matter, said the distillery actually owed $204,526, excluding any penalty. In 1932 Ball was found dead in Stanley Park in Vancouver, an apparent suicide by poison.

The best known officer in the Preventive Service was Captain La Couvée who continued to intercept rum-runners despite having to use his ship frequently for the pleasure trips of Ottawa officialdom. La Couvée had gone to sea at the age of fourteen and sailed for forty-seven years, thirty-two of them in customs patrol boats and cruisers. He joined the *Constance* in 1897 when the Preventive Service was formed and became master of the *Margaret* in 1915. He lost a leg in 1917 when it was caught in a tow rope. He cut off the leg himself with a knife. The next winter, on his wooden leg, he led a rescue party fourteen miles across ice in the Gulf of St. Lawrence to the crews of two trapped schooners. In 1927 alone, his last year of customs service, he made these seizures: 236 packages of liquor valued at $4,000 from the *Ronald B* in the Bay of Chaleur, 439 packages valued at $100,000 from the *Noxall* off Cape North, 1,980 packages valued at $185,122 from the schooner *Almedia* off Prince Edward Island, 1,438 packages valued at $72,000 off the Magdalen Islands, 266 packages valued at $3,000 off Miscou, New Brunswick, 287 packages valued at $17,850 off Ste Anne des Monts, Quebec, and 2,408 packages valued at $190,669 from the *Marion L. Mason* between New Brunswick and Prince Edward Island.

The Preventive Service had some of its toughest times just keeping flotsam and jetsam out of the hands of the public. (Under the Customs Act, it will be remembered, flotsam and jetsam is taxable.) On February 23, 1928, the schooner *Loyola* out of St. Pierre ran aground at Blueberry near Liverpool, Nova Scotia, with a cargo of 1,117 bags and 79 kegs of malt whisky. (Smuggled liquor was wrapped in straw and burlap bags for easier handling.) At low tide, the schooner was high and dry. Collector

More and one officer, the official records show, guarded the wreck "for the protection of the liquor cargo and the prevention of smuggling." But "the anxiety of the officers was increased by the attitude of a portion of the crowd which openly threatened to rush the guards, board the schooner and obtain possession of the liquor." Collector More managed to summon the RCMP for assistance and the cargo was saved — to be poured into the sea.

There was a bungalow overlooking Halifax's Bedford Basin which was long suspected by the Preventive Service of being a hideout for smuggled liquor. There were several beaten tracks from the shore to the cottage and from the cottage into the surrounding woods. But every time Customs raided the cottage, the officers found nothing. The cache was finally found by accident when the smugglers left in a rush. The "hide" was a big hole in the ground some distance from the cottage. A real tree had been nailed by the roots to a heavy lid. In their hurry, the smugglers had left the tree lying on its side.

One of the largest illicit stills ever found in Canada was discovered in the east end of Montreal. An innocent-looking brick bungalow with an ordinary basement was found to have two sub-basements. The first sub-basement contained cellulose-making machinery as a camouflage to cover the real operation in the sub-sub-basement: two stills and ten vats, each vat with a capacity of 700 gallons. The secret entrance was through an upright steel tank whose top lifted up by pulley. None of the liquor was taken out through the bungalow. Instead, a pipe led under the street from the sub-sub-basement to a former church rectory, and from there to a garage where deliveries could be picked up.

Now a new type of moonshiner has begun to operate in Canada, both on a small and large scale, with Manitoba and Prince Edward Island leading the way. The means of production is a still, the main ingredient barley, mangels, or cull potatoes, and the product gasohol. In 1981, in a test case, an individual still-operator in Ontario who was using alcohol apparently for fuel was charged with possessing a still without a licence, but the Crown withdrew the charge.

Smuggling takes many different forms, of course. Back in 1920-33, Canadians used to smuggle rye whisky into the United States. Recently, American rye, the grain, was being smuggled into Canada. It is legal to import U.S. rye for feed, but illegal to sell it under the quota system operated under the Canadian Wheat Board Act. Some Canadian prairie farmers with poor crops and unfilled quotas have apparently brought rye across the border from North Dakota and sold it for up to $1-a-bushel profit to grain companies with elevators near the border. These frontier points are the very sites of the liquor export houses of six decades ago.

The impulse to smuggle fosters an ingenuity praiseworthy in any other line of endeavor. New smuggling methods are devised almost every day, as when cattle being smuggled across the frozen St. John River between Clair, New Brunswick, and Fort Kent, Maine, were fitted with overshoes, so that it would appear that just the usual crowd of people had walked across the snow-covered ice to the bingo game.

SECTION IV

The Lives and Times of Customs and Excise Officers

CHAPTER I

"Conduct Yourself with Urbanity"

The Customs officer rifling through soiled vacation clothes and brand-new souvenirs at a crowded airport baggage counter or lonely frontier post is not trying to annoy the traveller. Rather as a representative of the oldest department in government, and springing from a long and honorable line of public servants, the officer is dedicated to carrying out the orders of the Parliament of Canada — protecting the revenue — while keeping smile and temper in place.

C.G. Stewart, landing waiter and searcher of His Majesty's Customs at the port of Quebec in 1828, received these instructions from London: "You are to conduct yourself with urbanity to all persons with whom you have any official intercourse; as also with deference to your superior officers; but should you discover any fraud or neglect of duty on their part, you are immediately to acquaint the Governor therewith, giving the parties accused copy of your representation, and also transmitting to us copy of the same, and of the proofs produced in support of such charge, otherwise you will be considered as a partaker of the offence, and be punished accordingly."

That was just one article of twenty-eight received from the Commissioners of His Majesty's Customs in the book of instructions for landing waiters and searchers in the British Possessions Abroad.

The Commissioners did not leave much to chance: "You are to give daily attendance at your office in the Custom-House (Sundays and holidays excepted) at such hour as may be ordered by the Collector and Comptroller, and enter your name and the time of your appearance in a book kept for that purpose." (There were only three annual holidays then: Christmas, Good Friday, and the Sovereign's birthday).

The instructions given in 1828 could be today's:

> On receiving warrants for the examination of passengers' baggage, you are to address an order to the waiters, as their authority for allowing the same to be unshipped, in which you are to express the number and description of the packages, taking care that they be accompanied by an Officer of the King's warehouse, where you are carefully to examine the contents of every such package, observing that all goods

found therein which are liable to duty are to be detained until the proper duties are paid.

You are to give all possible dispatch to the merchants' business, consistent with the safety of the revenue, who are always to be attended to in their proper turn, so that no undue preference be shown.

You are hereby enjoined not to take or receive, either directly or indirectly, by any means or on any account, any article landed by you, or any other officer, either as a present, or under the pretence of paying for the same; nor are you to take or receive any article whatever by way of present from any merchant or other person with whom you may have official intercourse.

And you are not to go on board of any vessel which may be discharging to partake of any refreshment, nor receive the same either in taverns, or elsewhere at the expense of the merchant, or master of such vessel.

In the civil service today, these instructions would be called conflict-of-interest guidelines.

The principal officer of the colonial customs house was the collector, who was in charge of the actual collection of duties and recording of all shipments. The name is still in use today, though some collectors would prefer to be called simply managers. The sub-collector was in charge at a smaller port. The comptroller acted as a check on the collector and to do this he kept a second set of books. The surveyor performed this task when there was no comptroller, but the surveyor's main duty was to assist the collector in the supervision of outside activities, in particular the work of searchers and waiters. The searcher developed into today's appraiser, the central figure in the customs operation because he sets values on imports and applies the appropriate duty. The waiter, whether landing waiter or tidewaiter, boarded all ships to prevent any illegal landing of goods before arrival at the quay. The position of the tidewaiter became that of the outdoor officer, and the landing waiter the examining officer. The jerquer searched vessels for contraband. The gauger tested — and still tests — for the strength of spirits so that the proper duty can be applied. The name comes from the "gauge in the cask." The locker supervised entry of goods into a bonded warehouse. The preventive officer watched for smugglers, usually in lonely coves and on wilderness trails. The main place of office work was (and is) the longroom. The name comes from the length — 190 feet — of the main office of the customs house in London in the early 19th century.

The surveyor was the channel through which the collector gave orders to the staff and received reports from the staff. A directive issued in 1892 by Commissioner W.E. Parmelee said: "The practice followed by collectors at some ports in giving orders direct to and receiving reports direct from subordinate officers in the surveyor's department has been found to lead to inconvenience and is detrimental to the public service." The surveyor was supposed to keep a fatherly eye on the staff: "As it is of the utmost importance to the public service that the general character of officers in this service, both in public and private life, should be respectable, he (the surveyor) is, as far as practicable, to make himself acquainted therewith, and should he discover that any of those under his survey have, in either case, been guilty of any offence derogatory to fair character and good conduct, he is, without fail, to acquaint the collector thereof, for the information of the Commissioner of Customs."

A new nomenclature has given us clerk and chief clerk, cashier, commodity specialist, keypuncher, auditor, manifest clerk and so on. The term inspector has undergone a change. The inspector until fairly recent times was the officer who went from port to port, unannounced, to keep the system honest. Internally, the inspector was known as the hangman. Today the inspector is the officer you meet at the border crossing or at the international airport.

Many of the best anecdotes in Customs and Excise concern visits by the inspectors, who always travelled in groups of two, three or four. It was a wise collector who set up an early warning system to apprise himself of inspectors' visits. At Grand Falls, New Brunswick, the collector's brother-in-law ran the taxi stand at the railway station and was the first to know of their arrival. George Large, former collector at Windsor, Ontario, recalled in 1982 that he used to be tipped off by the porter on the sleeper of the Toronto train. A quick telephone call from the train station was all the warning he needed to put everybody on the alert. One inspector always went directly to see the collector; another moved in on the cashier and balanced the books on the spot, drawing a green line to show where the audit should start. The inspectors sometimes used cars to cross the border and approach the target port from the American side. One evening at Chartierville, Quebec, many years ago, the inspectors, making a fast sortie from the United States, found the man in charge asleep on the counter. Worse, to ward off the evening chill, the man had wrapped himself in the office Union Jack.

Previous sections of this history have described the kinds of instructions which went out to the field on government policy and regulations. Governments have been equally assiduous in controlling the conduct and deportment of customs and excise staff. One of the earliest recorded orders concerning conduct appears in a commercial treaty between England and Holland in 1496: "The officers of either country, appointed for searching for contraband goods, shall perform it civilly, without spoiling them or breaking the chests, barrels, packs or sacks, under pain of a month's imprisonment."

But civility does not preclude seizure. In an English statute of 1660, relating to shipping, navigation, commerce and revenue in the "British Colonies and Plantations in America and the West Indies," the section on seizures began: "Any Officer of the Customs, authorized by Writ of Assistance under the superior or supreme Court of Justice having Jurisdiction with the Colony or Plantation, may take a Constable, Headborough, or other Public Officer inhabiting near the Place, and in the Day-time enter any House, Shop, Cellar, or other Place, and in case of Resistance, break open Doors, Chests, Trunks, and other Packages, there to seize and to bring any kind of prohibited or uncustomed Goods to His Majesty's Storehouse in the Port next to the Place where such Seizure shall be made." The phrase "in case of resistance" was later changed to the more sweeping "in case of necessity."

If customs officers had stiff laws to support them, still they were themselves subject to heavy penalty for not observing customs regulations. Taking a bribe, recompense, or reward, or conniving at any false entry meant being immediately "rendered incapable of serving His Majesty in any employment civil or military" and paying a fine of £500, a very considerable sum in the 17th, 18th and 19th centuries. An officer who allowed a foreign ship any of the privileges of a British ship "shall for the first offence be put out of office." Even allowing one merchant to get ahead of another in the customs queue brought a penalty of "double costs and damages."

We have seen how early legislators in Nova Scotia, New Brunswick and Canada saw the customs collector: an avaricious official enriching himself with exorbitant fees for filling out simple forms. How did the public see the customs officer?

Robert Hunter Jr., in his journal of a trip from Quebec to Carolina in 1785-1786, reported on the conduct of Captain Paul Minchins: "He gave himself some airs and us a great deal of trouble about the boats not having each a pass." Along the St. Lawrence and Great Lakes at that time, garrison troops acted as customs officers. At Niagara, Hunter said, "We had as much trouble with an impertinent corporal about our boat as if we had been in France."

A Frenchman saw it differently. Le Duc de la Rochefoucauld Liancourt, in his famous two-volume record of travels in North America in 1795-97, notes his meeting with a customs officer at Oswego just before Britain gave it up as part of the peace treaty ending the American revolutionary war. Under the protection of a garrison numbering two officers and thirty men, this official, a Mr. MacDonald, searched all vessels which sailed up or down the St. Lawrence. "As to the prohibited exports in merchandise," Liancourt writes, "they are confiscated, without exception, for the benefit of the custom-house officer, by whom they are seized. This naturally prompts his zeal, and increases his attention."

He looks askance at MacDonald, who came from a family of some social prominence (his brother was Speaker of the Upper Canada Assembly):

> A man of Mr. MacDonald's extraction, in France, would injure his character, in the public opinion, by accepting a place in the customs. In England they know better. There, no injurious idea attaches to any profession which concurs in the execution of the laws, and no blame attaches to a nobleman for holding a place in the commission of the customs, or turning merchant. He is, on the contrary, respected as much as if he belonged to the church, the army, or the navy, or were placed in any other honourable situation. Yet, if public opinion were altogether founded on just and reasonable principles, it should stigmatize all persons who hold sinecures without any useful employment and press consequently as dead burdens on the State.

The American, John Heckewelder, entering Upper Canada at Niagara in 1798, had no border troubles at all: "In the evening we passed the fort at Chippewa, the commander of which was very civil to us. We were no where asked for a pass, had any duties to pay, or were officially interrogated." Fifty years later, however, James Dixon, in his *Personal Narrative of a Tour Through a Part of the United States and Canada*, published in New York in 1849, drew a comparison between the officers of Canada and the United States unflattering for Canadians:

> The American officer never forgets that he is a citizen, and the citizen does not forget that he is a man; their intercourse is perfectly easy, free, unembarrassed; the one class never assumes an air of superiority; the other never lowers his status, or yields up his consciousness of equality, or his self-respect. On the other hand, the Canadian officer never removes from his standing of assumed dignity, or condescends to become the citizen; he rarely amalgamates with the people; and they, on their part, as seldom think of stepping beyond their line, and claiming equality. [The reader may like to place this view beside Miss Fitzgibbon's, (page 329 for the futility of judging behavior as belonging to national "types".]

Although very few first-hand accounts by revenue officers themselves have survived to give a flavor of their life and times, there are many letters which, though they deal mainly with day-by-day transactions at the port where they were written, hint at what it was like to be a guardian of the revenue. For example, it was very common in the late 18th and early 19th centuries for merchants and shipowners to appeal customs decisions. They were substantial people in the community and acted with an appropriate confidence. But so were the senior customs officers, which made the contest more or less equal.

A letter from Governor Thomas Carleton, dated at Fredericton July 23, 1791, is addressed to William Wanton, customs collector at Saint John. It says: "Isaac Bell and Samuel Miles, merchants and owners of the Schooner *Bell* of Saint John, have made application to me, accompanied with affidavits, respecting the seizure of the said schooner, representing that the two barrels of tobacco which they are accused of having illegally imported, were shipped at New York as flour and in flour casks, and that neither the master or owners of the vessel were privy to the fraud, and being satisfied concerning the truth of their representation, I think it highly equitable to consider them as not answerable for an offence in which they appear to have had no intentional participation; and I therefore recommend it to you to restore the vessel to the owners." Two days later, Carleton put similar pressure on Wanton in a letter concerning an incident involving the schooner *Sally*, owned by Aaron Beck and William Yeaton.

The next letter we have at hand is one addressed to the governor by Richard Batchellor, customs surveyor and searcher at Saint John. It is dated five days later, July 28. Batchellor says that Wanton has shown him both letters from Carleton, and he is, in effect, replying on Wanton's behalf. He continues, saying that no one was readier than he to obey the governor's command but the case of the *Sally* had already gone to court, with himself as prosecuting officer. As for the *Bell*, "I am sorry to be obliged to say" that the merchants' statements fell considerably short of the real facts attending the seizure. It was impossible to believe the owners were ignorant of the real contents of the flour barrels. The governor had been "induced" to order freeing of the schooner. "Be pleased, sir, to allow me the further indulgence to observe" that if the vessels were freed, future seizures would result in similar petitions and "greatly impede me in the execution of my duty and render me liable to personal danger and continual abuse." If the affidavits were sent to him as soon as possible, he would point out the essential defects in them and convince the governor that he (Batchellor) had acted correctly.

On August 6, the affidavits on behalf of the merchants were sent to Saint John. One starts out by saying that Bell and Miles had, by "an almost unparalleled exertion," raised the shipping business in Saint John to an "enviable degree" which had meant "lucrative revenue" benefitting the province. Then Godfrey Leydeck, the seizing customs officer, is attacked as extremely offensive and injurious to commerce and revenue. Indeed, it was very unsafe to have any property come into the port of Saint John what with Leydeck laying his "ungrounded informations." The merchants' affidavit concludes: "The detention of property and unavoidable expense attending the recovery thereof is such a clog to the wheels of business that [we] cannot in silence . . . continue [our] exertions under the mortifying situation of being subject to the caprice of a character who, having nothing at stake, vents his malignancy without control."

There is a gap in the correspondence and we can only assume that the governor's will prevailed. The next letter, dated August 14, 1792, a year later, is from Batchellor to Governor Carleton requesting leave of absence — "withdraw myself from official duty" was the officer's phrase. (At that time, governors in the colonies had to approve leaves of absence because some officers had been taking off a year or so on approval of the collector only.) Batchellor says he is asking for leave because "having a long time since laboured under a disorder in my bowel occasioned by a cold I contacted whilst on my official duty which had hitherto baffled all medicine and Dr. Paddock who had attended now informs me that having done his utmost, nothing can remove my complaints but a total relaxation from business and a change of air, whose certificate I have the honour to enclose as corroboration." It is his plan to go to the United States to get medical attention and rest.

The next letter, dated September 6, 1792, is from Wanton to Carleton: "We have this moment been informed that Mr. Batchellor has deviated from Your Excellency's leave and has taken passage at Saint Andrews on board the brig *Friendship* for Greenock, instead of going to Boston as we firmly believed he meant for his health, and this we declare was the only motive for delivering him your leave of absence."

We see the end of the affair a year later, August 6, 1793, when a letter from the customs house, London, announces a customs commission for one Colin Campbell as surveyor and searcher at Saint John "in the room of" Richard Batchellor, "who has resigned."

The same investigating team which Customs sent from London to investigate smuggling in British North America in 1812-14 reported on the day-to-day workings of the customs houses as well. For instance, they found that elderly and infirm officers could scarcely be budged from their jobs. There was no superannuation until 1870, and a customs officer clung to his post as long as he could. Thomas Nicholson Jeffery, the collector at Halifax, said his tidewaiter was so old (eighty-two) and infirm that he could no longer climb aboard ships. A replacement had to be hired for this duty at 3 shillings, fourpence a day, increased to four shillings to encourage the substitute to search for contraband. (Five shillings was the equivalent of $1 at that time.) The inquiry team also learned that Comptroller John Slayter at Halifax was "scarcely competent" because of advanced age. Collector Wanton at Saint John should be replaced because the "general powers of his mind were partaking of the gradual decay of the body." Wanton had not been at the office for a year but signed documents taken to his house; he died in 1816 at eighty-two.

The investigators said that holidays should be curtailed at Halifax. There were twenty-four of them, including Christmas and three days following, as well as Good Friday, Easter Monday and Easter Tuesday. The hours of business were 10 a.m. to 2 p.m., though Jeffery said that merchants could transact business until 4 p.m. "without even the payment of extra fees for such service." Customs revenue had been kept in a wooden box until Jeffery had bought an iron chest for it out of his own money. The collector was allowed £20 a year for an office but had to pay £50 and then furnish it at £100. Customs duties in 1810 had amounted to £2,468 of which all but £150 had been used for expenses. This "profit" Jeffery appropriated for himself, much to the annoyance of his comptroller, who expected half of it. Andrew Belcher, a member of the executive council (as Jeffery was), told the inquiry team that preventive officers in the outbays should be "unconnected with the people of the country." (This same argument was used in 1932 to justify removal of the Preventive Service from Customs and putting it under the Royal Canadian Mounted Police. It was argued by proponents of the move that preventive officers in outlying districts were too well acquainted with the inhabitants, making it socially awkward for the officers to report local smuggling.)

Jeffery became involved in a case of alleged fraud on the part of the collector at Sydney, Renna Cossit, whom Comptroller George Ainslie in Cape Breton suspended and accused of fraud, forgery and misconduct. On March 28, 1818, Ainslie wrote to His Majesty's Principal Secretary of State for the Colonies that Cossit had committed fraud "by introducing a clause with sympathetic ink in a receipt for money paid to him on his own account purporting that it was for the rum duty and of forgery in subscribing his sister's name as witness who was not even in the house when the transaction took place." Ainslie said Cossit had acknowledged fraud to many persons "with apparent exultation on the ground of its being a clever trick, deserving the applause of a jury." Furthermore, Cossit had been guilty of "almost incessant intoxication" for several years. Things were so bad, Ainslie complained, that "I cannot recommend any person on this island to succeed him." He would therefore recommend a British army officer who "will give a respectability to the office which the constant and daily intoxication of Mr. Cossit has long deprived it of."

Ainslie wrote further on April 8, that Cossit had refused to give up the revenue books, declaring that he never kept any, and that there was a deficiency of more than £500. When Ainslie had demanded that Cossit appear before him, Cossit had sent an insolent verbal message by a servant "that he did not choose to come." Cossit "frequently could not sign his name from the effects of his solitary debauch the preceding evening and I cannot avoid remarking that the people in general here are so linked together by other ties as well as roguery that it is very difficult to bring guilt to proof especially if the accused is a public defaulter; an almost universal combination is then made to screen him and robbery ceases to be so, here, when on the public purse."

Cossit, who had been collector at Sydney since 1813, entered his defence in a letter April 30, 1818. He said he had defended the king in America, had sacrificed property, and been obliged to abandon America and fly to other colonies. No investigation had been allowed him. All the revenue involved was a "paltry sum" of £23-4-0 which had given rise to Ainslie's charge of "unprudential conduct" and had "put me at the risk of eternal disgrace." The amount was duty paid on 464 gallons of rum. As for the charge of intoxication, Cossit asserted, "It is with regret and sorrow, I myself am in honor called upon to say that the charge is partially true. A very severe nervous walk and debility of limbs has been taken for intoxication."

Jeffery conducted an investigation. He did not relish going to Cape Breton. He sailed to Canso and then went overland, complaining of the lack of a proper carriage. He reported that the charges of fraud and forgery were without foundation and that Ainslie had been "most unfortunately misinformed." Jeffery also found that Cossit had four orphan sisters solely dependent on him. He had served since 1803 and should be given an annual allowance if dismissed. Jeffery added: "In small colonial governments like that of the Island of Cape Breton, eternal warfare exists between the executive, the officers of government and the people." Jeffery's last remark on the subject was: "I quitted Sydney with a most fervent prayer that I may never have cause again to visit it." The Board of Customs on September 25, 1818, ordered Cossit to be severely reprimanded and strictly enjoined to abstain from inebriety. But he kept his job.

The position of customs collector was not sought for the salary it commanded, as we have seen, but for the schedule of fees which could be charged for providing the necessary documents. The collectors at Halifax, Saint John and Quebec were rich men. When fees were abolished and replaced by salaries in 1825, a few posts earned high pay, though not as much as the old fees brought in, but the salary of a collector outside the biggest seaports was usually only about £100. The collector and other officers would count on receiving a share of the money realized through sale of seized goods.

This practice began in Britain, where there was once a sliding scale for seizures of liquor and tobacco, ranging from one-eighth of the revenue from the auctioned goods in a case where the goods were seized but nobody convicted, to the full amount where the goods were seized and all accused parties convicted. There was little chance of an officer receiving the full amount because juries, as noted by Ainslie in Cape Breton in 1818, were loath to convict smugglers or anybody who had robbed the public purse.

The 1823 ledger of seizures at St. Andrews, New Brunswick — a surprising number of records of that port have been preserved — shows that the proceeds from goods taken from the 59-ton schooner *Herald* realized £26, divided equally among three parties: the seizing officer, the lieutenant-governor of New Brunswick and the crown. Seized goods sold included 80 gallons of gin, £4-6-8; 21 gallons of brandy, £4-14-6; 133 pounds of tobacco, £3-6-6; five barrels of apples, 17 shillings; seven barrels of onions, 12 shillings; 10 barrels of potatoes, 3 shillings; 100 fresh codfish, 8 shillings; articles of clothing and hardware, and the schooner itself and its rigging.

Generally, the seizing officer's share was one-third. This is spelled out in a United Province of Canada order-in-council of 1850 which apportioned the net proceeds from the sale of seized goods. One-third went to the government, one-third to the seizing officer or officers, and one-third to the informer or informers. If there were no informers, two-thirds went to the seizing officer or officers. The collector got five per cent of the gross proceeds for arranging the sales and doing the bookkeeping.

William Hands, the first collector at Windsor, Ontario, was paid by being allowed to keep one-third of the revenue he took in. In 1840, this amounted to £1,795. In 1854, a new Act for the Management of Customs decreed that there would be four holidays a year and that the maximum salary would be £500. (In 1938, Collector Andrew H. Dalziel of Windsor joked that he would have liked to be in his predecessor Hands' position of receiving one-third of the port's revenue in salary — the collections that year at Windsor amounted to more than $20 million.)

Some officers had to be warned against over-zealousness in making seizures as a means of earning money. The Commissioners of Customs in London insisted, in 1831:

> We think it necessary to acquaint you that the severe penalties and forfeitures prescribed by the Acts of Parliament relating to the Revenue and Navigation are principally directed to cases of fraudulent or wilful violation of them and not to those of mere ignorance or inadvertence ... And we acquaint you that we shall hold you strictly responsible for all the consequences arising out of any prosecution which may hereafter be instituted at your port contrary to the manifest spirit and intention of this order; and you will take care to apprise every officer under your survey of this order.

CHAPTER II

Kerby of Fort Erie

Take the case of Colonel the Honourable James Kerby, collector at Fort Erie from 1834 to 1854. Fort Erie was one of eleven customs posts established by Upper Canada in 1801 on the United States border; many of Kerby's hand-written records of the post have survived.

Kerby was born near Sandwich, Upper Canada, in 1785 and led a militia battalion in the war of 1812-14. He was severely wounded and was twice awarded the Sword of Honor by the Assembly of Upper Canada. No other native Upper Canadian won so much distinction in the war. Besides maintaining his militia duties as a lieutenant-colonel after the war, he was postmaster, magistrate, businessman and town warden at Fort Erie and a member of the legislative council (1831). He got into Customs almost by accident. He didn't relish the work and was shot at by Canadian smugglers almost as often as by invading American troops in the war. But Kerby soldiered on. He believed in protection of the revenue. His rigid upholding of the law had him in legal hot water most of the time. The townspeople got up petitions to have him removed and they sued him frequently in the courts for trespassing and illegal seizure of goods. His appeals to his superiors in York and Niagara for support usually fell on stony hearts because these officials had to deal with the public uproar caused by Kerby's zeal.

"I am filling the office of collector of Customs, which is wearing me down fast," he wrote to a friend in 1837. "I am really worn down," he told Inspector-General John Macaulay in 1841. About the only break Kerby got was during the 1837 rebellion when he was called out for military duty at Niagara. During his absence of ten months, his deputy stole the collections, resulting in official censure of Kerby for not knowing his deputy was untrustworthy. Kerby's wife died in 1839, his son-in-law in 1841 and his only son in 1846.

From his detailed letters, one can easily visualize Kerby on night anti-smuggling patrol, standing in his sleigh, pistol in one hand with the other whipping on his horses across the frozen Niagara River in pursuit of villains trying to run whisky and tobacco from the American side. He was responsible for a 20-mile stretch of the Niagara frontier from Point Abino to Black Creek. He once was ambushed and shot in the neck and back near his riverfront home on a moonlight night. The *St. Catharines Journal* of February 19, 1846, reported: "Many attempts have been made to injure Col. Kerby, but this exceeds them all for coldblooded, fiendish atrocity."

The collectors at Fort Erie had all been from the Warren family; then, with the death of John Warren in 1831, a wave of applications hit the lieutenant-governor. Among the applicants writing to Sir John Colborne were Henry Warren, brother of John, Duncan Warren, a nephew, George Hardison, another nephew, Johnson Clench, whose father had just died leaving "a widow and several children unprovided for, most of whom are females," Thomas Baines, backed by Bishop John Strachan, William Smith, who had borne "a conspicuous part" in the 1812-14 war, and Daniel McDougal, wounded in the war and with a large family, one deaf and dumb. Kerby supported Hardison, saying Hardison would be in the best position to lend financial assistance to Warren's pregnant widow, who already had seven children.

Hardison showed promise. One time he chased the sleigh of John Butler, a York saddler, for twenty miles and seized tea and other articles smuggled across the Niagara River from Buffalo. Butler's excuse was ingenious. He had missed the Buffalo-Fort Erie ferry and had hired a boat to get across the river to visit his aging father near Fort Erie. He had planned to declare his goods at Niagara on his way home. His father had been a master saddler for the 18th Light Dragoons for nearly twenty years and would not have connived in any attempt to defraud the revenue. But Hardison seized the goods and, as the law called for then (and does now), the conveyance as well, in this case the team of horses, harness and sleigh.

By July 1, 1834, Kerby was compelled to say that it was "very grievous" to him as a magistrate and Hardison's backer to report that Hardison was a defaulter. If he didn't make good "his deficiency" (the amount was not mentioned) and if he were removed from office, Kerby himself would solicit the appointment. Hardison was sacked (he later became reeve) and Kerby's appointment to the job of collector appeared in the Upper Canada Gazette, effective September 22, 1834.

Two days later, Kerby made his first seizure, from one John Tidy of Ancaster, for declaring short weight and therefore short value on goods bought in Buffalo. Kerby informed Inspector-General George Markland that he had posted for auction Tidy's pair of horses, wagon and confiscated goods, including tea and cheese. He asked whether it would be all right for him to bid up prices at the auction if he thought the goods were going for too little.

There was sometimes a tug-of-war for the goods Customs was trying to seize and, as we shall see later, there were often attempts, sometimes successful, to retrieve the goods taken by officers. On November 22, 1834,

Kerby reported that one of his assistants, Francis Smith, had seized a small boat with twenty-five bags of tea "but the party being too strong against him, he was constrained to lose sight of the tea." On March 5, 1835, Kerby seized a sleigh, a pair of horses and two barrels of salt from Johiadah Schooley. He was not to hear the end of it for some time.

Schooley began denouncing Kerby around town on account of the seizure, so Kerby wrote to him March 21, urging him to make a formal complaint to the Commissioners of Customs at Niagara: "Upon their decision it will be known to the public who was right or who was wrong." Kerby also said: "I am well aware that you have spared no pains, wherever you have been, to impress upon the minds of the public that I in the execution of my duty as collector of Customs have distressed and oppressed you by seizing your horses and sleigh the night you crossed from Buffalo on the ice six miles from a port of entry ... Take care that I don't come upon you for the penalty; that will operate against you worse than the seizure." (The penalty for defrauding the revenue was then usually £100.)

On April 23, thirty inhabitants of Bertie Township sent off a petition to Lieutenant-Governor Colborne complaining about the "arbitrary and unjustifiable conduct" of Kerby who "should never be trusted with authority beyond his own premises." The petition added: "James Kerby for the short time he has been collector has given more cause for complaint than has ever occurred." It also maintained that Kerby's servant bid on seized goods at auction. Kerby described the charges as "void of truth" and "false imputations so injurious to my character, ... got up by a few designing men avowedly for the purpose of prejudicing the minds of the people against me." Then he said in his letter to Markland: "If they are suffered to go on in this way uninterrupted what security or protection have I or any other public officer to be thus unwarrantably abused and insulted by such a fractious set."

Markland upheld Kerby, deciding that the petition had been made "by some turbulent individuals who are desirous of producing embarrassment." But the Commissioners of Customs found in favor of Schooley, and Kerby had to return the horses and sleigh. Kerby was undeterred by this setback, making even more seizures while noting: "The ice is quite safe and it affords smugglers a great opportunity." He found a tub of dutiable salt fish buried in a barrel of duty-free potatoes. He seized barrels of smuggled whisky and gunpowder, tea, coffee, molasses, sugar, raisins, starch, cinnamon, assorted nuts, pepper, ginger, cigars, shoe brushes, clothing, wrapping paper, buffalo robes, calfskins, prunes, snuff boxes, shaving soap, cloves, rice, and matches.

But for nearly every seizure there was a petition to the lieutenant-governor, who had to launch an investigation, the starting point being a request for a full explanation by Kerby of his action. Kerby began spending more and more of his time writing letters to Niagara and York in his own defence. He dismissed the petitioners as "totally ignorant" men, whose "abusive remarks" and "efforts of malignity" would recoil on themselves. The commissioners in one case held that Kerby had acted "overzealously and enforced the law too vigorously under the conviction he had no discretionary power." Kerby was guilty of an "error in judgment and not any wilful inclination to injure individuals or exceed his duty under the pretext of his authority as a revenue officer." Markland told Colborne that, although Kerby was "legally warranted in his proceeding," his duty was "performed in a vexacious manner, harassing to persons going over to Buffalo on business." Still, it would scarcely be just to censure Kerby, Markland concluded.

If Kerby was harassing the citizens of Fort Erie, they had only begun devising means to harass him right back. For one thing, they kept Kerby so busy writing defences against their petitions that he got behind in his accounts and had to ask for more time to straighten them out. At sales of seized goods, they agreed not to bid against each other so that persons whose goods had been confiscated could buy them back cheaply, prompting Kerby to complain that such "highly improper conduct proved very injurious" to the revenue and to ask that the matter be put before the attorney-general for action.

Kerby retaliated. For instance, he seized Mrs. Charlotte Warren's ferry boat because the ferryman allowed persons with dutiable or prohibited articles to land without benefit of Customs. Then, when Frederick Rose came over on the ferry from Buffalo with a bag of flour and put the bag in his wagon, Kerby seized the team of horses and the wagon.

To spite him, the captains of the ferries *Water Witch* and *Waterloo* landed not at the new customs wharf but at another pier a quarter-mile away, forcing Kerby to trudge from his office and back. The passengers requested that Kerby write out a form for every single article, dutiable or not. A petition by some citizens to authorize landings at places other than the customs wharf was approved by the Commissioners of Customs. Kerby wrote on November 16, 1840: "I am now nearly broken down by the treatment of these people who study every way and means in their power to provoke and aggravate me in the execution of my duty and I beg leave most humbly to appeal to His Excellency for immediate redress and not allow a faithful subject of the crown to be thus treated with impunity by a party headed by persons who are determined to deprive me of my office if they can." Kerby did not wait for a reply from government house. Two days afterward he seized the *Water Witch* for not landing goods at the appointed place for examination. At the same time, he seized a small green boat and some goods from Alexander Dougan, the former deputy who helped himself to customs revenue.

The citizens of Fort Erie began to sue Kerby regularly for wrongful seizure of goods or trespassing. By August, 1842, Kerby had damages and costs of £184 outstanding against him. This was to come out of Kerby's own pocket, and he wrote to Inspector-General Francis Hincks that people "destitute of principle" were seeking his ruin. "My whole trouble and misfortune is that I acted fearlessly to the best of my humble ability in the just protection of the rights of the crown. I have thus been made a sacrifice to the gratification of these people when I know and feel that Government in justice to me as a faithful servant ought to support and bear me out."

It appeared at that time that the sheriff was going to seize Kerby's chattels to pay the damages, and Kerby asked that he be allowed to pay the claims out of customs revenue and reimburse the crown by instalments. Surely, he said, "His Excellency will not see my little earnings sacrificed to the hammer, to the mortification of my poor family." His salary was £150 a year. Kerby's younger brother, Andrew, paid the collector's debts.

On July 17, 1845, in the line of duty, Kerby seized a box of books, including one called the *Life of Marion* which Kerby described as "a very objectionable work for British readers." The books had been bought by "the association for the mental improvement of the youth of Crowland Township" and were ordered returned by the Commissioners of Customs except for those prohibited by copyright law. (British books pirated and published in the United States were prohibited in Canada.) Kerby lost two more cases that year and complained to J.W. Dunscomb, Commissioner of Customs: "It is a very great hardship that I should be made to sustain these several losses which are to a very considerable amount in the performance of my official duties — all of which have hitherto been disallowed me to my very serious injury. All my little earnings go to meet the several suits instituted against me in my official duty in the protection of the revenue."

On July 29, 1846, the executive council rejected Kerby's petition that the crown pay £396 18s 8p that Kerby owed for defending lawsuits. The petition said: "Your memorialist is advanced in life, has suffered in health, in person and in property to a large amount in the zealous and active discharge of his duties." He had acted under the instructions of the inspector-general and therefore "Government was pledged to bear the expenses of the prosecutions and damages to which he has been subjected."

At about the same time that the executive council rejected his request for a £50 increase in salary, Kerby reported an attempt on his life: "I received the contents of a gun in the back charged with duckshot which took effect and wounded." Kerby sought permission from Dunscomb to post a reward for information on the assailant, but apparently received no reply. He received a tip that a "grand rascal living three miles from Amherstburg" was responsible, and asked permission to leave his post to go after him. Again, no response.

On April 25, 1848, Kerby informed Dunscomb that his landing waiter, Orange Schryer, was being evicted by his landlord, H.H. Warner, tavern-keeper and "noted smuggler." Warner had told Schryer that as a revenue officer he was "injurious to his custom as an innkeeper."

Three weeks later, Kerby wrote the commissioner: "The present serves merely to acknowledge the receipt of the blank forms and aggregate books furnished for this office and to acquaint you that a very bold attempt was made upon me last night by twelve men with two boats, landed in front of my door, no doubt to rescue the seized property in my charge. They were received with vigilance and left the shore as they came. I have every reason to believe that the notorious smuggler H.H. Warner was the person who headed said party, having succeeded in a like attempt about three years ago."

In the early months of 1854, Kerby reported seizing twelve barrels of whisky from Adam Goldie, hiring another customs officer because of the opening of the Erie and Brantford Railroad, and obtaining an increase in pay for Schryer — to £100 a year from £50 after ten years' service.

On June 22, 1854, Richard Graham, customs surveyor and chief assistant to Kerby, wrote to R.S.M. Bouchette, Commissioner of Customs: "It becomes my duty to inform you that Col. the Hon. James Kerby, collector at this port, departed this life on Tuesday the 20th after a short illness. I have telegraphed to the Hon. the Inspector-General in substance the above. As there is no mail from this place today north, this will not leave till tomorrow."

In July, businessman William A. Thomson wrote to the governor-general and to Bouchette: "The late Col. Kirby [Thomson misspelled his name] as Custom House officer, although a gentleman, was by his unyielding habit a great drawback to the growth of commerce at the port of Fort Erie." Progress at Fort Erie had been "much retarded by the mulish principles under which the Customs were managed." He suggested that Graham be appointed collector, and he was.

Early in 1855, Thomas Worthington, inspector of ports, went to Fort Erie to report on the management of the port since Kerby's death. He told Bouchette in a letter dated February 7 that Graham "exercises all his discriminations in favor of the public" so that a "huge amount of duty may have been irrevocably lost to the revenue." Kerby probably would not have been averse to that being taken as his epitaph.

K erby had experienced nothing but trouble for sticking to the rules, but Graham, for all his laxness, did not appear to have any difficulty keeping his collector's job and held it for a quarter-century until 1881, when he was superannuated. Backsliding officers were rarely dismissed, usually because they were patronage appointments in the first place. We may take as an example the case, again in Fort Erie, of John Magwood, preventive officer.

As early as 1859, there had been complaints from citizens about Magwood's "obnoctious" behavior occasioned by his "dissipation and abusive language," particularly during municipal elections. Nelson Forsyth complained that Magwood was "not only unfit but a very improper person to hold an office under the government." Magwood's boss, Collector Graham, stood up for him, saying that Magwood had lost his job as constable because of Forsyth's influence in the village council and had therefore done all he could to defeat Forsyth at the next election. Magwood had "greatly rejoiced" when the polls closed and Forsyth had been defeated. Graham added that Magwood was a "warm-hearted Irishman who sometimes takes an extra glass and when in funds at election times is not the most polite or prudent person in the world." Besides, Magwood's salary was only $100 a year and he had to work as an auctioneer and at other jobs to provide for his family.

In 1861, John Douglas complained officially that Magwood had been drunk in the street and had used abusive language against him. Graham again made excuses. Douglas had used his influence to prevent Magwood from renewing a lease on a fishing station. Anyway, Graham had heavier concerns. The customs house had burned down and the only office space he could find was in a tenement at $3 a month. Later, he was able to rent a former saloon near the ferry landing at $100 a year.

In May, 1862, Worthington ordered Graham to "expedite the removal" of Magwood. There had been another complaint about his drunkenness in public and his abusive language. In this case, Magwood had gone into a tavern, accosted a man carrying a carpetbag, and ordered him to open it for inspection. When the man showed him the contents Magwood had exclaimed, "If I owned stuff like that I'd never show it to anybody."

Far from being dismissed, Magwood received a 100-per-cent increase in pay to $200 a year. (Graham was then making $1,000 annually and the other four members of the staff $500 each). On September 9, 1866, Magwood asked for a transfer to another port on the grounds that his life was being threatened repeatedly, but he remained on the Fort Erie staff until 1874, with a raise to $300 in 1872.

Meanwhile, in 1860, there was another incident at Fort Erie of smugglers taking their loot back after it had been seized by Customs. The following broadside (poster) appeared:

> $100 Reward will be paid by the undersigned to any person or persons giving information that will lead to the Arrest and Conviction of the parties present, aiding and assisting in the forcible taking and removal of a wagon load of smuggled goods from the Customs officers of this port, at Alexander Willson's Barn, in the township of Bertie, after the same had been seized, on the night of 6th October, 1860, Rich'd Graham, Collector of Customs, Port of Fort Erie, October 8, 1860.

Several men armed with clubs had grabbed the loaded wagon, after Graham and his assistants had seized it, and had run it down the lane and into the swallowing darkness.

The customs house staff took part in the repulsion of a Fenian raid at Fort Erie in early June, 1866. Graham reported to his superiors June 4 that "the raid has come to a close here and I am right side up." Orange Schryer had been taken prisoner twice but released both times unharmed. William Murray, "noble fellow," had penetrated the Fenian camp on a Friday night and taken seventeen prisoners and secured their guns. Only this one short letter by Graham is on record about the incident, and it appears that some exaggeration might have intruded. The noble Murray seemingly took prisoners when the Fenians were already giving themselves up.

Another incident involving the Fenians is described by Frederick Parker, collector at Frelighsburg, Canada East, in a letter June 21, 1866:

> I have the honor to inform you that during the raid by the Fenians on the Custom House and village of Frelighsburg, on the 7th and 8th inst., there being no force to oppose them, they made an attack on the Custom House, broke the office sign in pieces, also the door of the office. They opened all boxes, scattered the papers and letters in all directions, broke all the ink stands, stole all the pens and stationery, but did no further damage in the office except to put everything in confusion, the books, receipts, office blanks and returns. I have after a great deal of trouble picked up and sorted. They are not damaged. I have also saved all Government Money in my hands. On the Fenians entering the place, the leader sent me a deputation of the citizens of this place requesting me to surrender myself a prisoner, threatening to hang me if I did not comply, which I refused to do, and as they sent a strong force to capture me, and presented their guns, I retreated to the woods and with great difficulty escaped. They also broke into my

residence, stole all my clothing, a Masonic apron, my commission, all my private papers and receipts, besides doing me a great deal of other damage.

Parker was no stranger to assault. Lake Memphremagog connects Magog, Quebec, and Newport, Vermont, and was a favorite smuggling avenue, by boat in summer, sleigh in winter.

A preventive station was established on the lake at Georgeville, Quebec, which later became a full-fledged port of entry, in 1854. Parker, then preventive officer, once intercepted a cariole on the ice and seized it, the horses and the contraband goods. He then kindly offered the smuggler a lift home in the seized sleigh. The smuggler accepted, knocked Parker on the head, threw him out of the cariole and made off, leaving the customs man to make it on foot to the nearest village. By the time he summoned aid, the smuggler had long since fled to Vermont. Little wonder that the total value of seizures at Georgeville in 1854 was 13 shillings, three pence. (In 1840 in Lower Canada, the salary of a junior customs officer was £40 a year, plus 65 per cent of the proceeds from seized goods. There, as elsewhere, the new officer had to have two guarantors who agreed to make up any public funds he might lose or steal.)

There were sometimes special inducements for officers. On January 24, 1859, Commissioner Bouchette wrote to the collector at Niagara Falls that three preventive officers were being added to his staff because of increased winter smuggling there. Then he announced: "The Inspector-General, as an encouragement to the officers concerned in the proper discharge of this important part of their duties, has recommended that the Crown's proportion of seizures be given to the seizing officers at your port, thereby enabling the officers engaged to equip themselves efficiently for defence, and for quickly moving from place to place. I have also to inform you that the extra remuneration to be allowed to officers upon preventive duty away from their own ports will be as follows: for married men, one dollar per diem, for single men, fifty cents per diem."

In Nova Scotia, in 1864, the procedure was slightly different. Proceeds from the sale of seizures were applied so that: "the collector, out of the net proceeds of the sale, after paying the expenses of the proceedings, shall pay one-half part to the seizor and the remainder as the board shall direct, and the board may thereout grant a further sum to the seizor, or may recompense the informer, or any person assisting in the seizure."

The seizure form (No. 15) in the Canadas in the period about 1840 was about a foot square and printed on heavy paper. On the front of it, the seizing officer had to fill in the particulars in their assigned columns: time, place, goods, from whom seized, source, probable value and so on. But on the back were these fourteen questions which the officer had to answer:

1) Date of Seizure, and when delivered to Collector, if any delay occurs, explain the cause.
2) The Name and Rank of every Officer or person employed in the Customs concerned in making the Seizure.
3) The quantity and quality of the Goods, of what country they are the Production, and how the fact is ascertained.
4) Particular circumstances which led to the Seizure, and the cause of Forfeiture, and whether by information or not.
5) State the Act or Acts of Parliament specifying the Sections thereof under which the Seizure is considered liable to forfeiture.
6) Whether attended with any attempt to rescue, if any, state all particulars.
7) The probable value of the Vessel, Goods, etc., respectively.
8) If the Vessel, in which the Goods were imported, is seized, state her Name, and that of the Master, of what country, from what Place, by whom owned and her burthen according to British Admeasurement, and if British, when and where registered.
9) If the Goods were seized on board any Vessel, state her Name, and that of the Master, of what Country she is, and her burthen according to British Admeasurement, from whence, whether the Goods were reported by the Master, and if not, whether there is reason to believe they were purposely omitted.
10) If the Goods were seized in Boats or other Vessels employed in the unshipping or landing the Goods, state of what Vessel they were taken, with the Names of the Persons concerned in the transaction.
11) If the Goods were seized on Shore, state the Names of the Persons from whom seized, and whether the Horses, Cattle, or Carriages employed in the removal of the Goods have been detained.
12) If seized in any Building or other Premises, state by whom the same are occupied, and whether there is reason to believe the occupiers were privy to the Goods being lodged there, and the grounds thereof, or by whom they were lodged, or in whose possession they were at the same of Seizure.
13) When persons are liable to Prosecution for Penalties, state whether the parties from their situation in life will be enabled to pay the Penalty, and whether they have ever been before guilty of a similar offence.
14) State whether claimed, and if so, the state of the Proceeding, and the Amount of Law expenses, and all Charges incurred up to the time of reporting the Seizure.

In this period, officers had to sign attendance books — they were called appearance sheets — both morning and afternoon. Fines for lateness or absence were scaled according to salary. An officer making £100 a year or less was liable to a fine of two shillings if late and four shillings if absent all day. The fines were increased for every £50 of salary. For an officer earning £500 a year or more, the fine was 10 shillings for lateness and £1 for a day's absence. No salary or other allowance was forthcoming until the fines were paid. The 1830 order added: "It is to be understood, however, that notwithstanding the payment of fines, any dereliction of the Board's Standing Orders for ensuring the due attendance of the officers and clerks, will also be visited by such censure or punishment as the nature of the case may appear to deserve." If an officer were arrested for being in debt — "pecuniary embarrassment" was the term used in the order — his pay ceased and, though some had tried, he could not put time in prison against annual leave. Furthermore, there would be a full investigation to determine whether he could resume duty.

Illness was a constant worry because there was no special provision for sick leave. The usual procedure was to ask for leave of absence without pay. A collector in Lower Canada once wrote the commissioner that he was going into hospital for amputation of a gangrenous big toe. He had hoped to be back at work the day after the operation but the doctor had insisted he take eight days off. The collector said he would charge this time against his annual leave.

Throughout, there were constant instructions on how to act toward the public. Commissioner Dunscomb in 1844 issued this general advice for preventive officers:

> Bear in mind that your appointment has been made more with the view to prevent the violation of the laws in future than to take cognizance of past evasions of them. Upon assuming your duties at a station where no Customs House was previously established and where the inhabitants in your immediate neighborhood have been so long accustomed to obtain their supplies from the United States without the payment of any duty, principally from the circumstance of their residing at so great a distance from any Customs House, you will no doubt find the execution of your duties opposed to their feelings, and as the Revenue Laws are never regarded with favor by the public in general, your attention is particularly directed to the foregoing circumstances, which are likely to aggravate such feelings, as involving an additional reason, that in the strict enforcement of the Laws you give no just cause of complaint, of the manner in which you execute that trust; and you will avoid a fruitful source of complaint by exercising great caution, and which you are strictly enjoined to do, in making the most particular inquiry respecting all informations which may be given to you, before acting upon them, so as to avoid being made subservient to the vindictive feelings of individuals, who have frequently no other object in view but to harass their neighbors with whom they may have quarrelled.

When he became commissioner, R.S.M. Bouchette advised customs officers that they had a perfect legal right to examine women's satchels "but it is a right to be exercised with great delicacy and discretion."

Jean C. Belleau, collector in Iles-de-la-Madeleine in 1848, equated paying customs duties with furnishing a share of the public revenue and said that islanders who evaded duties were depriving themselves of "claiming their share of the public revenue for local purposes."

In early 1845 at Sault Ste. Marie, Collector Joseph Wilson instructed Baptiste Lesage to pay duty on some whisky. Lesage complained to Commissioner Dunscomb: "I told Wilson I would give him fish as I had no money in my possession. He said the Queen did not want fish, nothing but money."

In 1846, Collector William Macrae at St. Jean became involved with two of his officers in a protracted argument which finally had to be settled by Governor-General Earl Cathcart. Macrae had ordered the two to sweep out the office daily and light the fires in winter. The officers protested that this was beneath them and Cathcart agreed: the object of respectability in the customs house "can scarcely be attained by calling upon gentlemen holding a commission from Her Majesty's Representative in this Province to execute the menial duties to which they have made objection."

Always, there were the unforeseen problems.

In 1847, farmer David Carpenter asked for permission to winter his cattle on the Vermont side of the border. Customs agreed, on condition that Carpenter pay duty on the American hay his cows would consume while away from home.

On February 12, 1847, L.H. Masson, collector at Dundee, Canada East, made an eloquent plea on behalf of returning Canadiens. He wrote to Commissioner Dunscomb:

> There have been lately many calls made at this office from French Canadians, my Countrymen, who emigrated to the United States a few years ago, to enquire whether they could come back to their Native Land and bring back, without the payment of duty, some, one horse, some, one cow, or such other animal, their only property, of which they do not like to ... dispose of at this post, alleging their poverty prevents them from paying duties on the same.

Dunscomb acceded to the request. Masson wrote this letter in English, but he sometimes wrote in French. Internally, official replies were invariably in English. There does not seem to have been any directive requiring customs officers to use English in their reports and letters. But it was simply taken for granted that the working language of the department was English. There are references as early as 1760 about the inability of civil servants in Quebec to speak French. In 1886, Henry Kavanagh, inspector of ports, was asking about the French-language capabilities of some officers in the Eastern Townships where the majority language was then English.

Customs was responsible in the mid-1800s for collection of canal, road and bridge tolls. There were often complaints from the collectors as soon as winter set in that pedestrians and vehicles were crossing on the river ice to evade bridge tolls. In one case, three farmers got together and built their own road to circumvent one of the collection gates on the toll road. Bridge regulations of 1845 provided for fines of up to £5 for non-payment of tolls; for smoking on a wooden bridge; and for mooring rafts or vessels to bridge supports.

Perhaps a unique case, in 1866, was seizure of an entire hotel by Vincent Cazeau, collector in Beauce County. Duty had not been paid on American materials used in construction of the hotel. Customs released the hotel when the duty was paid.

In 1860, Customs at Prescott, Canada West, tried to seize 108 American-built Grand Trunk Railway locomotives on the grounds that duty on them had not been paid. Headquarters over-ruled Prescott on the grounds that such a seizure would inconvenience the public.

The government exercised patronage in all customs appointments. This is made very clear in the uproar created in 1860 by the merest suggestion by Quebec Collector Dunscomb (former commissioner) that the hiring of some junior employees might well be left to the collector. Commissioner Bouchette wrote him Aug. 7, 1860: "He (Finance Minister A.T. Galt) is of opinion that the patronage of the government properly extends, as of course, to all grades of employees from the highest to the lowest."

A year later, Dunscomb was ordered to hire Olivier Noël as a boatman on the customs vessel which took inspecting officers out to ships. Dunscomb had no objection to this, as the later correspondence shows, but he didn't act swiftly enough on the order, raising a suspicion that he had somebody else in mind for the job. George Etienne Cartier, attorney-general for Canada East, speaking (as he said) for Galt and John A. Macdonald, attorney-general for Canada West, wrote to Bouchette: "The Commissioner of Customs is instructed to direct the Collector of Quebec to employ Olivier Noël as a boatman." Bouchette accused Dunscomb of insubordination and there was a serious falling-out between the two old colleagues. Dunscomb told Bouchette that he thought he might have at least been spared Bouchette's "assumption of official superiority, setting aside any grateful remembrance you may have of the advice and assistance I so cheerfully extended to you upon your succeeding to my office." On a higher level, Prime Minister Alexander Mackenzie in 1874 discarded into Customs his minister of militia and defence, William Ross, as collector at Halifax. In 1880, Dunscomb told the royal commission on the civil service that there had been only two promotions in his office in twenty-five years because all vacancies were filled by patronage appointments from outside Customs. The merit principle was not accepted in government until the Civil Service Act of 1908.

At the time of Confederation in 1867, there were fifteen customs employees all told at headquarters in Ottawa (still Bytown in official customs returns), including Commissioner Bouchette at a salary of $3,200 a year, ten clerks at $500 to $1,600 and two messengers at $300 to $450. Dunscomb remained collector at Quebec at a salary of $3,240.

There were 181 ports of entry in 1867, manned by an outside staff (as it was then called) of 642. There were 81 ports in Nova Scotia, 47 of them one-man stations, with a staff of 169; 53 in Ontario, with a staff of 220; 29 in New Brunswick, with a staff of 121; 17 in Quebec, with a staff of 141; and a staff of 11 for collection of tolls on the Welland Canal. The gross revenue collected was $8,624,318, of which six per cent went for salaries and all other expenses of collection. Collectors' salaries ranged from $3,000 a year for the collector at Montreal to as little as $80 a year plus 10-per-cent commission on duties collected: Collector A.B. Thorne of Thorne's Cove, Nova Scotia, collected only $80.42 in duties in 1867-68, bringing his total pay to $88.04.

For contrast, here are the figures for 1883, fifteen years later and four years after Macdonald launched his national policy of taxing imports to protect domestic industry. The number of ports had nearly doubled to 350 (116 in Nova Scotia, 104 in Ontario, 50 in New Brunswick, 45 in Quebec, 23 in Prince Edward Island and six each in Manitoba and British Columbia). But the staff had grown to only 956 and fully one-quarter of them were concentrated at four ports, Quebec, Montreal, Saint John, New Brunswick, and Halifax, reflecting the very heavy reliance on ocean shipping for imports. Revenue that year was $23,172,309, a gain of $10,000,000 from 1879. The percentage of the revenue spent to collect it was down to 3 1/4.

The ports were widely scattered, of geographical necessity, and most of them were very remote from the source of their authority. All the more precise, then, was the control exerted over the individual officers in the field. A directive from Commissioner Thomas Worthington of inland revenue, issued April 20, 1869, announced that heavy travelling expenses incurred by excise officers made it necessary that the following rules be strictly observed:

> 1st — All journeys under four miles shall be deemed walking distances, for which no allowance will be made.
>
> 2nd — An allowance of $1.50 per diem will be made for the hire of a saddle horse, for the time necessarily occupied when the journey cannot be performed either by railway or steamer.

> 3rd — When the journey is performed by railway or steamer, then the actual fare both going and returning will be the sum allowed.
>
> 4th — An allowance of $1.50 per diem will be made for personal expenses when boarding out the full day — for half of the day, 75 cents.
>
> 5th — All unnecessary travelling to be strictly avoided, and the district inspectors are charged to see that this is attended to.

Worthington was at his collectors all the time to save expenses. In an earlier directive, July 7, 1868, he had said: "The heavy charge to which this Department has already been made liable by the indiscriminate use of the Telegraph in matters of unimportant business which might have been communicated equally well by requisition or letter makes it necessary to restrict the use of this mode of communication to business of urgent importance only; you will therefore be good enough to govern yourself accordingly."

Collectors had to be trusted in matters of departmental policy, a confidence always bolstered with stern warnings. On December 9, 1867, they were given "in strict confidence" the excise tax increases on liquor and petroleum which would not be placed before Parliament as resolutions until some months later. This was to enable them to apply the increases the moment they were announced by the minister. "PS," the letter read: "You will be held responsible for the consequences arising out of any improper use being made of any portion of the Resolutions now transmitted." On June 26, 1868, the minister warned, in a circular numbered 12 1/2, that unless collectors stopped submitting their returns in a "very careless and unbusiness-like manner" they would have to hire someone "at your own expense" to do the accounting.

An excise commissioner of unsparing vigilance, Alfred Brunel produced an incessant stream of instructions. His orders governing transfers, issued May 31, 1872, show that there was sometimes a penalty for being single:

> 1st — In the case of officers without families, they are to receive the actual necessary expenses of their journey to the place to which they are removed, and a sum not exceeding the cost of one week's board at the ordinary rate charged at respectable boarding houses at the place at which they are stationed. All other expenses are to be borne by themselves. Should they be recalled, the necessary expenses of the return journey are to be allowed.
>
> 2nd — When officers having families are required to remove from home on temporary duty, their necessary travelling expenses and the full amount of their board while on such temporary duty, at the ordinary rate charged at the place at which they may be stationed, are to be allowed.

3rd — When officers having families are notified that they are required to make a change of residence, without promotion, the necessary expenses of removing themselves, their families, and their furniture, together with one week's board for themselves and the members of their families, at the ordinary rate charged at the place to which they are removed, are to be allowed.

4th — When officers without families are removed on promotion, no travelling expenses are to be allowed.

5th — When officers having families are removed on promotion, the allowance of travelling expenses will be submitted to the department, to be specially dealt with as the circumstances of the case may required.

In circular No. 72, 1873, Commissioner Brunel informed newspaper editors: "I am directed by the Honorable the Minister of Inland Revenue to inform you that although your paper is included in the List of Newspapers that are to receive Government patronage, this is not to be understood as an authority to insert all advertisements relating to the business of this Department, many of which are of only local interest. You will be duly notified as to the advertisements of this Department which you are to insert, and payments will not be made for such as are inserted without special authority."

In directive No. 131, September 20, 1876, Brunel set out the rules governing official correspondence:

1 — Official papers are to be written on foolscap paper, leaving a convenient margin, i.e., from half to one-fourth, on the inside of the paper.

2 — When the letter does not extend beyond one page, only half a sheet is to be used. If the letter cannot be written on one page leaving a quarter margin, a second half sheet is to be used.

3 — Each letter is to be related to one subject only and must contain as full and complete information on that subject as possible.

4 — Each paragraph is to be numbered as shown in this circular.

5 — If there are any inclosures they must be described in the margin. The transmission of unnecessary inclosures is to be avoided.

6 — All official letters are to be folded in four folds as this circular is and forwarded in official envelope E2.

7 — In official correspondence and in reports the most concise and explicit terms are to be used; formal and unnecessary quotations from previous letters, repetitions and mere speculative opinions unsupported by evidence are to be avoided and in making statements the exact facts are to be rigidly adhered to, as the writer will be held strictly accountable for the accuracy of the information he forwards.

And so on, for six more numbered paragraphs. This directive was revised March 29, 1882, mainly to acquaint the staff with sixteen new sizes and colors of official envelopes, making the total thirty-one.

(It is interesting to compare Brunel's directive with a recent and similar Privy Council order in 1979, entitled "Guidance Manual for the Preparation and Handling of Cabinet Papers." The manual is one hundred and two pages long and contains this instruction: "Discussion papers are to be typed, single-space, on 8 1/2" x 14" paper, using both sides of the pages, English and French texts facing, French on the left, English on the right. Pages are to be numbered consecutively beginning with the cover pages. Allowance is to be made for left, right, top and bottom margins of 1 1/2 inches each. Pages are to be stitched together at the upper left corner and four-hole side punched. See Appendix B for specifications." Appendix B is a drawing of a sheet of paper showing the proper 1 1/2-inch margins. The punch holes are 3 1/2 inches apart. The top punch hole is 1 3/4 inches from the top of the page and the bottom punch hole is, of course, 1 3/4 inches from the bottom.)

On January 28, 1879, Brunel passed on this directive about politicking within the civil service:

> The Treasury Board have observed with much regret a growing practice on the part of gentlemen employed in the Public Service to endeavor to influence the Ministry to accede to their applications for increase in salary or additional retiring allowance, by means of the private solicitations of Members of Parliament and other persons of political influence ...
>
> It appears to the Board that any attempt on the part of the officer to approach them on these matters through the private intercession of persons unconnected with this Department is virtually imputing to the Board either that it is likely to turn a deaf ear to a reasonable application unless supported by political influence, or that it may be induced to accede to an unreasonable application if such influence be brought to bear upon it.
>
> The Board decline either alternative, and in order to prevent for the future any misapprehension upon this subject, they wish it to be understood by every public officer that any attempt made by him to obtain their sanction to his application by any such solicitation as hereinbefore referred to, will be treated by them as an admission on the part of such officer that the case is not good enough upon its merits, and such application will be dealt with by them accordingly.

Nothing missed Brunel's eagle eye. On June 27, 1879, he declared: "It has been reported to this Department [inland revenue] that some district inspectors and collectors have been in the habit of granting informal leave of absence to their subordinates for periods varying from one day to one week; and that it has been no uncommon thing to meet with excisemen at distances from their places of business quite inconsistent with their duties, without the Department having been informed of such absence. I am directed to call your attention to this practice, which is in opposition to the regulations of the Department and subversive of all discipline ... The Department will not sanction the indiscriminate granting of leave when the parties receiving it can show no greater cause for granting it than a desire to participate in some amusement." In future, he ordered, leave beyond the three-weeks annual leave would be granted only with the approval of headquarters.

He gave instructions, March 19, 1881, for excisemen travelling from place to place with weights and measures to inspect hay scales, weight bridges and the like. "The actual cost of the hire of horse and vehicle while actually and necessarily in use will be allowed by the Department," the circular said. "When the horse and vehicle are not in actual use the horse feed only, which is not to exceed 50 cents per day, will be allowed."

The next month he issued Circular 212 about the hours of work: office hours were 8 a.m. to 6 p.m. six days a week with one hour off for dinner. The only days off were Sunday and legal holidays. If an officer had to work on Sunday, he received $1 for the first hour and 50 cents for any subsequent hour. On holidays, the pay was $1 for the first two hours and 25 cents an hour after that. For time worked before or after regular hours Monday to Saturday, the overtime rate was 50 cents for the first two hours and 25 cents an hour subsequently. The department didn't pay this overtime. It was collected from manufacturers or other persons for services rendered.

One dispute over expenses got all the way to Parliament in 1876. A customs officer in the Kootenays was considered to have made excessive claims for the cost of firewood and maintenance of the government horse. An inspector was sent from inland revenue to investigate, travelling for two months from Victoria to St. Joseph's Prairie (Cranbrook), one thousand miles of it on horseback. He made his enquiries, found the claimed costs for firewood and the care of the horse to be reasonable, only to have his own expenses questioned by Ottawa. (The account of this episode was tabled in Parliament, and appears as an appendix.) Brunel seized upon the Kootenay incident to fire off a circular to his staff asking each station the cost of stoves, stovepipes, stove coal and firewood, and whether coal or wood was the more economical.

Meanwhile, the customs department poured out its own flood of directives, longer, if anything, than those issued by inland revenue. In 1870, Customs produced a set of instructions to out-door officers of which thirty-seven clauses applied just to the locker, the officer supervising a bonded warehouse. Clause No. 36 threatened dismissal for "tippling in the Warehouses or Vaults." (All thirty-seven clauses can be found in an appendix.) Even with all this, lockers were not greatly trusted. On March 8, 1884, Customs Commissioner James Johnson ordered that all lockers be shifted to other warehouses every six months. By this time, absenteeism had become so prevalent among all customs officers and clerks that Johnson ordered deduction of full pay for each day's absence, including all cases caused by sickness "unless the party uses due diligence in notifying his collector of the same."

The instructions to out-door officers in 1875 occupied thirty-nine pages. Instruction No. 6 said: "It is the imperative duty of all Officers of Customs to demean themselves with civility to all persons with whom they have any intercourse in the execution of their official duty, and to be careful that in the despatch of business, no undue preference be shown, but that the business of merchants, or others, be always attended to in proper turn, using such promptitude therein as may be consistent with the requisite accuracy of entries and all other official documents. Indulgence in intoxicating drinks, and the use of profane or otherwise offensive language will be regarded as among the most serious derelictions of duty."

The apportionment of the proceeds realized from seizures was always a problem. In 1871, special rewards were approved for discovery and seizure of illicit stills: four-fifths of the appraised value of the articles seized; up to $500 for information leading to conviction of persons owning or operating illicit stills; one half the assessed fines to the informer paid by the department in cases where those convicted cannot pay. Names of informers were not to be made public without their consent. In 1876, the general rules governing the sharing of proceeds were changed for the first time since 1850. Collectors whose salaries were under $2,000 a year were entitled to five per cent of the gross proceeds of a seizure if the seizure were made by another or other officers. If the seizure were made by the collector himself, he received the same share as other officers, that is, one-third. For a collector earning more than $2,000 a year, no percentage or share of the proceeds was allowed. We have not found a recorded case of a collector refusing a salary increase to keep his pay under $2,000 so that he could continue to share in seizure proceeds.

There was sometimes ill feeling between the collector and members of his staff about the distribution of the proceeds of seizures. Occasionally the collector would neglect to pay the seizing officer, who would have to complain formally to the commissioner. But these disputes were mild compared with the complaints of insistent informers about the size and promptness of their payments. Commissioner James Johnston wrote the collector in Niagara Falls in 1883 the following explanatory letter: "In reply to your letter, I beg leave to state that I could not officially say more in such cases than to quote the regulations, and especially as my experience has been very unpleasant in reference to dealing with informers.

They are apt to think that this department can in every case enforce the full penalties of the law; and if that is not done, no matter what may be the reason, they become very clamorous and offensive. I may, however, correct your impression of what the regulations say respecting fines or penalties. If you read them carefully you will see that fines and penalties are distributed as proceeds of seizures; hence an informer is entitled to share in them as well as in proceeds of sales.''

As we have noted in other sections of this book, customs officers often had much more required of them than their customs assignments: in 1799 in New Brunswick, for instance, customs officers were required to help watch passengers of incoming ships for any signs of ''yellow fever, putrid bilious fever or other pestilential or contagious distemper.''

In the early days of colonization, the officers had to enforce laws of France and England which dictated that colonial goods destined for the two parent countries must be shipped in, respectively, French and English ships. This task was considered far more important than the collection of any revenue because it went to the very heart of the maintenance of empires. The early customs man (it was a completely male establishment then) had to know, or at least be acquainted with, an enormous body of law. In 1825, in an ''Effort to rescue them from entire Confusion,'' no fewer than 443 customs acts — the digest of them alone ran to 1,375 pages — were repealed simultaneously and replaced by eleven new acts. France had gone through a similar process in 1791. Canada's consolidated laws of the customs of 1856 were modelled on — indeed, often repeated verbatim — the 1825 British revision, as were also the laws of Nova Scotia and New Brunswick.

When, in Upper Canada in 1816 and 1818, acts were passed to licence hawkers, pedlars and auctioneers, customs collectors were made responsible for collecting the licence fees and enforcement of the regulations. After the union of Upper and Lower Canada in 1841, such licensing gradually passed to municipal control. The customs branch of the inspector-general's office became responsible in 1844 for collection of canal tolls. In 1849 Customs handled sales of provincial roads to municipal councils and private companies, and in 1850 Customs took on management of ferries. All these responsibilities embroiled Customs in long political entanglements over road tolls, tenders for ferry services and canal charges. Because from its earliest days Customs had dealt with ships' arrivals, its officers were often made responsible as well for immigration duties, registration of ships and enforcement of shipping and navigation regulations. That has continued to modern times.

Customs officers had to be knowledgeable not only about the Customs Act and Customs Tariff but about scores of other statutes or those parts of them which applied to the officer's job. In 1885, for instance, Customs was made responsible for the Chinese Immigration Act which restricted entry to Canada, imposed a head tax, and required registration of all Chinese in Canada. (Revenue from Chinese immigration in 1890 was $55,408.)

By 1893, the customs officer had to have a working knowledge of the following acts beside his own: inland revenue; postal service; immigration and immigrants; Chinese immigration, and two amending acts; quarantine; inspection of ships; registration and classification of ships; certificates to masters and mates of ships, and two amending acts; shipping of seamen; shipping of seamen on inland waters; sick and distressed mariners, and one amending act; safety of ships and prevention of accidents on board thereof, and two amending acts; inspection of steamboats and examination and licensing of engineers employed on them and two amending acts; pilotage, and one amending act; wrecks, casualties and salvage; aid by U.S. wreckers in Canadian waters; coasting trade of Canada; government harbors, piers and breakwaters; port wardens; harbor masters; tonnage dues levied in Canadian ports; exemption of transports from port and harbor dues; fishing by foreign vessels; protection of navigable waters;

Inspection of petroleum, and one amending act; weights and measures; agricultural fertilizers, and one amending act; fisheries treaty between Britain and the United States; fisheries and fishing, and one amending act; an act to encourage the manufacture of pig iron in Canada from Canadian ore, and two amending acts; an act to encourage the development of the sea fisheries and the building of fishing vessels, and one amending act; an act respecting U.S. fishing vessels;

Shipping of livestock; an act to encourage the production of beet-root sugar; bounty on beet-root sugar; the revenue, the raising of loans authorized by Parliament and the auditing of the public accounts; to amend the consolidated revenue and audit act, and one amending act; civil service, and three amending acts; superannuation of persons employed in the civil service of Canada, and one amending act; government civil service insurance.

The customs department not only listed the acts but quoted all their relevant parts for handy use by its officers.

It might seem from this recitation of directives, laws and regulations that life in Customs would become more and more stunted and frustrating by even more meticulous direction and prohibition. But this was not necessarily the case by any means. At certain times and places, a vision of public service prevailed that drew the best from customs men. Such a story is that of John Carmichael Haynes, collector of Customs at Osoyoos, British Columbia.

CHAPTER III

John Carmichael Haynes, Agent of the Governor

Governor James Douglas of the colony of British Columbia had a marvellous knack of finding and appointing men who could represent his authority deep in the interior of his far-flung domain of mountain and forest. Reporting directly to him, most of these agents were noted for their willingness to do far more than ordered or asked — and in many fields other than those to which they were assigned. A Douglas man was, by definition, an all-round man — with bravura.

Haynes arrived at Victoria from Cork, Ireland, in 1859, and promptly got a job as a constable on the Fraser River gold diggings. After gold was found that year on Rock Creek near the border of British Columbia and Washington Territory, Governor Douglas had sent William George Cox there as magistrate, gold commissioner and collector of customs. Cox was handy with his fists and once knocked down an American who refused to recognize him as a customs collector. Haynes, already chief constable at Yale, was sent to assist Cox in 1860. A port of entry was established in the Similkameen Valley with Haynes as deputy collector.

Haynes was not one to sit in the customs house and wait for business to come to him. On April 28, 1861, he reported to Douglas from "Similkameen Revenue Station" that he had started to patrol the trails leading to the north and had seized sixteen horses in one pack train bound for the Cariboo goldfields. The owners had refused to pay duty on the horses or the goods, which included liquor and tobacco. The owners appealed to Cox, who allowed them each a horse and saddle and one pack horse to carry enough supplies for them to make the Cariboo. Governor Douglas congratulated Haynes but insisted on Cox paying for the horses and food he had given away. Cox sold the seized horses and goods which remained to pay the required duty.

Haynes very early showed that he considered collecting the revenue only one of many things he could do concurrently. In the same letter in which he reported the seizure — "the example made will in a great measure deter others from trying to evade the duties and thereby save the Revenue Department much trouble" — he applied for the jobs of magistrate and gold commissioner in the Similkameen. "Nothing on my part shall be left undone to promote the welfare and encouragement of the district," he added.

In July, 1861, Haynes sent Douglas specimens of gold he had picked up at mining operations above Rock Creek or which travellers passing his customs station had given to him. Two months later, he was acknowledging receipt of forms which required him to keep statistics on the population, farms, mines, manufactures, schools, prisoners, churches and "miscellaneous."

Cox received authority in September, 1861, to build a customs house, with living quarters, at Osoyoos (from the Indian Soo-Yoos, meaning two lakes coming together) on the American border at the south end of the Okanagan Valley. The specifications were provided from Victoria: of log construction, hewn on two sides, 30 feet long, 20 feet wide, 10 feet high, board floor, four windows, two with 12 lights (panes) and two with six lights, two rooms with doors and knobs, strong roof covered with shakes, cost not to exceed £130. The actual cost came to £114, including £5 for an extra door, unauthorized. It was the only building at Osoyoos, a rendezvous point from about 1812 on the early Okanagan fur route, but never a white settlement.

There was a rapid exodus of miners from Rock Creek and the Similkameen in 1861. Cox was transferred, and Haynes succeeded him as collector and gold commissioner at the age of 29, moving to the busier Osoyoos in the late fall of 1861. He was also responsible for maintenance of law and order and issuance of miners' licences, and had jurisdiction over Indian affairs and roads and trails.

On October 19, 1861, Haynes accounted for duties levied on 625 cattle, 356 horses and 92 mules since January 1 that year, and also reported at some length on the varieties of soil and agricultural capabilities on the benches of Okanagan and other lakes; he sent samples of wheat and oats grown in Keremeos by François Desebiquette, the Hudson's Bay Company factor there (in Haynes' meticulous hand, the cedilla in the name was carefully placed); he said he would gain some information of the geology of the district and send mineral specimens besides gold; he also sent his weather diary, noting that the mosquitoes and flies had been so troublesome from May to October that he had been unable to keep any of his horses near the station.

The winters were very severe. After his first winter at Osoyoos, Haynes reported March 31, 1862, that few imports had arrived at his station and "numbers" of men had perished on their way to the British Columbia goldfields. A month later, he wrote that there was a big rush to the Salmon River gold find. Immigration had thus fallen off at Osoyoos, and he would reduce his staff in the district to three from four or, "if finances don't improve, to two, as a means of relieving the Department from its present embarrassed state." He hadn't received any salary since September 30 last and was "therefore in debt for the necessities of life." The rest of his staff was in the same position. Twenty-four men had passed through Osoyoos en route to the Cariboo goldfields. The vicissitudes of goldseeking were illustrated in Haynes' very next letter, in which he reported that dejected miners were returning from the so-called strike on Salmon River.

On June 9, 1862, Haynes acknowledged receipt of instructions to inspect the obelisks and forest cuttings marking the international boundary. In that month, 271 men, 1,065 horses, 135 mules, 488 cattle and six tons, 975 pounds of merchandise had crossed into British Columbia from Washington Territory at Osoyoos. Haynes' salary was £20 a month (about $100) and Constables Lowe, Young and Collins made £16 each. His detailed accounts show these salaries as well as payments for feeding government horses during the winter, catching runaway horses, blacksmithing, carrying provisions to the station, expenses for constables away on duty (six shillings a day, including food and lodging for constable and horse).

On September 30, 1862, Haynes reported tersely, after what must have been an arduous journey of some weeks, that the obelisks were "in good shape." Seventeen miners still left at Rock Creek were making $2 to $4 a day panning for gold. In the following month, Haynes again asked to be named magistrate, partly on the grounds that the miners of the district were already calling him "judge." He acknowledged receipt of "rules and regulations for the working of the gold mines."

On February 28, 1863, Haynes reported a very severe winter: "no imports, no people, no revenue." All the trails had been blocked and travel was possible only by snowshoe. Smallpox had broken out among the Indians and more than twenty had died already: "With this letter I am sending for vaccine which I shall use as best I can."

On November 30, 1863, Haynes said that a Mr. Clements had passed through on his way to Walla Walla, Washington Territory, from Shuswap. He had examined six miles of Cherry Creek, a tributary of the Shuswap River, where gold had recently been discovered. Mr. Clements had brought coarse specimens with him worth two cents to six cents a pan or $10 a day. Another traveller, Mr. Melvin, reported ten men on Cherry Creek making $8 to $10 a day. The sixty-mile trail from Okanagan Lake to Cherry Creek was very passable except for a stretch of twelve miles. Haynes said he had dispatched Constable William Young to Shuswap to pick up as much information as possible. Meanwhile, he had been informed by the Hudson's Bay Company factor at Colville, Washington Territory, that miners were moving into the Kootenai north of the boundary. He had asked the factor for more particulars.

Constable Young returned in a month and reported on, among other things: the crop yield at the Catholic mission on Okanagan Lake, the state of the trail, weather, mining claims, inhabitants, dwellings, and Indian reserves. He concluded that there was an "encouraging field for those able and willing to explore difficult terrain."

Haynes was finally made a magistrate in 1864. Along with notice of his appointment, the mail brought more forms covering miners' licences and records of claims. Governor Douglas had apparently asked his advice on road-making, because on June 10, 1864, Haynes reported that he had surveyed the trail to Kamloops on both sides of Okanagan Lake, travelling by pack train, and proposed that the main road go on the west side.

Haynes was hardly back from this trip when he was instructed to go to the Kootenai district as quickly as possible and report on the amount of revenue likely to be collected at the border in that district and how best to prevent smuggling of any goods from the United States. Haynes resaddled his pack train and set out again on July 20.

The next we hear from him, five weeks later, he is at Wild Horse Creek, originally Stud Horse Creek, a mining camp built after a Métis gold strike in 1863 in the Kootenais about fifty miles north of the boundary. His report gives a glimpse of gold fever: the inrush of about 1,000 people, mostly Americans, in only four months; the staking of 500 claims; a report on each claim, with the number of men working it and how much gold was panned a day; the appointment of two constables, one as a peace officer at Wild Horse Creek, the other at Tobacco Plains to watch the trail from Bitter Root Valley in the United States; 22 trading licences issued, 12 liquor licences and 663 miners' certificates; (the revenue, he said, would be dependent on how long the gold lasted); talks with the Indians in the district; acquittal by a jury on a charge of murder of William Burniston, alias Powder Bill, in the shooting during an eating house brawl of Thomas Walker, who died, and Robert Evans, alias Overland Bob, who recovered; the necessity for a permanent magistrate. Constable Young was left in charge when Haynes left Wild Horse Creek in the fall, having collected more than $16,000, which he kept in a valise.

Arthur N. Birch, the colonial secretary, was so taken with Haynes' report that he visited Wild Horse later that autumn. He wrote in his own report: "All customs duties paid and no pistols seen." It was the ultimate accolade for a customs and law officer. But while Haynes was at Wild Horse, his wife died after giving birth to a son. Haynes found out from a newspaper given him by a traveller. He later remarried, and his second wife bore seven children.

Constable Young reported, December 1, 1864, that because of the severe early winter one packer who started out with forty animals got through with only eight and that "but for this the customs receipts would have been much larger." Young also reported a common civil service disaster: "Quite out of printed forms so unable to send accounts in more formal shape." He resigned the next year when there was a general reduction in civil service salaries. The Wild Horse strike petered out about the same time. In 1884, the English traveller W. Henry Barneby found only sixty persons still there. They received mail eight times a year.

In 1865, Haynes moved his combined residence and customs house to a site commanding a better view of all roads and trails and put on an addition incorporating two jail cells. The government refused to pay the £31 bill for insulation and papering, calling this "decoration." It later relented and paid half. On March 5, 1865, Haynes submitted a list of the stationery required for his customs office: 1 ream of blue foolscap, 500 official envelopes, 250 note envelopes, 25 cloth-lined envelopes (small), 8 cloth-lined envelopes (large), 8 quires of blotting paper, 3 pints of ink, 1 box of quill pens, 2 boxes of steel pens, 2 dozen penholders, 1 dozen lead pencils, 2 ink stands, 2 record books, 1 journal, 2 diaries, 4 memo books, 6 bottles of red ink, 2 letter clips, 1 paper cutter, 2 bottles of mucilage, 1 box of India-rubber bands, 2 boxes of sealing wax, 3 paper files and 1 dozen rolls of red tape.

On April 7, 1865, Haynes told the new governor, Frederick Seymour, that three of his horses had died as a result of the Kootenai trip. His request for $240 to replace them was granted. During the summer, Haynes successfully defended neighboring Indians when whites tried to grab their reserve lands for ranching. He also asked for and got permission to explore the tributaries of the Kettle River north of Rock Creek. He even found time, in a dispatch dated July 3, 1865, to give an inventory of his spartan station: 1 padlock with duplicate keys, 1 iron safe with duplicate keys, 1 patent padlock, 1 office seal, 1 grinding stone in good order, 1 Mexican saddle, 1 pack saddle, 1 paper cutter, 1 plane, 1 saw, 1 chisel, 1 axe, 1 Union Jack, 1 buckskin purse, 1 nest of pigeon holes, 1 horse blanket, much worn, 3 window blinds, 6 tables, 1 office desk, 4 stools, 1 boat, nearly useless, 1 metal stove, nearly useless, 1 cross-cut saw, 1 lasso, 2 candlesticks, 1 sketch of the Columbia River by Lieut. Mayne, 12 lengths of stovepipe, 1 telescope and case, 2 government horses, 1 bulletin board, 2 outside shutters, 3 shelves, 1 hand bucket, 4 tin vessels for carrying water and 1 carpet sack.

Haynes must have collected considerable revenue. The records for the Osoyoos customs house between November, 1861, and July, 1864, show importations of 7,720 cattle, 5,378 horses, 1,371 sheep and 948 mules.

The duty on cattle was $6 a head, though it is not clear what the duty was on the other livestock.

In 1866 Haynes was made a county court judge and later he was appointed to the legislative council of British Columbia. On October 14, 1871 — the year that British Columbia joined the Canadian confederation — Haynes showed what he thought of regulations which delayed business. He reported that he had overtaken the mail carrier, J. Johnston, on the Similkameen trail but that Johnston had refused to give him customs letters from the Kootenai, saying that they had to be delivered to the post office. He had taken the mail from "this person," whose conduct had been insolent and behavior insulting. "I trust he will not be paid or employed again on this route," Haynes said.

Haynes kept the same job under the new Ottawa administration. But he thought he didn't have enough to do to keep busy, so he gradually established his own ranch. He got his start in ranching by buying cattle from drovers who needed the money to pay duty on the remaining part of the herd. He ended up with 3,000 head at one time on a ranch covering 20,756 acres and known as Haynes Meadows through which flowed a stream called Haynes Creek. His American customs counterpart, Cullen E. Bach, reported that Haynes had paid more than $5,000 in customs duties one season on cattle exported to the United States.

The customs house burned down in 1878. Haynes' 290-pound neighbor, storekeeper Theodore Kruger, rescued the 1,200-pound safe, with revenue, and Haynes rebuilt. Kruger later became collector (1889 to 1899) and once accepted a cheque in payment of duties on imported machinery for a projected stamping mill. The cheque was made out incorrectly but by the time it was returned from Ottawa the mill was in operation and the owner had earned enough money to pay cash instead.

Haynes was on his way home from Victoria with his sons Fairfax and Valentine and daughter Mabel on his 57th birthday, July 6, 1888, when he fell out of the saddle with a heart attack. He died on the trail before the nearest doctor, a Dr. Chipps, could reach him. He was buried on a hillside of his ranch beside a cottonwood grove. Many Indians attended the funeral. In 1957, a cairn was built on the site of the first customs house. Four of Haynes' children were present for the unveiling. There was an Osoyoos border centennial celebration in 1961 to mark the beginning of Haynes' work there. Not many places have a celebration to mark 100 years (or any anniversary) of customs service.

It is interesting to note what became of one of Haynes' subordinates because it shows that Customs was well ahead of its time in hiring the handicapped.

W.H. Lowe acted as collector at Osoyoos when Haynes was sent to tame Wild Horse Creek. In 1865, he was appointed Chief Constable for a vast district of the southern Okanagan. In 1872, Lowe went east to marry his childhood sweetheart. The day before the wedding, he was dashing for a train and fell under it. Both arms were severed. Three days later, at the insistence of his fiancée, they were married. On January 1, 1873, he was appointed sub-collector at New Westminster at $1,400 a year. With the assistance of his wife, one other customs officer, and a host of friends, he performed his job to everybody's satisfaction.

In 1876, at the instigation of J. Cunningham, local Conservative MP, Lowe was accused of drunkenness. The community was outraged and Cunningham lost to a Liberal despite the Conservative sweep back to power in 1878. Lowe's friends signed a successful petition that he be retained and one of his friends, the famous Judge Matthew Begbie, wrote: "In your severe affliction, you may at least perceive this consolation that Providence, which for its own mysterious purposes permits slanderers to live unmaimed, has at least made it physically impossible for you to be or become a drunkard and that the slanderer has in your case stumbled upon a falsehood which carries with it its own refutation." Lowe died in 1882.

Just before we leave the 19th century, we might mention that salaries of collectors in the excise branch were scaled according to the amount of business done in the individual offices. Here is the scale for 1889: the maximum salary for a collector 1st class, that is, in a port doing more than $1,000,000 worth of business a year, was $2,800 annually. A collector 2nd class earned a maximum of $2,300 in a port which collected more than $500,000 in revenue. The scale went down to collector 7th class, earning a maximum of $1,000 a year in a port doing under $10,000 worth of business annually. The career objective was to win promotion to a higher class or a busier port (the two went together automatically). To win promotion to first-class officer required a passing grade of at least 80 per cent in examinations. The subjects included: book-keeping by double entry; addition, vertical and horizontal; inland revenue laws; arithmetic; mensuration; malt gauging and computation of quantities in bulk; use of hydrometer and saccharometer; malting and supervision of malthouses; tobacco and cigar manufacturing and supervision of factories; stamping, marking, warehousing and removal of excisable goods; petroleum inspection; distillation and supervision of distilleries; bonding manufacturers and testing of products. The collector annually made a "conduct" report on each subordinate comprising industry, sobriety, reliability, integrity and general behavior. Each was classed as very good, good, fair or indifferent and only a "very good" rating enabled a first-class exciseman to win promotion. The annual maximum increase permitted was $100.

Excisemen were not always confined to the office. Far from it. Mary Fitzgibbon in her book *A Trip to Manitoba* recounts her winter-long stay at a base railway construction camp of the Canadian Pacific after travelling up the Red River to Winnipeg by steamer and then by the bumpy Dawson Road to Lake of the Woods. It was the winter of 1878, prohibition was in effect, and smugglers were hiding whisky on islands in Lake of the Woods for retrieval when needed. A railway worker was caught peddling whisky in one of the camps and was arrested by the exciseman, known locally as the whisky detective. The smuggler was fined $50 or thirty days in jail. He said he had no money and would therefore accept jail. But the nearest jail was in Winnipeg more than a hundred miles away. There was no transportation and the smuggler declined to walk the distance. What to do? The whisky detective agreed to forfeit half the fine to which he was entitled for making the arrest and the construction foreman gave the judge the other $25 with the understanding the smuggler would work it off on the railway. There were no more arrests for smuggling in that district, at least not in winter.

Miss Fitzgibbon gives us this vignette of customs service after her steamer stopped at Pembina, today's Emerson. The customs officers of Canada and the United States came aboard at the same time. She writes: "They were good specimens of their different countries. The Canadian was a round, fat, jolly, handsome, fair man; the Yankee was tall, slight and black-eyed, with a cadaverous look. They did not give us any trouble, and I felt sorry for their lonely life."

In the chapter on the frontier, we have dealt with the exploits of clerk John Godson, the first customs officer on the Klondike Trail in 1897, and in the section on the history of the service we have discussed D.W. Davis, the first collector at Dawson, who couldn't stay away from prospecting himself. We might also mention Percy Peele, who spent fifteen years at Chilkoot, White Pass, Bennett Lake, Caribou Crossing and Whitehorse. He went outside every three years on leave. He spent forty-four years in Customs, retiring in 1937. In the early days of the Yukon, customs officers were paid a living allowance of $1,500 a year, which was usually more than their salaries.

One customs officer became so well known, internationally as well as at home, that he was given the unofficial title Busby of the Yukon. His official title, after the episode we are about to describe, became Inspector of the Yukon Frontier. In 1901, Edward S. Busby defended the Canadian flag so punctiliously that he caused an international incident which reached into the cabinets of three countries and exercised the citizenry of two of them. Busby was one of the few customs officers ever to make it into the Canadian Who's Who, which said of him in 1912: "courteous and firm and of unbending integrity."

CHAPTER IV

Busby of the Yukon

Busby was born at Southampton, Ontario, June 12, 1863, and was educated there and at Northern Business College, Owen Sound. He went to work for a railway company in Detroit and joined Canada Customs at Boston in 1897. In the heyday of the railroads, Canada stationed customs officers in most major shipping centres in the northern United States to clear goods under seal direct from the marshalling yards. Similarly, the United States had their officers in Canada.

Busby's grounding in railway operations and accounting served him well in his customs work. His superiors apparently thought well of him right from the start because in May, 1899, he was posted to Skagway, Alaska, tidewater terminus of the White Pass and Yukon Railway which opened service to Whitehorse in June, 1900. Skagway was the brawlingest town of the Klondike gold rush. The Canada-U.S. border was still unsettled — it was not fixed until 1903 — and pistol-carrying J.W. Ivey, chief U.S. customs officer in Alaska, had tried (vainly) to push the North West Mounted Police off White and Chilkoot Passes overlooking Skagway and plant his own customs posts farther north at Bennett and Lindemann Lakes.

Busby did not collect duties at Skagway. He was there to expedite Canadian shipments to the Yukon through the Alaska panhandle and thereby avoid inspection delays at White Pass. For convenience, his customs office was in the depot building of the Yukon and White Pass Railway. The building was the tallest in Skagway and the customs office was on the top floor. Busby, as he said afterwards, thought he would make it easier for shippers and brokers to identify his office if he hoisted a Canadian flag on the building.

Busby went about this enterprise carefully. First, he obtained an official customs flag — the red ensign with a golden crown in the fly — from the clerk of supplies in Ottawa. He then wrote to Solon W. McMichael, chief inspector of Customs, on April 25, 1901, for advice on hoisting the flag during business hours to provide a "source of information" and a "certain amount of prestige." McMichael said this would be perfectly all right because special officers of U.S. Customs located in Canada flew the American flag over their offices.

Busby had an iron flagpole put up on top of the building, and it was painted white with a gilt ball on top. He ignored the fact that U.S.

authorities had refused to permit the Canadian flag to be flown the year before when Lord Minto, the governor-general, passed through Skagway en route to the Yukon, and on June 22, 1901, he ran up the ensign just before his office opened.

The citizens had been watching the progress of the flagpole with interest and were not caught by surprise when the Canadian customs flag stood out in a fresh summer breeze. One George M. Miller, a Juneau lawyer, rushed into the depot building at 8:45 a.m., cut the halyard with a pocketknife, pulled down the flag, threw it into a recess of the building and left. Busby immediately accosted him and Miller handed him his card. (That very card survives today in the Public Archives of Canada.)

Busby obtained a new halyard and ran up the flag again. He then sat down and wrote two letters, one to Captain I.C. Jenks, commander of U.S. troops in Skagway, and the other to E.C. Hawkins, manager of the Skagway depot of the Yukon and White Pass Railway. To Jenks he complained of "the outrage committed upon the Canadian Customs Official Flag" by Miller "without cause or provocation," and reminded him that flag courtesies were permitted U.S. customs officers in Canada. "I now look to you," Busby said, "to see that the Canadian Customs situated at Skagway receive like treatment." He told Hawkins that such a "grave offence" and "insult" to the flag could not be overlooked and that "I look to you for the necessary protection to keep it floating during office hours." That very day Hawkins swore out a complaint against Miller of wilful and malicious damage to property. Miller had left hurriedly for Porcupine but was arrested and brought back to Skagway.

C.L. Andrews, U.S. collector of customs at Skagway, went to Busby's office (in an "agitated manner," Busby reported to his superiors) and demanded to know by what authority Busby had hoisted the British flag. Busby said the flag was not British but the Canadian Customs official ensign. Andrews said two U.S. customs officers on duty near White Pass in British Columbia had been taunted by Canadian customs and police officers for flying the Stars and Stripes. But he conceded that no one had interfered with the U.S. flag. Busby confided in John McDougald, Commissioner of Customs, that he felt Andrews was partly responsible for the incident because he was "a very narrow-minded man, bitterly opposed to anything British or Canadian." Miller and Andrews well represented U.S. west-coast jingoism at that time and not just the view of the "lower element" in Skagway, as Busby put it in a letter to A.R. Milne, collector at Victoria.

In any event, the flag was up again and a delegation waited on Busby in his office. The delegation, comprising Captain Jenks, Magistrate Shelbride and the city marshal, advised Busby to lower the flag or "they would be unable to control the mob" which had gathered outside. Busby agreed to keep the flag down for a "few days" pending a decision from Washington. The few days were to stretch into months.

After the visit from the delegation, Busby immediately informed Ottawa and Victoria of what had happened and begged the customs department not to give way: "If our flag is finally lowered after once being raised it will injure our prestige in this northern country." And again, by telegram to McDougald: "Strongly advise holding position taken otherwise will weaken effectiveness of service on Yukon frontier." But to Ottawa, and more particularly to London which then controlled Canadian foreign affairs, Busby was an embarrassment who was creating a scene at the worst possible time.

The *Daily Skagway News* of June 22, 1901, the day of the incident, ran a headline "Hauled Down British Flag!" and quoted Miller as saying: "I cut down the British flag on my own authority by virtue of rights resting in every American citizen." The newspaper went on:

> The United States has occupied this strip of land [Alaska panhandle] since 1867 and Canadian officials have gradually encroached, unrestrained by the American government. By leaps and bounds the Canadian Customs house had advanced toward the water. From Tagish, to Bennett to Log Cabin and lastly to the summit [of Chilkoot and White Passes] and when the Customs ensign of Canada was hoisted at Skagway it is small wonder that some John Brown would not wait for tardy action from Washington but cut down the flag. Skagway is a city whose patriotism has been tested time and again by the lazy indifference of their own government as against the aggressive activity of the Britons.

The next morning, the *Daily Alaskan* said: "Statements on the street were that the flag was raised to accustom Americans to it and to prepare them for the final surrender of this country to England."

On July 1 Commissioner McDougald got a note from Arthur Brophy, Lord Minto's private secretary, saying that the governor-general wanted to see him "as soon as possible." (Customs Minister William Paterson was away.) This was the start of a long series of diplomatic notes among Ottawa, Washington and London about Busby's flag. Chief Inspector McMichael chimed in from London, Ontario, to tell McDougald that the U.S. flag was being flown daily over the U.S. customs office there in the Grand Trunk Railway station.

There was another uneasy moment after Busby wrote a personal letter to J.M. Bowell, collector at Vancouver, with some unflattering remarks about the Americans and especially the citizens of Skagway. Bowell, judging the letter a good summation of Candian views, gave it to the *Daily World* of Vancouver, which printed it in its entirety. McDougald asked

Busby how he could make such an "unauthorized communication considering the international bearings of the matter." Busby replied that he was "surprised and pained" that Bowell would do him a "grave injustice." Collector Milne and Inspector McMichael went to Skagway in early August and reported to McDougald that they met U.S. customs officials and "that the flag incident was not referred to and our converse was generally of an agreeable character." Busby had been praised for his "promptitude and tact" in the transfer of goods.

Meanwhile, by July 13, the customs minister had prepared a report for the Canadian cabinet, which asked Lord Minto to forward it to the British ambassador in Washington for action. The British ambassador, Lord Pauncefote (formerly Sir Julian Pauncefote) was away and the British embassy was in summer quarters at Newport, Rhode Island. However, Gerard Lowther, chargé d'affaires, managed to get a reply off to Lord Minto by September 2. By that time, the complaint against Miller had been withdrawn.

Lowther said he had sent a note to the U.S. government, after receiving instructions from His Majesty's principal secretary of state for foreign affairs. The note ventured the hope that "due reparation will be made for an act of discourtesy to a British flag on territory in the temporary administration of the United States."

Alvey A. Adee, acting U.S. secretary of state, informed Lowther on September 7 that in July the secretary of the treasury (in the United States, Customs comes under the treasury) had detailed a special agent to investigate the incident. The agent had reported, among other things, that Hawkins, manager of the railway depot, had withdrawn his complaint against Miller July 17 on "instructions by Ottawa." The Canadian government later denied this, though it would seem that heavy persuasion was exerted on Hawkins, who had been as keen as Busby about raising the flag. The treasury agent also said Busby had been instructed by the Canadian government "not to insist on the display of the British flag contrary to popular feelings."

Adee expressed regret on behalf of the U.S. government for "the offence committed against the flag of a friendly power" and suggested as a means to prevent recurrence of such "untoward incidents" that "it might be found advisable to mutually discontinue the practice of customs officers flying their customs' flags within the jurisdiction of the other party."

Adee's note made the required rounds of Ottawa and London and on October 5 Joseph Chamberlain, secretary of state for colonies, told Lord Minto in a dispatch from Downing Street: "I presume that in view of the explanations afforded and the regret expressed by the United States government, your ministers share Lord Lansdowne's opinion that the incident may be regarded as closed."

The Canadian cabinet, meeting on December 23, concurred in Adee's suggestion. Lord Minto informed Lord Pauncefote. Lord Pauncefote informed the U.S. government. U.S. Secretary of State John Hay asked the U.S. Treasury to ask U.S. Customs to stop flying the Stars and Stripes in Canada. Lord Pauncefote told Lord Minto January 27, 1902, that the instructions to U.S. Customs had gone out from the U.S. Treasury. On February 11 Lord Pauncefote informed the Marquess of Lansdowne that Canada had instructed its officers stationed in the U.S. to discontinue flying the Canadian flag over Canadian customs offices.

The irrepressible collector Ivey, in Sitka, announced to the press that he was closing the Canadian customs office in Skagway and sending "bag, baggage, flag and other paraphernalia flying out of the country." He also closed the port of Unalaska to Canadian sealing schooners. The U.S. Treasury ordered him to rescind the order. He refused and was sacked.

Busby complained to McDougald about "malicious falsehoods" and "pure fabrications" by Ivey and the "conspirators of Skagway" but McDougald sent Busby a personal note saying "At present it is probably best to 'say nothing, but saw wood.' "

Miller was employed from time to time by U.S. Customs as a special officer at Skagway. He later moved to Seattle where he helped advance the argument that the Alaska-Yukon boundary should be at the 130th west meridian instead of the 141st, which would have put most of the Yukon Territory in the United States.

The Canadian office in Skagway was not closed. G.V. Zinkan replaced Busby and was still there in 1919. Busby was promoted inspector, Yukon Frontier, with headquarters in Whitehorse, and promoted again in 1902 as customs collector for the Yukon with headquarters at Dawson. Busby was chief inspector of Customs for Canada from 1912 to 1929 and lived to the age of 90. During the 1926 customs scandal, the opposition Conservatives maintained that the government had "sedulously" kept Busby out of Quebec for three years so that he would not uncover internal crookedness there.

On April 11, 1902, Busby wrote to McDougald from Whitehorse: "The Skagway papers continue to publish offensive articles against myself and Canadian officials generally, but no notice is being taken of them, and business in the Customs is going along nicely." But somebody was taking notice of what was going on in Skagway. On June 18, 1903, Prime Minister Sir Wilfrid Laurier told the Commons that fifty more Mounties had been sent secretly to the Yukon (making a total of 300) because a conspiracy, serious or otherwise, existed in Skagway for the invasion of the Yukon by "American desperadoes."

As the number of visitors to Canada began to grow, early in the century, inspectors at the border were reminded to be on their best behavior. For instance, Border Circular No. 10, issued in 1911, enjoined officers to observe these rules strictly:

> 1. Officers must be courteous in their dealings and conversation with the travelling public and with all transportation officials with whom they may have business.
> 2. Officers must not be discourteous by reason of provocation on the part of a passenger or other person seeking to land in Canada. If exception is taken by a passenger or other person to any part of the examination, it will be the duty of Border Inspectors to explain courteously the provisions of the Immigration Act.
> 3. Officers must not enter bars when in uniform, whether on duty or not, and must abstain from the use of intoxicants while on duty.
> 4. Officers must abstain from smoking or chewing while on duty.
> 5. The Department requires that Officers shall pay strict attention to a cleanly appearance, not only of uniform but of linen and boots.

During the next two decades, there continued to be heavy emphasis on courtesy toward the tourist, especially the American tourist. Directives, regulations, instructions, circulars, advisories and admonitions flowed from the West Block on Parliament Hill where Customs had its headquarters — until 1916 when it moved to the then new Connaught Building across the Rideau Canal from the Hill and where it is still located. One commissioner of Customs, John McDougald, hated the telephone, so during Commons question period his secretary, a man, sat in the press gallery in the Centre Block to listen for questions on customs matters, then rushed to the West Block for information. This winded emissary was usually able to rush back to the Commons with the answer for the minister before the question period ended.

The department was wholly serious about treatment of tourists at its ports; threats of banishment to the freight yards added force to an instruction sent out in April, 1928:

> Complaints have reached the Department from reliable sources regarding the demeanour and actions of certain officers of National Revenue whose duty it is to examine passengers and their baggage on trains entering Canada from the United States. While the fact is recognized that officers assigned to these necessary duties have a difficult task to perform, it must be borne in mind that discretion, tact and courtesy go hand in hand with proper performance of those

duties. An examining officer who allows his temper to show itself, and acts in a discourteous manner, will not be allowed to continue in that capacity. If he is retained in the Service he will be sent to the freight yards or the manifest room where his peculiar temperament will not offend others. The tourist season is about to open, and visitors to Canada by automobile and railway must be treated with constant courtesy by National Revenue officers whose duties bring them into contact with the travelling public. There is no place in the Service for an officer who is rude and discourteous, and the sooner this is realized the better it will be for all concerned.

In November, 1929, there came this warning:

Comments have reached the department concerning the manner in which a few of the officers in the Customs Postal Parcel Branches treat the public, more particularly ladies who call for parcels sent to them from abroad. These comments indicate that some of the officers so far forget themselves and the deportment which it is proper for them to observe at all times, as to make flippant or irrelevant remarks respecting the contents of the parcels examined by them ... No officer should be guilty of making flippant or irrelevant remarks to any one, and it is hoped that no occasion will arise for any such comments in future.

December, 1929:

When a tourist drives up to a Customs office on the frontier, it is the duty of the examining officer to go outside and interview the visitor. The Department has been advised that at certain offices the Customs officer sits at his desk and waits for the caller to come to him. It need hardly be stated that this treatment savors of discourtesy and must be abandoned forthwith.

Customs officers became so drilled in the necessity of treating tourists with courtesy, not to say deference, that one of them made up this ditty:

A machine rolls in from the U.S.A. — a family on the trail;
They carry a tent to save on rent, they have extra gas by the pail.
They carry their food, they carry their oil, they have blankets and pots;
They are rarin' to go and will spend their dough on the gratis parking lots.
You open the door, they put up a roar, you hand them a free permit,
They whine of red tape and call you an ape but you musn't mind a bit;
You dig up their gats from under the mats and insist that they check the rods;
If your temper they try, you musn't reply, they are tourists and therefore gods.

Courtesy might have been stressed, but the collection of the revenue was not allowed to languish. In 1929, a customs officer named Paterson and two assistants travelled 1,500 miles through Quetico Park in northwestern Ontario by canoe and motorboat and collected $900 in duty from tourists.

For a short time, until the flood of automobile traffic made it impossible, Customs was required to keep a ledger recording every car which entered Canada, including the date, owner's name and address, manufacturer's name, model and number, licence plate number, seating capacity and destination. A 1926 ledger from Four Falls, New Brunswick, has survived which records these makes: Oakland touring and sedan; Dodge touring and sedan; Essex coach and coupe; Ford touring, sport and roadster runabout; Buick touring and brougham; Studebaker touring and sedan; Chevrolet touring and sedan; Hudson sedan, touring and brougham; Mitchell touring; Star sedan and touring; Overland sedan and coupe; Chrysler sedan; Pontiac coach and cabrolet; Nash roadster; Reo coupe; Oldsmobile coach; Paige sedan; Whippet sedan and coach; Willys Knight sedan and coupe; Chandler sedan; LaSalle coupe; Diana sedan; Jewett brougham; Hupmobile sedan; Samson brougham; Cole coupe; and Maxwell Flint touring.

Wartime meant added duties for customs officers. In 1914, an elaborate procedure was laid down so that immediately on the outbreak of war all enemy merchant ships were held in port by Customs and all other ships which might be carrying munitions or other "contraband of war" to the enemy were detained until such goods were unloaded. The customs collector was to enlist the aid of the military or police if any ship tried to escape. Also in 1914, Ottawa sent out a warning that "large numbers of undesirable aliens" were coming into Canada with theatrical companies, circuses and vaudeville shows. Cash bonds were to be obtained from the managers of such troupes to ensure their departure, with all hands, from Canada. The amount of a bond would depend on the "number and character of the aliens." By a directive of October 5, 1939, all customs officers were authorized to detain or arrest any member of the enemy armed forces, including spies and saboteurs.

Wartime brought other problems. The work required of customs officers increased during the First World War because of various measures to increase revenue: the special war revenue act of 1915, the business profits war tax of 1916, and the income war tax act of 1917. Then, in 1918, Customs and Inland Revenue, which had functioned until then as separate departments, were merged under one minister. The royal commission into the 1926 customs scandal found that administrative changes in the organization necessary to meet all these changed conditions had not been made. The numerous regulations had not been revised or consolidated and many officers across Canada were working completely in the dark.

We have dealt with the scandal elsewhere in this book, but it is worth noting here that the royal commission found severe fault with the system whereby officers seizing goods received a share of the revenue (moieties) for their sale. The commission said:

> The officer of the Department known as the seizing officer was entitled to share in the moieties in case his salary was under a certain stated amount. This provision was intended to stimulate such officers to activity in connection with seizures but had the effect of lessening the interest of the other officers of the port and in some instances led to an arrangement whereby certain of the junior officers would make the seizure and share the moieties with the collector or other superior officer. This practice tends to weaken discipline, and the desirability of the system is questionable. We believe that if no officer was permitted to share either directly or indirectly in any of the moieties, it would have a beneficial effect on the service. It is one of the duties of all officers of the Department to detect any violations of the Customs Act or regulations, and to take all necessary actions to have the offender dealt with according to law, and this duty should be performed without any such incentive as would flow from the awarding of moieties. One of the chief objects of the moiety system of award is to induce those outside the service who have information or who are in a position to secure information to impart the same to the service. In many cases such informant never gets any award at all, although he has done his full duty and in most cases the distribution of the award when made is not made for many months, in some cases several years, after the information is given or the seizure made.

But awards to seizing officers continued to be paid for another twenty years — to 1947. The last such share-out amounted to $192,712. Awards are still made to informers outside Customs and Excise.

The commission also gave its attention to problems less grave than privilege and corruption, but to which government service is, by tradition, equally prone: An employee approaching retirement was given six months' leave of absence with pay, the position not becoming vacant until the end of the six months. The Civil Service Commission then filled the vacancy, usually by promotion, and this created another vacancy "and so on down the whole line of employees." This had resulted "in very serious disorganization" of the work of the department and of the ports. Moreover, promotions were confined almost exclusively to officials in the port where the vacancy occurred. This prevented the most competent officers being promoted or transferred. "Merit had been made subordinate to seniority and residence in a particular centre." The commission also found there was no relieving staff available so that when an officer was on leave or sick, his work became congested or neglected, resulting in delays and "detriment to the public service."

The commission recommended a "very substantial" reduction in the number of ports of entry. It listed the number of customs stations at March 31, 1926, at 773, as against 270 in the United States. The government heeded this advice and, by 1936, cut the number to 450. Today it is approximately 650. In 1949, the Public Accounts of Canada stopped listing the ports which cost more to run than the revenue taken in, though there still are some. There were two in this category in 1948, compared with thirty in Upper and Lower Canada alone in 1866.

At the height of the customs scandal in 1926, the department itself commissioned a Toronto chartered accountancy firm, Clarkson, Gordon and Dilworth, to examine departmental management. In its report, filed February 9, 1928, the firm also made objections to the system of paying moieties: "It tends to the making of unwarranted seizures, that is, the officer eager to earn the moiety and fearing someone else may step in before him is apt to make a seizure before he is sufficiently sure of his ground."

On getting rid of deadwood, the consultants said: "There is one difficulty of paramount importance and that is in regard to dismissals. At present, an Order-in-Council is required before any permanent employee can be dismissed, but such dismissals are nearly always for some specific offence other than inefficiency or laziness, and as a result many employees have been carried on the strength of the department long after their services have been found unsatisfactory."

On training: "There was no adequate supervision of the Preventive Service. In some instances the officer appears to have received no training, assistance or supervision of any sort, all that seems to have been done being to hand him the Customs Act and the Excise Act and turn him loose to protect the revenue as best he could."

The most telling point made by Clarkson, Gordon and Dilworth, and one which still goes to the heart of the department's operations, was this: "It has been to an increasing extent the experience of the Preventive Service that the recoveries to the revenue which can be made as a result of investigation work in the chief commercial centres by trained officers acting on information received are greatly in excess of those which can be made by any number of patrol officers working along the frontier." Put another way, this says: why keep an officer on the border to discover $5 worth of smuggled underwear when an auditor in the same time can uncover a $1,000,000 fraud?

Despite the depression, the 1930s seemed to have their lighter side for customs officers. Thomas Jarrott, an officer at North Portal, Saskatchewan, wrote a wry account of border customs work for the *National Revenue Review* in 1932:

> It is generally supposed that a Canadian Customs officer's chief duties at the border consist of searching hatboxes, grips and trunks of

passengers, for new Easter bonnets, silk dresses, radio tubes, cigars and cigarettes. These, however, are minor incidents in the round of his daily duties. He may be called upon at any time to appraise a spavined horse, and while the officer may never have studied dentistry, he must be able to tell the age of the horse by an examination of its teeth, present and absent. He may be asked to ascertain if a bottle of gasoline drawn from a tank car with a string tests high or low, and at what temperature a sample of kerosene will flash. Next, he may be delegated to arrive at the present value of an obsolete touring car. If a better make of car is presented for appraisal it will be necessary to determine the present selling price at the factory so as to arrive at the rate of duty. There is a schedule of depreciation for each year of use.

The officer's mental activities having been exercised, he may next get the opportunity for physical exercise by tramping up and down a snow-enshrouded railway yard to supervise the applying of Customs seals to a string of 40 tank cars of crude oil, with the temperature 40 below, the officer carrying a flashlight in one hand, a string of Customs seals in the other, and no third hand to rub his frost-bitten cheeks.

In the office, manifests must be dealt with, covering carloads, and less than carload shipments of freight and express destined to almost every point in the western provinces. The officer must not only know the Customs ports, but also his geography, in order that merchandise for the smallest town may be bonded on the correct port, to facilitate the quickest clearing of goods and avoid the carrying of goods farther than necessary.

When people arrive at the border by automobile or with cars of settlers' effects, the Customs officer is responsible for seeing that said persons are passed by immigration officers before clearing of cars. If stock, certificate from veterinary inspector must be obtained; if a hog, it must be quarantined for the requisite period. The officer must be familiar with the latest in quarantine regulations, must know from what States horses and other stock are not to be admitted, so that foot and mouth disease may be kept out of Canada. He must even watch for the importation of sausage skins, used sacks, bananas and other fruit and vegetables packed in straw, if coming from certain countries. Prison-made goods must also be watched for.

With the daily routine often there is mingled some comedy. When the nearest fumigation station to this border port was Winnipeg, a shipment of whiffletrees arrived, and was promptly sent to that city for fumigation. When United States settlers were pouring into Canada to secure homesteads, sometimes as many as 100 cars entering in one day, and passenger trains loaded with land agents and land-seekers, a certain passenger arrived and informed the officer that his wife's trunk was coming on later. He assured the officer that it contained nothing but his wife's wearing apparel. The officer took the check number, the trunk duly arrived and was placed on the railway platform for examination. The weight of the 'personal baggage' was too great and the trunk burst, revealing the contents to be a 250-pound threshing belt. An export reached the Customs office covering a carload of damp wheat. Typed on the export papers were the words 'Not fit for human consumption; for consumption in the United States.'

Border Customs work changes with the passing years. In 1909-10 the three long quarantine barns were filled with horses, sometimes totalling 600 head at one time. Now automobiles enter by the thousands in a year.

One of the most colorful officers at the time was Billy Beale, collector at Prince Albert, Saskatchewan, from 1914 to 1934. He had a waxed moustache, wore a bowler hat and spats, carried a cane, and had a white Pomeranian dog always at his heel. He wanted all the office desks in the customs house in a precise line, and he lined them up himself every morning. The pens and pencils in a wire rack all had to be pointing the same way. Forms in French from Ottawa were returned with a note that there must have been some mistake — the forms were in a "foreign language." Billy dropped dead in the street one Sunday morning on his way home from church.

In 1952, J. Earl Donnan published a booklet called *My First Forty Years with Canada Customs* in which he recorded these inquiries received by Customs, mainly during the 1930s:

"Am taking my dog into Canada. Does he require a birth certificate?"

"Which hotel in Montreal, the Mount Royal or the Windsor, affords the best view of Niagara Falls?"

"How can I address and seal a parcel so as to ensure that the Canadian Customs will not open and examine it?"

"What port of entry is likely to give me the lowest rate of duty as I take my merchandise into Canada?"

"How fast can your speed cops travel?"

"What are the most satisfactory methods of smuggling goods across the Border?"

"When may I be sure the Customs Officers will not be on duty at the Border?"

"Has Ottawa any Capital?"

"How much liquor can I drink in Manitoba?"

At about the same time, these replies to questions were kept for posterity:

Asked whether he was visiting Canada for pleasure, a traveller replied: "No, I'm seeing my wife's folks."

Asked if they were U.S. citizens: "No, just farmers."

Asked to state the length of residence in Canada: "Thirty feet by forty feet."

In 1939, at the outbreak of the Second World War, customs officers who had been greeting tourists to Canada suddenly found themselves transposed into watchful searchers for illegal exports which might be of use to the enemy. With the imposition of controls on foreign exchange, the officers had to seek full information on the amount of funds being taken out of the country. There is no doubt that this prying into the monetary affairs of the travelling public was the most distasteful job ever assigned to Customs, at least in recent times. Collector C.P. Wright at North Portal, Saskatchewan, said that the regulations should have been enforced by a special staff from headquarters in Ottawa or by trained prize fighters. In all his work, he said, he had found nothing which created so much public antagonism and resistance. (He was the collector at North Portal from 1913 to 1947). Customs officers often had to take funds from travellers, leaving them almost penniless, far from home and without a hotel or room to which to go or a bank from which they could obtain funds. A special arrangement had to be worked out for Indians living at Old Crow, Yukon Territory, who had always sold their furs and obtained provisions at Fort Yukon, Alaska; otherwise, the Indians would have faced a journey of three hundred miles to Dawson. The government went so far as to consider evacuation of the area but special permits were allowed for the community.

Customs work was particularly heavy in wartime at Canadian seaports. Customs, in conjunction with the Navy, exercised control over shipping, entered and cleared vessels and cargoes and searched all neutral ships. The wireless on all ships entering port had to be sealed. At Halifax, a security control station was established for all harbor craft. At Sydney, Nova Scotia, a medical service for merchant crews was inaugurated and placed under the direction of the customs collector. At Rimouski, Quebec, the collector was also naval reporting officer and personally decoded all admiralty messages; he was also the official mediator in disputes between master and crew on allied merchant vessels. At Windsor, Ontario, a customs officer captured an escaping German prisoner-of-war on the engine of a passenger train. At Winnipeg, the customs and excise staff was designated to issue Canadian passports. At Emerson, Manitoba, an international airport was built on the boundary so that planes could be delivered from the United States to Canada. Before the United States' entry into the war in December, 1941, the American neutrality act precluded air delivery of warplanes to Canada; so the planes were landed on the American side of the frontier at Emerson and hauled or pushed across the border onto the Canadian side, where pilots of the Royal Canadian Air Force awaited them. When the Alaska Highway was built in 1942, the customs staffs at Coutts, Alberta, and Edmonton went suddenly from clearing a few carloads of goods a day to handling whole trainloads. All sidings in Edmonton were filled with trainloads of equipment and trains had to be held at stations outside Edmonton. At Vancouver, in June, 1940, a customs search of a Japanese vessel uncovered a list with the names of a number of German agents in South America.

Nearly all the original customs houses in Canada were at seaports or on the land frontier. But as settlement expanded and industry grew, inland ports had to be established to handle commercial and other goods shipped to, or close to, their ultimate inland destinations. The advent of railroads and highways, and later air traffic routes, increased this trend and today more than 500 of the 650 customs ports are inland. The elimination of most commercial entries at the land frontier meant that border clearances for travellers became the main function at frontier stations, and this remains the case today.

After the Second World War, travel expanded enormously; more tourists came to Canada, more Canadians travelled abroad. Originally, travellers' clearances dealt only with matters related directly to Customs and Excise — that is, protection and collection of the revenue. The administration and enforcement of laws and regulations pertaining to immigration, agriculture, health and so on were performed by officers of those departments located at the customs ports of entry. This caused long delays for travellers and necessitated separate questioning and examination by several different inspection agencies — and duplicated federal costs. On Oct. 1, 1969, this intolerable situation was resolved by making customs officers responsible for questioning of travellers on behalf of all federal departments concerned. In difficult cases, travellers are referred to the officers of the appropriate government departments who are located in all major centres. Customs policy is self-compliance by the traveller with the law and verification — courteous verification — by the customs officer that the law has been observed. The verification process means that about ten per cent of travellers are required to undergo selective baggage examination.

Today the department administers, besides its own acts and regulations, the provisions of 57 other acts of Parliament prohibiting or regulating imports. From the 19th century's comparatively simple and clear issue of free trade versus protection we have advanced through a blizzard of international and bilateral trade treaties, customs unions, common markets and domestic tariff policy to today's labyrinth of regulations required for the efficient operation of a national revenue service.

Customs officers are responsible, among other things, for: clearing of exports to foreign countries; clearing of aircraft, ships, cargo containers, freight cars and trucks arriving and departing; the computation and receipt of duties on imports; the valuation of imports for duty purposes;

the ascertainment of the fair market value of goods in foreign countries; the cost of production of goods in foreign countries; the assessment of special or dumping duties; the classification of goods under one or other of the thousands of items in the customs tariff; the allowance of discounts from list or published prices for the determination of value for duty purposes; the determination of whether goods are of a class or kind made or produced in Canada; the making of regulations for the marking of goods with the name of the country of origin; the study of currency fluctuations in foreign countries to determine value for duty purposes, and so on.

The most difficult questions are mainly those of classification and of valuation. There are hundreds of thousands of kinds of goods, and more are being invented or manufactured every day. All these articles come under one or the other of items in the customs tariff and the customs officer must place them under the right items. Naturally, continual disputes arise between the importers and customs. Importers seek classifications which will put their imports under tariff items which are free of or low in duty. Customs officers must be careful to guard the revenue — but not to make importation unnecessarily difficult by deciding every doubtful case in favor of the national treasury. Additional difficulty is caused by the fact that many of the duties are imposed on goods of a class or kind made or produced in Canada. These duties are protective. The moment a duty becomes a protection rather than a revenue-raiser, not only the crown and the importer are interested in the proper classification for duty purposes. A third party — the Canadian producer — now is involved. Customs officers may in this case be the arbiters between the importer and the Canadian manufacturer. The battle for lower or higher classifications goes on continually. The Tariff Board is always there as a court of appeal for any aggrieved party, whether the importer, the manufacturer, or the customs department.

Proper valuation of goods for duty is at least as important as the tariff rates themselves. This is particularly true under the Canadian system in which fair home market value and dumping duties play so vital a part. It has been the fate of customs officials since the very beginning of the service to be accused by protectionist domestic manufacturers of being too liberal to importers and accused by free-trade importers of putting up too many unnecessary barriers against imports. The customs tariff contains about 3,200 major classifications, subdivided into more than 16,000 commodity descriptions. There are four tariff structures, each with its own set of rates, established mainly by various international agreements such as the General Agreement on Tariffs and Trade — some countries are party to more than one agreement. The upshot of all the careful weighing and assessing and making informed judgments is that ten thousand men and women at seven hundred locations of the Customs and Excise division collect $18 billion a year for the national revenue. By comparison, in 1937 a staff of 7,049 at 450 locations collected $317 million.

Although Customs in Britain began employing women in 1842, (British Excise in 1873 called them "female typewriters") Canada Customs was almost exclusively male until 1947, when the government imposed foreign exchange controls which necessitated personal searches in much greater numbers than ever before. Up to that time, and especially during the Second World War, it had been the practice to have a few women on special duty call at major border points for searching women. That Customs and Excise, and indeed all government departments, opposed hiring women is well illustrated in this two-paragraph mention of women under the title "female clerks" in the 1881 report of the royal commission into the civil service (all seven commissioners were, of course, male):

> Whilst we see no reason whatever why female clerks should not be quite as efficient public servants as men, we are forced to confess that there are several obstacles in the way of their employment which we fear it will be very difficult if not impossible to overcome. For example, it would be necessary that they should be placed in rooms by themselves, and that they should be under the immediate supervision of a person of their own sex; but we doubt very much if sufficient work of similar character can be found in any one Department to furnish occupation for any considerable number of female clerks, and it would certainly be inadvisable to place them in small numbers throughout the Departments.
>
> Should circumstances hereafter arise warranting the employment of female clerks, we see no objection to their being appointed as clerks of the third class, under such regulations as the Civil Service Commissioners may, with the sanction of the Governor in Council, make, as to competitive examination, age, health and character.

There are some letters on file from the 1920s in which officers in the field urged headquarters to consider hiring women for inspection work. Inspector Fred W. Allen reported after an inspection tour of most ports in December, 1926, that he had seen only one female officer; that was at Sault Ste. Marie, Ontario. By 1982, 39.1 per cent of all employees in Customs and Excise were women.

Up to very recent years, training of officers who deal directly with the public was done on the buddy system: the trainee put his ear close enough to pick up the conversation between a traveller and an experienced officer. Clayton H. England of Niagara Falls, who served 42 years in Customs and Excise, recalled in 1982, when he was 82 years old: "I was just given a hat and told to go to work." Veteran inspectors have said that the buddy system did not always work because the purportedly experienced officer breaking in the recruit was sometimes a mine of misinformation and the trainee had to learn all over again. Since 1980, Customs and Excise has had a training college, at Rigaud, Quebec, which, within two years, was providing 25,000 days of training a year for about seven hundred officers, including customs inspectors and superintendents, excise officers, audit supervisors and middle managers, as well as seven to ten concurrent technical courses. Projected expansion calls for doubling the number of trainees a year.

The basic insignia of Canada Customs has always been the same: a portcullis under a crown on a gold maple leaf. Under the portcullis is "Canada" and under that "Customs-Douanes." These words were added as recently as 1978 on the understandable premise that few people seeing the badge would know the significance of the portcullis by itself. The connection of the portcullis, or gate, with Customs dates from 1604 when a London merchant brought suit against James I for increasing customs duties without the consent of Parliament. The merchant lost, the judges deciding that "the seaports are the King's gates, which he may open and shut to whom he pleases."

Uniforms date from early in this century but rules that officers at frontier highways and bridges and rail and boat terminals must wear them on duty were apparently not strictly observed. When he was 93 in 1980, Arthur Bruce, former collector at Shelburne, Nova Scotia, recalled that during his long tenure from 1918 to 1952 he had a uniform for only two or three years. "Ottawa was always cutting back and they simply didn't replace my uniform," he said. The standard allowance in 1931 was two uniforms a year at $27.50 each. The uniform used to be navy blue but was changed in the 1970s to a brighter blue. Bilingual shoulder flashes are worn as well as hat badges.

The rules of conduct for customs and excise officers are little changed from a century ago, though the language of officialdom has become a little less tart — and perhaps more woolly. The 1982 code of conduct and appearance requires that:

> Employees should be sensitive to the expectations and needs of the public served and should act in a business-like fashion in every official activity involving their conduct with others. Sensitivity to the needs of the public requires that employees of Customs and Excise conduct themselves in a pleasant, polite and business-like manner with all members of the public with whom Customs and Excise does business, even under difficult conditions and in times of personal stress and in the face of provocation which does not involve a violation of the law.
>
> In this regard, employees will not make any abusive, derisive, threatening, obscene or other insulting, offensive or provocative gesture or remark to or about another person in their presence.

An intricate customs problem was posed by the entry of Newfoundland into Confederation in 1949. It necessitated the integration of the Newfoundland and Canadian customs tariffs and the assimilation of the Newfoundland customs staff into Canada's.

Gordon Howell recalled in 1981 how it was done. In 1949, he was head of Customs in Newfoundland, chief commissioner of immigration, chairman of the liquor control board and an adviser to the Newfoundland delegation which arranged the terms of union. He became a member of Canada Customs at Confederation and, before his retirement in 1972, was assistant deputy minister, field operations, in charge of a staff of about 7,000 (compared with about 150 in Newfoundland in 1949).

Howell said that one of the terms of union had to do with liquor, because Canadian liquor was 70 proof but Newfoundland rum was 100 proof: "There was no restriction on proof in Newfoundland such as there was in Canada, even though the Canadian restriction was never written into law. Well, we worked out a compromise with the Canadian officials. All the gin, whisky, rye and that kind of stuff would be Canadian 70 proof. But we reserved the right to bottle rum at any strength we liked. It was one of the terms of union which was never published."

Howell considers that customs duties played a bigger part in Newfoundland's decision to join Canada than is generally realized. Joseph Smallwood, apostle of Confederation who became the province's first and longtime premier, promoted the attraction of the Canadian family allowance which Newfoundlanders would start to receive at Confederation. "But he called more attention to the customs duties," Howell said. "Joey would address the housewives particularly at meetings: 'You'll be able to order from the Eaton's and Simpson's catalogues and the goods will come first class right to your door without going through Customs because there won't be any more duties on goods from Canada. You can order from Canada duty free.' Well, that was true enough. What Joey didn't mention was the Canadian sales tax. We didn't have a sales tax until we came into Confederation."

Before Confederation, the bulk of Newfoundland's imports had come from Britain and the United States. But the switch was made to imports from Canada because customs duties between Canada and Newfoundland ended with Confederation. "Before Confederation," Howell said, "we had customs men at fifty outports, all one-man ports except Port aux Basques and Corner Brook. The day after Confederation, we needed only about a dozen of those outports, so we had to bring in our officers from these harbors where they had lived all their lives. It was quite a wrench for all of them. It was more than a wrench for a lot of people. It was a shock. Nobody had a mortgage in the outports. You simply bought a house or built it yourself. You cured your own fish and grew your own vegetables. Now all these officers had to give up that life. But not one man who was required to move declined to move.

"Remember Gander in those days, the big trans-Atlantic refuelling stop? Customs didn't have all that much to do there because most passengers were in transit. The waits in the old hangar there used to be pretty long. I remember one day when I was there I met Yehudi Menuhin among the passengers waiting for their plane to be gassed up. I asked him, just on the spur of the moment, whether he would play for his fellow passengers. He gave a forty-five-minute concert in that draughty old hangar.

"Do you know that we were still using shipping documents for airplanes after the war? The purser on a ship had five days to prepare those documents for Customs. The purser on a plane had to do up the same documents in about the same number of hours. It was interesting being part of revving Customs up to the speed of aviation."

APPENDIX I

Border Customs Ports

Customs houses on the Canada-United States border date from the end of the 18th century. The first, though not flush on the border like today's posts, was opened at St. Jean, Quebec, in 1788. Even then, the boundary was vague and all its bits and pieces were not finally settled until early in this century. There are older customs posts in Canada, such as St. John's, Newfoundland, Quebec, Annapolis Royal, Nova Scotia, and Saint John, New Brunswick, but this list deals only with the frontier ports of entry.

From east to west, the 114 border points (with their U.S. counterparts) are:

New Brunswick

Campobello — An island linked to Lubec, Maine, since 1962 by the Franklin D. Roosevelt International Bridge (the U.S. president had a summer home on Campobello), it was the rendezvous for New England and Maritime smugglers in sailing-ship days. Most of the 1,200 islanders hold dual citizenship because nearly all the children are born in the United States (the hospital at Machias, Maine, is 53 kilometres from the bridge).

St. Stephen and ***Milltown*** — Opposite Calais, Maine, they were amalgamated in 1973. The towns were settled in 1779 and became a big shipbuilding and lumber centre (there were forty-two sawmills in 1842). The first bridge connecting Canada and the United States was built here in 1820. A British customs office was established at St. Stephen in 1801 or 1802. The first Canadian collector, Henry Webber, took office in 1870. His grandson, Leonard Webber, was collector from 1956 to 1961 and served in Customs for forty years. The first customs office in Milltown was established in 1896.

Ste. Croix — The name is taken from the river and island first named by de Monts in 1604. On the island, whose name now is Dochet, was established the first white settlement north of Florida. The customs house was first located here about 1900 and was operated by one man from his home. Opposite Vanceboro, Maine.

Forest City — About twenty miles northwest of Ste. Croix, opposite Forest City, Maine.

Fosterville — On the northern tip of Grand Lake, the village was founded in 1889 and the first postmaster was William Foster. The old, thirty-two-foot wooden bridge on the boundary was reputed to be the shortest span linking the two countries. Opposite Orient, Maine.

Woodstock Road — The customs house here, opposite Houlton, Maine, dates from about 1875 though Woodstock itself, fourteen miles from the border, had an office as early as 1830, was the first inland port in New Brunswick, and in 1837 collected £63 and 16 shillings (about $300). Charles Campbell, the customs officer from approximately 1896 to 1906, was supplied with a horse and wagon to patrol the border. He was one of several officers on the Canada-U.S. boundary who had roving missions and operated entirely away from the customs house. As late as 1920, one customs officer handled all customs work at his home.

Bloomfield — This is another customs point, near Lakeville and opposite Monticello, Maine, which existed for decades as a one-man operation from a house. The first regular office was not opened until 1939.

Centreville and ***River de Chute*** — Twenty-one miles northwest of Woodstock, Centreville was founded in 1862; its early names were Perkins Corners and Wheelers Corners. The customs port was created in 1936 and is opposite Bridgewater, Maine. The sub-station at River de Chute is opposite Easton, Maine.

Perth-Andover and ***Four Falls*** — These points handle traffic to and from Fort Fairfield, Maine. Andover dates from 1846. There is no record of when a customs house was first established at Andover but an 1873 customs warehouse entry exists showing fifteen barrels of kerosene consigned to Presque Isle, Maine. In those days, there was no railway in northern Maine and goods were shipped up the St. John River by steamboat and towboat, unloaded at New Brunswick river-front villages and hauled by horses to their Maine destinations.

Grand Falls and ***Gillespie Portage*** — First mentioned in explorers' literature in 1688, Grand Falls was originally Grand Sault, then Great Falls; in Maliseet Indian it was Chikchunikabik, for place of destruction, after Mohawk canoes were lured over the falls by Maliseet women. Gillespie Portage, opposite Limestone, Maine, was opened in 1929 and named after the first customs officer there, L.P. Gillespie. The Grand Falls highway office, opposite Hamlin, Maine, was opened in 1953.

St. Leonard — Dates from 1847 and was named after Magistrate Leonard R. Coombes. Opposite Van Buren, Maine.

Edmundston — Frequently misspelled Edmunston, it is named after Sir

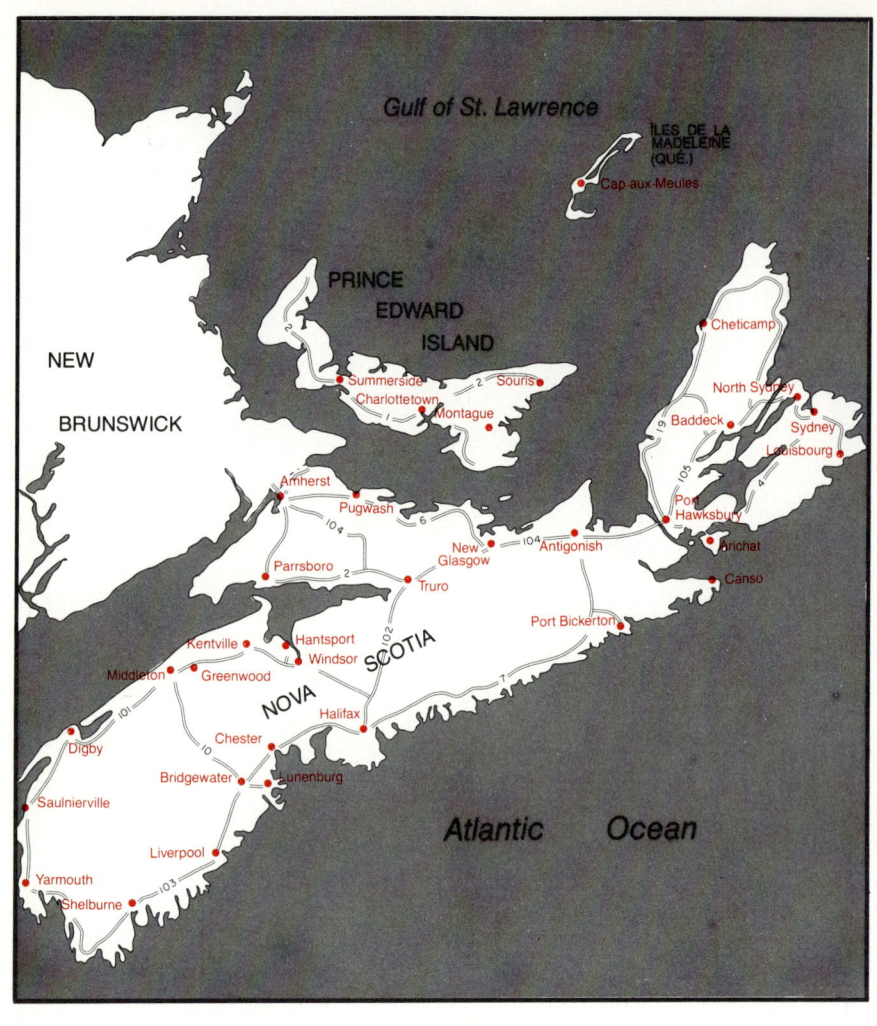

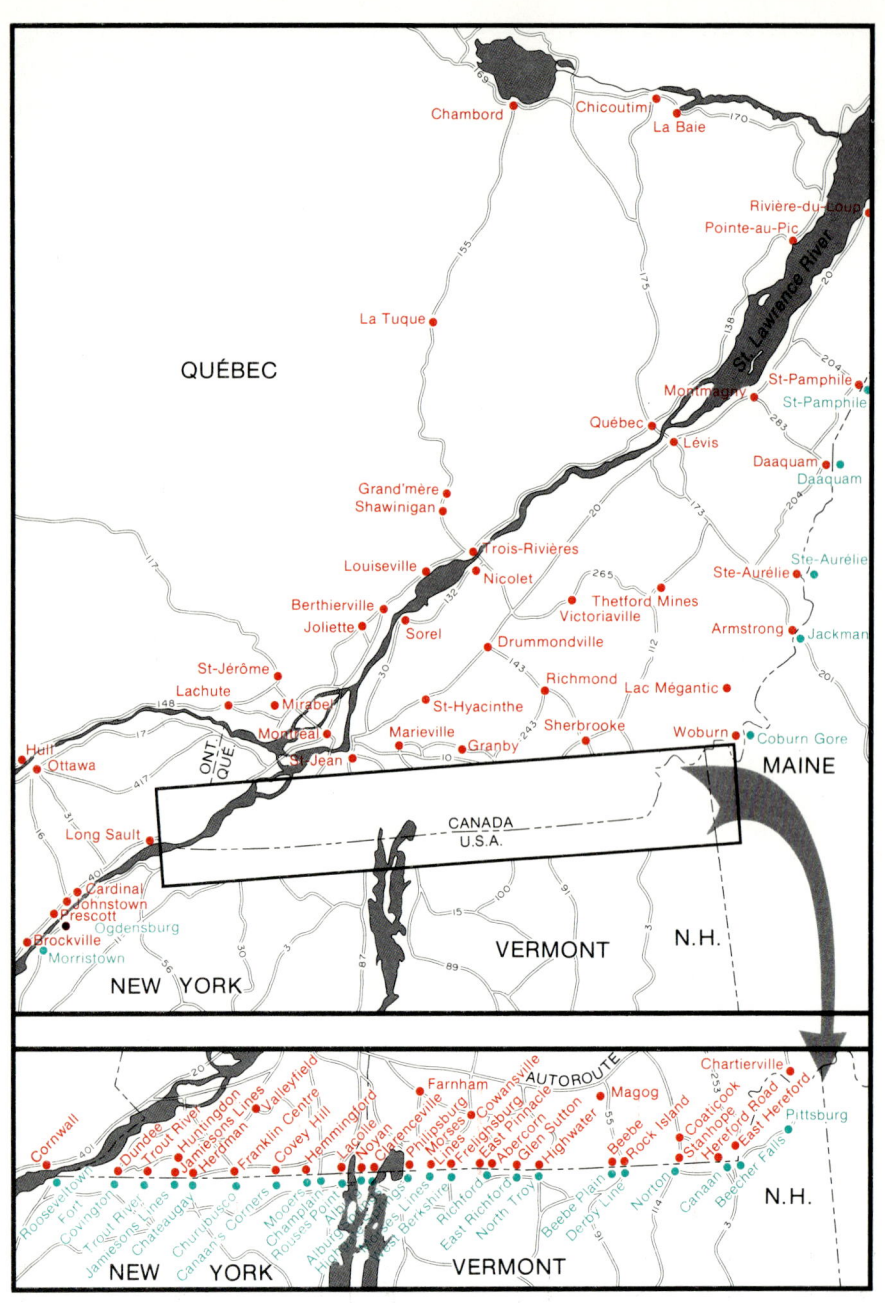

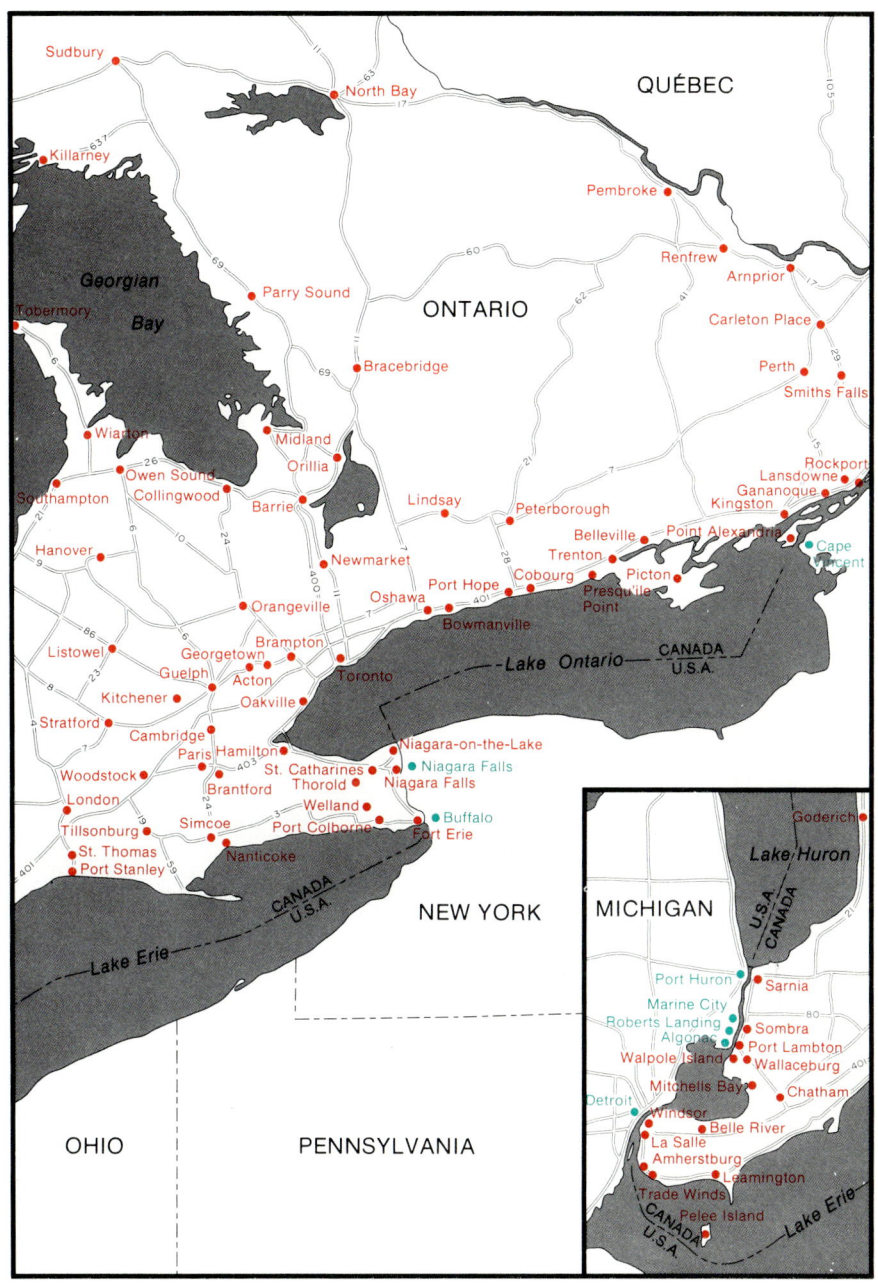

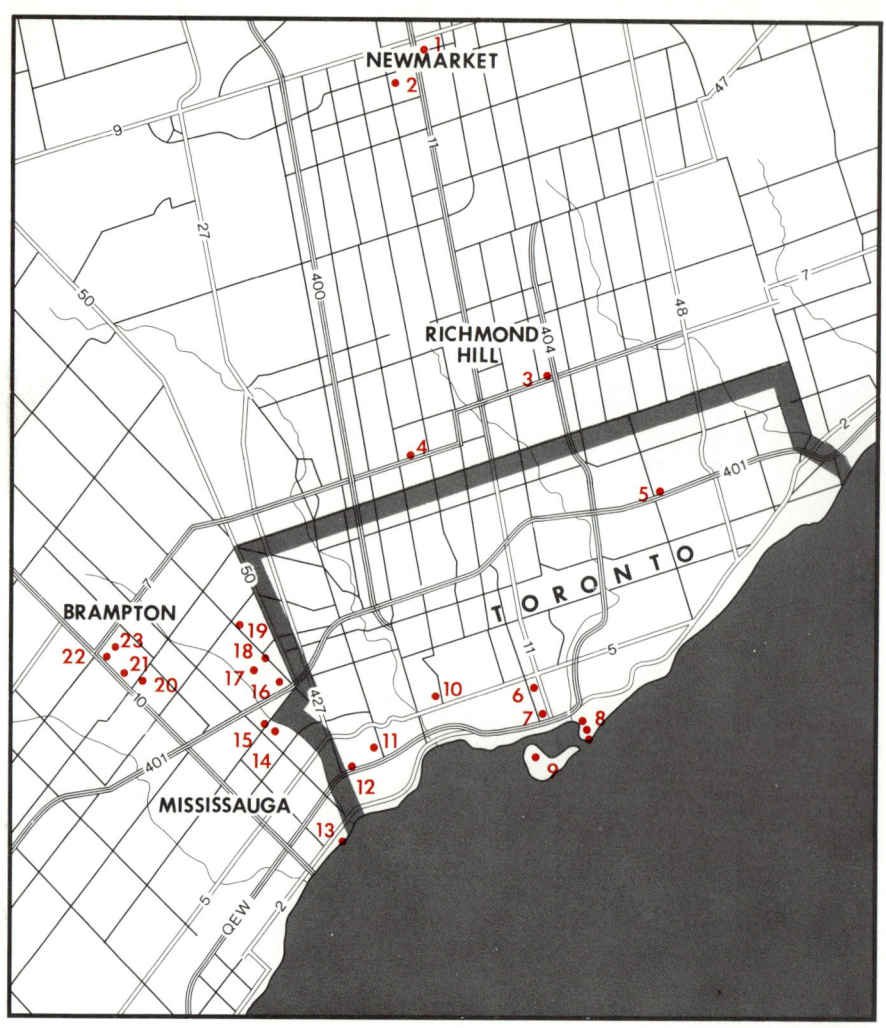

TORONTO

Legend

1. Newmarket Port Office
2. Walkers Warehousing Limited Sufferance
3. Buttonville Airport
4. C.N. Concord
5. Toronto Sufferance Truck Terminal
6. Main Office — Port of Toronto — Regional Offices
7. Toronto International Mail Unit Clearance
8. Marine Operation
9. Toronto Island Airport
10. West Toronto Postal Clearance
11. C.P. Obico Intermodal Services
12. Mid Continent Truck Terminal
13. Canadian Arsenals — Postal Sortation
14. Gateway Postal Plant
15. Interport Sufferance Warehouse
16. Terminal II International Traffic
17. Terminal I International Traffic
18. Commercial Operations Terminal
19. Toronto International Centre of Commerce
20. Peel Terminal
21. MG Sufferance Warehouse
22. Brampton Area Port
23. Brampton Postal Clearance

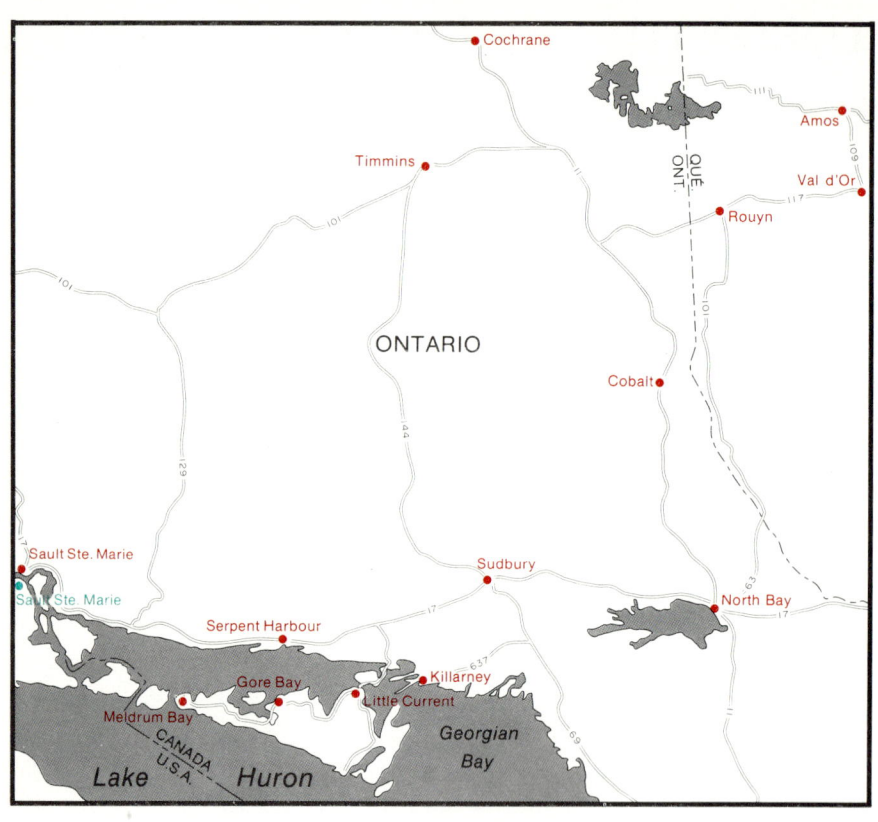

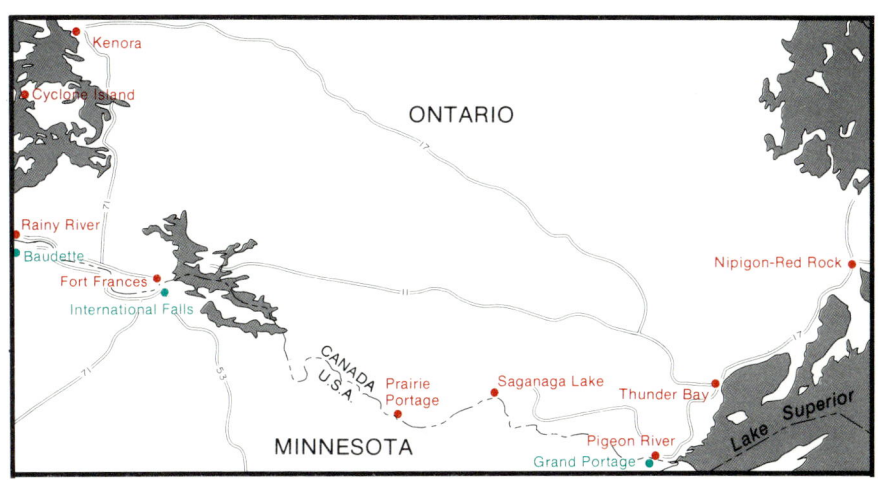

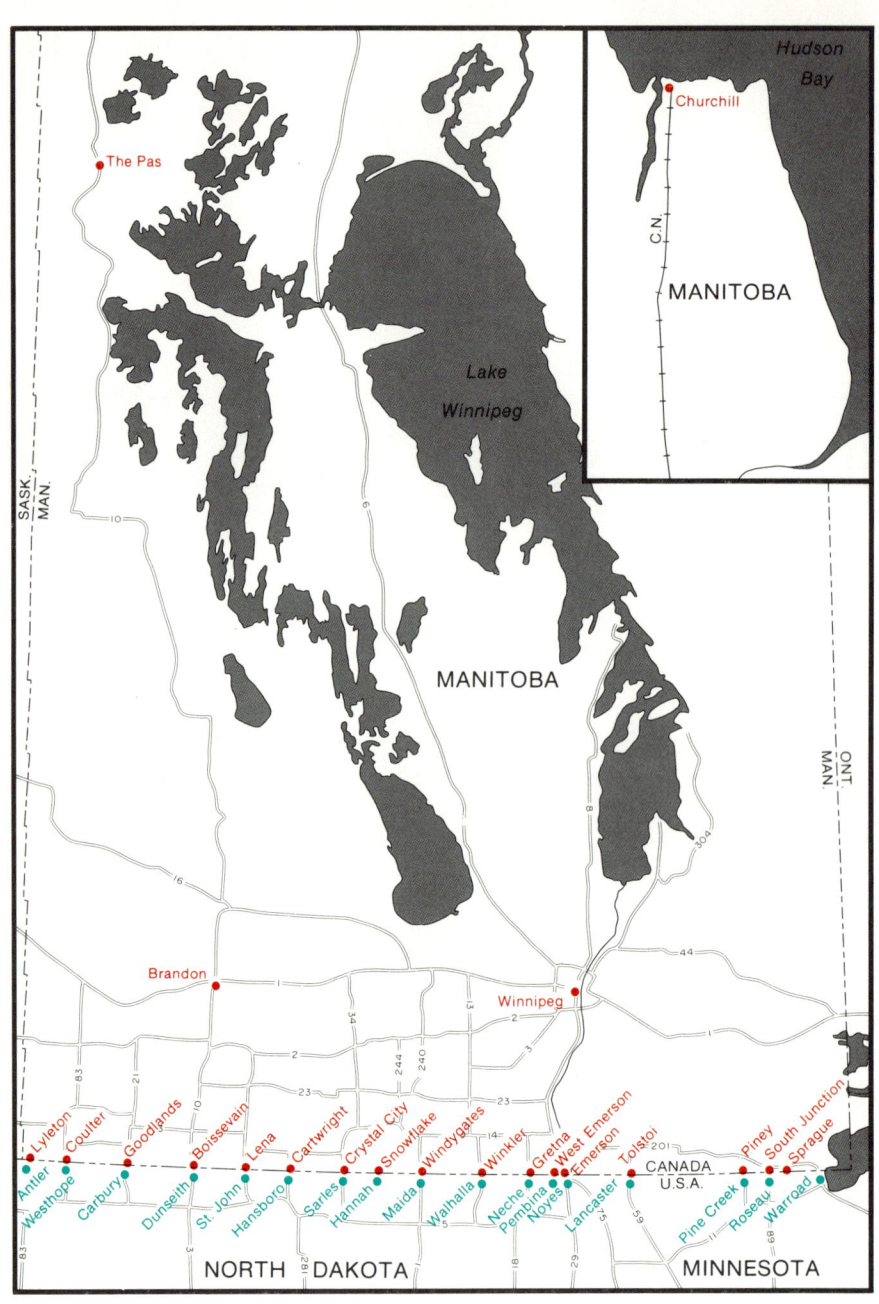

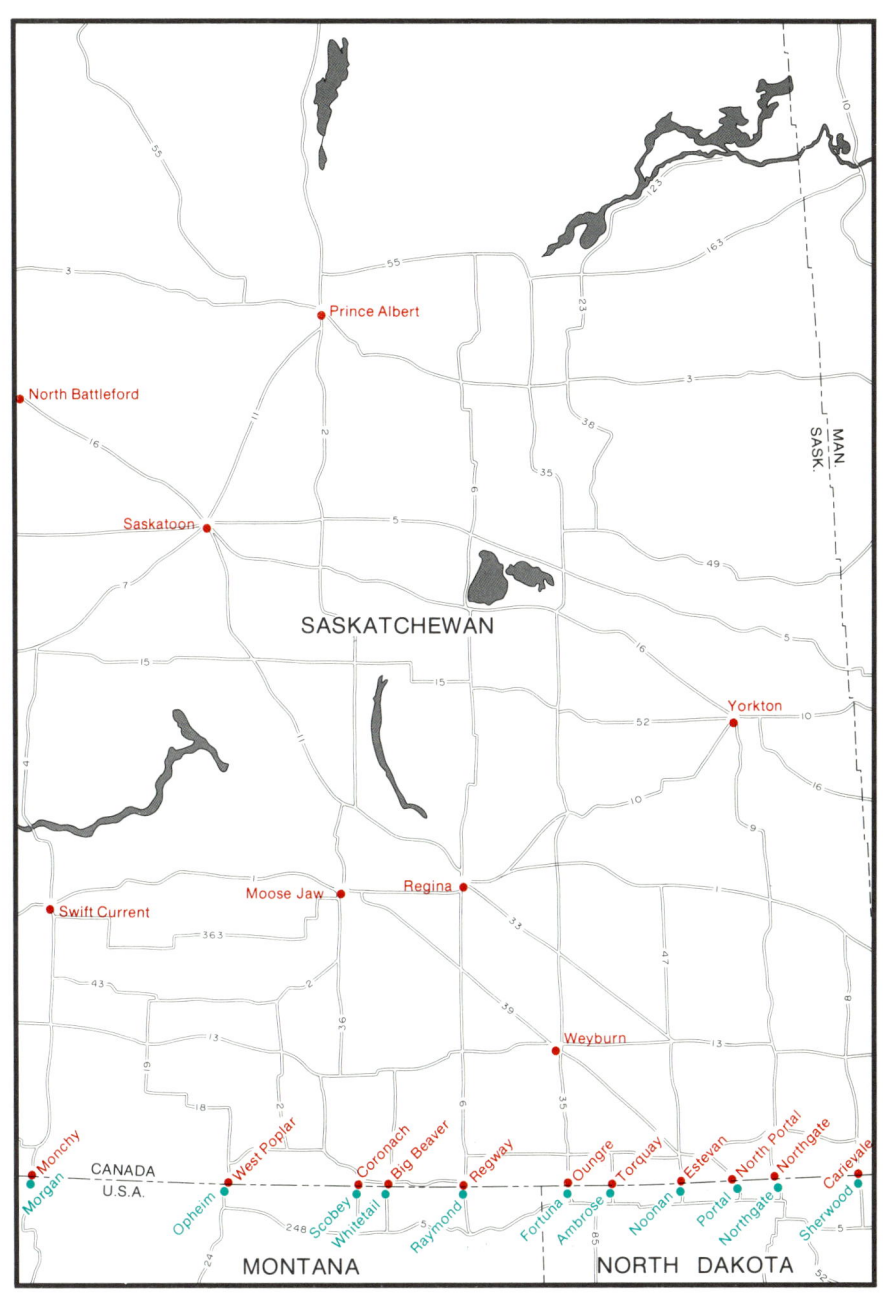

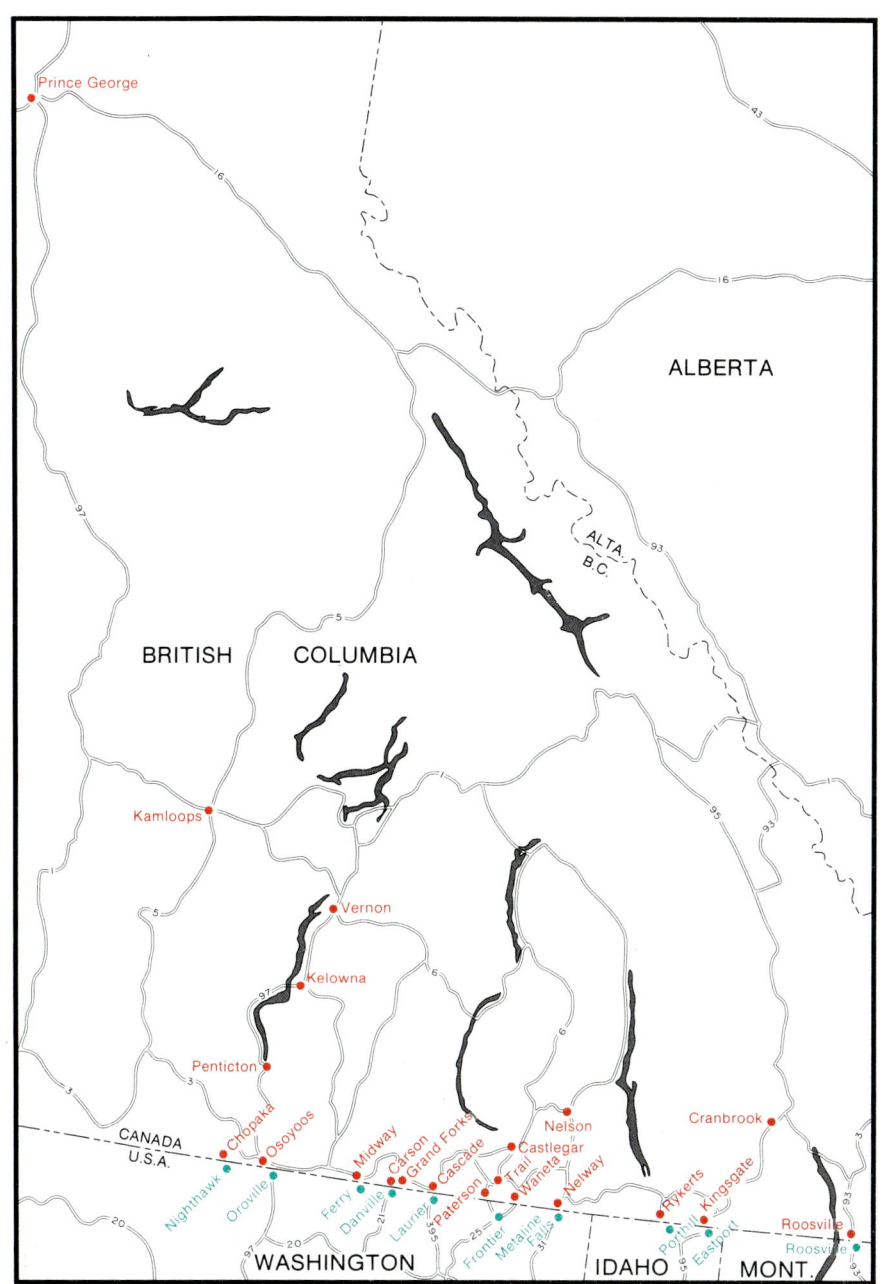

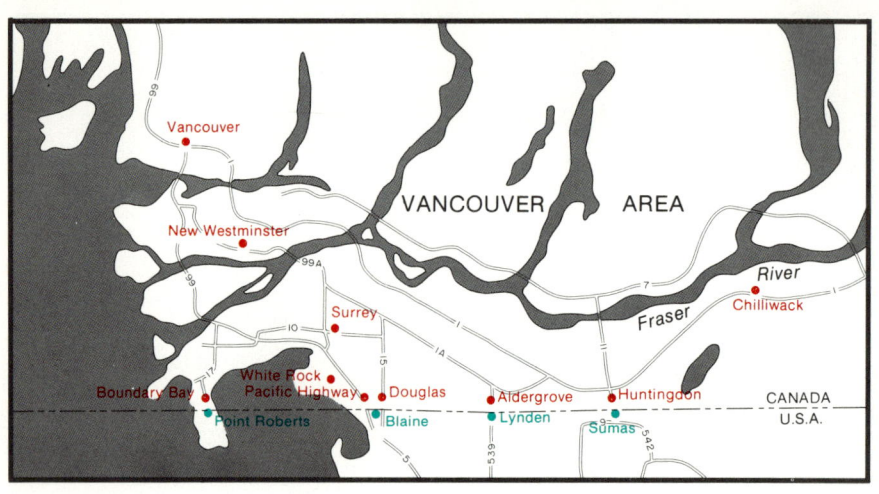

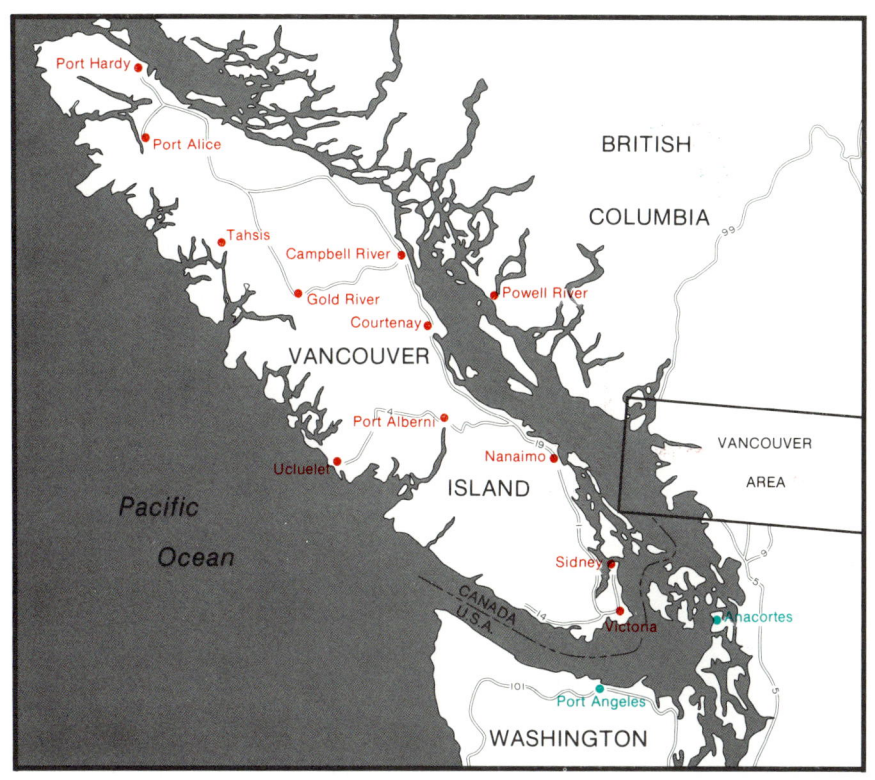

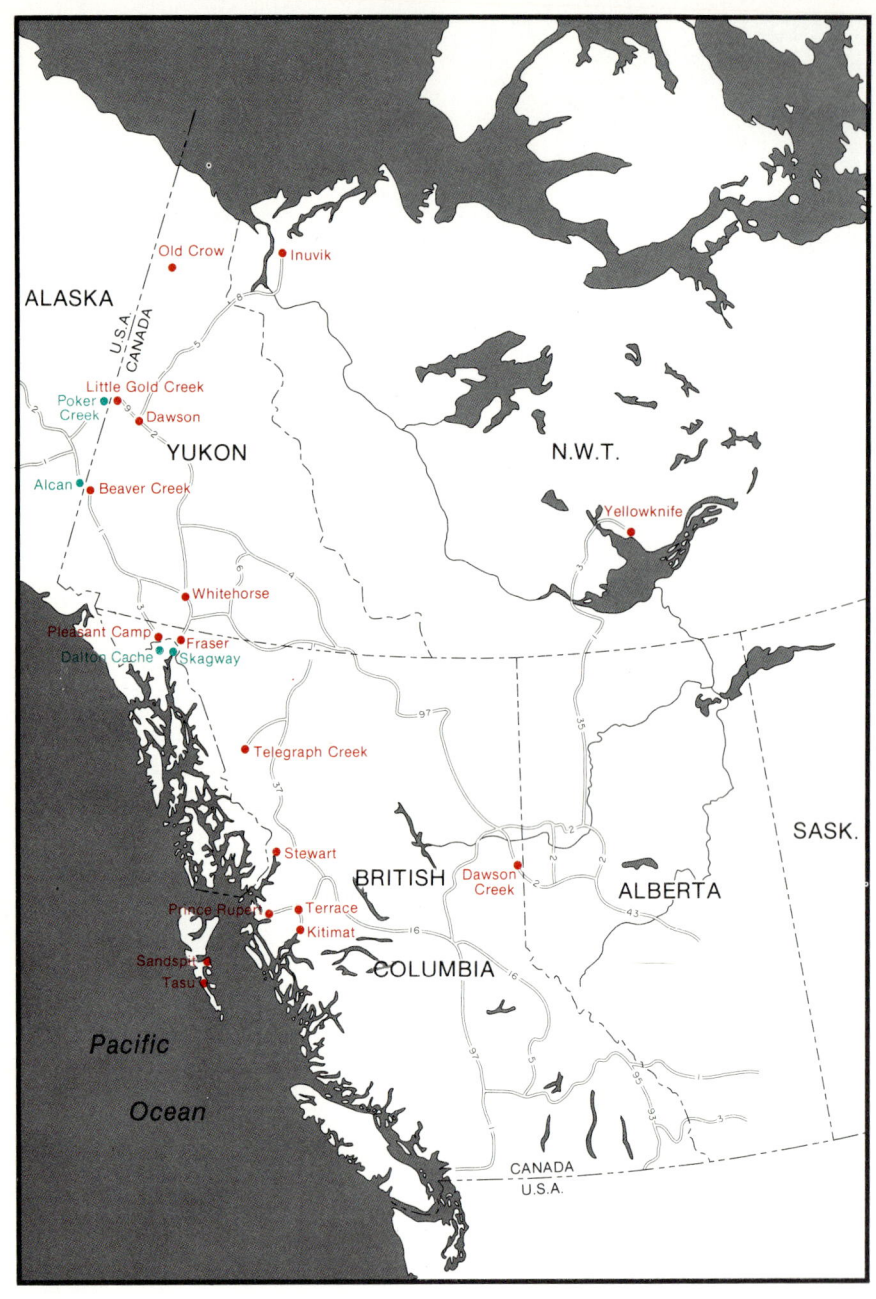

Edmund Head, lieutenant-governor of New Brunswick in 1848-54. Its original French name was Petit Sault. Opposite Madawaska, Maine.

Clair — Dates from 1890 when the Temiscouata Railway was completed and the railroad station was named Clair for Peter Clair, who donated the land on which it was built. The customs port was called Middle St. Francis until 1905. The first highway bridge to Fort Kent, Maine, opposite, opened in 1930.

Quebec

Quebec has border points with four American states: Maine, New Hampshire, Vermont and New York. For literally hundreds of miles, there is no trans-border highway linking Quebec and northern Maine. From the Quebec village of *Pohénégamook*, opposite Estcourt, at the northern tip of Maine, south to Armstrong, Quebec, the only border crossings are logging roads required by U.S. firms to get timber out of the Maine woods. The only available connecting roads are Canadian. The three logging-road crossings are at the Quebec points of *St. Pamphile*, *Daaquam* and *Ste. Aurélie*.

Then come:

Armstrong — Customs has been in Beauce County since 1835 when stagecoach service opened between Quebec and Boston. But the first customs house was at Ste. Marie, 60 miles from the border. The collector was Thomas Jacques Taschereau, brother of a cardinal, and one of his roving preventive officers was James Armstrong, after whom the village and customs port are named. The second customs house at Armstrong was still ten miles from the boundary and officers had to contend with a wide no-man's-land in seeking smugglers. The present customs office on the border was built in the early 1960s. Opposite Jackman, Maine.

St. Augustin de Woburn — Opposite Coburn Gore, Maine, through which Benedict Arnold marched for his attack on Quebec in 1775. The first customs office was opened in 1929.

Chartierville — Opposite Pittsburg, New Hampshire. (Many customs records for the Eastern Townships of Quebec were lost when they were donated by the central Sherbrooke office to a wartime paper drive in 1940.)

East Hereford — In the southeast corner of Quebec, opposite Beecher Falls, Vermont. The first customs house was established in the 1830s to handle stagecoach traffic from New Haven, Connecticut, to Quebec.

Hereford Road — Opposite Canaan, Vermont.

Stanhope — Established as a customs preventive station in 1897, though the office at Coaticook, fifteen miles from the border, opened in 1853. Opposite Norton, Vermont.

Rock Island — Stagecoach service between Montreal and Boston necessitated a customs office in adjacent Stanstead Plain in 1821, the second in Lower Canada after St. Jean. The office moved one mile to the border in 1909 though it was first located on the second floor at the rear of the post office building and had no view of the boundary at all. Rock Island is cheek-by-jowl with Derby Line, Vermont, and in the 1920s the two towns became a favorite centre for textile smugglers because bolts of American cloth could literally be thrown from an American warehouse into a Canadian factory. Rock Island was a focal point in the 1926 customs scandal which brought down (temporarily) the Liberal government.

Beebe — Named for David and Calvin Beebe who settled here in 1798, Beebe shares one of its streets with Beebe Plain, Vermont. One side of the street is Canadian, the other American. The customs office was established in 1909 but earlier offices at Georgeville (1854), Magog (1864), and Cedarville (1866), handled water traffic on Lake Memphremagog. This traffic included boat excursions from the United States numbering as many as 1,200 people, each group accompanied by a band.

Highwater — The customs house appears to date from 1872. It once occupied a former hotel called The Line House. Opposite North Troy, Vermont.

Glen Sutton — The first office here was opened in 1928 in a farmhouse. Opposite East Richford, Vermont.

Abercorn and ***East Pinnacle*** — Opposite Richford, Vermont. The Abercorn customs office was first opened by a doctor in 1845.

Frelighsburg — Named after Abram Freligh who settled here about 1795. Opposite West Berkshire, Vermont.

Morses Lines — The name comes from a settler, Morse, who built a line store on the border about 1810. A U.S. post office was located in the same building. A customs station was opened in 1937, replacing Pigeon Hill where the customs officer had to supply an office at his own expense on a salary of $900 a year. Opposite Morses Lines, Vermont.

Philipsburg — Named after Philip Ruiter, a United Empire Loyalist who settled here in 1809, Philipsburg was on the stagecoach route between Montreal and New York and customs service dates from 1842. The first daily bus service between the two cities opened on the same route in 1929. The first three female officers joined the staff here in December, 1947. Opposite Highgate Springs, Vermont.

Clarenceville — Named after the Duke of Clarence, son of mad George III. The duke visited Canada in 1787. Opposite Alburg Springs, Vermont.

Noyan — This port opposite Alburg, Vermont, was, early in the century, a central point for customs inspection of freight and passenger trains. Three railway lines — Rutland; Quebec, Montreal and Southern; and Grand Trunk — used to pass through Noyan. In 1917, railway traffic began switcing to Lacolle and highway traffic averaged about 25 cars a year. But highway construction increased in the 1920s and business picked up again.

Lacolle — This port handles three trans-border highways between Montreal and New York. The first hard-surfaced highway built by the Quebec government was finished in 1913 between Montreal and Lacolle (the second was from Sherbrooke to Rock Island). At that time, wealthy car owners would travel in groups from New York to Montreal, accompanied by one or two trucks carrying spare parts. A single customs officer used to handle highway traffic at Lacolle. Now it requires hundreds in shifts around the clock. Opposite Champlain and Rouses Point, New York.

Hemmingford — Opposite Mooers, New York.

Covey Hill — The first customs house was built in 1925. Opposite Cannon's Corners, New York.

Franklin Centre, *Herdman*, *Jamiesons Lines* and *Trout River* — Opposite, respectively, Churubusco, Chateauguay, Jamiesons Lines and Trout River in New York.

Dundee — Originally part of the St. Regis Indian reserve, Dundee was first settled in 1793. The customs house, most westerly in Quebec, dates from 1844. Opposite Fort Covington, New York.

Ontario

Up to now, it will have been seen that the big majority of border crossings are at tiny hamlets whose names do not appear on most maps. Most border points in Ontario are cities and the crossings bridges.

The Americans began establishing customs houses along the border with Upper Canada in 1799 and Canadians had little choice but to follow suit. By the end of 1801, eleven ports of entry had been created, at Cornwall, Johnstown (Prescott), Kingston, Newcastle, York (Toronto), Queenston, Niagara, Fort Erie, Turkey Point (Port Dover), Amherstburg and Sandwich (Windsor).

Cornwall — The New York Central railway bridge was planked over in 1934 to provide the only international vehicular bridge (at that time) between Montreal and Niagara Falls. It was replaced in 1958 by the Seaway International Bridge. The American entry point is Rooseveltown, New York.

Prescott — A ferry operated as early as 1770 between here and Ogdensburg, New York. In 1917, there were seventeen customs and excise officers at Prescott, seven of them full time at Wiser's Distillery. The bridge between Prescott and Ogdensburg was opened in 1960.

Lansdowne — The Thousand Islands International (or Ivy Lea) Bridge was opened in 1938 by Prime Minister Mackenzie King and President Roosevelt. Ivy Lea is a summer resort just west of the bridge and opposite Alexandria Bay, New York.

Niagara Falls — A fort was built at Niagara in 1687 by Jacques René de Brisay, Marquis of Denonville. In the early 1800s there were several customs points along the Niagara Frontier, including Queenston, Port Robinson (on the first Welland Canal) and Chippewa, where James Secord, husband of Laura Secord, was appointed collector in 1820. The first steam ferries between Niagara Falls, Ontario, and Niagara Falls, New York, operated about 1846. The first bridge, the Whirlpool Rapids Bridge, opened in 1848 and the customs office was a hard chair at the end of the bridge because the bridge company refused to provide shelter. Numerous bridges have been built since, some of which blew down or were destroyed by ice. The Rainbow Bridge was opened in 1941, and the latest Queenston-Lewiston bridge in 1962.

Fort Erie — White settlement here began about 1750 with building of a stockade by the French a mile south of the present Fort Erie. The international railway bridge between Bridgeburg, which amalgamated with Fort Erie in 1932, and Black Rock on the American side opened in 1873. The Peace Bridge joining Fort Erie and Buffalo, New York, was opened in 1927.

Windsor — Antoine Laumet, Sieur de Lamothe Cadillac, built a fur-trading fort across the river at Detroit in 1701 and 22 settlers from Quebec began Windsor in 1749. Windsor is Canada's southernmost point and south of Detroit. It has traditionally been the busiest port of entry in Canada. In 1881, Hiram Walker of Detroit got tired of spending 90 minutes going from home to his distillery on the Canadian side and installed his own ferry service. It remained in operation until 1942 despite construction of the Ambassador Bridge, opened in 1929, and of the Windsor-Detroit tunnel, opened a year later and the first vehicular subway between the two countries. Four-fifths of the liquor smuggled to the United States during American prohibition (1920-33) took the Windsor-Detroit route.

Sarnia — Originally known as "The Rapids," Sarnia takes its name from the ancient Roman name for the Channel island of Guernsey. The name was suggested in 1836 by Sir John Colborne, lieutenant-governor of Upper Canada and former governor of Guernsey. In that same year, an innkeeper named Crampton was appointed the first customs collector. He was sent packing empty-handed from the first schooner he boarded to collect cargo duties. The schooner's captain later succeeded Crampton as collector. A railway tunnel to Port Huron, Michigan, was built in 1894. The International Blue Water Bridge was opened in 1938.

Sault Ste. Marie — The original community where Lake Superior rushes into Lake Huron comprised some 2,000 Algonquin Indians. The Jesuit mission was established in 1668. "The Soo" was a fur-trading post and the North-West Company built the first canal around the rapids in the St. Mary's River in 1798. The present canal on the Canadian side was completed in 1895. The first customs house opened in 1843. The ferry service to Sault Ste. Marie, Michigan, was replaced in 1962 by the international bridge.

Pigeon River — This was the entrance to the best portage route from Lake Superior to the Canadian west. The portage was on the south (American) side of the river and when the United States in 1804 imposed duty on all goods carried over the portage, Canada's fur traders transferred to the inferior Dog River route out of Thunder Bay. The first Canadian customs post was established in 1917 — in a tent. Opposite Grand Portage, Minnesota.

Fort Frances — Named in 1830 for the wife of Governor George Simpson of the Hudson's Bay Company when they visited the post. It has been a customs point since 1895. The bridge to International Falls, Minnesota, was opened in 1912.

Rainy River — The customs house dates from 1902. Opposite Baudette, Minnesota.

There are thirty-six border crossings on the prairies. Many of them comprise only the customs house and the home or homes of the staff.

Manitoba

Sprague — The customs office here opened in 1901, mainly to handle rail traffic of the Duluth, Winnipeg and Pacific Railway and the Port Arthur-Duluth-Winnipeg branch of Canadian Northern. Northbound passengers arrived at the border early in the morning but were not interviewed by the customs officer, who travelled on the trains, until just before Winnipeg. Sprague is in the southeast corner of Manitoba opposite Warroad, Minnesota.

South Junction — Opposite Roseau, Minnesota.

Piney — Customs service dates from 1922. The first officer operated part-time and was paid $200 a year. Opposite Pine Creek, Minnesota.

Tolstoi — The first settlers came from the estate of Count Tolstoi in Russia. Customs service is of recent beginning — 1950. Opposite Lancaster, Minnesota.

Emerson — The customs house was established in 1871, the year after Manitoba became a province. But four fur-trading companies had had posts on the banks of the Red River at or near Pembina (now Emerson) as early as 1801: Hudson's Bay, North-West, XY and American. Emerson grew from a village of one hundred in 1875 to a town of 3,000 in 1881 with seventy-five places of business, including six hotels and a daily newspaper, and six resident clergymen. In 1874, the name was changed to Emerson because American philosopher and essayist Ralph Waldo Emerson was the favorite author of William Fairbanks, one of the two Minnesota businessmen who founded the townsite a year earlier. The International Boundary Commission found in 1873 that the Canadian customs house was on U.S. soil but it was 1879 before it was moved to Canada. A coulee northeast of town still bears the name of the first collector, F.T. Bradley. The first official jail on the prairies was established here in 1879, mainly to accommodate illegal whisky traders from the United States. In that same year, writer P. Mitchell from Montreal observed that Emerson customs officials were "not nearly so obtrusive or troublesome as American customs officers." Emerson has been flooded by the Red at least eight time since 1882. In the 1950 flood, the customs staff went to work by boat. Opposite Noyes, Minnesota.

Emerson West — The office here was opened in 1931. Opposite Pembina, North Dakota.

Gretna — The customs office in Gretna, named after Gretna Green, Scotland, dates from 1883 but there was an earlier preventive station dating from 1876 in the district and known as Smuggler's Point. Opposite Neche, North Dakota.

Winkler — Customs offices on the prairies frequently moved to accommodate railway and highway construction (or removal). The Winkler office was earlier at nearby Haskett, where it had been since 1908. Winkler is named after Valentine Winkler, elected to the Manitoba legislature for Rhineland in 1892. Opposite Walhalla, North Dakota.

Windygates — The customs office dates from about 1929. Opposite Maida, North Dakota.

Snowflake — The name is an English translation of an Indian word. It was a customs point in 1889 under the North West Mounted Police. The first customs officer, James Connor, lived on a farm six miles from Snowflake. He arrived at the office by horse and buggy (sleigh in winter) with enough provisions for the week; he returned home Friday evening and the office was left unattended during weekends. Opposite Hannah, North Dakota.

Crystal City — Named for the clearness of the water in Crystal Creek, the town was founded in 1879, mainly by Thomas Greenway of Centralia, Ontario, who later became premier of Manitoba. Customs service was established in 1889. Opposite Sarles, North Dakota.

Cartwright — It is named after Canada's finance minister in 1873-78. It was founded in 1879 and an early resident was Robert J.C. Stead of Middleville, Ontario, who established the weekly *Rock Review and Cartwright Enterprise* in 1899 when he was 18. Stead was later one of Canada's best-known novelists. Early customs work was done by the Mounties and the first regular customs office was opened in 1914. Opposite Hansboro, North Dakota.

Lena — The customs office was established here in 1930 after being located an unsatisfactory twenty miles from the border at Killarney for forty-one years. Opposite St. John, North Dakota.

Boissevain — Named after Adolph Boissevain, senior member of an Amsterdam company which sold early Canadian Pacific Railway shares in Europe. The customs office was opened in the town in 1912 but in 1930 was moved twenty miles south to the border, where there is an international peace garden. Opposite Dunseith, North Dakota.

Goodlands — The customs station was opened in 1932 after being located farther north at Deloraine from 1889. Opposite Carbury, North Dakota.

Coulter and *Lyleton* are in the southwest corner of Manitoba. Both are named after postmasters. Opposite, respectively, Westhope, North Dakota, and Antler, North Dakota.

Saskatchewan

Carievale — The name is Scottish for "lovely valley." The first settlers arrived in 1882 and the first ordained minister (Methodist) was J.S. Woodsworth, founder of the Co-operative Commonwealth Federation. All customs officers had their offices in the homes where they boarded until 1930, when an office was built. Opposite Sherwood, North Dakota.

Northgate — The customs office was opened in 1913 to serve the Grand Trunk Pacific Railway. Opposite Northgate, North Dakota.

North Portal — The customs station was opened in 1893 when the railway arrived and handled the arrivals of thousands of prairie settlers. It was first located in the CPR depot, which was also used as church, dance hall, concert hall and municipal council chambers. The first separate customs building consisted of an office and a coal bin and it was always flooded when it rained because it was lower than the highway at the front door. Opposite Portal, North Dakota.

Estevan — Named in honor of George Stephen and William Van Horne, first and second presidents of the CPR. The first customs house was opened in 1913 and the lone officer, M.J. Roche, enlisted in the armed forces in 1915, served overseas for four years, returned to his job in 1919 and remained at Estevan until 1952, when he retired. Opposite Noonan, North Dakota.

Torquay — Named in 1913 after the seaside resort in England. The customs office was established in 1915, after being located earlier in Dupuis, then Marienthal, and then Outram. Opposite Ambrose, North Dakota.

Oungre — Named after Dr. Louis Oungre, manager of the Jewish Colonization Association which brought in settlers. The first customs house opened in the early 1930s. Opposite Fortuna, North Dakota.

Regway — This was a one-man outport from its opening in 1931 until 1946. Until 1949, a windmill provided the electricity. Opposite Raymond, Montana.

Big Beaver — Named for extraordinarily large beavers found in a nearby pond when the railway arrived. Opposite Whitetail, Montana.

Coronach — Named by early English settlers in 1908 for an Epsom Derby winner, Coronach is on the old Powder River Trail. The first customs office was established in 1914. Opposite Scobey, Montana.

West Poplar — The first customs office was opened in 1917. Opposite Opheim, Montana.

Monchy — Named after a small village in Flanders where Corporal H.G. Richards, a Saskatchewan homesteader, was killed in 1915. Opposite Morgan, Montana.

Climax — Named by settlers from a village of the same name in Minnesota. A customs officer and a Mountie were stationed near the border about 1910 and made their quarters at a farmstead. Before grain elevators were built, the huge pile of wheat prompted the board of trade to adopt the slogan Climax, the Million-Bushel Town. When travelling road shows played Climax, the stage was formed by placing boards over the pool tables in the Silver Dollar Hotel. The customs office was built in 1927. Opposite Turner, Montana.

Willow Creek — Customs service began in 1905 but the first office, built in 1917, was in a gully out of sight of the highway it was supposed to control. A new office was built in the early 1940s. Opposite Willow Creek, Montana.

Alberta

Wild Horse — The North West Mounted Police began operations for Customs in the southeastern corner of Alberta in 1904. A regular customs officer did not appear on the scene until 1925. Opposite Wild Horse, Montana.

Aden — This customs port is so isolated that inspectors refuse to live here and no residence has been built. Customs service dates from 1929. Opposite Whitlash, Montana.

Coutts — The Alberta Railway and Coal Company brought its service, and Customs, to Coutts in 1890. Opposite Sweetgrass, Montana.

Del Bonita — Construction of a highway from Magrath, Alberta, to Cut Bank, Montana, brought establishment of the customs office here in 1939. Opposite Del Bonita, Montana.

Carway — Construction of another highway, from Cardston, Alberta, to Glacier Park in Montana, meant opening a customs office here in 1925. Before the office was built, William Roberts, the first officer, operated from a tent on the Lowe ranch for four months. When the road was snowbound, Roberts rode the eighteen miles to Cardston on horseback to mail his reports. The name Carway was coined from Cardston and highway by Herbert Legg, district inspector of Customs who purchased the one-acre site (for $50) for the border office. Opposite Piegan, Montana.

Chief Mountain — The highest customs office in Canada at 5,649 feet, Chief Mountain is a summer entry point to Waterton Lakes National Park and was opened in 1936. Opposite Chief Mountain, Montana.

British Columbia

British Columbia has some of the oldest customs ports in Canada, dating from its colonial days. And two of them, at Fraser and Pleasant Camp, played a vital part in the Klondike gold rush of 1898.

Roosville — The customs office in the southeastern corner of British Columbia moved between 1896 and 1898 from Tobacco Plains to Crow's Nest Landing to Phillips, renamed Roosville in 1917 after postmaster Fred Roo, though Michael Phillips had been the first postmaster. Opposite Roosville, Montana.

Kingsgate — The colony of British Columbia had a customs man in this area as early as 1864. The Kingsgate office was established in 1906. Opposite Eastport, Idaho.

Rykerts — In 1883, J.C. (Charlie) Rykert left Victoria with the titles of customs officer, immigration inspector, gold commissioner and registrar of shipping and with orders to establish a customs house on Kootenay River. He built it of hand-hewn logs and it remained in use until 1930. Rykert retired in 1924 and died in 1931. He and his wife are buried on the site of their original home. Opposite Porthill, Idaho.

Nelway — Mining boomed in interior British Columbia in the latter half of the 19th century and most of the people who passed through the frontier posts were prospectors, their suppliers, and railway builders. Nelson became a customs port in 1895 and gradually frontier outposts were opened at Nelway, opposite Metaline Falls, Washington, and at the following five points:

Paterson and ***Waneta*** — Opposite Frontier, Washington. Paterson, originally Sheep Creek, was renamed in 1900 in honor of William Paterson, minister of Customs. His brother, A.N. Paterson, was the customs officer at Paterson. Waneta's original name was Fort Shepherd and a customs officer was on duty there first in 1865.

Cascade — The customs station opened in 1897. Opposite Laurier, Washington.

Carson — Opposite Danville, Washington.

Midway — Customs arrived in this area, at Rock Creek, in 1860. The Midway office was opened in 1897. Opposite Ferry, Washington.

Osoyoos — John Carmichael Haynes was appointed the first customs collector here in 1861. He was collector and magistrate until his death in 1888. In 1961, there was a border centennial celebration to mark the beginning of Haynes' work. Opposite Oroville, Washington.

Chopaka — The first customs house was established in 1861 by Haynes before he moved on to Osoyoos the same year. The service was not re-established until 1907 with the coming of the railway. Opposite Nighthawk, Washington.

Huntingdon — Customs began operations in 1896 at Huntingdon, named after the Quebec community which was the home town of Benjamin Douglas (1839-1900), president of the New Westminster and Southern Railroad. Opposite Sumas, Washington.

Aldergrove — W.H. Vanetta established the first customs office in his own house in 1886. Opposite Lynden, Washington.

Pacific Highway and *Douglas* — This twin port opposite Blaine, Washington, is thirty miles south of Vancouver and was established in 1913. But customs service in the area dates from 1880 when a station was begun at Elgin. The Douglas office was opened in 1891. Douglas is the site of the International Peace Arch.

Boundary Bay — This was the first point marked when the 49th parallel was surveyed as the boundary from the coast to the Rockies. The first customs office was opened in 1914 in the home of officer E.T. Calvert, who patrolled the surrounding area by boat and on horseback. The southern tip of the peninsula on which Boundary Bay is located covers about seven square miles and is U.S. territory. Opposite Point Roberts, Washington.

Stewart — The customs office was established in Stewart at the head of the Portland Canal in 1910, seven years after the Canada-Alaska border was fixed. Opposite Hyder, Alaska.

Fraser — A new highway between Skagway, Alaska, and Carcross, Yukon Territory, brought opening of the customs house in 1979. It is two miles from the site of the original customs office in White Pass on the Trail of Ninety-Eight. Opposite Skagway, Alaska.

Pleasant Camp — The North West Mounted Police opened the first customs house on the Dalton Trail in 1898. Customs service was re-established in 1946 three years after construction of the highway from Haines, Alaska, to Haines Junction, Yukon Territory, on the Alaska Highway. Opposite Dalton Cache, Alaska.

Yukon Territory

Beaver Creek — This is Canada's westernmost community. The customs house was established, first at Snag Creek, four miles away, in 1946, four years after construction of the Alaska Highway. Opposite Alcan, Alaska.

Little Gold Creek — The most northerly frontier post in Canada, Little Gold Creek is on the Top of the World Highway sixty miles west of Dawson. Opposite Poker Creek, Alaska.

APPENDIX II

The Customs Act of 1886

The powers and duties of Customs officers as set out in the Customs Act of 1886, clauses as numbered then:

133. Every officer and person who is employed under the authority of any Act relating to the collection of the revenue, or under the direction of any officer in the Customs Department, or who is an officer of the said department, shall be deemed and taken to be duly employed for the prevention of smuggling; and in any suit or information, the averment that such person was so duly employed shall be sufficient proof thereof.

134. Every such officer or person as mentioned in the next preceding section, and every sheriff, justice of the peace, or person residing more than ten miles from the residence of any officer of Customs and thereunto authorized by any collector of Customs or justice of the peace, may, upon information, or upon reasonable grounds of suspicion, detain, open and examine any package suspected to contain prohibited property or smuggled goods, or goods respecting which there has been any violation of any of the requirements of this Act, and may go on board of and enter into any vessel or vehicle of any description whatsoever, and may stop and detain the same, whether arriving from places beyond or within the limits of Canada, and may rummage and search all parts thereof, for such goods; and if any such goods are found in any such vessel or vehicle, the officer or person so employed may seize and secure such vessel or vehicle, together with all the sails, rigging, tackle, apparel, horses, harness and all other appurtenances which, at the time of such seizure, belong to or are attached to such vessel or vehicle, with all goods and other things taken therein or thereon; and the same shall be seized and forfeited.

135. Any officer of Customs, or person by him authorized thereunto, may search any person on board any vessel or boat within any port in Canada, or on or in any vessel, boat or vehicle entering Canada by land or inland navigation, or any person who has landed or got out of such vessel, boat or vehicle, or who has come into Canada from a foreign country in any manner or way, if the officer or person so searching has reasonable cause to suppose that the person searched has goods subject to entry at the Customs, or prohibited goods, secreted about his person; and every one who obstructs or offers resistance of such search, or assists in so doing, shall incur a penalty of one hundred dollars; and any person who is on board of or has landed from or got out of such vessel, boat or vehicle, or who has entered Canada from a foreign country in any manner or way, may be questioned by such officer, as to whether he has any such goods about his person, and if he denies having any such goods, or does not produce such as he has, and any such goods are found upon him on being searched, the goods shall be seized and

forfeited, and he shall forfeit treble the value thereof: Provided, that before any person can be searched, as aforesaid, such person may require the officer to take him or her before some police magistrate, justice of the peace, or before the collector or chief officer of the Customs at the port or place, who shall, if he sees no reasonable cause for search, discharge such person, but if otherwise he shall direct such person to be searched; and if such person is a female, she shall not be searched by any but a female; and any such magistrate, justice of the peace or collector of Customs may, if there is no female appointed for such purpose, employ and authorize a suitable female person to act in any particular case or cases.

136. Every officer required to take any person before a police magistrate, justice of the peace, or chief officer of Customs as aforesaid, shall do so with all reasonable despatch; and if any officer requires any person to be searched without reasonable cause, such officer shall incur a penalty not exceeding forty dollars.

137. Any officer of Customs having first made oath before a justice of the peace that he has reasonable cause to suspect that goods liable to forfeiture are in any particular building, or in any yard or other place, open or inclosed, may, with such assistance as is necessary, enter therein at any time between sunrise and sunset, but if the doors are fastened admission shall be first demanded, and the purpose for which entry is required declared, when if admission is not given, he may forcibly enter; and after in either case entry is made, the officer shall search the premises and seize all goods subject to forfeiture; and such acts may be done by an officer of Customs without oath or the assistance of a justice of the peace, in places where no justice resides, or where no justice can be found within five miles at the time of search.

138. If any building is upon the boundary line between Canada and any foreign country, and there is reason to believe that dutiable goods are deposited or have been placed therein, or carried through or into the same, without payment of duties and in violation of law, and if the collector or proper officer of Customs makes oath before any justice of the peace that he has reason to believe as aforesaid, such collector or officer may search such building and the premises belonging thereto, so far as the same are within the limits of Canada, and if any such goods are found therein, the same shall be seized and forfeited; and every person who is guilty of a violation of the provisions of this section shall incur a penalty not exceeding one thousand dollars and not less than two hundred dollars.

139. Officers of Customs may board any vessel at any time or place and stay on board until all the goods intended to be unladen have been delivered; and they shall have free access to every part of the vessel, with power to fasten down hatchways, the forecastle excepted, and to mark and secure any goods on board; and if any place, box or chest is locked, and the keys are withheld, the officer may open the same:

2. If any goods are found concealed on board they shall be seized and forfeited, and if any mark, lock or seal upon any goods on board is wilfully altered, opened or broken before the delivery of the goods, or if any goods are secretly conveyed away, or if hatchways fastened down by the officer are opened by the master, or with his assent, the master shall incur a penalty of four hundred dollars, and the

vessel may be detained until the said penalty is paid, or satisfactory security is given for the payment thereof.

140. The collector or other proper officer of the Customs may station officers on board any ship while within the limits of a port, and the master shall provide every such officer with suitable accommodation and food, and, in default of so doing, shall incur a penalty of two hundred dollars.

141. Any judge of the Exchequer Court of Canada, or any judge of any of the superior courts in any Province of Canada, having jurisdiction in the province or place where the application is made, shall grant a writ of assistance upon application made to him for that purpose by Her Majesty's Attorney General of Canada or by a collector of Customs, or by any superior officer of Customs; and such writ shall remain in force so long as any person named therein remains an officer of the Customs, whether in the same capacity or not:

2. For the purposes of this section, any judge of the Court of Queen's Bench, in the Province of Manitoba, shall have jurisdiction over the North-West Territories and the District of Keewatin, and shall grant a writ of assistance for use therein, in like manner and with like effect as he might grant such writ for use in the Province of Manitoba. 46V., c. 12, s. 177.

142. Every writ of assistance granted before the coming into force of this Act, under the authority of Acts relating to the Customs now repealed shall remain in force, notwithstanding such repeal, in the same manner as if such Acts had not been repealed. 46V., c. 12, s. 178.

143. Under the authority of a writ of assistance any officer of the Customs, or any person employed for that purpose with the concurrence of the Governor in Council, expressed either by special order or appointment or by general regulation, may enter, at any time in the day or night, into any building or other place within the jurisdiction of the court from which such writ issues, and may search for and seize and secure any goods liable to forfeiture under this Act, and in case of necessity, may break open any doors and any chests or other packages for that purpose.

144. Any officer or person in the discharge of the duty of seizing goods, vessels, vehicles or property liable to forfeiture under this Act, may call in such lawful aid and assistance in the Queen's name, as is necessary for securing and protecting such seized goods, vessels, vehicles or property; and if no such prohibited, forfeited or smuggled goods are found, such officer or person, having had reasonable cause to suspect that prohibited, forfeited or smuggled goods would be found, shall not be liable to any prosecution, action or other legal proceeding on account of any such search, detention or stoppage.

(There were also four clauses for the protection of officers (145 to 148) and another (213) containing the penalty for assaulting or obstructing customs officials):

145. No action, suit or proceeding shall be commenced, no writ shall be sued out against, nor a copy of any process served upon any officer of the Customs or person employed for the prevention of smuggling for anything done in the exercise of his office, until one month after notice in writing has been delivered to him, or left at his usual place of abode, by the attorney or agent of the person who intends to sue out such writ or process, — in which notice shall be clearly and ex-

plicitly contained the cause of the action, the name and place of abode of the person who is to bring such action, and the name and place of abode of the attorney or agent; and no evidence of any cause of such action shall be produced except of such as is contained in such notice, and no verdict or judgment shall be given for the plaintiff, unless he proves on the trial, that such notice was given; and in default of such proof, the defendant shall receive a verdict or judgment and costs.

146. Any such officer or person against whom any action, suit or proceeding is brought on account of anything done in the exercise of his office, may, within one month after such notice, tender amends to the person complaining, or his agent, and plead such tender in bar to the action, together with other pleas; and if the court or jury, as the case may be, find the amends sufficient, judgment or verdict shall be given for the defendant; and in such case, or if the plaintiff becomes nonsuited, or discontinues his action, or judgment is given for the defendant upon demurrer or otherwise, such defendant shall be entitled to full costs of defence:

2. The defendant, by leave of the court in which the action is brought, may, at any time before issue joined, pay money into court as in other actions.

147. Every such action, suit or proceeding shall be brought within three months after the cause thereof, and laid and tried in the place or district where the acts complained of were committed; and the defendant may plead the general issue, and give the special matter in evidence.

148. If in any such action, suit or proceeding, the court or judge before whom the action is tried certifies that the defendant in such action acted upon probable cause, the plaintiff in such action shall not be entitled to more than twenty cents damages nor to any costs of suit, nor in case of a seizure shall the person who made the seizure be liable to any civil or criminal suit or proceeding on account thereof.

213. Every person who, under any pretence, either by actual assault, force or violence, or by threats of such assault, force or violence, in any way resists, opposes, molests or obstructs any officer of Customs, or any persons acting in his aid or assistance, in the discharge of his or their duty, under the authority of this Act, or any other law in force in Canada relating to Customs, trade or navigation, or who wilfully or maliciously shoots at or attempts to destroy or damage any vessel belonging to Her Majesty, or in the service of Canada, or maims or wounds any officer of the Army, Navy, Marine or Customs, or any person acting in aid or assistance of such officer, while duly employed for the prevention of smuggling, and in execution of his or their duty, and every person who is found with any goods liable to seizure or forfeiture, under this Act or any other law relating to Customs, trade or navigation, and carrying offensive arms or weapons, or in any way disguised, and every person who staves, breaks or in any way destroys any such goods, before or after the actual seizure thereof, or scuttles, sinks or cuts adrift any vessel, or destroys or injures any vehicle or animal, before or after the seizure, or wilfully and maliciously destroys or injures, by fire or otherwise, any Customs House, or any building whatsoever in which seized, forfeited or bonded goods are deposited or kept, is guilty of felony.

APPENDIX III
Customs Instructions in 1870

Customs instructions in 1870 to the locker, the officer in charge of a bonded warehouse:

I.

You are to remember that your position in the Service will depend as much on your perfect acquaintance with all branches of your duty, and your zealous performance of them, as on your general good conduct; you are frequently to read over and duly observe these and such other instructions as you may from time to time receive from the Department, or your superior officers, to whom you are to apply for information and directions in all cases of doubt or difficulty respecting your duty.

You are faithfully and diligently to conduct yourself, and you shall not do or suffer to be done — abet, or conceal any act or thing prejudicial to the Revenue or contrary to the Rules and Regulations of the service, taking notice that you will be called upon to make good any loss which the Revenue may sustain through your negligence or misconduct.

II.

You should bear in mind the oath you have taken on your appointment viz: "I, do swear to be true and faithful in the execution, to the best of my knowledge and power, of the trust committed to my charge by my appointment as Locker, and that I will not require, take or receive any fee, perquisite, gratuity or reward or emolument, whether pecuniary or of any other sort or description whatever, either directly or indirectly, for any service, act, duty, matter or thing done or performed, or to be done or performed in the execution or discharge of any of the duties of my said office or employment on any account whatever, other than my salary, or what shall be allowed me by law, or by order of the Governor of this Dominion in Council — So Help Me God."

III.

You are to reside within two miles of the Custom House, and to apprize the Collector of the Port of your place of abode, and whenever you change your residence, you are, without delay, to acquaint him therewith in writing.

IV.

If prevented from attending your duty by sickness, or other unavoidable circumstance, you are, by the prescribed time of your appearance, to acquaint the Collector therewith in writing, stating the address at which you are to be found, the nature of your illness, or other circumstance by which your absence is occasioned.

V.

If through sickness you are unable to resume your duty at the expiration of any period of leave which may have been granted to you, you are to forward to the Collector an application for sick leave, accompanied by a medical certificate. The Department will punish any officer who may forward an application for sick leave without sufficient cause, or transmit a certificate incorrect or exaggerated in its statement of illness. You are also to observe that all applications for leave must be forwarded in sufficient time to admit of the decision thereon being received by you prior to the date from which the absence is to commence.

VI.

You are at all times, when on duty, to appear cleanly and respectably dressed, and in uniform, if so directed.

VII.

You will be held responsible for the safe custody of any locks, keys, spits, stamps, gauge rods, testing instruments, tools, or any other property belonging to the Government entrusted to your care, and if any of these articles be lost whilst in your charge, you will be liable to make good the same.

VIII.

Sobriety is strictly enjoined and all games whatever are prohibited when on duty.

IX.

You are to pay due respect and obedience to your superior officers, and to behave with civility to all persons with whom you may be officially concerned. Every neglect of duty on your part will be recorded and brought before the Department, whenever your case may be considered for promotion or otherwise.

X.

Strict obedience is enjoined, under pain of dismissal, to the following directions, viz:

1) If not prohibited by law to vote at Parliamentary Elections you may record your vote, — but not otherwise interfere.
2) Not to act directly or indirectly as a Broker or Agent for any merchant, master of a vessel or other person.
3) Not to borrow money from merchants or others who transact business at the Custom House.
4) You shall not receive or permit any person to receive for you, any fee, gratuity or reward of any kind from any master, merchant or others, for making out documents, which you are not officially required to do, or for furnishing information to merchants or others, in connection with your duty, on any account whatever.
5) You are not to hold any Municipal office.

XI.

You are not to keep any house of public entertainment, or any shop for the sale of customable or exciseable goods, or of any goods manufactured on the premises.

XII.

You are not to hold any agency to loan, insurance, or other Companies, without the express sanction of the Department.

XIII.

You are to take notice that in the event of your availing yourself of the provisions of the insolvent laws, in any respect, you will be considered as having by so doing forfeited your office or situation.

XIV.

You are strictly prohibited from making any application for promotion, or increase of salary, except through the recognized channels — nor shall you solicit the influence for those purposes, of persons engaged in trade.

XV.

You are not to enter upon any negociation for an exchange of situation with any officer without the previous knowledge and sanction of the collectors of the Ports concerned, — and you will be liable to dismissal, if any pecuniary consideration form part of the agreement.

XVI.

You are forbidden to make retail purchases at wholesale stores, nor are you to buy or sell goods in bonded Warehouses under your charge or in which you may be employed.

XVII.

You are not to compromise any assault committed upon you, whilst in the execution of your duty, but you are at once to state the whole circumstances to the Department, through your superior officer.

XVIII.

If in the performance of your duty, you are required to keep any official book or record you are on no pretence whatever to take the account on loose papers or a slate, or with chalk; and you are to use your best endeavour to avoid mistakes; should, however, errors occur, you are not to make any erasures in your book, but to cancel the error with a pen, by drawing a line through it, so as to leave it legible, and inserting the correction in a plain manner over or under the original entry; and the alteration must be attested by your initials. You are also most strictly forbidden to tear out a leaf from, or in any manner to mutilate or deface any book you may be required to keep; but you are to preserve the same with all possible care, during the time it is in your possession; and you are carefully to examine such books when they are first delivered to you, to ascertain that they are perfect as you will be held responsible if any leaf be afterwards found wanting.

XIX.

You are not to act upon any document for the delivery of goods in which any alteration has not been attested by the initials of the officer or clerk issuing the order.

XX.

Should Bond be required of you, you are on the bankruptcy, insufficiency or death of either of your sureties coming to your knowledge, immediately to give notice thereof to the Collector in writing, and offer fresh security for approval, observing that if you fail to do so within one month, you will incur a heavy penalty and the forfeiture and loss of your situation.

XXI.

While an officer of the Customs, you cannot be compelled to serve in any other Public or Municipal office, or on a jury or inquest or in the Militia.

XXII.

The only Holidays in the Customs Service are New Years, Good Friday, Christmas, Queen's birth-day, a General Fast or Thanksgiving by Proclamation and such other days as may be appointed as Holidays by the Governor in Council.

XXIII.

Should you feel yourself aggrieved by the conduct of the Collector or any other officer, in a matter connected with your public duty, and you are unable to adjust your differences, you will acquaint the Collector or other proper officer, and furnish the party concerned with a statement of your complaint, in writing, for the purpose of being transmitted to the Department, through the Collector, — and in the event of that officer refusing to forward the same, or should any undue length of time elapse without a decision thereon being communicated to you, you will transmit a copy of your complaint to the Department direct acquainting the Collector or other officer concerned with your intention to do so. But the necessity of cordial co-operation with the other officers of the Revenue cannot be too strongly impressed upon your mind so as to avoid collision, which must be disadvantageous to the service and discreditable to the parties concerned.

SECTION 2.

XXIV.

You are to give regular attendance at the Custom House, and in the Warehouses to which you may be appointed, from 9 A.M. to 4 P.M., and if employed and necessary until 6 P.M. You are both morning and evening to sign the appearance sheet, stating the precise time of your arrival and departure — and you are not to quit your duty without leave, which is to be noted on the appearance sheet, by your superior officer.

XXV.

When any part of a Warehouse is specially approved for certain goods only, you are not to allow other than such goods to be deposited therein.

XXVI.

On receiving goods into the Warehouse, you are to take care that the marks and numbers agree with the "Receiving Order," the receipt of which is to be recorded on the document as well as the date on which the goods were received. Packages unmarked are not to be admitted. If Blue books are furnished to the Lockers of your port, the foregoing particulars are to be recorded therein.

XXVII.

You are not to suffer that any package or portion of any goods be taken out of the Warehouse under your charge, before you have received the Collector's "Order" for their delivery, nor without the sanction of your superior officer shall you allow samples to be taken out.

XXVIII.

On the delivery of goods out of the Warehouse, you are, if Blue books be not supplied, to tick off the mark and number of each package carefully, on the "Delivering Order," adding the date of the transaction and your initials (as more than one Locker may be employed on the same order) — all which are to be sent, when completed, to the proper officer at the Custom House.

If the goods be delivered for exportation, for ships stores or removal to another Warehouse in your Port, you must see that a Locker or Tidewaiter attends to guard them. The receipt is to be signed by the officer in charge of the Vessel, the railway station, or the Warehouse to which removal has taken place.

XXIX.

On delivery of goods for Exportation, if it appear to you that any package has been opened, or should for any other cause be re-examined, you are to suspend the delivery and give notice immediately to your superior officer.

XXX.

In case of goods received back into a Bonded Warehouse, you should see that there has been no alteration in the Packages or abstraction of the goods, and you are to certify the receipt of the goods on your "Delivery Order" (and make an Entry thereof in such Book as may be supplied to you for such purposes), and forward it to the proper officer. If however you have reason to believe that any package has been tampered with, you are to call the attention of your superior officer to the circumstance immediately.

XXXI.

You are to take care that all goods be stowed in the Warehouse so that they shall be kept properly separate, and a sufficient passage left between them, to which the marks and numbers are to be turned on the right and left — that stock may be taken, or the Bond checked conveniently, and otherwise according to the established regulations, and you are not to allow a change to be made in the appearance of any package, intended for exportation without authority, or give any Delivering Order or Warrant into the possession of the Merchants, their clerks or servants.

XXXII.

You are to give vigilant supervision and strict attention to all operations carried on in Warehouses under your charge; for the safe custody and correct delivery of all goods therein, you will be held responsible; you will be expected to point out every distinct importation when required.

XXXIII.

You are not to open more than one door or gate at the same time, without leave, nor are you to open such door or gate of a Warehouse or Bonding yard unless for the purpose of viewing, receiving or delivering goods, nor is it to remain open after legal hours without permission, unless in case of emergency, or where the delivery can be completed in half an hour under your superintendence.

XXXIV.

If you should be directed to take samples of spirits, they are not to be given out of your charge until delivered into the hands of the Landing Waiter or Gauger. You are to report the particulars of all cases of loss of wine or spirits that do not appear to have arisen from natural waste.

XXXV.

When any of the locks provided by the Government for Bonded Warehouses, or Yards, shall be no longer in use, you are to return them at once to the surveyor.

XXXVI.

You are not to allow tippling in the Warehouses or Vaults by Revenue Officers or others, — and if you be found guilty of drunkenness while on duty you shall be dismissed.

XXXVII.

When the business of the day is over, you are to see that all loop holes, windows and outer doors are properly secured or locked, and to take the keys to the officer appointed to receive them — any breach of this article will be deemed a serious offence.

APPENDIX IV

A Customs Affair of 1876

The report of revenue inspector Charles Thomas Dupont in 1876 on the operating expenses of a log customs house in the remote British Columbia interior — and the report's attendant correspondence and expense accounts — is a story of pioneer customs life, and of bureaucracy gone mad.

It took Dupont, a former preventive officer, fisheries inspector and Indian agent on Manitoulin Island, two months to make the trip from Victoria to St. Joseph's Prairie in the deep Kootenays and back, more than 1,000 miles of it on horseback, to investigate what were considered in Ottawa and Victoria exorbitant costs for a stove ($40), firewood ($6 a cord), and hay for the government horse ($50 a ton).

The correspondence begins in 1873 with vouchers submitted by H.E. Seelye, the $1,800-a-year customs officer at Kootenay, to get back money spent by him to try to keep the winter cold out of his log house, which was also the customs office. Dupont reached St. Joseph's Prairie May 27, 1876, to find that Seelye had died March 28, his urgent request for medical leave denied. Dupont carried out his investigation in any case, with the help of Seelye's widow. He had also been instructed by James Johnson, Commissioner of Customs, and Wymond Hamley, collector at Victoria, to visit the outports of Fort Shepherd, Osoyoos and Burrard's Inlet (Vancouver) as well as the Kootenay.

Dupont's original report and the related correspondence are in the sessional papers of the Parliament of Canada, Vol. X, No. 9, 1877. Presented here are extracts from Dupont's letters to Johnson, beginning with those of July 8 and 12, 1876, two weeks after his return to Victoria:

> Gold mining is the only industry that is carried on in the Kootenay District. There may be said to be no farming or stock raising. The settlements are the mining camps at Wild Horse and Perry Creeks. There are besides a few scattered adventurers prospecting for gold, or traders doing business chiefly with the Indians. Apart from the Indians the population is exclusively adult, and with the exception of five women (wives of settlers) male. In all there are not in the district over 60 white persons, 100 Chinese, and about 350 Indians. The district is the most isolated of any in British Columbia, separated from the more settled portions of the Province by ranges of mountains, on whose western slope is situated the chief mining camp of

Wild Horse Creek. The only outlet is to the south, in which direction there is easy access to Montana, and a trail comparatively easy to travel, although rocky and through brush and timber for about 175 miles leading to Washington Territory, when a country so open and level is reached that for hundreds of miles waggons can be drawn over natural roads. As a consequence the entire trade of Kootenay in flour and provisions, as well as every other description of goods, is with the United States, nothing whatever being imported from other portions of this Province. The amount of gold produced at Kootenay is in the neighbourhood of $200,000 per annum, and competent judges among the miners are of opinion that gold exists so generally in its creeks and rivers as to insure the permanency of Kootenay as a mining district. The Customs revenue is not likely, however (unless some great discovery of gold should be made), to increase or exceed the cost of its collection. An excitement may at any moment be created by new discoveries, which would cause a rush of miners to this district. . . .

I have the honour to report in respect to claims for $180 for firewood, that I find the price charged ($6 per cord) to be the regular price of the country; that the quantity charged for, fifteen cords per annum, is the proportion of Mr. Seelye's total consumption of fuel that he thought would be an equitable charge against the Department.

The winter at Kootenay is extremely cold and long — mercury remaining congealed for days at a time. There is frost every month of the year, and at the time of my visit (June 1st), at every house in the neighbourhood as well as at the Custom House, fires had to be kept up for comfort. On the 25th May, I rode for miles through quite deep snow on the Kootenay trail. The only firewood that can be procured is pine, which burns away very rapidly. The Custom House in which also the late Mr. Seelye had his residence is a wooden building, roughly constructed, and no doubt difficult to keep warm, and I can quite believe the statement made to me by Mrs. Seelye, that the total annual consumption of fuel had exceeded thirty-five cords. I think if a fire had been kept up in the office during the season of cold weather there would have been consumed more than fifteen cords of wood per annum.

I enquired of the Local Government agent at Kootenay (Mr. L. Booth), what his expenses had been for fuel for his office, and he stated that his account had been from $140 to $160 per annum, and that they had been allowed and paid. I believe that the fifteen cords of wood charged for in November, 1872, referred to in Collector Hamley's letter of 2nd February, 1875, might easily have been consumed (as Mrs. Seelye states they were) in the autumn of 1872, and in the spring of the following year, and that the charge made in 1873 and disallowed by Mr. Hamley was a just one.

I beg, therefore, very respectfully to recommend the payment of the charges of $90 in 1873 and $90 in 1874 for fuel.

In respect to the charges for fodder, for ranching &c., a horse belonging to the Department . . . I believe the account to be just, and would respectfully recommend that it should be paid. . . .

Claim No. 6 is for a stove and lamp, and for construction of a woodshed. A stove, or some means of heating the office, was a necessity. The objection in this instance is rather to the kind of stove bought, namely, a cooking stove. The office communicates with the one room of the house used as a sitting and dining and general room, and Mrs. Seelye explained that it was kept warm from fire in this room; that Mrs. Seelye supposed that if the purchase of a stove was warranted, and so long as the office was comfortably heated, the Department would not mind in view of their isolated position what description of stove was bought. . . .

The woodshed was an absolute necessity, and the charge, though high, is only in proportion to the rates of the district. . . .

The 500 feet of lumber charged for in claim seven was used in making furniture and otherwise about the house, Mr. Seelye making the various articles himself. The house at Kootenay possesses a minimum of comfort in every respect. There did not seem to me to have been any extravagant expenditure upon it, and with less it would have been untenantable.

I found that work charged for had been actually done, and I would respectfully recommend that the claims be allowed. . . .

Fort Shepherd on the Columbia River is an out-station of Osoyoos, Mr. Wm. Moore acting as officer here; he receives $30 per month. Mr. Moore reports and sends his returns to Mr. Sub-Collector Haynes. As the Columbia River is navigable from Colville in Washington Territory, to a point some distance beyond the boundary of British Columbia, I consider an officer being stationed at Fort Shepherd as desirable. This spring the steamer *Forty-Wives* has ascended the river with a large party of Chinamen for the purpose of prospecting for gold. If these men are successful in their search they will remain in the country and increase the importations, entries of which would be made at Fort Shepherd. I was unable to visit the station at Fort Shepherd except by ascending the Columbia River from Fort Colville, where the trail which I was obliged to take to reach Kootenay, strikes that river. This would have occupied so much time that I deemed it better to pass it by. . . .

Burrard's Inlet is only 9 miles from New Westminster, and there is a daily stage and mail between the two places. . . .

There are at Burrard's Inlet two extensive lumbering establishments, and a number of vessels are annually entered there. There is at present no office for the Customs, and much inconvenience is caused by parties having to seek the officer at his house. I would respectfully recommend that he be authorized to rent an office. A suitable one could be obtained for a rental of from $5 to $7.50 per month. . . .

Your instructions being to make a full inspection of the business transacted at each station, and mine being the first Customs inspection since Confederation, I have entered somewhat minutely into particulars for your information.

I have the honour to forward herewith a map of this Province, showing the position of the different Customs Stations, and the trails by which goods are brought in from adjacent portions of the United States. The trail dotted red across the Shepherd Mountains ceased to be travelled, as, in consequence of the height of Shepherd Mountain, the snow lies so deep and for so long a period of the year that only for a very short season could it be used; and such a quantity of timber falls across the track during the time it cannot be used, involving such labour in cutting it out, that the more frequently travelled, although longer route through Washington Territory and a portion of Idahoe, is preferred.

In consequence of the deep snow on the Hope Mountain at the season of my trip, I was obliged to proceed via Yale per waggon road (marked yellow) to Kamloops, from whence I made the journey over trail marked red via Colville and Spokane on horseback, encountering the greatest freshets and highest waters that has been known by white settlers on this coast, greatly increasing the distance by the necessity for frequent detours. I returned to Victoria by way of the Columbia River and Puget Sound, that route being the one by which I could most expeditiously get back. In all I travelled — by steamer and railway, 800 miles; by stage, 475 miles; on horseback, 1,022 miles.

Having exonerated Seelye of any wrongdoing, Dupont put in his expense account for his two-month trip: $1,321.36, with 19 vouchers to back it up. It was disallowed by Customs Minister Isaac Burpee despite Johnson's recommendation that it be approved. The expenses, said Burpee, were "unnecessarily large," with an "elaborate" camping outfit.

Dupont defended himself vigorously in a long letter to Johnson October 20, 1876:

I did not seek the making of this trip nor recommend its being made. I was not consulted about it or informed as to the ideas of the Department as to its probable cost, or the mode of travelling to be adopted. I had no volition in the matter; it was not part of my ordinary duty, and I was in no way responsible for its being made. It is true that in reply to your first letter of instructions, I stated, unasked, that the "most economical estimate of the cost of the journey at the proper season of the year would be $600." I did not contemplate in this what may be called an investment in camp material for the Department, but the net outlay for which nothing would remain to the Department by the trip. In any case I did not contract to make the trip for this sum, and, as a matter of fact, I could not and cannot make it for such a sum. The country was an unknown one to me; it was my first experience in making such a trip, and the error I made was in thinking I could make it for so much less than had been expended by other officials, although it is possible, with my acquired experience, I could make it for less another time than its cost in this instance, which, after deducting the cost of camp material on hand and a horse, the property of the Department, on pasture in the upper country (all of which I am ready to hand over to any one authorized to receive them) is $998, inclusive of $225.40 paid for stage fares and freight to Kamloops, in consequence of the season of the year necessitating my proceeding via that place.

I cannot but feel that, under all the circumstances, the impossibility of the Department at Ottawa understanding the nature of the trip and what was necessary. My rank and length of service (15 years) in the Dominion Civil Service, my being an officer of another Department, and not having been remunerated in the slightest degree for this work for the Customs, it would have been only just to have afforded me an opportunity of explaining anything not comprehensible, rather than, after the lapse of nearly three months, and then only in reply to a second letter, summarily declining to reimburse me the unavoidable outlay I had incurred. The inconvenience of having for so long had to advance so large a sum as $721 is to me of itself great, but added to this the direct consequence of having had to make this trip has been pecuniary loss to me, as I was compelled to hire a man at the rate of $2.50 a day to protect certain interests about my place during my two months' absence, that, had I been at home, I could have attended to myself after office hours.

I now beg to explain in regard to those particulars to which objection is taken in your letter of the 3rd instant.

1st. As to my mode of travelling. There are but two possible ways of proceeding to Kootenay. One is via the Columbia River by steamer and railway to Walla Walla, and thence with horses and a camp outfit to Kootenay. The other way by trails through British Columbia with horses and a camp outfit.

Your instructions requiring me to visit Osoyoos, and every Customs out-port I could take en route to Kootenay, and make a full inspection of the business transacted at each, I had of necessity, either going or returning, to proceed over the trails through British Columbia.

In either case horses and a camp outfit had to be provided, without these it would have been simply impossible to have gone, and the question resolves itself into whether I provided an unnecessary amount of these or not.

I purchased two tents, one for myself, and one for my men. Three pairs of blankets, being one pair for each man, and one pair for myself, having in addition a buffalo robe of my own, and costing the Department nothing. I purchased canvas sheets or tarpaulins to lay on the wet ground under the blankets. Sacks and boxes in which to pack blankets and provisions, without which they could not have been fastened on the horses, or kept from getting filthy. I also purchased necessary camp cooking materials, and two axes. How this can be characterized as an "elaborate outfit," I am at a loss to understand, with less I could not have gone or been asked to make such a journey, and if its costs ($198.31) seem large, you must ascribe it to correct cause, the costliness of everything in this Province.

In addition to this camp outfit I purchased one horse for myself to ride, at a cost of $125, believing that on so long and fatiguing a journey I had a right to secure an easy riding horse, especially as should there be a loss upon him when sold, it would not amount to more than it would have cost for hiring. The camp outfit and the horse, as I have already said, are on hand, the property of the Customs Department.

In respect to the attendants I took with me, two men, — one a white man and one an Indian, and which you characterize with my outfit as being elaborate — I beg very respectfully to say that any one acquainted with the nature of this method of travelling would admit that two men were necessary. One man alone cannot "pack" a horse. Two always have to do it conjointly, there being a regular system of lashing and packing that requires two trained men. Constant attention is also necessary at the horses during the day, and the loads have to be frequently re-adjusted, and at night, in addition to making camp, procuring firewood, and cooking, there is a great deal of labour in looking after and attending to the horses. As well as the men I had to, and did, work in camp — (all three of us, in addition to long days of dangerous and hard riding, in wet clothes, all day from the necessity of swimming and fording swollen rivers), having abundance of occupation. But I am not a "packer" and I did not know how to pack a horse, neither did I know the route, or was it possible for me to go without a guide, in which capacity I had one of the men, he assisting in every other way that he could.

In your letter of the 3rd instant, you say I account for the elaborate outfit and attendance which I deemed it necessary to procure on the ground of the unfavourableness of the season; but that my instructions were sent me long before, and that I was not restricted to a season when such expenses would be necessary. I beg again, Sir, to assure you that neither my outfit or attendance was elaborate, and no matter at what season of the year the trip had been made, such an outfit and attendance would have been indispensable. If you will be good enough to refer to my letter with my account you will perceive that what I accounted for on the ground of the season of the year was the expenses to Kamloops. F.J. Barnard & Co's bill $225.40 and steamer and hotel fares, amounting to about $100, additional.

I also stated that the freshets and floods I had to encounter had increased the expenses of the trip, a statement that no one conversant with the parts will doubt, the high water of this spring having been greater than was ever before known, so unforeseen as to be ruinous to thousands, and which I never contemplated having to contend with, or I would not have felt bound to encounter such danger and difficulty by starting when I did.

The inference to be drawn from your statement that I had received my instructions "long before" would be that I might have made the trip sooner. My letter of December 4th, 1875, so fully explains how impossible it would have been to have done this that I must most respectfully protest against this imputation. It could not have been expected that I should have made a trip of this character in winter, involving from 1,000 to 1,200 miles snow-shoeing, sleeping at night in the snow and in no other way could I have done it, since your first communication, dated 5th November, 1875, duly reached me here on the 22nd of that month when winter had set in. Had I done so the expenses would have been much greater. As it was I started so early that I had to lengthen my journey because of the snow on the Hope trail and I had to ride in several places through quite deep snow.

On the other hand had I delayed starting until after the season of high water, or until the Hope trail was passable for horses I could not have left Victoria until after the 1st July, because my duties in the Inland Revenue Department, connected with the renewal of licenses, required me to be there on the 1st July, which I could not have been had I not started when I did, the trip taking two months, and because, although the Hope mountain trail is favourable by the beginning of June, the unusual high water of this year did not subside until the beginning of July. In your first letter you directed me to proceed "as soon as possible," and as part of the duty assigned to me was to relieve Mr. Seelye, a dying man, and provide for the protection of the revenue, the season of the year being at hand when trade between Kootenay and the United States would recommence, I did not feel that I should be complying with your wishes or acting in the interest of the service by delaying my departure any longer than I did, but I could not have started at an earlier date. . . .

No one could have been more anxious to end the trip or get home than I was, yet it took me twelve days from Walla Walla to Victoria, because of interruptions of communications. The railways were under water, passengers were ferried about the streets of towns to second stories of hotels, and one of the largest at Walla Walla floated down the Columbia River two nights after I slept in it. I cannot conceive the Department would think it just that an officer, on a mission by its instructions, should bear the expenses of such unforeseen difficulties.

Had there been such things as freight pack trains via Osoyoos to Kootenay (which as a matter of fact there are not), I could not have travelled by such a means, without giving any other reasons, for the sufficient one that it would have taken me four months to accomplish the journey, and I could not have been gone so long from my other duties. . . .

As further evidence of the character of this trip and the expenses attendant on it, I beg to enclose you a certified copy of an account paid by the Local Government to James Wardle, the expressman, for bringing from Kootenay to Victoria on his October trip (the best season of the year for making it) a writ of some papers, all of which were contained in a good sized envelope. The amount paid him was $300.

In respect to the number of horses I took with me, there can be no complaint by the Customs Department. As far as Osoyoos I had seven horses, one for myself and one for each of my men to ride, and four to pack. Six of them, being, from previous hard work, unfit for the railway service, were lent to me by John Robson, Esq., Paymaster and Surveyor of the Southern Pacific Railway Survey, and did not cost the Customs Department one cent for hire or feed, as in this method of travelling the horses have to find their feed. The seventh horse was the one I purchased. I had to send back the Canadian Pacific Railway Survey horses from Osoyoos, and from that point I continued my journey with four horses and one man, having sent one of my men (Seymour) back to Kamloops with the Canadian Pacific Railway Survey horses, and being assisted the remainder of my journey by Wardle, the expressman, and his men.

In every way I endeavoured to keep down expenses. I used my own saddle and bridle and borrowed others as well as "Aparajoes" for the pack horses. I have charged $5 per day for hotel expenses (a sum barely insufficient to cover them) whereas the rate allowed in this Province is $6 per day. It is quite apparent the nature of the trip I had to make was not and is not understood when I am told my "mode of travelling was such as was never contemplated much less sanctioned by the Department."

On March 12, 1877, the House of Commons ordered the government to produce the correspondence between Dupont and itself and as a result the file was spread before Parliament.

The Tables of Trade and Navigation of the Dominion of Canada for the fiscal year ended June 30, 1878, showed this entry under "Charges on revenue — Customs": J. Gordon, H. Gallagher, C.T. Dupont and others, Travelling Expenses, etc. $4,740.27.

BIBLIOGRAPHY

Anderson, Alexander C. *The Dominion at the West.* Victoria, 1872.
Anderson, Frank W. *The Rum Runners.* Surrey, B.C., 1980.
Andrews, Israel D. *Communication for the Secretary of the Treasury ... on the Trade and Commerce of the British North American Colonies.* Washington, 1853.
Armstrong, L.O. *Southern Manitoba and Turtle Mountain Country.* n.p. 1880.
Association des Officiers des Douanes et Accise, Division de Montréal. *L'Edifice des douanes Montréal.* MS. Montréal, 1936.
Association pour l'histoire de l'administration des Douanes. *L'Administration des Douanes en France sous l'ancien régime.* Paris, 1976.
____: *L'Administration des Douanes sous la Révolution.* Paris, 1978.
Atton, Henry and H.H. Holland. *The King's Customs.* 2 vols. London, 1908, 1910.
Bailey, Alfred G. "The Basis and Persistence of Opposition to Confederation in New Brunswick." *Canadian Historical Review,* December, 1942.
Banks, John. *Smugglers and Smuggling.* 1871; rpt. Newscastle Upon Tyne, 1966.
Barneby, W. Henry. *Life and Labour in the Far, Far West.* v.p. 1884.
Begg, Alexander. *History of British Columbia.* Toronto, 1894.
Berton, Pierre. *The Klondike Fever.* New York, 1958.
Biggar, E.B. *Reciprocity.* Toronto, 1911.
Biggar, H.P. *The Early Trading Companies of New France.* Toronto, 1901.
Bigsby, John J. *The Shoe and Canoe, or Pictures of Travel in the Canadas.* 2 vols. London, 1850.
Blake, Gordon. "The Customs Administration in Canadian Historical Development." Paper presented at the annual meeting, Canadian Political Science Association, Montreal, June 6, 1956.
____: *Customs Administration in Canada.* Toronto, 1957.
Boucher, Pierre. "Histoire véritable et naturelle des moeurs et productions du pays de la Nouvelle France vulgairement dite le Canada." Paris, 1664. *Mémoires de la Société royale du Canada,* 1896.
British Columbia. *Journals of the Legislative Assembly,* 1873 to 1883.
____: *Description of the Kootenay District.* Victoria, 1884.
____: Provincial Archives. *Correspondence of the Government of the Colony of Vancouver Island, 1849-1866*; and *Correspondence of the Government of the Colony of British Columbia, 1858-1871.*
Brown, Frank. *A History of the Town of Winkler, Manitoba.* Winkler, Man., 1974.
Canada. Department of Agriculture. *A Hand-Book of Information for Intending Emigrants.* Ottawa, 1877, 1879.
____: *A Guide Book for Intending Settlers.* Ottawa, 1886, 1887.
Canada. Department of Customs. *Acts and Tariffs.* Ottawa, 1890.
____: *Customs Orders-in-Council.* Ottawa, 1893.
____: *Customs Tariff.* Ottawa, 1887, 1907.
____: *Digest of Orders-in-Council.* Quebec, 1875.
____: *Instructions for Officers of Her Majesty's Customs.* Ottawa, 1875.
____: *Instructions for Out-Door Officers.* Ottawa, 1870.
____: *List of Ports, Outports and Preventive Stations.* August, 1890.
____: *Record of Seizures made at the port of Dawson 1899-1969.*
____: *Record of Seizures made at the port of North Portal, 1904-1927.*
____: *Special Statutes Affecting Duties of Customs Officers.* Ottawa, 1886.

Canada. Department of Employment and Immigration. *The Pier 21 Story, Halifax 1924-1971*. Halifax, 1978.
Canada. Department of External Affairs. *Treaties and Agreements affecting Canada in force between His Majesty and the United States of America with subsidiary documents 1814-1925*. Ottawa, 1927.
Canada. Department of Inland Revenue. *Regulations for the Governance of the Excise Branch*. Ottawa, 1913.
Canada. Department of Mines and Resources. By W.F. Lothian, *Yukon Territory*. Ottawa, 1947.
Canada. Department of Mines and Technical Surveys. By Norman L. Nicholson, *The Boundaries of Canada, Its Provinces and Territories*. Ottawa, 1954.
Canada. Department of National Revenue. By J.F. Telford, *A History of Federal Sales and Excise Taxes*. MS. Ottawa, 1978.
____: *Commodity Taxation*. MS. Ottawa, 1979.
____: *National Revenue Review*. Vols. I to XV (1927-1942).
____: By W.J.C. Wright, *Customs and Excise in Canada: History and Development*. MS. Ottawa, 1964-1966.
Canada. *House of Commons Journals*. Sessional Papers 86, 1867-68; 133, 1877; and 34, 1885.
Canada. *Imperial Economic Conference 1932*. Ottawa, 1932.
Canada. By Arthur Harvey, *A Statistical Account of British Columbia*. Ottawa, 1867.
Canada. *Instructions regarding the Detention of Enemy and Neutral Merchant Ships in time of War*. Ottawa, 1914.
Canada. By H.L. Langevin, *British Columbia*. Ottawa, 1872.
Canada. *Memorandum on the Commercial Relations, past and present, of the British North American Provinces with the United States of America*. n.p., 1874.
Canada. North-West Mounted Police. *Report, 1898*. Ottawa, 1899.
Canada. By Maurice Ollivier, *British North America Acts and Selected Statutes 1867-1962*. Ottawa, 1962.
Canada. *Public Accounts*. Ottawa, 1868 to 1981.
Canada. Public Archives. *Documents Relating to Canadian Currency, Exchange and Finance during the French Period*. Ed. Adam Shortt 2 vols. Ottawa, 1925.
____: *Guide to Canadian Ministries since Confederation*. Ottawa, 1957, and supplement, 1966.
____: Manuscript Group 21, file 8831.
____: Manuscript Group 29, Department of National Revenue.
____: *The Oakes Collection, New Documents by Lahontan*. Ottawa, 1940.
____: *Ordinances Made and Passed by the Governor and Council of the Province of Quebec 1763-1791*. Ottawa, 1917.
____: Record Group 16, Department of National Revenue.
____: By H.J. Warre, *Overland to Oregon in 1845*. Ottawa, 1976.
Canada. *Report of the Special Committee investigating the Administration of the Department of Customs and Excise*. 2 vols. Ottawa, 1926.
Canada. *Royal Commission on Customs and Excise, Interim Reports 1 to 10* and *Final Report*. Ottawa, 1928.
Canada. Senate Committee on Foreign Affairs. *Canada-United States Relations*. Vol. II Ottawa, 1978. Vol. III Ottawa, 1982.
Canada. *Tables of Trade and Navigation of the Dominion of Canada*. Ottawa, 1876 and 1883.

Canada. *Tariff Relations between the United States and the Dominion of Canada, Correspondence and Statements.* Ottawa, 1911.
Canada. By John Peter Turner, *The North-West Mounted Police, 1873-1893.* 2 vols. Ottawa, 1950.
Calder, J. William. *Booze and a Buck.* Antigonish, 1977.
Cameron, John. *The Canadian Tariff.* Toronto, 1856.
Carievale, Northwest Territory, 1903-1978. Carnduff, Sask. 1978.
Carson, Edward. *The Ancient and Rightful Customs.* London, 1972.
de Charlevoix, Pierre François Xavier. *Journal of a Voyage to North America.* London, 1761.
Chicago Record Co. *Klondike: The Chicago Record's Book for Gold Seekers.* Chicago, 1897.
Civil Service of Canada. *The Civilian.* Special Issue. Ottawa, 1914.
Classen, H. George. *Thrust and Counterthrust: The Genesis of the Canada-United States Boundary.* Toronto, 1965.
Climax Before and After 1905-1955. Climax, Sask., 1955.
Coke, E.T. *A Subaltern's Furlough, descriptive of scenes in various parts of the United States, Upper and Lower Canada, New Brunswick and Nova Scotia.* London, 1833.
Coronach Historical Committee. *From the Turning of the Sod: the Story of the Early Settlers in the Rural Municipality of Hart Butte No. 11.* Winnipeg, 1980.
Cox, Ross. *The Columbia River, or Scenes and Adventures during a residence of six years on the western side of the Rocky Mountains among the Various Tribes of Indians hitherto unknown together with a journey across the American continent.* 2 vols. 3rd ed. London, 1832.
Coûtume de Paris, An Abstract of the Criminal Laws that were in force in the Province of Quebec in the Time of the French Government drawn up by a select Committee of Canadian gentlemen well skilled in the Laws of France and of that Province by the desire of The Honourable Guy Carleton, Esquire, Captain-General and Governor in Chief, of the said province. London, 1773.
Craig, Gerald M. *Early Travellers in the Canadas 1791-1867.* Toronto, 1955.
____: *Upper Canada 1784-1841.* Toronto, 1963.
Creighton, Donald. *The Commercial Empire of the St. Lawrence 1760-1850.* New York and Toronto, 1937.
____: *British North America at Confederation.* Ottawa, 1963.
____: *John A. Macdonald: The Old Chieftain.* Toronto, 1955.
Cruikshank, E.A. *Memoir of Colonel the Honourable James Kerby, His Life in Letters.* Welland, 1931.
Customs and Excise Officers' Association. *Customs and Excise Examiner.* Ottawa, 1951-1965.
Dales, J.H. *The Protective Tariff in Canada's Development.* Toronto, 1966.
DeGroot, Henry. *British Columbia, its Conditions and Prospects.* San Francisco, 1895.
Dominion Customs Ready-Reckoner and Importer's Guide. Halifax, 1888.
Donnan, J. Earl. *My First Forty Years with Canada Customs.* Ottawa, 1952.
Doyle, James ed. *Yankees in Canada.* Downsview, Ont. 1980.
Dunlop, William. *Statistical Sketches of Upper Canada.* London, 1832.

Earnshaw, William. *A Collection of the Statutes now in force relating to Shipping, Navigation, Commerce and Revenue in the British Colonies and Plantations in America and the West Indies from 12 Charles II to 57 George III included with a copious index.* London, 1818.

Eastman, H.C. and Stefan Stykolt. *The Tariff and Competition in Canada.* Toronto, 1967.

Eccles, W.J. *The Government of New France.* Canadian Historical Association. Ottawa, 1965.

Emerson Chamber of Commerce. *Emerson 1875-1975.* Altona, Man., 1975.

Farjeon, J. Jefferson. *The Complete Smuggler.* London, 1938.

Fisher, Peter. *The First History of New Brunswick.* 1825; rpt. Fredericton, 1921.

Fitzgibbon, Mary. *A Trip to Manitoba.* Toronto, 1880.

Fraser, Geo. J. *The Story of Osoyoos 1811 to 1952.* Penticton, B.C., n.d.

Frégault, Guy. *Canadian Society in the French Régime.* Canadian Historical Association. Ottawa, 1954.

____: *La Civilisation de la Nouvelle France.* Montréal, 1944.

____: *Le XVIIIe Siècle Canadien.* Montréal, 1968.

Galbraith, John S. *The Hudson's Bay Company as an Imperial Factor 1821-1869.* Los Angeles, 1957.

Garneau, F.-X. *L'Histoire du Canada depuis sa découverte jusqu'à nos jours.* Troisième édition, Québec, 1859.

Gervais, C.H. *The Rumrunners: a prohibition scrapbook.* Thornhill, Ont., 1980.

Gilroy, Marion. "Customs Fees in Nova Scotia." *Canadian Historical Review,* March, 1938.

____: "The Imperial Customs Establishment in Nova Scotia 1825-1855." *Canadian Historical Review,* September, 1938.

Gourlay, Robert. *Statistical Account of Upper Canada.* 2 vols. London, 1822.

Gray, Hugh. *Letters from Canada.* London, 1809.

Gray, James H. *Booze.* Toronto, 1972.

Great Britain. *Financial Relations of Upper and Lower Canada 1791-1821.* London, 1822.

____: *House of Commons Report from the Select Committee on the Civil Government of Canada.* London, 1827.

____: *Instructions by the Commissioners of His Majesty's Customs to the Landing Waiters and Searchers in the British Possessions Abroad.* London, 1828.

____: Public Record Office, London. Customs Group 34.

____: *Reports of the Commissioners of a Special Revenue Inquiry during the years 1812, 1813 and 1814.* London, n.d.

Haliburton, Thomas C. *An Historical and Statistical Account of Nova Scotia.* Halifax, 1829.

____: *The Old Judge, or Life in a Colony.* Vol. 2. London, 1849.

Hamilton, J.C. *The Prairie Province: Sketches of Travel from Lake Ontario to Lake Winnipeg.* Toronto, 1876.

Hamilton, Lord Frederic. *The Days Before Yesterday.* London, n.d.

Heriot, George. *Travels through the Canadas.* London, 1807.

Hind, H.Y. and others. *The Dominion of Canada.* Toronto, 1868.

Historical and Scientific Society of Manitoba. *Original Letters and Other Documents relating to the Selkirk Settlement.* Winnipeg, 1889.

____: *Some Red River Settlement History.* Winnipeg, 1887.

____: *The Abortive Fenian Raid on Manitoba.* Winnipeg, 1888.
History of the Border Country of Coutts 1890-1965. Lethbridge, n.d.
Hopkins, G. Harold. *Echoes of the Past.* MS. West Vancouver, 1976.
Howison, John. *Sketches of Upper Canada.* Edinburgh, 1821.
Hughes, H.C. *The History of the Port of Toronto.* MS. Toronto, 1960.
Hume, J.D. *The Laws of the Customs.* London, 1825.
Hunter, Robert Jr. *Quebec to Carolina in 1785-1786.* Ed. Louis B. Wright and Marion Tinling. San Marino, Calif., 1943.
Innis, Harold A. *The Fur Trade in Canada.* rev. ed. Toronto, 1956.
____: *Select Documents in Canadian Economic History 1497-1783.* Toronto, 1929.
____: *Select Documents in Canadian Economic History 1783-1885.* Toronto, 1933.
International Boundary Commission. *Joint Report upon the Survey and Demarcation of the Boundary between the United States and Canada from the Source of the St. Croix River to the Atlantic Ocean.* Ottawa, 1934.
____: *Joint Report upon the Survey and Demarcation of the Boundary between the United States and Canada from the Northwesternmost Point of Lake of the Woods to Lake Superior.* Washington, 1931.
____: *Joint Report upon the Survey and Demarcation of the Boundary between the United States and Canada from the Northwesternmost Point of Lake of the Woods to Lake Superior.* Washington, 1931.
____: *Joint Report upon the Survey and Demarcation of the Boundary between the United States and Canada from the Gulf of Georgia to the Northwesternmost Point of Lake of the Woods.* Ottawa, 1937.
____: *Joint Report upon the Survey and Demarcation of the Boundary between the United States and Canada from the Western Terminus of the Land Boundary along the Forty-Ninth Parallel, on the west side of Point Roberts, through Georgia, Haro, and Juan de Fuca Straits, to the Pacific Ocean.* Washington, 1921.
____: *Joint Report upon the Survey and Demarcation of the Boundary between Canada and the United States from Tongass Passage to Mount St. Elias.* Ottawa, 1952.
____: *Joint Report upon the Survey and Demarcation of the International Boundary between the United States and Canada along the 141st Meridian from the Arctic Ocean to Mount St. Elias.* n.p., 1918.
International Waterways Commission. *Report upon the International Boundary between the Dominion of Canada and the United States through the St. Lawrence River and Great Lakes.* Ottawa, 1916.
Jesuit Relations and Allied Documents. R.G. Thwaites edition. Cleveland, 1896-1901.
Kalm, Peter. *Travels in North America.* Ed. Adoph B. Benson. Toronto, 1966.
Kennedy, Clyde C. *The Upper Ottawa Valley.* Pembroke, 1970.
Kennedy, W.P.M. *Documents of the Canadian Constitution 1759-1915.* Toronto, 1918.
King, Alexander. *Travels & Adventures in Canada and the Indian Territories between the years 1760 and 1776.* New ed. by James Bain. Toronto, 1910.
King, Andrew. *Estevan The Power Centre.* Saskatoon, 1967.
Lachance, André. *Le Bourreau au Canada sous le régime français.* Québec, 1966.
Lajeunesse, Ernest J. *The Windsor Border Region.* The Champlain Society. Toronto, 1960.
Lambert, John. *Travels through Canada and the United States in the years 1806, 1807, 1808.* 2 vols. 3rd ed. London, 1816.
Leftwich, Bertram Ralph. *A History of the Excise.* London, n.d.

Legg, Herbert. *Customs Services in Western Canada 1867-1925*. Creston, B.C., 1962.

Liancourt, Duc de la Rochefoucault. *Travels Through the United States of North America, the Country of the Iroquois and Upper Canada in the years 1795, 1796 and 1797*. 2nd ed. London, 1800.

Long, H.G. ed. *Fort Macleod, The Story of the Mounted Police*. Fort Macleod, 1958.

Lower Canada. *Edits, Ordonnances royaux et arrêts du Conseil d'Etat du Roi concernant le Canada*. Québec, 1803.

____: *Ordonnances des Intendants et arrêts portant règlements du Conseil Supérieur de Québec*. Québec, 1806.

Macdonald, D.G.F. *Lecture on British Columbia and Vancouver's Island*. London, 1863.

Macdougall, W.B. *Illustrated guide, gazeteer and practical hand-book for Manitoba and the North-West*. n.p., 1882.

MacNutt, W.S. "The Coming of Responsible Government to New Brunswick." *Canadian Historical Review*, June, 1952.

Manitoba Archives. Hudson's Bay Record Society. *Minutes of the Council of Assiniboia*. Fort Garry, 1832 to 1853.

Martin, R. Montgomery. *History of Nova Scotia, Cape Breton, the Sable Islands, New Brunswick, Prince Edward Island, the Bermudas, Newfoundland*. London, 1837.

Masters, D.C. *Reciprocity, 1846-1911*. Canadian Historical Association. Ottawa, 1961.

McAdorey, Arnold. *Niagara's Story of Customs*. MS. Niagara Falls, Ont., 1960.

McGregor, John. *British America*. London, 1832.

McKitrick, T.G. *Corner Stones of Empire: The Settlement of Crystal City and District*. Crystal City, Man., 1970.

McLean, Simon J. *The Tariff History of Canada*. Toronto, 1895.

Miles, H.H. *The History of Canada under the French Régime*. Montreal, 1872.

Miller, Don. *I Was a Rum Runner*. Yarmouth, N.S., 1979.

Mitchell, P. *Notes of a Holiday Trip*. Montreal, 1880.

Mossing, Carol A. *Our Diamond Heritage 1905-1965*. Torquay, Sask., 1965.

Moray, Alastair. *The Diary of a Rum Runner*. Boston and New York, 1929.

Morton, Arthur S. *A History of the Canadian West to 1870-71*. v.p., n.d.

Murphy, Emily F. *The Black Candle*. Toronto, 1922.

New Brunswick. *Acts of New Brunswick 1786-1835*. Fredericton, 1836.

Nova Scotia. *Journals and Proceedings of the House of Assembly, 1819-1820*.

Okanagan Historical Society. *Sixth Report*. Vancouver, 1936. *22nd Report*. Vancouver, 1958.

Patton, Janice. *The Sinking of the I'm Alone*. Toronto, 1973.

Pennsylvania Historical Commission. *Travels in New France by J.C.B.* Harrisburg, 1941.

Porritt, Edward. *Sixty Years of Protection in Canda 1846-1912: Where Industry Leans on the Politicians*. 2nd ed. Winnipeg, 1913.

Province of Canada. *Customs Acts, Tariff and Regulations*. Quebec, 1854.

____: *Journals of the Legislative Assembly 1841, 1843*.

____: By J.W. Dunscomb, *The Provincial Laws of the Customs*. Montreal, 1844.

____: *Public Accounts.* Quebec, 1854 to 1866.

____: *Report of the Select Committee appointed to receive and collect evidence and information as to the right of the Hudson's Bay Company under their charter, the renewal of the licence of occupation, the character of the soil and climate of the Territory, and its fitness for settlement.* Ottawa, 1857.

Prowse, D.W. *A History of Newfoundland.* London and New York, 1895.

Reid, Allana G. "General Trade Between Quebec and France during the French Regime." *Canadian Historical Review*, Vol. XXXIV, 1953.

Robinson, Geoff and Dorothy. *The Nellie J. Banks: Rum-Running to Prince Edward Island.* Summerside, 1980.

Rodney, William. *Kootenai Brown.* Sidney, B.C., 1969.

Rondeau, Rev. Clovis and Rev. Adrien Chabot. *History of Willow Bunch, Saskatchewan, 1870-1970.* Winnipeg, 1970.

Rose, Clifford. *Four Years with the Demon Rum.* Fredericton, 1980.

Rothney, G.O. *Newfoundland: From International Fishery to Canadian Province.* Canadian Historical Association. Ottawa, 1959.

Saskatchewan. *Report of the Royal Commission to inquire into statements made in statutory declarations and other matters.* Regina, 1931.

Severance, Frank H. *An Old Frontier of France, the Niagara Region and Adjacent Lakes under French Control.* Vol. 1. New York, 1917.

Shaw, Frederick Davis. *Daily Journal for 1896.* MS. St. Mary's, N.W.T.

Shirreff, Patrick. *A Tour through North America.* Edinburgh, 1835.

Shore, Lt. Henry N. *Smuggling Days and Smuggling Ways.* London, 1892.

Skelton, O.D. *Canada and the Most Favored Nation Treaties.* Kingston, Ont., 1912.

Smith, Graham. *Something to Declare: 1,000 Years of Customs and Excise.* London, 1980.

Smith, William. *History of Canada from its first discovery to 1791.* 2 vols. Quebec, 1815.

Société littéraire et historique de Québec. *Collection de mémoires et de relations sur l'histoire ancien du Canada d'après des manuscrits récemment obtenus des Archives et Bureaux Publics en France.* Québec, 1840.

Stacey, C.P. *The Undefended Border: The Myth and the Reality.* Canadian Historical Association. Ottawa, 1960.

Sulte, Benjamin. *Le Commerce de France avec le Canada avant 1760.* Mémoires de la Société royale du Canada. 1906.

Taylor, C.C. *Toronto Called Back.* Toronto, 1892.

Teignmouth, Lord and Charles Harper. *The Smugglers.* 2 vols. London, 1923.

Thomas, Lewis Herbert. *The Struggle for Responsible Government in the North-West Territories 1870-97.* Toronto, 1956.

Tyrrell, J.B., ed. *Documents Relating to the Early History of Hudson Bay.* Champlain Society. Toronto, 1931.

Umfreville, Edward. *The Present State of Hudson's Bay.* 1790; rpt. Toronto, 1954.

Upper Canada. *Journals of the Legislative Assembly 1818.*

Verrill, A.H. *Smugglers and Smuggling.* London, 1924.

Walker, David E. *The Modern Smuggler.* London, 1960.

Walker, Frank. "President for a Day." *The Beaver*, December, 1949.
Wallace, Carl. "Albert Smith, Confederation, and Reaction in New Brunswick 1852-1882." *Canadian Historical Review*, December, 1963.
Weir, William. *Sixty Years in Canada*. Montreal, 1903.
Weld, Isaac. *Travels Through the States of North America and the Provinces of Upper and Lower Canada during the years 1795, 1796 and 1797*. London, 1799.
Whitelaw, Marjory, ed. *The Dalhousie Journals*. Vol. 2. Ottawa, 1981.
Willoughby, Malcolm F. *Rum War at Sea*. Washington, 1964.
Wilson, Charles. *Mapping the Frontier*. Ed. G.F.G. Stanley. Toronto, 1970.
Zaccano, J.P. *French Colonial Administration in Canada to 1760*. MS. Pittsburgh, 1961.

INDEX

Abbott, Douglas, 136
Abercorn, Que., 370
Acadia, 29, 30, 187, 220
Acadian Recorder, 48
Adee, Alvey A., 335-6
Aden, Alta., 175-6, 377
Age-strip, 137
Agricultural Products, 68, 72 75-6, 79, 84, 97-8
Ainslie, George, 298-300
Air traffic, 143
Air transport, 139-40
Aklavik, N.W.T., 181
Alaska Highway, 174, 179, 181-2, 211, 345
Alaska panhandle, 194, 197, 199, 200, 210, 332, 334
Albany, N.Y., 31, 140, 187, 221, 225-6
Aldergrove, B.C., 379
Alert, N.W.T., 182
American Revolution, 47
Amnesty, 225-6
Anderson, J.T.M., 280
Andrews, Israel D., 75
Andrews, C.L., 333
Annapolis Royal, N.S., 45-6, 101, 351
Annexation, 73-5, 84, 92, 95
Annexation Manifesto, 73
Anti-dumping, 86
ap Amerycke, Richard, 14
Appearance sheets, 311
Appraiser, def., 292
Arctic, 170-1, 181-2
Armit, William, 176
Armstrong, Que., 151, 283, 369
Aroostook War, 186, 190, 194
Arrearages, 38
Arthur, Sir George, 233
Ashburton, Lord, 190
Assiniboia, 158-64
Association for the Promotion of Canadian Industries, 74
Atlantic Import Company, 275-7
Atlas Shipping Company, 275, 277

B-13 forms, 282-3
Baddeck, N.S., 139
Begbie, Judge Matthew, 329
Baird, William T., 190
Baker, I.G. and Co., 169-70, 177

Baldwin-Lafontaine Ministry, 44
Barnston, Que., 244
Barrington, N.S., 47
Basswood Lake, Ont., 262
Batchellor, Richard, 296-7
Bath, Ont., 58
Beale, Billy, 343
Beauce County, Que., 313
Beaver, 18, 26, 31, 225-7
Beaver Creek, Y.T., 211, 380
Bedford Basin, 287
Beebe, Que., 268, 370
Bégin, Intendant, 226
Bégin, Michel, 70
Belcher, Robert, 179, 206-9
Belleau, J.C., 64, 312
Bennett Lake, B.C., 204-7
Bennett, R.B., 148, 156, 280
Bertie Township, Ont., 303
Better terms, 92-3
Bienfait, Sask., 281
Big Beaver, Sask., 376
Biggar, H.P., 24
Bigot, François, 32, 70, 228
Bigsby, John J., 71, 103
Bird, James, 159-60
Bisaillon, Joseph E.A., 268, 270
Black, John, 234
Blair, Charles P., 266
Blanchet, J.G., 65
Bloomfield, N.B., 352
Boissevain, Man., 375
Boivin, George, 267, 269, 272
Bonanza Creek, Y.T., 200
Bootlegging, 265, 269, 272, 281-2
Borden, Sir Robert, 84, 108
Botham, James, 243
Boucher, Pierre, 27
Bouchette, R.S.M., 100, 107, 137, 153, 306, 309-14
Boundary Bay, B.C., 379
Bourreau, le, 222
Bowell, Mackenzie, 74, 86, 108
Bowell, John, 244, 334-5
Bowyer-Smith, Henry, 48, 49
Bradley, F.T, 165
Brandy parliament, 223
Breadner, R.W., 145-6
Bribery, 294
Brisebois, A.E., 169
British American Brewing Co. Ltd., 274

British Columbia, 93, 96-9, 195, 323, 378-9
British Columbia Distillery Co. Ltd., 286
British Columbia Vinegar Co. Ltd., 273
British Party of Montreal, 42
Brockville, Ont., 57-8
Bronfman, Harry, 275-6
Bronfman, Sam, 151-2
Bronfman Brothers, 152, 267, 273, 275, 280-1
Brown, John George (Kootenai), 168, 185
Brown, James Thomas, 270
Brown, George, 78, 93
Bruce, Arthur, 283, 348
Brunel, Alfred, 55, 101, 315-8
Brydges, Charles John, 167-8
Buchanan, Isaac, 74
Bunker, G.N., 142-3
Bureau, Jacques, 267-8, 270, 276, 278, 280
Bureau du Domaine, 32
Burlington, Ont., 59, 60
Burns, Robert, 132
Burpee, Isaac, 394
Burrard Inlet, 391, 393
Busby, Edward S., 7, 330-6
Byng, Governor-General, 270-1

Cabot, John, 14, 19
Calais, Maine, 188
Caldwell, Henry, 62
Caldwell, Maj. William B., 162
Calgary, Alta.,178, 281
Cameron, Donald, 199
Cameron, John, 75, 133
Cameron, Malcolm, 61, 243
Campobello, N.B., 91, 185, 235, 239, 351
Canada, United Province of, 27, 42, 56, 72, 74, 78, 91, 104, 107, 109, 163, 237, 245, 300
Canada Customs Act, 146, 226, 286, 341
Canada Drug Co., 273, 275
Canada Temperance Act, 255-6
Canada Trade Act, 40
Canadian Colonial Airways Ltd., 140

407

Canadian Customs Official Flag, 333
Canadian Manufacturers' Assn., 74, 85, 145
Canadian preference, 72
Canso, N.S., 45-6, 299
Cape Breton Island, 25, 29 30, 47, 67, 187, 240, 299
Capone, Al, 281
Carbonear, Nfld., 237
Carcross, Y.T., 180, 211
Card money, 227-8
Cardston, Alta., 174-5
Cariboo Gold Fields, 323, 325
Carievale, Sask., 375
Carleton, Thomas, 11, 52, 295-7
Carling Export Brewing and Malting Co. Ltd., 274
Carmack, George W., 178, 200
Carr, William Guy, 256, 265
Carson, B.C., 378
Cartier, Jacques, 19, 22
Cartier, Sir George Etienne, 95, 313
Cartwright, Sir Richard, 66, 78-82, 85-6
Cartwright, Man., 375
Carway, Alta., 377
Cary, Joseph, 61
Cascade, B.C., 378
Cassiar Gold Rush, 198
Cazeau, Vincent, 313
Centreville, N.B., 352
Champlain, Samuel de, 22-3, 222
Charlottetown, P.E.I., 49, 105, 144, 240
Chartierville, Que., 293, 369
Chauvin, Pierre, 22
Chechik, Meyer and Moses, 273
Cheticamp, N.S., 285
Chief Mountain, Alta., 123, 377
Chilkoot Pass, 178-81, 201-2, 205-7, 209-10
Chinese, 99, 250-2, 321
Chipps, Doctor, 328
Chisholm, John, Sr., 59-60
Chisholm, William, 56, 58-9
Chopaka, B.C., 379
Choquette, Buck, 197
Christie, Alexander, 160
Civil Service, 63, 112, 147, 313-4, 317
Civil Service Commission, 340
Clair, N.B., 369

Clarenceville, Que., 371
Clarkson, Gordon and Dilworth, 341
Cleveland, Pres. Grover, 81
Climax, Sask., 376
Coast Doctrine, 199, 210
Cobequid, N.S., 46
Cocaine, 251
Code of Conduct, 348-9
Coke, Lt. E.T., 51, 233-4
Colbert, Jean-Baptiste, 27-8, 115, 224
Coleman, Alta., 265
Collector, def., 292
Columbia River, 18, 26, 158, 193-4
Commercial frauds, 279
Commercial Protective Assn., 267-8
Commercial Union League, 81-2
Commis, les, 220
Compagnie de la Nouvelle France, 24-6, 223
Comptroller, def., 292
Condé, Prince de, 23
Conflict of Interest, 178, 292
Connaught Building, 268, 337
Constantine, Charles, 177-8
Contraband of War, 339
Corméré, Baron de, 17
Corn Laws, 68, 72
Cornwall, Ont., 61, 187, 371
Coronach, Sask., 376
Corruption, 269
Cossit, Renna, 298-9
Coulter, Man., 375
Coutts, Alta., 171-5, 345, 377
Coutume de Paris, 221
Covey Hill, Que., 371
Cox, Ross, 18
Cox, William George, 323-4
Creighton, Donald, 19, 26
Crown Lands, 52
Crystal City, Man., 375
Cull, James, 59
Customs Act of 1886, 91, 111-2, 321, 381
Customs and Excise, def., 15
Customs and Excise duties, 11
Customs Consolidation Act of 1841, 104
Customs duties, 15, 34, 36, 45, 51, 53, 60, 64-6, 77, 81, 86, 91-2, 96, 104, 109, 134, 136
Customs duties, def., 13
Customs fees, 62, 299

Customs insignia, 348
Customs laws, 44, 54
Customs officers, assaults on, 242-4
Customs officers, hours of work, 318
Customs officers, travelling expenses, 314
Customs officers, bribery, 294
Customs officers, uniforms, 347
Customs officers, code of conduct, 344-8
Customs officers, promotions, 328
Customs, patronage, 52, 313
Customs revenue, 37-9, 44, 97
Customs Scandal of 1926, 7, 11, 144, 253-88, 335, 340, 371-9
Customs seals, 342
Customs uniforms, 348
Customs, women in, 347
Cutler, Lyman A., 196
Cypress Hills, Alta., 164, 169

Daaquam, Que, 369
Dales, J.H., 86
Dalhousie, Lord, 62, 231
Dalton Trail, B.C.,204, 206, 208, 211
Dalziel, Andrew H., 300
Daniel, Charles, 25
Davis, Donald Watson, 177-9
Dawson, Y.T., 154-5, 177-80, 202, 211, 336
Dawson, S.J., 163
Dawson Route, 165
de Caen, William, 23
de la Barre, Governor, 225
de Monts, Pierre de Gua, Sieur, 23, 187
Deadwood, 341
Defaulters, 56
Del Bonita, Alta., 377
des Groseilliers, Médard Chouart, 220
Detroit, Mich., 57, 139, 254
Diamond, Sam, 272-3
Dicks, Capt. Edward, 284
Diefenbaker, John G., 152, 156, 280
Digby, N.S., 101
Dingley Tariff, 83
Dixon, James, 72, 295
Domaine, 220
Dominion Distributors, 273, 275

408

Donnan, J. Earl, 343
Dorchester, Lord, 63
Dorval Airport, 143
Douglas, Governor James, 195-6, 323-4, 326
Douglas, B.C, 379
Drawbacks, 106
Ducondu, J.H., 268
Dufferin, Lord, 81, 98-9
Duncan, Walter, 267-9
Dundee, Que., 80, 312, 371
Dunlop, William, 60
Dunn, Alexander, 54
Dunscomb, John William, 102, 104, 129-31 243, 246-7, 305-6, 311-14
Dupont, Charles Thomas, 391, 394, 398
Duty-free goods, 66, 68, 75, 84, 88, 91, 129, 161, 181
Dyea, Alaska, 200-1, 203-6

East Hereford, Que. 369
East India Company, 34, 68, 231
Eastern Townships, 65, 69, 151, 242-3, 245, 313
Eastman, H.C., 86,
Ebey, I.B., 196
Edmonton, Alta., 344
Edmundston, N.B., 352
Egan, W.M., 274
Elgin, Lord, 75
Emerson, Man., 171, 186, 330, 344, 374
Emerson West, Man., 374
England, Clayton, H., 345
Ernst, Selwyn A., 273
East Pinnacle, Que., 370
Eskimos, 176
Estcourt, Lt.-Col. James Bucknell, 191
Estevan, Sask., 276, 376
Euler, W.D., 144-6, 155-6, 254, 280
European Economic Community, 88
Evans, William, 71
Excise, def., 12, 132
Excise Act, 134, 341
Excise duties, def., 97, 133-4
Excise duties and taxes, def., 12
Excise Tax Act, 134, 136,
Excise taxes, 45, 133, 135-6, 254,
Excise taxes, def., 134

Fairbanks, Charles, 50

Farming (revenue), 14, 30, 44
Farrow, Robinson R., 256, 267-8, 270, 276, 278
Fenian Brotherhood, 91, 186, 193, 308
Ferme générale (la ferme), 16-7
Fielding, W.S., 82, 84-5, 139
Fish, Hamilton, 96, 192
Fishing Rights, 75
Fitzgerald, Sgt. T.F., 181
Fitzgibbon, Mary, 330
Flathead, B.C., 176
Floggings, 16, 222
Flotsam and jetsam, 112, 286
Forbes, Dr. Charles, 106
Ford, John, 244
Foreign exchange, 344, 347
Foreign policy, 81
Forest City, N.B,, 351
Fort Benton, 164, 166, 168-70, 177
Fort Calgary, Alta., 169
Fort Cudahy, Y.T., 177
Fort des Prairies, 26
Fort Erie, Ont., 7, 61, 110, 301-2, 304-8, 372
Fort Frances, Ont., 373
Fort Garry, Man.,158, 161-2
Fort Hamilton, Alta., 164, 168
Fort Kent, Maine, 190, 288
Fort Kipp, Alta., 164, 167-8
Fort Macleod, Alta.,165-9, 171, 174-5, 177-8
Fort Montgomery, N.Y., 185, 190
Fort Norman, N.W.T., 140
Fort Rouge, Man., 31, 157-8
Fort Shepherd, B.C., 391, 393
Fort Walsh, 169
Fort Whoop-up, Alta.,164-5, 168, 177
Fortescue, James, 176
Fortier, Hector, 42-3
Forty Mile River, Y.T., 177-8
Fosterville, N.B., 352
Four Falls, N.B., 339, 352
Fox, John, 64, 244
Franco-Canadian Import Co. Ltd., 274
Franklin Centre, Que., 371
Fraser, B.C., 211, 379
Fraser River, 194
Fredericton, N.B., 52, 110
Free ports, 96, 105-6
Free trade, 52, 66, 68, 71, 74-5, 78, 80, 80-5, 104, 345-6

Free Trade Acts, 68
Freight yards, 337-8, 342
Frelighsburg, Que, 308, 370
French, G.A., 166
Frobisher, N.W.T., 182
Frontenac, Louis de Baude, Compte de, 28, 224
Fundy, Bay of, 22, 67, 89, 106
Fur Trade, 17, 19, 22-33, 66, 129, 157-8, 191-2, 220-7

Gabelle, 12-3, 17
Gage, Gen. Thomas, 64
Gainsborough, Sask., 281
Gainsborough Liquor Co., 275-6
Gainsborough Liquors Ltd., 275-6
Galleys, 15, 221-2, 225
Gallup, Milt, 283
Galt, A.T., 76-7, 87, 313
Gananoque, Ont., 58
Gander, Nfld., 350
Gaspe, Que., 26, 105, 237
Gauger, def., 292
General Agreement on Tariffs and Trade, 85, 88, 347
Georgeville, Que., 309
Gesner, Abraham, 77
Gillespie Portage, N.B., 352
Glacier Bay, B.C., 210
Gladman, George, 163
Gladstone, 68
Glen Sutton, Que., 370
Goderich, Ont., 61
Godson, John, 7, 201-11
Gooderham and Worts, 274
Goodlands, Man., 375
Goodman, George, 240
Gourlay, Robert, 34, 37-8, 233
Graham, Richard, 110, 306-8
Grand Falls, N.B., 293, 352
Grand Portage, 25, 30, 191-2
Grande Ordonnance criminelle, 222
Gray, Hugh, 66, 230
Great West Wine Co., 273
Gretna, Man., 374
Grey, Lord, 44, 90

Haines, Alaska, 180, 211
Haliburton, Thomas C., 30, 50, 103
Halifax, N.S., 7, 30, 45-7, 51, 57, 91, 94, 103, 105, 131, 144, 234-5, 254, 344

409

Hamilton, Alvin, 152
Hamilton, Ont., 59
Hands, William, 56, 300
Harbour Grace, Nfld., 238
Harney, Gen. William, 196
Harvey, Arthur, 97
Harvey, Sir John, 44, 54, 190
Hatch, Harry, 152
Hawkins, E.C., 333, 335
Hawks Harbour, Nfld., 237
Hay, John, 336
Haynes, John Carmichael, 7, 322-8
Head, Sir Edmund, 90-2, 94
Head, Sir Francis, 42
Heckewelder, John, 295
Hemmingford, Que., 371
Henry, Alexander, 18, 25
Herdman, Que., 371
Hereford Road, Que., 369
Heriot, George, 37
Herschel Island, N.W.T., 181-2
High River, 164, 167
Highwater, Que., 370
Highjackers, 284
Hincks, Sir Francis, 94, 233, 305
Hind, H.Y., 157, 163
Hocquart, Intendant, 226, 233
Hoffman and Dunford, 274
Hopkins, Harold, 282, 284
Hours of work, 318
Howe, Joseph, 50-1, 91-2, 94, 100, 215
Howe, C.D., 143, 147
Howell, Gordon, 349
Howison, John, 34
Howland, William P., 107
Hudson Bay, 26, 176, 191, 220
Hudson's Bay Co., 29, 95, 157-64, 167, 176-8, 191, 193, 195-8, 220, 230, 324-5
Hunter, Jospeh, 198
Hunter, Richard, 198
Hunter, Robert Jr., 188, 294
Huntingdon, B.C., 379
Huntingdon, Que., 243
Huron, Lake, 25

I'm Alone, 265
Ilsley, J.L., 156
Immigrants, 69, 81, 107, 165, 248-52, 321
Import duties, 28-9
Income Tax, 135, 185-6, 275

Indians, 17-9, 22, 24, 26, 29, 31, 66, 157, 160, 162, 164, 169, 173, 221-7, 325, 328, 344
Informers, 229, 319, 340
Inspector, def., 293
International Boundary Commission, 71, 165, 193-4, 211, 270
International Waterways Commission, 191
Inuvik, N.W.T., 182
Isaacs, J.M., 285
Ivey, J.W., 207, 332, 336

Jamiesons Lines, Que., 371
Jarvis, A.M., 206, 208
Jefferson, Pres. Thomas, 231
Jeffery, Thomas Nicholson, 7, 47-8, 51, 57, 62, 240-1, 297-9
Jenks, Capt. I.C., 333
Jensen, Paul, 140-2
Jerquer, def., 292
Jessopp, H., 130
Jesuits, 17, 26, 223, 227
John Jay Treaty, 66
Johnson, James, 154, 249, 318-9, 391, 394
Johnson, Samuel, 34
Johnstone, William, 48
Johnstown, Ont., 57
Juan de Fuca Strait, 194-5

Kalm, Peter, 187
Kavanagh, Henry, 313
Kelly, Capt. John ('Machine Gun'), 278
Kennedy, Clyde C., 18
Kerby, Col. James, 7, 61, 301-7
King, Mackenzie, 144-5, 147, 152, 156, 250, 267-71, 278-9
Kingsgate, B.C., 378
Kingston, Ont., 29-31, 41-2, 58, 224
Kirke, David, 24
Klondike Gold Rush, 178-80, 186, 198, 200-11, 332
Klondike Trail, 7, 200, 206, 208
Knowles, Cyril, 267, 275-6
Knox, P.C., 83
Knox, Thomas. 64
Kootenays, B.C., 318, 391-2

La Couvée, Capt. Alfred, 7, 146, 149, 269, 278, 286
La Vérendrye, 30
Labrador, 29, 33, 159, 191, 237-8
Lacolle, Que., 371
Laffery, L.I., 274
Lafitau, Joseph Franòis, 18
Lahontan, Baron, 31
Lambert, John, 64, 188, 230-1
Landing waiter, def., 292
Lansdowne, Ont., 372
Large, George, 282, 293
Laurier, Sir Wilfrid, 82-4, 108, 336
Laval, Bishop, 223-4
le Jeune, Paul, 17-8, 26
Leacock, Stephen, 255
Legg, Herbert, 174
Legge, Francis, 46
Lena, Man., 375
Lesage, Baptiste, 312
Lescarbot, Marc, 19
Lethbridge, Alta., 164, 168, 171-5, 177
Liancourt, Duc de la Rochefoucault, 60, 63, 294
Lillington, Capt. Israel, 284
Liquor laws, 255-6
Little Gold Creek, Y.T., 185, 211, 261, 361, 380
Liverpool, N.S., 46, 48, 235, 286
Locker, 319, 385
Locker, def., 292
Lockhart, C.B., 265-7, 278
Log Cabin, Y.T., 180
Logan, A.T., 256
London, Ont., 95
Long Maj. Stephen, 193
Longroom, 130, 292
Louisburg, N.S., 29-31, 46
Louisiana, 191
Low, Harry, 274
Lowe, W.H., 325, 328-9
Lower Fort Garry, Man., 165
Lowther, Gerard, 335
Lunenburg, N.S., 46, 265, 269
Lyleton, Man., 375
Lynn Canal, N.W.T., 200

Macaulay, John, 57-9, 301
MacBrien, Sir James, 149
Macdonald, D.G.F., 195
Macdonald, national policy of, 70, 74, 78-82, 84-5, 129, 314

Macdonald, Sir John A., 78-82, 87, 90-1, 94-6, 129, 165, 313
Macdougall, W.B., 248
Mackenzie, Alexander, 78-9, 92, 314
Mackenzie River, 26
Macleod, James F., 165-6, 168-9
Macphail, Agnes, 155
Macrae, William, 312
Magdalen Islands (Îles-de-la-Madelaine), 237, 244
Magog, Que., 309
Magwood, John, 307-8
Maine, 23, 94, 175, 185, 189-91
Maitland, Ont., 57, 243
Malton Airport, 143
Manahan, Anthony, 58-9
Manitoba, 95, 99, 163-4, 176, 373-5
Manitoba Refineries, 271
Maple Creek, Sask., 169
Marijuana, 249, 251
Markland, George, 56, 302-4
Martin, R. Montgomery, 50
Massachusetts, 45, 187, 189-90
Masson, L.H., 312
Matoff, Paul, 281
May, Capt. George, 148
McAlpine, John, 48
McCann, James J., 182
McDougald, John, 200, 204, 206, 209-10, 333-7
McGraw, Constable, 201-2
McGregor, John, 50, 65
McLelan, A.W., 92
McMichael, Solon W., 332, 334-5
Medicine Hat, Alta., 168
Meighen, Arthur, 270-1, 278
Memphremagog, Lake, 309
Merritt, William Hamilton, 74
Metis, 157, 160, 162-3, 221, 326
Mexico Export Co., 274
Michilimackinac, 25
Midway, B.C., 378
Miller, Don, 285
Miller, George M., 333, 335-6
Milltown, N.B., 238, 351
Milne, A.R., 200, 202, 206-10
Minto, Lord, 333-6
Mixed marriages, 219
Moieties, 340

Molasses Act, 45, 220
Molson's Brewery Ltd., 277
Monchy, Sask., 376
Moncton, N.S., 144
Montreal, annexation of, 40-2
Montreal, Que., 25, 32, 40-2, 64, 69, 70, 72-3, 94, 104, 140-2, 157, 171, 187, 221-2, 226-7
Montreal Gazette, 40
Moose Factory, Ont., 176
Moose Jaw, Sask., 170
Morphine, 251
Morses Lines, Que., 370
Most-favored-nation, 88
Murray, William, 308
Murray, Gen. James, 63, 102
Mutchmor, Dr. J.R., 153

Nanaimo, B.C., 286
Nanisivik, N.W.T., 182
Napanee, Ont., 242
Narcotics, 111, 215, 249-51, 268, 272, 286
Natanson, Zisu, 272-3
National Brewing Ltd., 277
National Policy League, 74
National Revenue Review, 141, 341
Navigation Act, 45
Navigation laws, 75
Neilson, John, 232-3
Nellie J. Banks, 284
Nelway, B.C., 378
Nevitt, Dr. R.B., 167
New Brunswick, separation of, 78
New Brunswick, 11, 23, 29, 39, 47, 49, 51-4, 67-8, 74-5, 77-8, 89, 92-4, 99, 105-6, 186, 189-91, 235-6, 238, 351-2, 369
New Carlisle, Que., 237
New England, 30, 34, 45, 77, 187, 229
New France, 17, 19, 22-4, 27-32, 69, 70, 157-8, 186-7, 191, 220-8
New Glasgow, N.S., 256
New Westminster, B.C., 329
Newfoundland, 19, 20, 23, 45, 51, 54, 67, 74-5, 77-8, 93, 229, 237-8, 256, 349
Newport, Vt., 309
Newton, John, 34
Newton, Hilbert, 45
Niagara (Falls), 29-31, 36, 186, 217, 234, 242, 249, 295, 301, 372

North Portal, Sask., 174, 341, 344, 376
North West Mounted Police (NWMP), 165-70, 173, 175, 177, 180, 199, 200, 204-8, 225, 332
North West Territories, 93, 95, 207
North-South Institute, 86
North-West Co., 157, 192, 230
Northgate, Sask., 376
Northumberland Strait, 96
Northwest Angle, 192, 196
Nova Scotia, 29, 30, 34, 39, 44-53, 67-8, 74-5, 77-8, 89, 92, 94, 99, 105, 189, 234-5, 239-40, 254, 309
Novascotian, The, 48
Nowlan, George, 147
Noyan, Que., 371
Nursey, Walter R., 268

O'Keefe Beverages Ltd., 272
Oakville, Ont., 56, 58-9
Ochiltrie, Lord, 24-5
Official correspondence, 316
Okanagan Valley, 342
Old Crow, Y.T., 344
Ontario, Lake, 29, 188
Ontario, 93-4, 96, 99, 188, 255, 371-3
Opium, 68, 97, 129, 249-51, 286
Oregon Territory, 185, 194
Oregon Treaty, 194-5
Osoyoos, B.C., 197, 322, 324-5, 327-8, 378, 391, 393, 395, 398
Oswald, Richard, 188
Ottawa, Ont., 17, 43, 110, 140, 279, 314, 343
Ottawa River, 17, 18, 23, 26, 63
Oungre, Sask., 376
Outdoor Officer, def., 292

Pacific Highway, B.C., 123, 379
Papineau, Louis-Joseph, 38-40
Parker, Frederick, 308-9
Parmelee, W.E., 292
Paterson, B.C., 378
Paterson, William, 82-5, 200, 334
Patronage, 313
Pauncefote, Lord Julian, 335-6

411

Payne-Aldrich Act, 83
Peabody, Francis, 53
Peace River, 26
Pearson, Lester B. 158, 280
Pecuniary embarrassment, 311
Pelissiers Ltd., 277
Pembina, 160, 162, 165, 193
Pepys, Samuel, 46
Perceval, Michael Henry, 62
Perry, A.B., 207
Perth-Andover, N.B., 352
Philipsburg, Que., 370
Piche, Joseph U., 274
Pictou, N.S, 105
Pigeon River, Ont., 192, 373
Piney, Man., 374
Piracy, 265, 284
Plaisance, Nfld., 29
Playing cards, 68, 112, 134, 227
Pohenegamook, Que., 369
Point Roberts, B.C., 194
Polk, Pres. James, 194
Pornography, 152-5
Port Churchill, Man., 171
Port Royal, N.S., 23
Pothier, de Rouville, 103
Potts, Jerry, 166
Poutrincourt, 23
Prairie Drugs, 273
Prescott, Ont., 57, 233-4, 243, 313, 372
Press Gallery, 152
Preventive Officer, def., 292
Preventive Service, 148-50, 218, 251, 254-5, 270, 286-7, 298, 341
Prince Albert, Sask., 343
Prince Edward Island, 29, 47, 51, 67, 74-5, 77-8, 93, 96, 99, 239-40, 255, 284
Pritchett, George, 198-9
Privateering, 54
Prohibited goods, 91, 109
Prohibition, 246, 253-65, 330
Promotions, 329
Protection of the Revenue, 11, 45, 291, 301
Prowse, D.W., 20, 229
Pyramid Harbour, 210

Qu'Appelle, Sask., 171
Quarantine, 321, 342
Quarantine stations, 170-1
Quebec, 93, 99-100, 189, 369-71
Quebec City, 23-8, 32, 36, 38-9, 41-2, 56, 60-5, 70, 72, 104-5, 186, 210, 220, 222, 246
Quebec Gazette, 129-30, 229
Quetico Park, Ont., 338

R-100, 141-2
Rabinovitch, Harry, 273-4,
Radisson, Pierre Esprit, 220
Railways Subsidies Act, 86
Rainy Lake, Ont., 18
Rainy River, Ont., 373
Randell, John T., 265
Raymond, Albert Reid, 268
Reciprocity, 66, 74-5, 78-85
Red Parlor, 85-6
Red River, Man., 31, 157-8, 160, 162-3, 165, 193, 196, 230
Regina, Sask., 170, 273
Regina Vinegar Co., 272-3
Regina Wine and Spirits Co. Ltd., 273, 275
Regway, Sask., 376
Reid, J.D., 278
Responsible government, 39, 44, 56, 69, 104
Richelieu, Cardinal de, 24
Richelieu River, 36, 188
Riel, Louis, 163
Rigaud, Que, 348
Rimouski, Que., 344
River de Chute, N.B., 352
Rivière du Loup, Que., 247
Roberval, Seigneur de, 22, 222
Robie, S.B., 106
Robinson, John Beverley, 39, 49
Rock Creek, B.C., 195, 323-4, 327
Rock Island, Que., 269-70, 370
Roosville, B.C., 378
Rose, Clifford, 256
Rose, John, 92
Rose, W.B., 173
Ross, Alexander, 160-1
Ross, William, 314
Rouse's Point, 185, 190
Rouyn, Que., 140
Royal Canadian Air Force (RCAF), 148-51, 170, 182, 287, 298
Royal Canadian Rifles, 162
Royal Commission, Customs Scandal of 1926, 371-9, 285-6, 339-40
Rum Row, 253, 265, 284-5
Rum-running, 150-2, 253-67, 282-5

Rush-Bagot Agreement, 186
Russia, 193-4, 197
Russian-American Co., 197
Rykerts, B.C., 378

Sable Island, N.S., 23
Sagard, Gabriel, 18
Saguenay River, Que., 26
Saint John, N.B., 11, 47-9, 51, 53, 75, 93-4, 101, 105. 109, 144, 235, 351
San Juan Island, 185-6, 188, 190, 195-6
Sanders, G.E., 170
Sandwich, Ont., 56-7, 391
Sangster, James, 196
Sarnia, Ont., 373
Saskatchewan, 150-1, 267, 280-1, 375-7
Saskatchewan River, 26, 30-1, 191
Sault Ste. Marie, Ont., 105, 312, 347, 373
Schooley, Johidiah, 303
Schryer, Orange, 306, 308
Scott, Gen. Winfield, 190, 196
Seagram, Joseph E. and Sons Ltd., 274
Searcher, def., 292
Seelye, H.E., 391-4, 397
Selkirk, Lord, 157
Separation, 98
Separation from Britain, 73
Settlers' effects, 99, 129
Seward, William, 197
Seymour, Frederick, 327
Shaw, Frederick Davis, 174-5
Shirreff, Patrick, 57
Sifton, Arthur Lewis, 108
Sifton, Clifford, 198, 204, 206-8
Sim, David, 7, 108, 142, 144, 146-8, 150, 152, 155-6
Simard, Wilfrid, 283
Simcoe, Governor, 60
Similkameen River, B.C., 194, 197, 323, 328
Simpson, George, 158-9, 162
Sitting Bull, 169, 175
Skagway, Alaska, 179-80, 198, 200-6, 208, 210-11, 332-7
Skookum Jim, 200
Slaughter market, 77
Slayter, John, 46, 297
Smallwood, Joseph, 349
Smith, Al, 191
Smith, Albert, 90
Smith, Goldwyn, 82

412

Smith, William H., 58
Smoot-Hawley Tariff, 88
Snag Creek, Y.T., 211
Snowflake, Man., 375
South Junction, Man., 374
Sparks, R.P., 268
Spearman, J.W., 238-9
Special Committee of 1841, 57-8
Special Revenue Inquiry, 1812-1814, 234
Special War Revenue Act, 133-4, 136, 338
Spence, Thomas, 164
Spencer, G.B., 164
Spracklin, Rev. J.O.L., 265
Sprague, Man., 373
Squirrel Whiskey, 281
St. Andrews, N.B., 54, 105-6, 187-8, 236, 238-9, 300
St. Augustin de Woburn, Que., 369
St. Aurelie, Que, 369
St. Clair, N.B., 288
St. Denis, Que, 69,
St. Eustache, Que, 69
St. Hubert, Que., 140-3
St. Jean, Que., 35-6, 63, 65, 67, 104, 188, 230, 237, 351
St. John River, 75, 94
St. John's, Nfld., 20, 49, 54, 105, 238, 351
St. Joseph's Prairie (Cranbrook), B.C., 318, 391
St. Laurent, Louis, 152, 156
St. Lawrence River, 19, 22-4, 26, 41, 72, 74-5, 103, 148, 187, 189, 191, 220, 243
St. Leonard, N.B., 256, 352
St. Pamphile, Que., 369
St. Pierre and Miquelon, 14, 32, 149, 229, 240, 254, 265, 281, 284
St. Regis, Que., 191-2
St. Stephen, N.B., 238-9, 351
Stanhope, Que., 370
Stanstead, Que., 65, 80
Starnes, Cortlandt, 148
Ste. Croix, N.B., 23, 351
Ste. Croix River, 188-9, 191
Steele, Sam, 179, 206-7, 209
Stevens, Harry, 268
Stewart, B.C., 379
Stewart, C.G., 291
Stikine River, B.C., 197-9
Stills, 246, 281, 287, 319
Strickland, D'Arcy, 179, 206, 208-9
Stykolt, Stefan, 86

Sub-collector, def., 292
Succession duties, 135
Superannuation, 297
Superior Lake, Ont., 25
Surveyor, def., 292
Sweetgrass Hills, 172-3
Sydney, N.S., 105, 144, 241, 344

Tadoussac, Que., 22-3
Taft, Pres., 83
Tagish, Charlie, 199
Tagish, Lake, 200-2, 204-9, 211
Talon, Jean, 27-8, 32, 223
Tarif de guerre, 16
Tariff, general, 177
Tariff, for Revenue only, 78
Tariff, National, 89
Tariff, Canada's first, 91, 112
Tariff, Commons debate on, 81
Tariff Board, 129, 153, 346
Tariffs, protective, 71-86, 97, 145, 345-6
Tariffs, customs, 29, 36, 40, 45, 67-8, 97, 159, 321
Taxes, commodity, 133, 136
Taxes, direct, 133
Taxes, excess profits, 135-6
Taxes, indirect, 133
Taxes, sales, 134-6, 186, 275, 349
Taxes, stamp, 134-5
Taxes, value added, 134
Taylor, C.C., 81
Taylor, W.F., 276
Telegraphs, 315
Temperence laws, 245
Tennant, Henry, 172-3
Territorial limit, 253, 269
Thompson, David, 191
Thompson, James, 65
Thompson, Jim, 170
Thompson, Sir John, 82, 108
Thorpe, Willis, 205-6
Tidewaiter, def., 292
Tilley, Sir Leonard, 80, 90, 107
Timber trade, 67, 72, 90
Tobacco Plains, B.C., 326
Tobacco stamps, 136-7
Tolls, 313, 320
Tolstoi, Man., 374
Toronto, Ont., 42, 58, 72, 74-5, 81, 85, 104, 273
Toronto Globe, 155
Torquay, Sask., 376

Tourism, 137-9, 337-8, 344-5
Trail of Ninety-Eight, 179, 211
Transfer payments, 100
Travelling expenses, 314
Treaty of Paris, 13, 32, 187, 191
Treaty of Washington, 96, 186
Trimble, James, 97
Trois Rivières, Que., 25, 27, 221
Trout River, Que.,371
Trumble, Beverly (Babe), 265
Tupper, Sir Charles, 82, 87, 108, 199
Turner, John, 199
Turner, John Peter, 168

Undervaluation, 279
Uniacke, John Richard, 47, 51, 105, 234-5
United Empire Loyalists, 66-7, 235
U.S. Congress, 67, 75, 84, 92, 97, 210

Valuation, 346
Vancouver, B.C., 143, 244, 249-51
Vancouver Island, 96-7, 106, 195
Veniot, Peter John, 151
Verner, John, 243
Victoria, B.C., 96, 98-9, 106, 195, 200, 208, 249, 251, 323
Voyageurs, 25, 29, 63, 221

Waiter, def., 292
Walker, Hiram and Sons Ltd., 274
Walsh, James M., 167, 169, 178, 201, 208-9
Waneta, B.C, 378
Wanton, William, 11, 53, 295-7
Warner, H.H., 300
Warre, J.H., 161
Washington, D.C., 75, 82-4, 87, 210
Washington Territory, 196, 323
Waterton Lakes, 169, 185, 194, 197
Weatherwax, J.B. (Waxy), 166, 168
Webster, Daniel, 190

413

Weld, Isaac, 63
Welland Canal, 69, 75
Wells, Alaska, 180
West Block, Parliament Buildings, 337
West Poplar, Sask., 376
Whisky Gap, Alta., 175
Whisky detectives, 330
Whisky special (Whisky six), 282
Whisky trade, 167-8, 225
White, Fred, 205
White Pass, 179-81, 332
White Pass and Yukon Railway, 211, 332
White slaves, 250
Whitehorse, Y.T., 180, 211, 332, 336
Wild Horse, Alta., 377
Wild Horse Creek, B.C, 326-7, 329
Willow Creek, Sask., 377
Wilson, Lt. Charles, 194-5
Wilson, Joseph, 312
Windsor, Ont., 252, 254, 265, 273-4, 280, 293, 300, 344, 372
Windsor, N.S., 46-7, 51, 101, 239
Windygates, Man., 374
Winkler, Man., 374
Winnipeg, Man., 95, 143-4, 158, 171, 267, 344
Wood, Zachary Taylor, 180, 205-7
Wood Mountain, Sask., 169-71
Woods, Lake of the, 25, 30, 191-3, 330
Woodstock, N.B., 151, 190, 236
Woodstock Road, N.B., 352
Working language, 312
Workman, George S., 72
Worthington, Thomas, 107, 133, 306-7, 314-5
Wrangell, Alaska, 197-9
Wright, Henry, 48-9, 53, 109
Writs of Assistance, 15, 109-10, 112, 294, 383

Yarmouth, N.S., 282
Yates, Reginald, 267
Yorkton Distributors, 273, 275
Young, Const. William, 325-7
Young, J.H., 86
Yukon, 7, 177-81, 197, 332-7, 380
Yukon River, 177, 202, 207